REFORMATION AND THE GERMAN TERRITORIAL STATE

Changing Perspectives on Early Modern Europe

James B. Collins, Professor of History, Georgetown University
Mack P. Holt, Professor of History, George Mason University

(ISSN 1542–3905)

Changing Perspectives on Early Modern Europe brings forward the latest research on Europe during the transformation from the medieval to the modern world. The series publishes innovative scholarship on the full range of topical and geographic fields and includes works on cultural, economic, intellectual, political, religious, and social history.

Reformation and the German Territorial State

Upper Franconia, 1300–1630

William Bradford Smith

UNIVERSITY OF ROCHESTER PRESS

First published 2008
Transferred to digital printing and reprinted in paperback 2016

University of Rochester Press
668 Mt. Hope Avenue, Rochester, NY 14620, USA
www.urpress.com
and Boydell & Brewer Limited
PO Box 9, Woodbridge, Suffolk IP12 3DF, UK
www.boydellandbrewer.com

Hardcover ISBN-13: 978-1-58046-274-7
Hardcover ISBN-10: 1-58046-274-X
Paperback ISBN-13: 978-1-58046-566-3
ISSN: 1542–3905

Library of Congress Cataloging-in-Publication Data

Smith, Wm. Bradford (William Bradford)
   Reformation and the German territorial state : Upper Franconia, 1300–1630 / William Bradford Smith.
      p. cm. — (Changing perspectives on early modern Europe, ISSN 1542-3905 ; v. 8)
   Includes bibliographical references and index.
   ISBN-13: 978-1-58046-274-7 (hardcover : alk. paper)
   ISBN-10: 1-58046-274-X (hardcover : alk. paper)
   1. Franconia (Germany)—Church history. 2. Reformation—Germany—Franconia.
3. Church and state—Germany—Franconia. 4. Franconia (Germany)—History. 5.
Franconia (Germany)—Politics and government. I. Title.
   BR857.F725S65 2008
   274.3'3106—dc22   2007042723

Portions of chapter 4 appeared previously under the title "Anticlericalism in Bamberg on the Eve of the Peasants' War," in *Constructing Publics: Cultures of Communication in the Early Modern German Lands,* ed. James Van Horn Melton (Aldershot: Ashgate, 2002), 48–65. Portions of chapter 5 appeared previously under the title "Lutheran Resistance to the Imperial Interim in Hesse and Kulmbach," *Lutheran Quarterly* 19 (2005): 249–75.

A catalogue record for this title is available from the British Library.

This publication is printed on acid-free paper.
Printed in the United States of America

Dewey Gordon Smith
In Memoriam

CONTENTS

Illustrations

ABBREVIATIONS

Annotationes	*Annotationes Domini M. Pauli Reinelii Diaconis Selbensis Anno 1612* (= StAB, A 245/I, 40/I)
AEB	Archiv des Erzbistums Bamberg
AO	*Archiv für Geschichte Oberfrankens*
ARG	*Archiv für Reformationsgeschichte*
BHVB	*Berichte des Historischen Vereins Bamberg*
BDLG	*Blätter für deutsche Landesgeschichte*
B. u. A.	*Briefe und Akte zur Geschichte des Dreissigjährigen Krieges*
CCB	*Corpus Constitutionem Bambergensium* (= StAB, B 26^c, 1)
CCC	*Corpus Constitutionem Carolinum*
CEH	*Central European History*
CUL	Cornell University Library, Department of Rare Books and Manuscripts
Falkenstein	Johann Heinrich von Falkenstein, ed. *Antiquitatem Nordgaviensium. Tom. IV, Codex Diplomaticus od. Probationun.* Leipzig, 1788.
GO	*Geschichte am Obermain*
JFFL	*Jahrbuch für fränkische Landesforschung*
JMH	*Journal of Modern History*
Kist, *Matrikel*	Johannes Kist. *Das Matrikel der Geistlichkeit des Bistums Bamberg.* Würzburg, 1955ff.
L	Johannes Looshorn. *Geschichte des Bistums Bamberg,* 6 vols. Bamberg, 1889–1906.
MGH	*Monumenta Germaniae Historica*
MJGK	*Mainfränkische Jahrbuch für Geschichte und Kunst*
MZ	Rudolf Graf Stillfried and Traugott Maerker, eds. *Monumenta Zollerana, Urkundenbuch zur Geschichte des Hauses Hohenzollern.* 8 vols. Berlin, 1852ff.

NBD	*Nuntiatur Berichte aus Deutschland*
PfA	Pfarreiakten
RI	*Regesta Imperii*
Rep.	Repertorium
RTA	*Deutsche Reichstagsakten*
SCJ	*Sixteenth Century Journal*
StAB	Staatsarchiv Bamberg
StBB	Staatsbibliothek Bamberg
U	Urkunde
Urbar A	Walter Scherzer. "Das älteste Bamberger Bischofsurbar 1323/28 (Urbar A)." *BHVB* 108 (1972).
Urbar B	Constantin Höfler, ed. *Friedrich von Hohenlohe, Rechtsbuch (1348)*. Bamberg, 1852.
VSWG	*Viertelsjahrschrift für Sozial- und Wirtsschaftsgeschichte*
WA	Martin Luther. *Werke. Kritische Ausgabe* (Weimar Ausgabe)
WA (B)	Martin Luther. *Werke, Kritische Ausgabe. Briefwechsel* (Weimar Ausgabe)
Wachter	Wachter, Franz. *General-Personal-Schematismus der Erzdiözese Bamberg, 1007–1907*. Bamberg, 1908.
ZBKG	*Zeitschrift für bayerische Kirchengeschichte*
ZBLG	*Zeitschrift für bayerische Landesgeschichte*
ZGW	*Zeitschrift für Geschichtswissenschaft*
ZHF	*Zeitschrift für historische Forschung*
ZKG	*Zeitschrift für Kirchengeschichte*

Acknowledgments

In the nearly twenty years I have been working on this subject, I have incurred not a few debts of gratitude. The Faculty Development Committee of Oglethorpe University generously provided a series of grants to support my research in Germany and at Cornell University. Most of the research was done in Bamberg at the Staatsarchiv, the Staatsbibliothek, and the Archiv des Erzbistums Bamberg. I would like to thank Dr. Franz Machilek at the Staatsarchiv, Dr. Bernard Schemmel at the Staatsbibliothek, and Dr. Josef Urban at the Archiv des Erzbistums for their assistance and advice. Thanks go as well to the staffs of the Special Collections Department at Cornell University Library, and the Herzog August Bibliothek in Wolfenbüttel. Pat Graham, director of the Pitts Theology Library at Emory University, allowed me unfettered access to the Richard C. Kessler Reformation Collection. Special thanks go my dear friend Stephanie Phillips of the Oglethorpe University Library for her skill and tenacity in finding obscure books and articles through Interlibrary Loan.

James Van Horn Melton first suggested to me the idea of studying religious confession, and I have greatly appreciated his friendship, guidance, and hospitality over the years. I owe a special debt to my "invisible friends," J. Russell Major and James Allen Vann III, both of whom had a profound influence on my view of history. Other scholars who have given me valuable advice and criticism along the way include Robin Barnes, Thomas A. Brady, Jr., William Beik, Rudolf Endres, Klaus Guth, Joel Harrington, Wolfgang Reinhard, Elisabeth Roth, Hans Sebald, Thomas Tentler, Peter Wallace, and Douglas Unfug. Mack Holt and Marc Forster played key roles in helping to get the book into print; they have also served as models of scholarly excellence and collegiality. Suzanne Guiod of the University of Rochester Press guided me through the publication process. Copyeditor Barbara Curialle did a fine job cleaning up the manuscript and spotting potentially embarrassing mistakes. David Mark Whitford read portions of the manuscript and saved me from serious error on a number of points. Michael Tinkler has been kind enough to put me up during my visits to Cornell and offered a number of suggestions on questions of Catholic theology. Alan Rogers has offered much thoughtful advice and intellectual prodding over the years, especially with regard to my work on witch-hunting. My parents provided support and encouragement, instilled in me a love of history, and taught me the value of honest work. My greatest thanks go to Misha for her kindness, patience, love, and good humor over these many years. Without her, there would be no book.

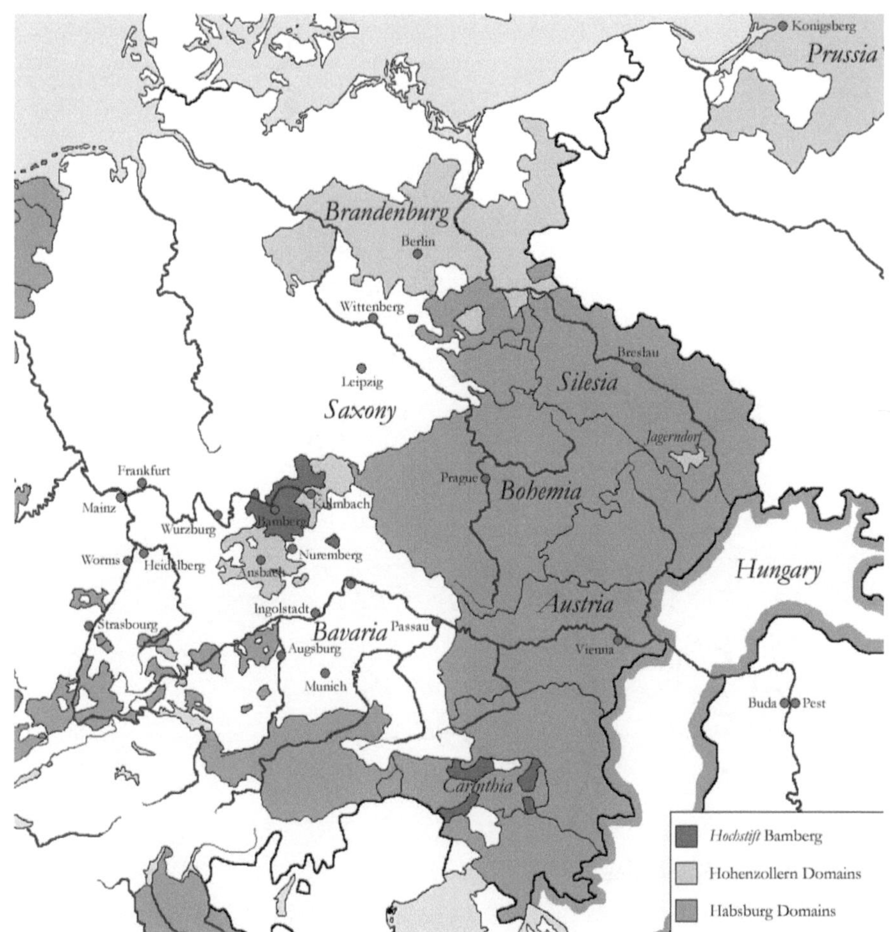

Map 1. The States of Upper Franconia and the Empire

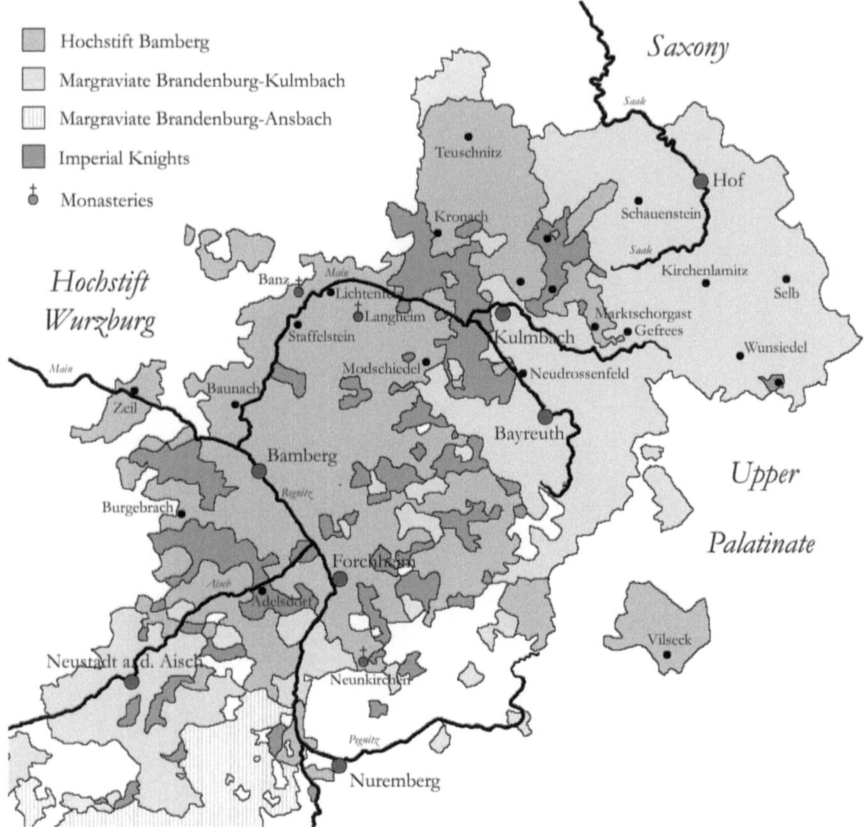

Map 2. Upper Franconia

Table I.1. The Hohenzollern Dynasty

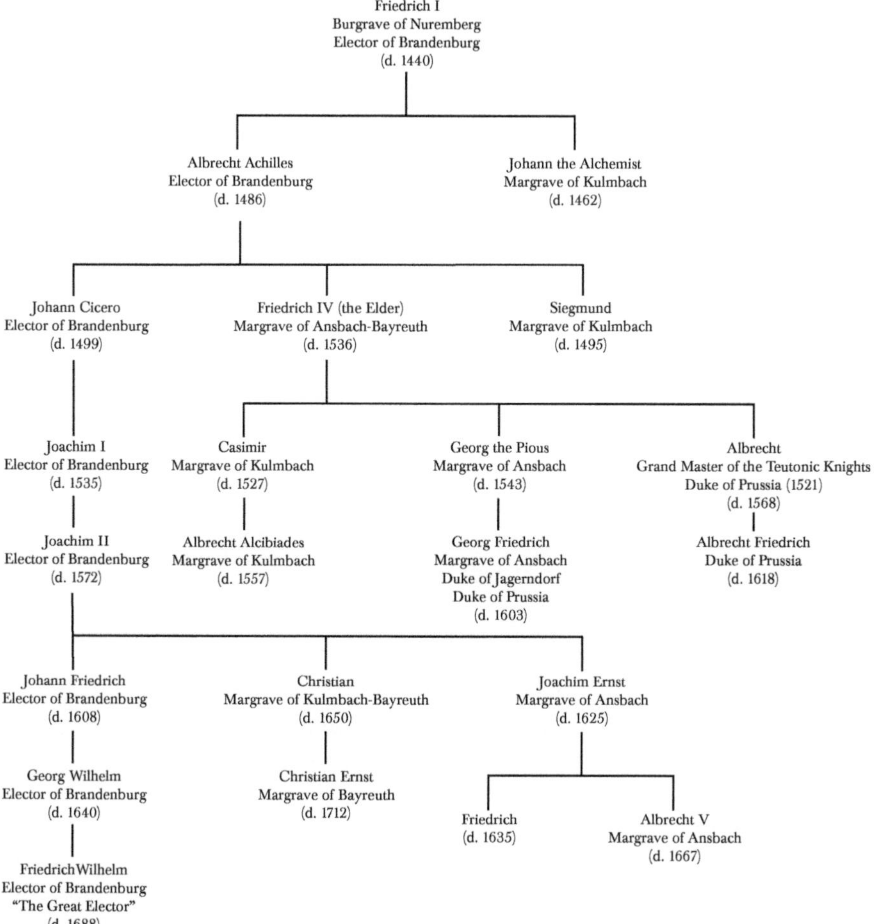

Introduction

Religious reform and the rise of the territorial state mark the two distinguishing characteristics of German history in the transition between the Middle Ages and the modern world. But just as 1517 no longer stands as the beginning of the Reformation, neither does 1555 mark the beginning of territorial state building.[1] The twin processes of religious reform and territorial formation have a much longer history, beginning in the later Middle Ages and continuing through the early modern period. The essential relationship between the rise of the territorial state and the reform movements of the fourteenth through the early seventeenth centuries provides the primary focus of this study. Our investigation centers on the diocese of Bamberg in upper Franconia. During the Reformation, the diocese was split in half: the parishes in the domains of the Franconian Hohenzollerns became Lutheran, while those under the secular jurisdiction of the bishops of Bamberg remained Catholic. The history of the region provides an excellent opportunity to compare the origins and course of Catholic and Protestant reform in the late Middle Ages and the early modern period. In particular, what this book seeks to understand is the role that religious reform played in the formation of the territorial state. Although much of recent scholarship has explored the impact of the sixteenth-century reformations on the development of the modern state, our concern here is rather with the ways in which those reform movements were themselves inseparable from the historical circumstances that gave rise to the territorial state. The history of upper Franconia suggests that the questions Whose realm? and Whose religion? proved to be far more complex than they would first appear to modern observers. Well before the Reformation, in the formation of the territorial states, the social and intellectual foundations were laid for the religious and political upheavals of the confessional era.

The relationship between reformation and state building has proved a rich topic for students of early modern Germany. Over the last quarter century, a host of scholars have addressed the theme with an eye to the confessionalization thesis developed by Heinz Schilling and Wolfgang Reinhard. Schilling and Reinhard sought to assign a meaningful place to religion in the transformation of European society. In that regard, their work should be considered part of a more general trend among scholars who have acknowledged the essential role of religious beliefs and practices in the social world of early modern Europe.[2] Recognizing the centrality of religion to the process of modernization, Schilling and Reinhard framed a general theoretical model that would allow "the totality of society in the early modern epoch to be captured."[3] Confessionalization represents a synthesis of the concept of "social discipline," developed by Gerhard Oestreich, and the idea of confessional formation (*Konfessionsbildung*) presented by Ernst Walther Zeeden.[4] From a methodological standpoint, the thesis arose out of a conscious reengagement with the sociology of Max Weber and Ernst Troeltsch.[5] As defined by Schilling, confessionalization

> designates the fragmentation of the unitary Christendom (Christianitas latina) of the Middle Ages into at least three confessional churches—Lutheran, Calvinistic or "Reformed," and post-Tridentine Roman Catholic. Each formed a highly organized system, which tended to monopolize the world view with respect to the individual, the state, and society, and which laid down strictly formulated norms in politics and morals.[6]

Confessionalization involved the development of confessional churches and their doctrines, institutions, rites, and traditions. More important, it stands among the motive forces driving the transformation of the old European society of orders into modern industrial society.

The confessionalization thesis has had a significant effect on our view of the sixteenth and seventeenth centuries. That said, the thesis has not been without its critics.[7] Some have condemn the thesis on the charge of "*etatismus*," arguing that Schilling and Reinhard overemphasized the role and effectiveness of the state.[8] Part of the problem derives from the definition of the "state." The modern state is "efficient" and "rational," and the institutional manifestation of both tendencies is that it is "bureaucratic."[9] The combination of modernization, rationalism, and bureaucratization is firmly rooted in Weber, but that begs the question of whether Weber's characterization of the modern state is valid. Some have argued that Weber "awarded bureaucracy two undeserved gifts, rationality and leadership," whereas his idealist conception of the state obscured the fact that bureaucracies are notoriously inefficient, often incapable of overcoming inertia or taking any sort of initiative.[10] This is not meant to deny a significant role to bureaucratic structures in modern governance. But since modern states are administered by professional bureaucracies, we tend to assume that political development necessarily led in that direction.[11] But there was a time when things were otherwise, and not all aspects of early modern governance point inexorably toward the establishment of highly centralized bureaucratic forms of administration. This is particularly true of Germany, where government always involved the interplay of many different levels—local, territorial, and imperial.[12] Although the development of the three Estates on both the imperial and territorial level was one of the main political dynamics in at least the early years of the Reformation, little attention has been paid to the estates and the role of representative institutions in standard works on confessional history. A notable exception here has been recent studies of the Counter-Reformation in the Habsburg territories, where the connections between the political authority of the estates, their notion of status, and their confessional loyalties has been carefully analyzed.[13] We also need to be cautious about overemphasizing the modernity of early modern political culture. The creation of a unified, disciplined body of subjects—one of the presumed results of confessionalization—appears as a precondition for the development of modern industrial society, but arguably not until the nineteenth century can we really say that such a society existed. And although such terms as *state* and *sovereignty* certainly were current in the sixteenth century, they tended to be used primarily in the context of personal dominion rather than to refer to institutions or political abstractions.[14] The famous remark attributed to Louis XIV—*l'état, c'est moi*—would be nonsensical in modern parlance, but is a commonplace within sixteenth- and seventeenth-century political discourse.[15]

A second criticism of confessionalization, as well as other permutations of the modernization thesis, has to do with chronology. Here the complaints are twofold. The confessionalization thesis moved the discussion of the transformation of Europe from the late eighteenth and early nineteenth centuries back into the early modern era, presenting the decades around 1600 as decisive and seeing the Thirty Years' War as the end of the confessional era.[16] Against this notion, Marc Forster had argued that "the process of popular religious differentiation . . . accelerated after 1650." It was only in the eighteenth century that the process might be considered complete.[17] The principal danger here would seem to lie in judging religious life in the late seventeenth and eighteenth centuries on the basis of sixteenth-century categories. Of course the opposite is also true: insofar as it takes the religious situation of the eighteenth and early nineteenth centuries as its destination, the confessionalization thesis could be seen as projecting later developments—in particular the hardening of orthodoxy in the Lutheran context and the professionalization of the clergy in the post-Enlightenment *Beamtenstaat*—back into the Reformation era.[18] The date for the beginnings of confessionalization is likewise a point of controversy. Although few would "wax nostalgic about the time when Luther's hammer still announced the initiation of the Reformation," in studies of confessionalization, the early years of the Reformation are scarcely noted.[19] And although 1555 no longer stands as the dividing line between the Reformation and the confessional era, few would seek to explore the origins of confessional churches much before 1540.[20] Among those who do, the Revolution of 1525 remains as a firm boundary between the "communal Reformation" and the "magisterial" and "princely" Reformation that followed.[21] Nevertheless, strong continuities link the early and later phases of the Reformation. These threads, moreover, bring us back into the fifteenth century, emphasizing fundamental ties between the late medieval *reformatio* and the reformations of the sixteenth century.[22] And although the broader definition of the "Age of Reform" seems fairly well accepted, scholars have been reluctant to extend their examinations of confessionalization back into the early sixteenth century, much less into the fifteenth and fourteenth centuries.

Thomas A. Brady, Jr., has seen such an approach as symptomatic of a general "flight from Reformation history," rooted in a refusal to confront directly the disputes over theology that define the era.[23] This is not to say that scholars have ignored the connections between religion and politics in pre- and early-Reformation Germany. A wealth of studies on the imperial cities followed in the wake of Bernd Moeller's seminal essay.[24] Peter Blickle's studies of the "communal Reformation" have offered vistas into the place of religion in the life of the autonomous peasant villages of southwestern Germany. Both Blickle and Moeller stress the association between particular theological perspectives, especially the teachings of Zwingli, and the ideals and forms of towns and villages in the later Middle Ages. Although some have questioned the applicability of the communalism thesis to northern Germany, there is no doubt that Blickle's work has forced scholars to reexamine long-held assumptions about religious life in rural Germany. More significant, the researches of Moeller, Blickle, and their varied interlocutors have directly engaged questions of theology, probing the direct connections between specific theological positions and social and political patterns.

Most works on confessionalization tend to downplay theological factors in order to accentuate the common aspects of Catholic, Lutheran, and Calvinist state formation. Reading much of the literature on confessionalization, we might wonder whether religion was important at all, except as a means of ensuring political authority. In the most extreme cases, religion is viewed primarily as an instrument for furthering the interests of a particular social group, denying religion any role in society *as religion*. The last tendency is perhaps the most problematic, insofar as the failure to examine religion as a system distinct from other political and social forces masks the extent to which religious values were in tension with more "concrete" social and political aims.[25] Indeed, the approach of many scholars betrays an ambivalence about religion generally, insofar as "religious behavior . . . has little place in the forward movement of modern man."[26] Such a perspective risks seriously misrepresenting the nature of early modern society and politics. The reformations of the fifteenth and sixteenth centuries may have had to do with the state, and may have had to do with society, but at their core they were about questions of doctrine; the social and political implications of the reforms were secondary to or derivations of their spiritual aims.

It seems clear that the ideas, institutions, and practices of the confessional churches were "anchored in a formal confession of faith [*Bekenntnis*]." On account of the differences between the formal doctrines of the three confessions, "church" ultimately had to mean something different in each context.

The "church," as it is known to most people, is the place where through rituals and ceremonies formal doctrines are expressed in visible form. In people's experience, the church is neither an abstraction nor simply an institution. It is above all a place and scene of action, and both the physical shape of the place and the kinds of actions that occur within it emphasized the distinctions between the rival confessions.[27] Here we must be careful not to separate ritual from ideas, or to emphasize the social-communal aspects of religious behavior apart from formal theological concepts. The public character of ritual does not negate the fact that for the individual believer, participation in the outward forms of religious life could have highly personal meaning. In this sense, Patrick Collinson's remarks about the sixteenth-century English view of the church would seem equally appropriate to the German perspective: "the Church was constituted, not by the Christians of whom was composed, nor by the sincerity of their profession, but by the purity of the doctrine publicly preached and upheld by authority."[28] These three aspects—doctrine, ritual, and authority—are largely inseparable, but ultimately the latter two derive their specific characteristics from and are hence dependent on the former. Religious practices have theological implications, whether clearly articulated or not. In this regard, the common distinction between "elite" and "popular" religion becomes rather less meaningful.[29]

Perhaps the most glaring omission in standard treatments of confessionalization is the larger political context. Rarely if ever do studies focusing on religion and the territorial state consider the impact of the Holy Roman Empire on territorial and local events. Although it is true that we can best see the development of modern political and social institutions in the territories, the role of the empire in shaping the territorial states should not be underestimated.[30] Arguably, it was only within the context of the empire that the territorial state could emerge. The empire was an "incubator" where smaller states could develop and retain their independence.[31] Throughout the confessional era, imperial institutions and policies continued to have an immediate impact on the internal politics of the states.[32] Compared with the national monarchies of England and France, in the empire we can see additional layers of political authority, complicating our understanding of the categories ruler and subject. The empire offers an opportunity to view the interaction between the center and the periphery in a more nuanced way. The multiplicity of states, each of which had to develop its own strategies with respect to internal policies, foreign affairs, and relations with the imperial regime, offer opportunities for comparative analysis.

Comparative history is a virtue more preached than practiced, in part because the results often take the appearance of what one historian has deemed a "historiographical Wimbeldon."[33] The work that follows may best be described as a braided narrative, tying together the events in the two territories and at the various levels of society. The chapters are arranged more or less chronologically, but each has a thematic focus as well. The overall structure of the narrative is less an examination of a process than an account of an argument, used here in the familiar sense of debate, but also in the older sense of "plot" or "story."[34] The period under consideration derives its internal coherence—its plot, in other words—from the ongoing argument over religious reform and its impact on society and politics. The chronology is taken from the sources. The protocols of the vicar general's court in Bamberg (*Protokollenbücher der Vikariatsgericht*), assembled between 1540 and 1630, comprise a detailed history of nearly every parish in the diocese from the late thirteenth century onward.[35] In the 1620s, when Friedrich Förner, suffragan bishop of Bamberg, considered the history of religious reform, he saw distinct parallels between the origins of the Thirty Years' War and the outbreak of the Hussite war.[36] Förner's Lutheran contemporary Paul Reinel, in his ecclesiastical history of his hometown of Selb, sought to reconcile the devotional practices of his fifteenth-century ancestors with the standards of Lutheran orthodoxy.[37] Reading through the writings of Förner and Reinel, and the other texts and documents relating to religious reform in upper Franconia, we can see very clearly the long argument and the extent to which later generations understood their own reforms in light of the past. Close consideration of the sources, moreover, remind us that there was always something experimental about the territorial churches. They remained "works in progress" throughout the confessional era; in that regard, "confession" was not a static concept, but a social and cultural dynamic.

At this stage, certain terms require explanation. Upper Franconia (Oberfranken) constitutes the northeast corner of the present Free State of Bavaria. It comprises the upper Main valley and the surrounding hill country. To the north lay Thuringia and the Vogtland, to the east the Egerland and Bohemia. It is hilly country, with great forest tracts as well as some of the steepest railway grades in Germany. From the late Middle Ages onward, the area was more or less evenly divided between the bishops of Bamberg and the Hohenzollerns. Throughout the work I have chosen to refer to the episcopal domains by their German name, Hochstift, a term which may either mean "diocese" or "prince-bishopric." The term contains a certain ambiguity insofar as it was used to refer to both the secular and spiritual domains, even though the two were not coterminous. This is the term used by contemporaries, though later on the form "our see and principality" (unser Stift und Fürstentum) becomes more common. For our purposes here, Hochstift has a certain utility in that it captures, in a way that is largely untranslatable, the combination of and tension between the spritual authority of the bishops and their power as princes of the empire.

In the case of the Hohenzollern lands, there is a like confusion over nomenclature. From the twelfth century to 1415, the Franconian Hohenzollerns were styled "burgraves of Nuremberg." The Hohenzollern burgraviate was made up of a string of holdings forming an arc from the Swabian frontier to the Vogtland. In the middle stood the city of Nuremberg, hence the standard division between the lands above and below the *Berg*. To the west lay the Unterland, centered on Neustadt an der Aisch. Further to the southwest was the Niederland, with the residence city of Ansbach. These two regions constituted the lands "below" Nuremberg. To the north and east was the *Land ober dem Gebirg*, or the Oberland, containing the towns of Kulmbach, Bayreuth, and Hof. Each of the three regions–the Oberland, the Unterland, and the Niederland–formed discrete territories until the end of the Old Reich. After Burgrave Friedrich VI acquired the mark of Brandenburg in 1415, all of his descendants held the title "margraves of Brandenburg." After 1440, the Franconian principalities were ruled by a cadet line of the electoral house, and more often than not, the lands were divided among various heirs. Given the potential for confusion over titles, throughout the work I generally use the term *Oberland* as a geographical descriptor rather than the adminstrative terms burgraviate and margraviate in their various permutations.

Of all the terms used in this book, the thorniest is that which appears in the title: *reformation*. "Reformation" is a word that appears in various contexts throughout the sources and literature of the period under question. It is used extensively in the period before 1517 and thereafter by both Protestants and Catholics to describe their own efforts. To this word must be added a lush undergrowth of related terms–reform, renewal, restoration–again employed in an often bewildering variety of ways. For the sake of convenience, I have chosen to stick to fairly standard historiographical conventions, using the Latin *Reformatio* to apply to the secular and spiritual reform movements of the fifteenth century, reserving "Reformation" for the emergence of Protestantism after 1517. In the Catholic case, I have tended to opt for "Counter-Reformation," not only because it remains the most common term, but also because it captures the essence of many of the reforms in late-sixteenth-century Bamberg, consciously directed against the Protestant heresy.[38]

Much of the difficulty in terminology derives from the concept of reform itself. Reform has a double edge; it is at once about restoration and about innovation.[39] At the same time, although often associated with one or another theological position (such as "reformed theology"), "reformed" is a relative concept. To be a reformer does not necessarily require subscribing to a specific set of doctrines. It is rather about a certain habit of mind, one deeply rooted in Christianity itself. It has been noted that messianic religion shows two fundamental characteristics. The spirit of messianic expectation is restorative in that it looks to bring the world back to a purity that existed in the past, however the past might be defined. It is also utopian in that the world to come would not be simply a return to a past condition but rather its perfection. The two faces of the reformist temperament reflect two faces of messianic expectation. Hence "in a personal sense every Christian is, or should be, a reformer."[40]

The emphasis on the personal side brings us to what is, for this present work, a central concern. Reformation and state building are concepts that are most frequently applied to the development of institutions and the discussion of political and theological abstractions. We tend to place the most visible institutional forms at the center, viewing forms of religious and political life that do not conform to the model as "departures" and "adaptations" when we are feeling generous and as "errors" and "distortions" when we are not. It would be truer to reality "to think in terms of a different model, putting the individual religious experience in the centre, surrounded by various forms of religious life, of which each was not less important for those involved in them than the more highly organized communities were for their members."[41] None of this diminishes the importance of institutional change—indeed, much of what follows necessarily deals with institutions. Rather, in confronting the history of religious reform, we ought to remain mindful that we are dealing with a subject that was always about both elites and the common person, about high and low culture, about the the community and the individual.[42] The history of religion and politics is not about ideas or institutions in the abstract, but about the connections between ideas and institutions and human life.

Chapter 1

TERRITORY AND COMMUNITY

The formation of the territorial state provides a central–if not the central–dynamic in the history of late-medieval Germany. The charters and other documents collected in the protocol books of the vicar general's court provide ample evidence for the growth of the territorial state from the mid-thirteenth century onward.[1] They indicate a demographic shift in the later Middle Ages, as new settlements were founded and some older ones were abandoned. They show the final dissolution of the manorial constitution and the emergence of free villages and towns. In the patterns of endowments and patronage, they chart the rise of the territorial nobility and the third estate.[2] The development of the territorial state is often taken as a sign of political chaos–the codification of anarchy–following the death of Frederick II.[3] In truth, the process of territorial state formation was well under way during the reigns of the later Hohenstaufen emperors. Far from serving as indicators of political collapse, the emergence of the territorial states revealed a growing sophistication of governance. Jan Dhondt's characterization of the rise of territorial principalities in post-Carolingian Neustria may well be used to describe the situation in post-Hohenstaufen upper Germany: the rise of territorial states marks an intensification of lordship on the local level.[4]

But there was more to the development of the state than politics. The charters preserved in the *Protokollenbücher* suggest that the line between secular and spiritual lordship was often difficult to discern. In this regard, the theoretical foundations of the territorial states were not all that different from those of the empire of which they were a part. The theory of empire in the fourteenth and fifteenth centuries retained many of the universalist-religious claims inherited from the Carolingians and Ottonians.[5] Lupold of Bebenburg, bishop of Bamberg from 1353 to 1363, described the emperor as "advocate and defender" of the church, linking his power to his responsibility for the preservation of orthodoxy.[6] The 1399 decree against Emperor Wenceslas IV cites the emperor's failure to resolve the Great Schism as the first cause for his deposition.[7] And the imperial concern for religion was not limited to the higher realms of politics. Charters from the fourteenth and fifteenth centuries reveal the imperial hand in endowments and the confirmation of ecclesiastical benefices.[8] At the heart of the imperial conception of sovereignty, then, was not simply care for worldly concerns, but the care of souls.[9]

The territorial princes shared in this concern. Drawing on the imagery of Revelation 4:5, the Golden Bull of 1356 likens the electors to the branches of a candelabrum, sevenfold but unified, like the Holy Spirit of God, giving light to the whole of the empire through their office.[10] Although probably few princes conceived of their office in such elevated terms, territorial rulers were deeply involved in ecclesiastical matters through their patronage and protection of churches and monasteries. And as countless noble testaments from the fifteenth through the seventeenth centuries remind us, the foundation of princely virtue was piety and the fear of God.[11] This is not to say that the authorities of the princes and the emperor were identical. Rather, insofar as the princely state emerged in the context of the medieval empire, its political institutions and culture always carried the imprimatur of the Reich, and that influence invariably involved a link between secular power and religious duties. The formation of the territorial state, then, did not simply mark the emergence of a new kind of polity but involved the creation of a sacred society.

The foundations of the territorial states of upper Franconia were laid down in the twelfth and early thirteenth centuries during the ascendency of the Hohenstaufen emperors.[12] The territorial princes derived their authority in part from their role as imperial officeholders. Their claims to jurisdiction over the regions that would later make up the territorial state were legitimized by a series of imperial edicts. Eckbert of Meranien, bishop of Bamberg from 1203 to 1237 and the builder of the Bamberger Dom, was among those bishops named in the *confoederatio cum principibus ecclesiasticis* of 1220.[13] The Hohenzollerns had a particularly close relationship with the Hohenstaufens and were among the Swabian notables who had profited from their patronage. As imperial counts and provincial judges *(Landrichter)*, both the bishops of Bamberg and the Hohenzollern burgraves could call local nobles to their court and held the right to resolve property disputes and distribute fiefs.[14] In addition to offices and privileges, the Hohenstaufen emperors provided the princes with a model of rulership that was widely copied. Effective territorial rulers in their own right, the Hohenstaufens had constructed a unified and powerful state in Swabia in the eleventh and twelfth centuries. Through their use of various means—the systematic foundation of towns and cities, the assumption of advocacy rights *(Vogtei)* over monasteries, and the judicious appointments of ministeriales as castellans and administrators on familial estates—the Hohenstaufen were able to consolidate their landholdings and use them as a springboard for their ambitions within the empire and beyond its borders.[15] Later territorial princes applied the same methods to the consolidation of their own territories in the later thirteenth and fourteenth centuries.

∽

The territory of the prince-bishopric of Bamberg, the Hochstift, grew together out of the fragments of four older counties: the Radenzgau, Volkfeld, Grabfeld, and Rangau. These had been seized from the rebellious counts of Schweinfurt and given in perpetuity to the bishops of Bamberg in the early eleventh century. To the east lay the terra sclavorum, including portions of the Bavarian Nordgau, the Egerland, and the Thuringian Sorbenmark. The area under the bishops' control grew steadily over the next two centuries, largely on account of the extinction of most of the noble families in the Radenzgau. The most important of these families were the dukes of Andechs-Meranian, who established a large and cohesive domain in the upper Main valley. The death of the last member of the Andechs-Meranian dynasty in 1248 resulted in a long, bitter struggle among the bishops, the counts of Orlamünde, the lords of Truhendingen, and the Hohenzollern burgraves of Nuremberg, over the families' estates.[16]

The Hohenzollerns quickly emerged as the bishops' main competitors in the upper Main. In the 1190s Friedrich of Zollern was appointed burgrave of Nuremberg. Burgrave Friedrich III (1261–97) acquired Bayreuth and was enfeoffed with the imperial *Landgericht* of Nuremberg in 1273.[17] After the death of the last count of Orlamünde in 1340, the Hohenzollerns acquired Kulmbach along with the *Ämter* of Berneck, Gefrees, and Wirsberg.[18] The Orlamünde inheritance—nearly all allodial land—formed the core of what came to be known as the *Land Oberhalb des Gebirgs,* or more simply, the Oberland.[19] Emperor Charles IV raised the Hohenzollern burgraves to the princely estate in 1363.[20] Subsequently, with Charles's support, the burgraves were able to acquire a wide string of territories in the Fichtelgebirge, including the towns of Münchberg, Naila, Wunsiedel, Weissenstadt, Kirchenlamitz, and Hof.[21]

By the middle of the fourteenth century, the physical outlines of the Hochstift Bamberg and the Hohenzollern Oberland were fairly well established. Neither territory yet constituted a "state" in the modern sense, however. Rather, each might better be described as "a complex . . . of smaller legal units that might or might not evolve into a unified *Land.*"[22] Like the empire it was a part of, the early territorial state was a cellular body, a coalition of noble lordships and townships bound to the prince in what Theodore Mayer called an "institutionalized personal association."[23] The multiple overlapping layers of lordship led the seventeenth-century jurist Anton Winter to the observation that "in Franconia there are territories within territories."[24]

The associative character of the early state may be seen in documents in which the prince addressed the estates. As late as the first decade of the sixteenth century, the bishops of Bamberg were wont to refer to the knights as "our associates in our see (*stifftsgenoß*)."[25] In this regard, the early territorial state resembled the imperial Landfriede coalitions of the later Middle Ages.[26] The prince was the leader of the coalition and provided legitimacy to the nobles through his formal recognition of their rights and status. What ultimately distinguished the prince from the members of the coalition was not necessarily the extent of his landholdings or the quality of their lineage but the imperial titles that allowed him to exercise authority over nobles and prelates within the province associated with his office.[27]

The elaboration of territorial administration during the fourteenth century reflected, in part, the rising prominence of the territorial princes. The expansion of lordly power was closely linked to the actions of "creative political personalities," princes and administrators who through their actions and policies left a distinctive mark on the outward shape and internal organization of the territories.[28] We might regard these German territorial states, no less than those of Renaissance Italy, as "works of art." Still, in spite of their successes, the princes faced the same problem as their Hohenstaufen forebears: it was practically impossible to govern without the assistance of local notables.[29] Consequently, just as Hohenstaufen administrative practice created the princely estate, so too did the process of territorial consolidation favor the rise of a new order: the territorial nobility.

The upper Franconian knights represented a fairly homogeneous group. They were characterized by "knightly" birth and designated *milites* or *ministeriales,* terms that indicated that the family was of servile background, unlike the older "free-born" nobility (*Adel*).[30] Nearly all were of *ministeriale* origin and seem to have been descended from free peasants living on imperial estates between Bamberg and Nuremberg.[31] Their names frquently refer to household offices: Truchsess (steward), Schenk (cupbearer), Marschalk (marshal). Several families retained allodial land well into the fourteenth century, including castles. In their ascent into the ranks of the nobility, the *ministeriales* and knights benefitted from the extinction of the older noble houses. The castles and estates of the older families passed to the bishops and burgraves, who in turn doled them out to their knights and *ministeriales* as fiefs or, more commonly, as part of an indenture.[32]

Service as princely castellans and Amtleute offered the knights a useful buttress to their own lordship. In the narrowest sense, princely officeholding increased the effective authority of nobles over peasants on their estates while providing them additional sources of revenue.[33] The nobles could also increase their autonomy by securing the support of multiple benefactors. Not infrequently knights held estates in several territories and could play one prince against another in the quest for higher office and other badges of status. Amtmänner and castellans were often sworn members of the regional Landfriede coalitions and could claim that they operated under the immediate sanction of the emperor or his *Hauptmann*. Such service afforded the knights imperial recognition of their status, independent of the territorial princes they ostensibly served.[34]

The powers and privileges of office allowed noble dynasts to pursue their own brand of territorial consolidation. Allodial estates and free castles made up the core of the noble estates in upper Franconia, which were extended through the construction of new settlements. The first wave of colonization came in the eleventh and twelfth centuries, followed by a second, more extensive period of forest clearing in the late thirteenth and fourteenth centuries. In the Veldener Forest, all but seven of the eighteen settlements listed in the *urbarium* of 1323 had been established after 1200.[35] These new villages were known as *Rodunge* and are chiefly recognizable by their names, containing the roots Hagen, Hurst, Wald, Reut, or Rode. The Rodunge were often exempt from the jurisdiction of princely courts.[36] Some were settled by Jews driven from Nuremberg and Bamberg following the pogroms of the 1370s and eighties. The Jews generally enjoyed a degree of protection, although their status created tension between the nobles and the princes.[37]

In consolidating their estates, the knights employed many of the same methods developed by the Hohenstaufen emperors and later used by the territorial princes. The lords of Schlüsselberg founded the towns of Waischenfeld and Ebermannstadt. The Gräfenbergers received a privilege from Charles IV allowing them to grant charters to Baiersdorf, Auerbach, Lauf, and Betgenstein.[38] Nobles were also active in supporting local churches. Although few had sufficient funds to support monasteries as did the territorial princes, they were able to build chapels and endow chantries. Some noble families had fairly extensive patronage rights. The lords of Wallenfels were patrons of three parishes—Lichtenberg, Steeben, and Wartenfels—and later founded chapels in Naila and Geroldsgrün and chantries in Stadtsteinach and Wartenfels. In all, twenty-three communities were served by priests appointed by the Wallenfels dynasty.[39]

One of the more dramatic examples of noble territorial formation was the lordship of the Förtsch von Thurnau family. The Förtsches were *ministeriales* of the dukes of Andechs-Meranien. In the early fourteenth century, the family controlled five castles: Thurnau, Maineck, Mönchau, Berndorf, and Peesten. Although the burgraves of Nuremberg claimed that it lay within their domains, Thurnau was essentialy an autonomous Amt. The independent status of Thurnau was confirmed by a charter issued by Emperor Wenceslas in 1398. The Amt Maineck lay in the Hochstift Bamberg, though here again, the status of the castle and surrounding area was subject to dispute.[40] Family members freely served both the bishops and the burgraves. In 1389, Martin Förtsch von Thurnau appears among the servants (*Diener*) of the bishops of Bamberg in a list of officials who has sworn to uphold the Landfriede of Eger. In 1404, the same Martin is listed among the "men and servants" of Burgrave Johann III of Nuremberg.[41] In 1300, the family held patronage rights over four parishes: Azendorf, Limmersdorf, Peesten, and their seat at Thurnau. These parishes included seventeen villages and hamlets. Over the course of the fourteenth century, the Förtsches established chapels at Burgellern, Berndorf, Mönchau, and Hutschdorf, and founded a hospital in Limmersdorf.[42] Taken together, the complex of castles, villages, parishes, and estates constituted a fairly cohesive territorial lordship that straddled the border between the Hochstift and the burggraviate.

The lords of Thurnau are an extreme example, but they are not unrepresentative. Throughout upper Franconia, noble dynasts sought to expand and consolidate their estates. Territorial officeholding was essential to their aims, just as imperial titles and offices provided the foundations for princely state building. Herein lies the paradox of late-medieval state building: the increase in state power tended to encourage particularism as local notables used the powers and privileges of office to carve out little territories for themselves and their heirs.[43] The knights were thus engaged in precisely the same sort of activity as their princely masters. In this regard, the same political dynamics that characterized the late-medieval empire—territorial formation and the struggle to maintain balance between the emperor and the princes (*Kaiser und Reich*)—were reflected in microcosm within the territories. But although the knights might have aspired to extend their domains, they faced the same fundamental problems that limited the power of the princes. The material strength of the nobles still derived from their landholdings, both familial estates and fiefs. The effective administration of these estates rested on careful management of local affairs. The bases of power remained local.

The territorial state of the later Middle Ages was a cellular body. If we look closely at the cells that made up the late-medieval territories, we can see a diverse range of communities—towns, villages, and smaller settlements—grouped together into administrative districts such as Ämter and parishes. Political life in upper Franconia in the later Middle Ages was centered on the small rural settlements that were home to the vast majority of the population.[44] The village of Büchenbach presents a fairly typical picture. One of the oldest townships in the Hochstift, Büchenbach first appears in a mid-eleventh-century list of estates belonging to the cathedral chapter in Bamberg and was certainly part of the old royal demesne granted to the chapter in 1008.[45] In 1348, the village of Büchenbach comprised between eighteen and twenty peasant farms.[46] A 1468 urbarium indicates that the village included twenty-two full mansi, although it is unclear how many individual households there might have been. Forty households seems plausible, suggesting a population of around two hundred souls.[47] At that time the Amt of Büchenbach included an additional thirteen hamlets, mostly isolated farmsteads, with about a hundred inhabitants among them. A number of these were Rodunge, as indicated by their names.[48] A few date from the first wave of clearings in the eleventh century, but most appear to have been established after 1300. Overall, the pattern seen here is fairly common throughout the region: nucleated villages with between one hundred and three hundred residents surrounded by a penumbra of smaller settlements. The village and surrounding hamlets were often fragments of older manors; in other cases the smaller communities were new foundations marking an expansion of the original village. On the margins were the Wilde Rodunge, communities set up by peasants in a deliberate effort to avoid seigneurial dues.[49]

The central feature of territorial administration in the late thirteenth and early fourteenth centuries was the castle, staffed by princely officials who administered princely domain lands and presided over local courts. These local officials were referred to by a range of titles—*iudex, Zentrichter, advocatus, Vogt, officialis, officiatus, Amtmann*—used rather indiscriminately well into the sixteenth century.[50] With the exception of "judge," the titles used to designate local officials derived from ecclesiastical parlance. An *advocatus* or *Vogt* was a layman charged with the defense of a church; an *officialis* or Amtmann was a member of a monastic community exercising a particular function (*officia*) and supported by a collection of prebendarial estates. By the end of the thirteenth century, the terms *officia* and *Amt* referred to a territorial unit made up of villages paying income to the church.[51] In Bamberg, the first use of *officia* in this context appears in a charter from 1259 in which the cathedral chapter's holdings in Fürth, hitherto referred to as a manor, are described as *officiam praepositure in Vuertte*.[52] By 1300, the terms *officia* and *Amt* had come to be applied to subunits of the territorial state. The Franconian *Landfriede* of 1316 describes officials who held court at castles (*veste*) as "*Amtleut*." In the *urbaria* of 1323 and 1348 the words *castra* and *officia* are used alongside one another, but in the later document, *officia* is by far the more common term. By the fifteenth century, the term *officium* was the standard Latin designation for administrative districts.[53]

The change in terminology reflected a transformation in the character of local government. Over the course of the fourteenth century, there was a tendency for the center of the Amt, originally sited in the castle, to move downhill to the village.[54] In the process, village officials assumed greater responsibility for day-to-day matters of provincial administration. In larger villages there was usually a judge (*Schultheiss*), one or two mayors (*Bauer*- or *Dorfmeister*), a council, and a court dealing with civil matters.[55] In 1404, Volkach had a Schultheiss and two *Bawernmeyster*, along with a seven-member council representing "the poor people and entire community."[56] Peasants living in the surrounding hamlets and in isolated farmsteads were generally under the jurisdiction of the village court. Criminal jurisdiction, in particular the four "higher cases" of murder, arson, robbery, and assault, were to be referred to the court of the Amtmann, although this did not always happen.[57] In practice, the Schultheiss served as the chief official in the Amt as the office of Amtmann gradually assumed the character of a sinecure for the nobility. By the end of the fifteenth century, judicial affairs were almost entirely in the hands of officials whose roots were in the village.[58]

The development of the office of Schultheiss led to a form of dualism in local administration. The Dorfmeister was the "most prominent" (*Vorstehende*) man in the community, elected by his peers. The Schultheiss was appointed, either by the prince or the noble lord. He was a man of the village to be sure, but one whose authority derived from being the lord's "overseer and steward" in the community. The more powerful the lord, the more likely that the Schultheiss, not the Dorfmeister, would be the most influential man in town, even if he had neither the means nor the kinship ties to merit the respect of his neighbors.[59] Here we can see the role of external authorities altering the internal structure of the village, but note that the effect is to introduce an artificial locus of authority, one potentially at odds with the ordinary structures of the village.

Through the granting of offices and the establishment of administrative institutions, princes could have a significant impact on the internal structure of rural communities. The most extreme expression of the formative power of princely patronage can be seen in the creation of territorial cities, the *Landstädte*. The bishops and burgraves both granted privileges to select villages, encouraging them to develop into towns. The foundations of such small cities, with their own walls and markets, marked an adaptation of the *Städtepolik* of the emperors and became a fixed part of the process of territorial consolidation in Swabia, Alsace, and Franconia.[60] Kulmbach, Bayreuth, Hof, and Lichtenfels had been founded by the princes of the Andechs-Meran dynasty as economic and political centers for their lands in upper Franconia.[61] The Hohenzollern burgraves followed suit, granting Kassendorf, Wonnsees, Rosstal, and Wunsiedel the right to build walls and hold markets. These towns helped define the frontiers of the Hohenzollern domains at strategic points.[62] Weismain, Herzogenaurach, Kronach, and Marktschorgast played similar roles in the Hochstift.[63]

Although the Landstädte played a significant role in the administration of the territories, they were nonetheless little more than large villages, often with no more than three hundred residents.[64] Writing in 1612 about the foundation of Wunseidel three centuries earlier, Paul Reinel mused that "at the beginning the town was likely just a castle surrounded by a few peasant hovels."[65] What distinguished these small towns from the surrounding villages was their role in the territorial government. Many of the burghers served as princely officials, as indicated by the prevalence of such personal names as Ammann,

Vogt, Hoffmann, Zollner, and Ungelter in the *urbaria* of the fourteenth century.[66] The economic and social advantages offered by the Landstädte made them attractive to immigrants from the countryside. The names of several residents of Stadtsteinach indicate that they had come from the surrounding villages. Some half dozen burghers had names deriving from the hamlet of Meingarsreuth, described in the *urbarium* of 1323 as deserted.[67] Here again we can see the disruptive potential of princely patronage. Throughout upper Franconia, small settlements were either partly or completely abandoned as the residents moved into the growing Landstädte. In this light, a comment in a fifteenth-century document from Schönfeld is revealing. The pastor reminds the cottagers and laborers in his village that they are not permitted to place themselves under the protection of other lords. Meanwhile, the names of four of the cottagers suggest that they had already done so, fleeing to Schönfeld from villages in the Hohenzollern domains.[68]

The rural communities of upper Franconia present a mixed picture in the later Middle Ages. Their physical shape and internal organization reflected the actions of the princes. This is especially true of the Landstädte, whose prominence derived almost entirely from princely patronage. On account of the influence of outside powers on communal institutions, it has been observed that in upper Franconia the "commune" as a distinct and autonomous political entity practically did not exist.[69] Practically, but not entirely. There were always communities that lay outside of the formal structure of the Ämter, especially in the highland regions.[70] Moreover, there are signs of a the development of a certain kind of civic consciousness in the towns and smaller communities. Residents of towns and villages alike tended to refer to themselves as "burghers." Over the course of the fifteenth century urban institutions, such as confraternities and guilds, proliferated in the villages. Peasants refered to their village "*Rathaus*" while they proudly displayed their communal coat of arms.[71] In other word, just as with the nobility, dependence on the prince for status did not necessarily preclude the development of a consciousness of estate among the rural population. And although it is not always possible to see a distinctive civic consciousness in the political realm, we can see it clearly in matters of religion.

Late-medieval parishes, like the Ämter, were administrative subunits of the territorial diocese. The parish church provided the most visible source of communal identity in late-medieval Franconia. Churches were generally the most permanent buildings in villages, providing not only the focal point for worship, but also serving as venues for community events. As burial places, the churches provided the clearest link to the history of the community.[72] Rural parishes generally included one or two villages along with a number of smaller settlements. Some of the villages incorporated into large parishes might have their own chapel, albeit without a permanent vicar. The pastor of the mother church was responsible for either traveling to the filial chapels or appointing chaplains in these communities. The failure of some priests to provide adequate pastoral care to the more distant corners of large parishes was a common source of aggravation. The residents of Ampfenbach complained in 1566 that the pastor of the mother parish of Burgebrach had not celebrated mass in their chapel since 1329, more than two centuries earlier.[73]

In response to the expansion of rural settlements, sixty-seven new parishes were incorporated in the diocese of Bamberg in the fourteenth and fifteenth centuries. Nearly half of these foundations (thirty-five) occurred between 1370 and 1440, with the largest concentration in the years around 1400.[74] In smaller communities, residents sought at least to provide for a chaplain or permanent vicar.[75] Records from the second half of the fourteenth century show a surge of pious foundations and endowments directed at local churches (see table 1.1). In the archidiaconates of Hollfeld, Bamberg, and Kronach, peasants and burghers endowed twenty-six chantries and vicarages in the years 1350 to 1399. Although the number drops off slightly between 1400 and 1449 (twenty-two), between 1450 and 1499 commoners made thirty-five major endowments.[76] The chapels and altars built with communal funds provided a much more natural focus for the community's religious identity than the distant parish church. The village council frequently was responsible for finding a chaplain and maintaining the chapel and altars. Through its oversight of the fabric of the church, the community came to exercise greater influence over its religious life.[77]

As important as these donations were, few villages had the means to create new parishes without assistance. Throughout the diocese of Bamberg, noblemen played a significant role in the creation of the "communal" church. In Ebing, a long-running dispute with the mother parish of Rattelsdorf led to an attempt to provide the village with a chaplain. The residents of Ebing attempted, without success, to establish a chapel; only through the generosity of Martin Förtsch von Thurnau was the foundation confirmed.[78] In Schönfeld, the Förtsch von Thurnau family endowed a chantry in 1390 that became the focus of donations by villagers and other local nobles. On the basis of these grants, Schönfeld was incorporated as an independent parish in 1397.[79]

The foundation of chapels and masses represent but one aspect of late-medieval religiosity. Looking beyond endowments to the more common expressions of piety, we should note that religious devotion in upper Franconia followed fairly familiar—and orthodox—patterns.[80] Of particular interest is the appearance of confraternities in the rural communities in the fourteenth and fifteenth centuries.[81] Rural confraternities represented an extension of mendicant piety, marked by public penance, private study, and prayer.[82] Women as well as men were active in these local religious organizations.

Table 1.1. Ecclesiastical Endowments in the Archidiaconates of Bamberg, Hollfeld, and Kronach, 1300–1529

Patrons	1300–1349	1350–99	1400–1449	1450–99	1500–1529
Nobles	14 (56%)	20 (37%)	18 (25%)	16.5 (27.5%)	7 (23%)
Burghers	6 (24%)	26 (48%)	22 (31%)	35 (38%)	16 (53%)
Confraternities	0 (0%)	0 (0%)	3 (4.5%)	3.5 (6%)	1 (3.3%)
Clergy	4 (16%)	4 (7.5%)	17.5 (25%)	4 (7%)	5 (17.3%)
Bishop of Bamberg	0 (0%)	1 (2%)	1 (1.4%)	0 (0%)	0 (0%)
Margrave of Brandenburg	1 (4%)	3 (5.5%)	9.5 (13%)	1 (1.5%)	1 (3.3%)
Totals	25	54	71	60	30

Source: Guttenberg-Wendehorst, *Bistum Bamberg.*

A confraternity in Vilseck, established in 1480, counted twelve women among its original members. More than half of the lay members named in the chapter's necrology were women.[83]

The most common form of lay confraternity in Franconian towns and villages was the Corpus Christi brotherhood, often styled "Brotherhood of the Angel Mass."[84] During the fourteenth and fifteenth centuries, Corpus Christi brotherhoods were organized in more than twenty towns and villages in upper Franconia.[85] In most cases, the foundation of the confraternity was closely linked to ecclesiastical endowments. The history of the Corpus Christi brotherhood in Selb is fairly typical. An Angel Mass was endowed by the "council and commune" of Selb in the first half of the fifteenth century. This was followed by the formation of a confraternity that remained active up until the Reformation.[86] In Bayreuth, the foundation of a Corpus Christi brotherhood in 1447 directly preceded the establishment of an Angel Mass.[87]

Where confraternities were established in filial communities, they might be seen as attempts to create an independent, communally based religious society outside of and free from the formal parish organization. In the diocese of Bamberg, evidence suggests that certain kinds of confraternities constituted an alternative to diocesan institutions.[88] The first clerical fraternity was established in 1344 and included clerics and lay people from the towns of Lichtenfels, Kronach, and Staffelstein. The communities in question made up the core areas of the archidiaconate of Kronach, one of the four major administrative subunits of the diocese. Over the course of the fourteenth century, the authority of the archdeacons had come into question, in part on account of clerical resistance to the bishops' aggressive tax policies. In its form and structure, the confraternity mirrored the more formal structures of the archidiaconate. Clergy within the province were expected to assemble on a regular basis for local chapter (*Landkapitel*) meetings. These were primarily intended to enforce reforms and discipline clergymen who were lax in their duties. The confraternity's statutes likewise required its members to meet three times yearly. The members dealt with matters of reform and used their meetings as opportunities to resolve disputes between clerics or between clerics and lay people. In other words, the confraternity was established to serve many of the same functions of the *Landkapitel,* the difference being that the confraternity was a voluntary association administered by the local clergy, rather than an official body under the supervision of episcopal officials.[89]

The clerical fraternity established at Lichtenfels was a practical response to problems of the diocesan administration. The archidiaconate of Kronach was large and spread out over fairly rugged country. It had no clear geographical center; rather, the parishes were concentrated in three areas, along the upper Main, Scorgast creek, and the upper Saale valley. The Lichtenfels confraternity served the churches in the first region. In the early fifteenth century, confraternities were established in the latter two regions: Stadtsteinach-Kupferberg-Marktschorgast (in 1402) and Kronach-Teuschnitz (1435).[90] Both confraternities were organized along the same lines as that in Lichtenfels and followed the same statutes. These voluntary associations at the local level were intended to provide a higher level of support for the parish clergy and to raise the standards of pastoral care. In both respects, but especially in their concern for the laity, the confraternities may be seen as expressions of the reforming impulses that gripped the church in the later Middle Ages, as popular institutions developed alongside the more formal diocesan synods.[91]

The spirit of reform may also be seen in the greater interest in scholarship in the small towns of upper Franconia in the later fourteenth and fifteenth centuries. After 1350, a small number of students from the diocese of Bamberg began to make their way to study at the University of Prague. After 1400 the trickle became a flood, with Leipzig replacing Prague as the prime destination for young scholars. Between 1408 and 1528, 940 students from the diocese went off to study at Leipzig, 774 of whom came from towns in the Hohenzollern Oberland. Although the largest number of students were from the larger towns of Kulmbach, Bayreuth, and Hof, quite a few came from towns and villages with fewer than three hundred residents.[92]

The students who went off to university were a socially diverse group. Many were of limited means: of 109 students from Kulmbach who studied at Leipzig between 1419 and 1517, eighty-seven received stipends to offset half of their fees, while eight were admitted as *pauperes.*[93] It was possible for young scholars, even those of relatively humble origins, to achieve prominence. Johann Balkmacher of Schauenstein rose to the position of dean of the arts faculty at Leipzig in 1468. Between 1491 and 1493, four other students from small towns in the Oberland–Johann Troger of Gefrees, Eberhard Pistoris of Berneck, Johann Rudiger of Creußen, and Nikolaus Kleinschmidt of Schauenstein–served on the university faculty, Kleinschmidt as rector of the arts faculty.[94] Friedrich Sesselmann (ca. 1410–83) was a burgher's son from Kulmbach who studied at Leipzig and Bologna, earning doctorates in both canon and civil law. In 1447 he served as ambassador to Rome for the German Electors and ended a long and storied career as bishop of Lebus and chancellor of the mark of Brandenburg.[95]

Sesselmann's career was clearly exceptional. Most students returned to Franconia after only one or two semesters and served as parish priests. This in itself suggests a larger social and cultural dynamic. The young men who had studied together formed a self-conscious group of scholars, not unlike the well-known sodalities of the early German humanists.[96] On the local front, popular criticism of scholars notwithstanding, it was generally accepted that higher education should provide better pastors and preachers.[97] The students who went off to university and returned to the parishes provided a vital connection between the centers of high culture and rural communities.

Considered together, the growing interest in education and the spread of confraternities indicates a popular engagement with learned culture and more cosmopolitan forms of piety.[98] The development of a distinctive religious consciousness in towns and villages may be seen as both cause and result of a genuine attempt to reform the church on the local level. Key factors in this local reform movement were greater lay participation in all facets of religious life, greater local control over church finance and discipline, and an emphasis on devotional practices that were adjunct to the mass. The evidence suggest that in the age of the Schism and the councils, rural society was formulating its own answers to the questions that plagued the church.[99] Communal identity in the later Middle Ages was closely associated with the ideals of religious reform, conceived of in terms that extended beyond the nominal boundaries of the *Gemeinde*.

The history of the parish and Amt of Marktschoragst provides an excellent example of the interrelation between territorial formation and changes in religious life at the local level. Lying astride the borders of the Hochstift and the Hohenzollern domains, Marktschorgast was one of the original parishes in the diocese of Bamberg. The center of the parish lay in the *terra sklavorum*, the old Sorbish mark on the eastern edge of the diocese. In 1109 the parish included the town of Marktschorgast and the older Slavic villages of Pulst, Pöllitz, and Wasserknoden. By the fourteenth century new settlements and Rodunge had increased the size of the parish considerably.[100] This placed strains on the rector's ability to serve all of the members of his

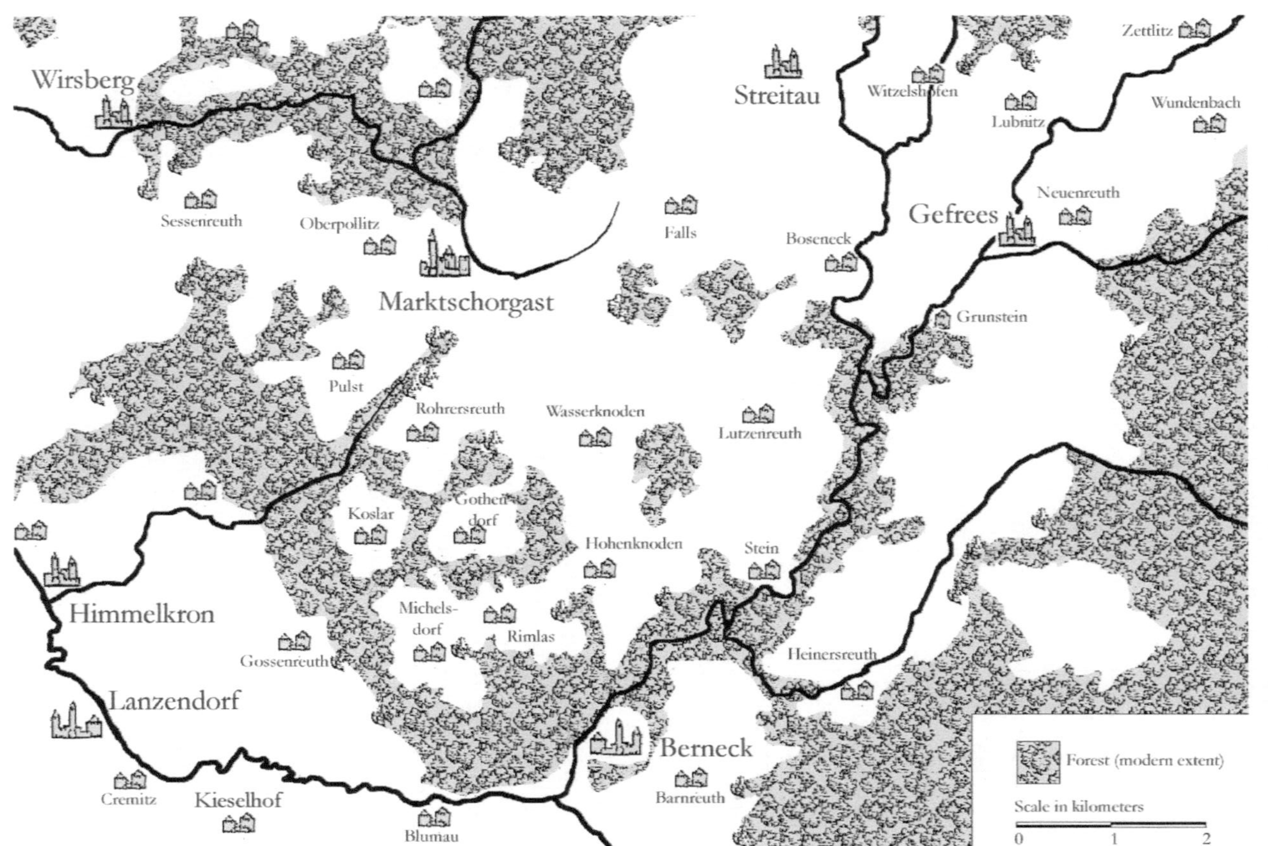

Map 3.   Marktschorgast and Its Environs

parish. In this regard, some rectors displayed less ardor than others. In 1341 the drunken pastor of Marktschorgast fled with the alms chest and defied attempts to bring him to justice.[101]

Following this incident, several communities sought to emancipate themselves from the parish with help from the Hohenzollern burgraves. The first was Berneck, where a self-standing parish was established in 1365.[102] That same year the residents of Gefrees, following the lead of their neighbors in Berneck, sought to establish an independent parish.[103] They were unsuccessful, and in the years that followed, relations between Gefrees and Marktschorgast deteriorated. In 1406 officials in Marktschorgast claimed that Gefrees and Stammbach were not simply part of their parish, but lay within their Amt as well. They produced evidence that since the time "before the great dying" the court in Marktschorgast had heard criminal cases originating in the two villages and certain outlying hamlets.[104] The burghers renewed their claim in 1413, arguing that Gefrees and Stammbach–along with the hamlets of Hermannsreuth, Metzlersreuth, Neuenreuth, Wundenbach, Weissenbach, and Zettlitz–lay within the jurisdiction of the bishops of Bamberg.[105] In 1419 the burghers brought forward more witnesses who testified that their court had heard criminal cases arising in Zettlitz, Pöllitz, and Stammbach during the 1370s and 1380s. From the perspective of the officials in Marktschorgast, the evidence plainly demonstrated that all these communities, unquestionably within their parish, were also part of their Amt.[106]

In their efforts to expand their Amt, the burghers of Marktschorgast were engaging in a form of state building from below. It was the burghers, not the bishop, who began the dispute. Their claims to secular jurisdiction, however, were based in large measure on the ecclesiastical jurisdiction of their parish. In other words, the goal was to make the secular *Gemeinde* conform to the spiritual community. In response, the residents of Gefrees redoubled their efforts to acquire their own priest. In 1442 Hermann von Hirschberg, Amtmann of Weisenstadt, and Albrecht von Wallenrode, a local nobleman, granted several estates to support a new mass. Seven years later Hans Gerber, a burgher from Gefrees, turned over the tithes from Böseneck to support the chantry. Two burghers administered the prebends.[107] In 1466 four brothers of the Roth family endowed a Lady Mass, to be administered by the mayor and council of Gefrees. The Roth family gave additional lands from their estates at Lübnitz in 1477 and 1482.[108] As a result of these endowments, nearly all of the hamlets and farms that lay between Gefrees and Markschorgast had financial ties to the chapel in Gefrees. In 1475 Heinrich Fuchs, formerly the chaplain in Marktschorgast, testified that a chantry priest in Gefrees was administering the sacraments to the residents of Zettlitz, Böseneck, Witzelshofen, Lübnitz, Neuenreuth, and Grünstein.[109] Following a second dispute in 1492, Bishop Heinrich Groß von Trockau ordered the pastor of Marktschorgast to appoint a chaplain to perform services in Gefrees on Sundays and holy days.[110] Meanwhile, the supporters of the new chantries established a confraternity.[111] In 1513 Jakob Gut, vicar of the Lady Mass since 1498, endowed an Angel Mass and founded a second confraternity, the Corpus Christi brotherhood. Both confraternities were active until the Reformation.[112]

While the residents of Gefrees were busying themselves endowing chantries and forming confraternities, a number of young men from the village entered the priesthood. Johann Roth, founder of the Lady Mass, was the first priest we know of from Gefrees. Johann Franck and Conrad Stretz were both ordained in 1466. About that same time, Johann Sammett, a member of a prominent Gefrees family, entered the University of Leipzig.[113] Johann Troger went off to Leipzig in 1479 and eventually rose to the rank of *magister,* earning a position in the philosophical faculty.[114] During his tenure, two brothers, Nikolaus and Pankraz Weis, followed him from Gefrees to Leipzig. Both brothers received their master's degrees, and Pankraz secured a place on the theological faculty.[115] In the years following 1500, several more sons of Gefrees entered the University of Leipzig. Johann Sammett's nephew Bernard was among them, as was Bartholomäus Gerber, the son of the administrator of the Lady Mass.[116] Altogether, twenty-three students from Gefrees attended the University of Leipzig between 1460 and 1528, the majority between 1475 and 1517.[117] For a rural, agrarian community, this figure seems astounding.[118]

It has been argued that during the later Middle Ages, "religion, piety, and the church were appreciated in the consciousness of peasants only insofar as they pertained to the village."[119] That does not appear to be true of Gefrees. As indicated by the number of university matriculations, quite a few residents had an appreciation of the church that transcended purely local concerns. The presence of students and teachers from Gefrees at the university had, moreover, a demonstrable impact of the developing religious identity of the community. At least two chaplains in Gefrees appear to have been recruited directly from Leipzig. The first was Johann Troger's classmate Jakob Gut, the founder of the Corpus Christi brotherhood.[120] The second was Johann Gangolf of Kulmbach, the last Catholic chaplain and the first rector of the new—and Lutheran—parish of Gefrees.[121]

Although the Lutheran Reformation takes us too far into the future, the coming of the Reformation in Gefrees does appear to have marked the culmination of a long series of actions whereby the residents of the village sought to break away from the mother church in Marktschorgast and establish their own parish. The political events revolve around territorial consolidation, but note that the attempts by the burghers of Marktschorgast to expand their *Amt* could be seen simultaneously as a manifestation of princely centralization *and* of communalism, here expressed in a form of local particularism. The burghers of Marktschorgast were engaged in much the same sort of activities as the knights, using their authority as princely officials to increase the number of rural communities under their control. In that regard, the political history of

Marktschorgast and Gefrees displays in microcosm many of the same features that characterized the history of the late-medieval empire.

One noteworthy feature of the contest between Marktschorgast and Gefrees is the way in which the residents of the latter community formed common cause with the nobility. Insofar as the cooperation between noble patrons and the leading families of the village were directed toward realizing a particular vision of religious community, the events of the fifteenth century would seem to prefigure the alliance of the second and third estates during the Reformation era. The focus of their activities was an effort to create a self-standing parish; the goal was to make the institutions of the local church correspond more closely to those of the secular *Gemeinde*. At the same time, the specific activities, such as the foundation of chantries and confraternities, had distinct theological implications; the sudden growth of learning in Gefrees argues that a reasonable number of parishioners were aware of the theological implications of their actions. In other words, the emergence of the notion of estate among the nobles and townspeople of upper Franconia appears closely linked to the development of a particular kind of religious consciousness: the formation of the Estates and confessional formation (*Ständebildung* and *Konfessionsbildung*) represent two aspects of a larger process.[122] This consciousness emerged during the course of a debate over spiritual and secular lordship and the shape of the sacral community. The tale of Marktschorgast and Gefrees reveals the centrality of the idea of reform as the central organizing principle of political activity.

Chapter 2

Rebellion, Representation, and Reform

The formation of the territorial state in upper Franconia was connected to a broader transformation of society at the local level. That transformation, moreover, had significant religious overtones, so much so that we have been able to describe local changes as manifestations of the late-medieval reformatio. As suggested in that claim, however, the reforms we observed in towns and villages such as Marktschorgast and Gefrees did not occur in a vacuum. In this chapter and the next, we will sketch out the specific events that drove the reform movements, first in the Hochstift Bamberg and then, in the next chapter, in the Hohenzollern lands. In both territories, events on the imperial stage in the late fourteenth and fifteenth centuries had a significant impact on both political consolidation and religious reform. Franconia figured prominently in the political system of the Luxemburg emperor Charles IV.[1] Under Bishop Lamprecht von Brunn, Bamberg played a leading role in the imperial Landfriede. The various crises that followed Charles' death, however, fundamentally altered the nature of both imperial and regional politics. Before 1378 the emperors were primarily interested in restoring imperial authority and maintaining the peace. The Great Schism, the collapse of imperial authority under Wenceslas and Ruprecht, the outbreak of the Hussite War, and a range of local rebellions that accompanied these events were catalysts for a much more ambitious program of religious and political reform than would have been conceivable a century earlier.[2]

Yet although external circumstances played a significant role in shaping the reform movement in the Hochstift Bamberg, the specific contours of the reform derived from political tensions within the episcopal city itself. Bamberg was the religious, administrative, and economic hub of the Hochstift. The center of the city was the tenth-century *castrum babenberg*. Henry II chose Bamberg as the site of his capital, building a cathedral and an imperial palace on the site of the old castle. The *castrum* became the site of the cathedral precinct (*Domstift*), the first of five ecclesiastical immunities within the city.[3] The cathedral chapter was the most significant political power in the late medieval city and Hochstift. Initially it comprised a group of canons regular who served the bishop and administered the cathedral, but by the beginning of the twelfth century, bishops were obliged to seek the chapter's advice on a number of matters.[4] In the middle of the thirteenth century, the chapter acquired the right to elect bishops.[5] From the election of Berthold von Leiningen (1257–85) onward, the canons required that newly elected bishops swear to uphold a capitulation of election (*Wahlkapitulation*). In all of the *Wahlkapitulationen* of the period between 1328 and 1422, the chapter attempted to limit taxes, spending, and the alienation of diocesan property.[6] The canons saw themselves—not the bishops—as the "hereditary lords" of the diocese and the city, and understood it as their responsibility to curtail the actions of their more ephemeral episcopal superiors when they seemed to threaten the long-term peace and stability of the Hochstift.

In addition to the cathedral precinct, there were four other ecclesiastical immunities in the city, built around the collegial churches of St. Gangolf, St. Stephen, and St. James, and the Benedictine abbey of Michelsberg. All four immunities came to form semi-autonomous boroughs within the city with their own courts and markets. With the exception of St. Gangolf, all of the immunities were on the left bank of the Regnitz. Straddling the river was the *civitas babenberg,* divided by the two major branches of the river into three large units: Sand, Insel, and Theuerstadt. On the fringes lay the two settlements of Zinkenwörth and Wunderburg, which were not formally incorporated into the city until 1413.[7] Unlike cities such as Nuremberg, Augsburg, or Cologne, Bamberg was not enclosed by a city wall, mainly because the bishops and the canons would not permit the burghers to build one.[8] Without a wall to define growth patterns, the city grew in a haphazard fashion, filling in gaps between the immunities and spreading over the islands and plains on the right bank of the Regnitz.[9]

There were significant economic differences between the immunities and the *civitas.* The *civitas* was a community of merchants and artisans. The immunities, by contrast, had a markedly rural character. In St. Gangolf, a large number of residents—perhaps as many as one hundred households—made their living as gardeners. A plan of the city drawn up in the late sixteenth century shows that large areas of St. Gangolf's were taken up with agricultural lands. In the immunities of St. Stephen and St. James, the houses are pictured with large yards containing gardens and orchards. And the wilderness was not far removed: in 1513 ten wild pigs swam across the Regnitz from St. Stephen's and ran amok through the center of town.[10]

The pigs should remind us that even the most urbanized areas of late-medieval Germany preserved a rural, if not a wild, character. The *civitas* Bamberg comprised a number of small, distinctive communities separated by river channels and stretches of woods and swampland. From the mid-twelfth century onward, the divisions between the *civitas* and the immunities intensified. A privilege of 1154 established the freedom of the "servants of the clergy" in the immunities from prosecution in the courts of the *civitas.*[11] Berthold von Leiningen freed the lay residents of the immunities—popularly known as "muntaters"—from ordinary taxation in 1261. After 1275 the burghers of the *civitas* were liable for taxes on business conducted in the immunities, but the muntaters had no tax burdens themselves. Criminals could flee to the immunities to avoid prosecution. Tensions grew between the *civitas* and the immunities, leading to armed conflict in the closing decade of the thirteenth century.[12]

After 1330, events tended to favor the burghers. Louis the Bavarian negotiated a peace settlement in 1333 that confirmed the city's right to self-government.[13] In 1340 Bamberg was included in the Franconian Landfriede alongside the imperial cities of Nuremberg and Rothenburg.[14] The city's privileges were renewed again in 1355 by Charles IV, who freed the burghers from the jurisdiction of "any secular judge or Amtmann . . . the Roman emperor excepted."[15] Meanwhile, Charles undercut the authority of the cathedral chapter, appointing two bishops of Bamberg with papal support. Neither Ludwig von Meißen (1366–74) nor Lamprecht von Brunn (1374–98) were encumbered by any sort of *Wahlkapitulation*. Consequently, both were able to pursue much more vigorous domestic and foreign policies than their predecessors.[16]

The reign of Lamprecht von Brunn proved of critical importance for the reform movements of the late fourteenth and early fifteenth centuries. Lamprecht was among the closest advisors to Charles IV and had previously served as bishop of Brixen, Speyer, and Strasbourg before assuming the episcopate in Bamberg. His arrival coincided with the outbreak of a political crisis that threatened the peace and stability of all of middle and southern Germany. In 1371 Charles IV purchased the mark of Brandenburg to ensure the election of his son Wenceslas to the imperial throne. To pay for the mark and the election, Charles mortgaged a number of imperial cities. In protest, the imperial cities in Swabia and Franconia formed a league on July 4, 1376.[17] In order to finance a war against the league, Lamprecht levied an excise tax on wine, from which no one—burgher, muntater, cleric, laymen, commoner, or nobleman—could claim exemption.[18] There was nothing unprecedented in this measure. In 1341, with the full support of the cathedral chapter, Bishop Lupold von Bebenburg had issued a similar tax on the *civitas* and immunities to support the Landfriede.[19] This time, however, the burghers and muntaters were united in their opposition to the tax. Together, they seized the gates and drove Lamprecht from the city. Only with help from the bishop of Würzburg could Lamprecht put down the revolt and return to Bamberg.[20]

A series of good harvests ensured that when Lamprecht reintroduced the excise tax in 1382, there were few complaints. A major fire in 1392 and an outbreak of plague two years later triggered a second uprising. The burghers were angry that the tax was not being collected in the immunities and appealed to both the pope and the emperor for support. In August 1397,

Pope Boniface IX issued a bull reversing the treaty of 1275. Henceforth, all people "whether they reside in the *Stadtgericht* or the immunities, are to be jointly referred to as burghers of Bamberg and treated as such" insofar "as they are both under the common protection and lordship of a single bishop."[21] Wenceslas IV confirmed Boniface's bull a few weeks later. In this case, since the tax had been issued in response to an imperial decree, Wenceslas seemed willing to do whatever was required to ensure its collection.[22] Ultimately, neither a schismatic pope nor a drunken emperor were able to provide the burghers with any tangible aid. The second revolt was crushed; the immunities remained intact.[23]

Shortly after the suppression of the revolt, Lamprecht von Brunn resigned, leaving behind a serious deficit and a legacy of rebellion and ill will. Later generations remembered him primarily on account of the excise taxes he attempted to impose—the sixteenth-century poet Martin Hofmann noted that "to this day this [sort of tax] is called *Lambertinus*."[24] Determined to prevent further conflicts, the canons imposed a brutal *Wahlkapitulation* on his successor. Albrecht von Wertheim (1398–1421) was stripped of most of his fiscal authority and offered little resistance when the dean and chapter assumed greater responsibility for the day-to-day running of the Hochstift. The next bishop, Friedrich III von Aufseß (1421–32), was a benign, middle-aged scholar with little interest in diocesan affairs. His *Wahlkapitulation* was even stricter than that of his predecessor. The "perpetual edict" of 1422 established a coregency between the bishop and canons, giving the latter almost complete control over fiscal administration.[25]

In light of the revolts in Bamberg and neighboring Würzburg,[26] as well as the larger conflict between the princes and the Swabian City League, the canons' actions seemed prudent. Fiscal restraint and the preservation of traditional privileges and immunities were, in their eyes, the key to maintaining stability and order.[27] Conflicts within the chapter in the past had limited its effectiveness, but by the first decade of the fifteenth century most problems had been resolved.[28] Still, since the taxes that the canons objected to had been levied to support the Landfriede, what appeared to the chapter as prudent fiscal policy could, from the imperial perspective, be construed as outright resistance to the emperor's edicts; certainly the emperors from Louis the Bavarian to Wenceslas saw it that way. Closer to home, the chapter's defense of the immunities in the wake of the revolts only accentuated the divisions within the city.

One indicator of the growing divisions between the immunities and the *civitas* was the spread of confraternal piety in the years surrounding the revolt of 1397. The cathedral clergy formed a brotherhood in 1380, extending membership to lay muntaters a few years later. The canons of St. Stephen's, St. James's, and St. Gangolf's established their own confraternities in imitation of that in the Domstift in the 1390s. Necrologia indicate that about one-third of the members were lay people.[29] In the *civitas,* endowments by burghers to local churches follow the same patterns noted above in the countryside. Of fourteen major endowments (chantries and vicarages) made by burgers between 1300 and 1430, ten date from the years 1393 to 1427.[30] A confraternity associated with the Carmel became a special focus of devotion in the first years of the fifteenth century. The necrologia for the Carmel brotherhood indicate that lay members outnumbered clerics nearly ten to one.[31]

The formation of confraternities may be seen as a means of integrating the ecclesial and civic communities. Given the circumstances, the near simultaneous appearance of confraternities within the various wards of the city in the aftermath of the rebellions suggests that such integration came at the expense of more general civic unity, giving religious expression to the divisions between the *civitas* and the immunities. These acts of faith could be seen as political acts, attempts to construct an alternative community no less significant than the more obvious rebellions of the 1370s and nineties. The centrality of the Carmel in the religious life of the city after 1400 is also noteworthy. It has been suggested that in some contexts, relations between mendicant orders and urban communities may be linked to the growth of evangelical heresy.[32] The evidence here is far too slim to form any conclusions. Nevertheless, the links between the rebellious burghers and the Carmel suggest that the critique of the canons' authority was framed not simply in political terms, but in religious ones as well.

The outbreak of the Hussite War upset the fragile balance between bishop, chapter, and city that had been framed in the years after 1400. With a major war on the horizon, the princes of Franconia were forced to raise armies, repair fortifications, and amass supplies. These things cost money, something in very short supply in the debt-ridden Hochstift. In 1421 Bishop Albrecht reached an agreement with the burghers of Bamberg for a property tax to finance the repair of a number of castles. In the countryside, towns were relieved of tax burdens for several years so that they could build or repair fortifications.[33] The country towns benefitted greatly from this policy, but it placed a disproportionate share of the general tax burden on the city of Bamberg. By the end of 1427, the city was growing restive as the bishop required ever more funds for a campaign against the Hussites.[34]

A military victory might have defused the burghers' concerns, but one was not forthcoming. The Franconian army sent to repel the Taborite invasion of Meissen was savaged by troops led by Andreas Procopius. During the winter of 1429–30, Taborite forces overran upper Franconia. Hof fell at the end of January 1430, and in the following week several other towns were taken and destroyed, among them Münchberg, Bayreuth, Marienweiher, Marktschorgast, and Kulmbach.[35] The Hussites arrived in Bamberg on February 2. The city was indefensible. The bishop and canons had fled to Forchheim. The town council found a burgher who could speak Czech to negotiate with the Hussite invaders. The city was spared, but only after the burghers agreed to a ransom amounting to some 12,000 gulden.[36]

In the aftermath of the invasion, the burghers presented Bishop Friedrich III and the chapter with a proposition calling for the consolidation of the five immunities and the *civitas*. In part, the burghers justified the measure as necessary to raise funds to fortify the city. They further demanded that "all secular courts . . . should become one court, and hereafter remain in unity." The proposal was approved by the bishop and a rump chapter of thirteen canons. The canons allied with the burghers argued that the city government should be placed "in the hand of one bishop." As matters stood, people fled to the immunities to avoid taxation, leading to "notable injuries." Moreover, "certain of the richest and most honorable men from the immunities" had agreed to the reform, since "disunity brought more trouble than freedom was worth."[37] The dissenting canons were not convinced. Meeting in Staffelstein, they condemned such "novelties," citing agreements from 1339 and 1410 in which the bishops and burghers had recognized the liberty of the immunities. "Base and crazy folk" were merely trying to stir up discord between the laity and the clergy. The immunities had been established precisely to protect the church from such rogues.[38]

In April, 1431 the two sides presented their cases before the emperor Sigismund and the cardinal-legate, Julianus Caesarini. Both the cardinal and the emperor were impressed by the deputation from the *civitas,* made up of burghers and prominent muntaters. Satisfied that the muntaters, the burghers, the bishop, and the majority of the canons were in agreement on the matter, Sigismund issued a Golden Bull, ordering the dissolution of the immunities and their incorporation into the *civitas*.[39] Sigismund arrived in Bamberg during Holy Week to promulgate the bull. He hoped that the bishop of Würzburg and Margrave Friedrich of Brandenburg could allay the concerns of the dissenting canons, but to no avail. The canons decried the Golden Bull as "poison" and refused to submit.[40]

Sigismund left Bamberg after Easter to negotiate with the Hussites at Eger. In his absence, opposition to the Golden Bull grew. Although the leading muntaters maintained that consolidation of the city was necessary for the "common good," it soon became clear that they did not represent the view of most residents of the immunities.[41] By the end of August, the muntaters refused to honor summonses to the Stadtgericht. As tensions grew, Bishop Friedrich announced—somewhat disingenuously—that the Golden Bull had been issued without his knowledge and then promptly abdicated. The canons now elected a bishop more amenable to their point of view. Anton von

Rotenhan (1432–59) had proven his skill at dealing with disgruntled burghers in Würzburg some years earlier, and the canons were confident that he would be able to prevent execution of the Golden Bull.[42] But Anton did not arrive in the city for another year, during which time the confrontation between burghers and muntaters became increasingly violent. In March 1433, the burghers arrested several leading residents of the immunities for refusing to swear an oath to the city council. Two weeks before Easter, some fifty heavily armed burghers rode out to the vineyards and gardens of the muntaters, arresting anyone from the *civitas* working there. During Holy Week, at least four hundred burghers stormed St. Gangolf's Immunity, smashing in the doors of anyone who refused to recognize the authority of the Stadtgericht.[43]

The burghers called on the emperor, Pope Eugene IV, and the Council of Basel to enforce the Golden Bull. Eugene was favorably inclined to the burghers' pleas and reissued the bull of Boniface IX, which had abolished the immunities. His letter never quite made it to Bamberg. When the papal messenger arrived in the city, he delivered the bull to an individual who claimed to be the mayor. In fact it was the dean of St. Gangolf's Church, who subsequently delivered the papal letter to Bishop Anton.[44] The Council of Basel provided even less help. It began to question whether or not the emperor had any jurisdiction in the case after all, and demanded that Anton come to Basel to clarify matters.[45] Throughout spring and summer of 1434, the council heard arguments from all quarters. The most serious indictment against the burghers was framed by the bishop of Würzburg, Anton's brother Bishop Christoph of Lebus, Margrave Friedrich I of Brandenburg, and the Elector of Saxony. The princes claimed that many women had been injured during the burgher's attacks on muntaters in Zinkenwörth, Theuerstadt, and Wunderburg. One woman had "lost her wits"; another had died of shock. Several "honorable ladies, widows, and pregnant women" had been pulled "naked from the baths" and thrown into the street. Clerics had been abused, churches had been despoiled. Burghers had prevented baptisms, and many children had perished unbaptized.[46] Although the burghers denied the charges, the council was swayed by the princes' complaints, as well as those of Bishop Anton and the dissident canons. On October 9, 1434, the Council of Basel fined the burghers 60,000 gulden and placed the city under the interdict.[47]

Sigismund and Eugene IV both condemned the council's action. They argued that the chapter had acted contrary to ancient custom in its dealings with the previous bishops.[48] The burghers compared the council to "Turks, heathens, and Tartars" and claimed that the ban was contrary to "divine, ecclesiastical, secular, and natural law." Their only intention had been "with the will and consent of the *rat* and *gemein*" to serve the best interests of all the bishop's subjects. Eugene lifted the ban of excommunication in May 1435, just as the burghers had begun to parlay with Bishop

Anton about dropping their suit.[49] Emboldened by the bull of absolution, the burghers now broke off negotiations. On June 23, 1435, they stormed the Michelsberg. Although the abbot agreed to their terms, turning over 300 gulden worth of plate, the commanders could not restrain their men. The abbey was sacked and burned.[50]

Anton now raised a relief army and marched on the city. After a few tense days, on July 7 Margrave Friedrich arranged a truce. The council agreed to lift the ban on the city, while the burghers quit work on the walls and swore loyalty to the bishop. Two years later the various parties agreed to a settlement worked out at the Reichstag of Eger. Sigismund grudgingly withdrew the privilege he had given to the burghers to build walls, but demanded that the immunities would remain subject to taxation.[51] The compromise eviscerated the Golden Bull, and when Sigismund died on December 9, 1438 the burghers found themselves in an uncertain situation. The appointment of the bishop of Würzburg, Johann II von Brunn, to mediate the dispute raised their hopes. Johann von Brunn and Anton von Rotenhan were old enemies, and the burghers felt confident that Bishop Johann would take their side as they rejected Anton's terms. A second round of discussions began in the spring of 1439, this time led by the Society of the Rose, an association of Franconian knights. The knights, bishop, and chapter now constituted a united front. On the other side, conflicts within the *civitas,* in particular between members of the council and the artisans, robbed the burghers of any chance for success. When negotiations concluded in June 1440, the immunities had been restored.[52]

In the immediate aftermath of the Immunities Contest, Anton von Rotenhan met with a deputation representing the cathedral chapter as well as the see's "prelates, knights, and *mannschafft.*" The assembly expressed serious concern over the fiscal condition of the Hochstift. The Hussite War and the Immunities Contest left the Hochstift with "hard and horrid debt"–over 300,000 gulden–on account of "usurious interest, extortion, payments, expenses, and manifold other damages, wars, assaults, insurrections, and bad luck."[53] Tax revenues had fallen sharply, largely on account of privileges granted to the Landstädte. Anton attempted to raise cash by mortgaging properties and selling privileges, but these measures found little favor with either the canons or the knights.[54] Since Anton had failed to find an "honorable and effective way" to alleviate the debt, the chapter appointed a council of regency which, with the advice of the prelates and the knights, would take over the fiscal administration of the Hochstift.[55] With the support of Margrave Johann the Alchemist of Kulmbach, the regents exiled the bishop to Carinthia in 1442.[56]

The council of regency quickly proved incapable of administering the Hochstift effectively. Conflicts between the cathedral dean, Gottfried Schenk von Limpurg, and the estates undermined the new regime. When Gottfried assumed power as coadjutor in Würzburg, the knights and prelates in Bamberg began to fear that he intended to unite the governments of the two sees under his leadership. In June 1443, the estates dissolved the regency. The knights and prelates condemned the "recent dissonance and division," laying the blame squarely on the dean and chapter. By the end of the year, Anton had been recalled from exile and restored to power.[57]

Bishop Anton's reign witnessed the emergence of a new factor in territorial politics. Although the rebellions of the 1370s and 1390s had been restricted to the city of Bamberg, the Hussite War and the Immunities Contest had affected the territory as a whole. From 1433 to 1439 the episcopal government was resident in Forchheim, the second city of the Hochstift. Other towns, such as Lichtenfels and Weismain, hosted meetings among the bishop, the chapter, foreign rulers, and local knights. The burghers of Bamberg seemed to have sensed a change, and increasingly described their actions as necessary for the "good order" of the entire Landschaft.[58] In 1446 ten Landstädte–Forchheim, Herzogenaurach, Höchstadt an der Aisch, Kronach, Lichtenfels, Weismain, Burgkunstadt, Hollfeld, Waichenfeld, and Schesslitz–formed a league that adjudicated a dispute between the town council and the artisan community in Bamberg.[59] After Anton's death, the towns were included in a union of estates, organized by the knights and prelates, all of whom hoped to maintain influence under the new bishop.[60]

Prince-bishop Georg I von Schaumberg was elected on May 18, 1459, a week after the formation of the union of estates. With greater success than his predecessor, Georg I was able to play the estates against the chapter.[61] Georg courted the towns, granting them generous tax exemptions, allowing them to improve their fortifications, and extending market privileges.[62] During his reign we see the first use of the term *Landtag* to describe the territorial diet, now including not only the knights and prelates but the towns as well.

The Landtag played a significant role in negotiations among the Hochstift Bamberg, Würzburg, and Margrave Albrecht Achilles of Brandenburg. Bamberg had allied with Bavaria, Würzburg, and Henneberg against Albrecht Achilles in 1460, but a year later agreed to a separate peace with the margrave at Zwernitz. The cathedral chapter opposed the Treaty of Zwernitz, arguing that they could not abandon their brethren in Würzburg. Given that several canons in Bamberg were members of the chapter in Würzburg, their position should have come as no surprise. On a more substantive level, the canons claimed that Bishop Georg had borrowed money from Duke Ludwig the Wealthy of Bavaria. Having now broken the terms of their alliance, the bishop would surely be called on to repay the debt.

The estates met at the Benedictine monastery at Banz to answer the chapter's accusations. The location was noteworthy because the diet was held outside of the capital city. The knights spoke first, led by Georg von Giech, who declared that anyone who claimed that the bishop had ever received money from Bavaria "lies like a scoundrel." Johann Truchsees von Pommersfelden agreed, stating that none of them had ever wanted a war with Albrecht Achilles. Albrecht was willing to make peace and abandon claims to jurisdiction over the Hochstft; Johann thought that would be sufficient. The representatives from the *civitas* reminded the chapter that the bishop of Würzburg had seized thirteen ships owned by Bamberg merchants with cargos valued at more than 70,000 gulden. Certainly the burghers owed Würzburg no debt of gratitude. The mayor of Kronach, Johann Packer, had the last word: "My lord, it is my belief that we ought to [accept the treaty]. So as now the prelates, the knights, and we from the towns are as one, and our gracious lord with us, we wish to bring this matter to a close, since we are they who must decide."[63]

With the support of the nobles and towns, Georg was able to compel the chapter to accept the Treaty of Zwernitz. Throughout the conflict, Georg had found it expedient to hide behind the diet and let the estates press his claims. A few years later, the bishop used the same tactic in his negotiations with Albrecht Achilles. In the process, he realized that there were distinct limits to the estates' support. After negotiating a secret treaty with the margrave, Georg found himself pressed by the diet on the terms of the agreement. The estates informed Georg that the "Landschafft would be entirely willing to help"—so long as the bishop followed their counsel. If the bishop had promised Albrecht anything beyond what was in the Treaty of Zwernitz, however, the diet would not accept responsibility. Any negotiations Georg made on his own were his problem. After receiving this rebuff, Georg let the diet conduct the final negotiations with Albrecht on their own. When pressed by the margrave on his apparent repudiation of the secret treaty, Georg excused himself by saying that he could not go against the estates in the matter.[64]

The reign of Georg I von Schaumberg marked the apogee of episcopal authority in the fifteenth century. He was praised by a contemporary as "a great man, sober, mature, just, possessing great religious zeal."[65] After his death, the fortunes of the episcopate declined sharply. The chapter was divided between a vocal minority, allied with the cathedral dean and seriously engaged with diocesan politics, and the majority of canons, who could have cared less. Philipp von Henneberg (1475–87) was elected as a compromise candidate. With the possible exception of his two brothers, none of the canons particularly cared for him. The will of the minority and the lassitude of the majority was made manifest in the *Wahlkapitulation* prepared for Philipp, without doubt the most oppressive ever foisted on a bishop of Bamberg.[66]

During the first five years of Philipp's reign, the chapter became increasingly polarized. The bishop, with support from a small group of canons, tried to extricate himself from the coils of the *Wahlkapitulation*. On November 24, 1480, Pope Sixtus IV struck down the *Wahlkapitulation* as "false, illicit, and injurious to the church in Bamberg."[67] The pope then appointed the abbots of Michelsberg and Langheim as executors of his decree, ordering them to make sure that the chapter backed down and made no effort to enforce the *Wahlkapitulation*.[68]

The canons were incensed. A member of the bishop's council, Dr. Theodorich Morung, tried to bribe some of the canons into accepting the papal decree, but this hardly helped matters. In October 1481, the contesting sides opened negotiations under the mediation of Bishop Wilhelm of Eichstätt. Bishop Wilhelm declared that the dean's party in the chapter was nothing less than an illicit conspiracy.[69] With the threat of excommunication hanging over their heads, the dean and the other canons agreed to continue negotiations, albeit under protest. The estates now became involved, informing the dean that if mediation failed, then the diet would take up the matter. When talks with Bishop Wilhelm stalled in January 1482, the diet convened itself and tried to mediate the dispute.[70] A compromise was worked out in mid-January 1482, but it amounted to only a few superficial changes in the *Wahlkapitulation*.[71] With the death of Sixtus IV, the dean and his associates felt free to disregard the estates and the mediators. The *Wahlkapitulation* remained in force.

The canons might celebrate their victory over Philipp von Henneberg, but ultimately the chapter emerged from the conflict with its reputation seriously tarnished. Reflecting on the canons' bellicose nature, one wit observed:

> In the *Domstift* is a good living.
> There they should be singing
> And looking after their parishes
> A book is more fitting in their hands than a halberd.[72]

The bishops, meanwhile, consistently found themselves limited by the power of the chapter. For a time it appeared that the territorial diet held the key to the restoration of episcopal authority. Anton von Rotenhan and Georg von Schaumberg had some success playing the diet against the chapter, but events showed that the bishops could not always count on the loyalty of the estates. In the long run, the bishops found ecclesiastical reform a much more effective weapon in their struggles with the chapter and the estates. In the age of the Schism and the councils, it was the power of the bishops *in spiritualibus* that provided the surest means to secure their authority as princes.

From the time of Lamprecht von Brunn, ecclesiastical reform in the diocese of Bamberg was directed toward three major targets: the monasteries, the secular clergy, and the diocesan administration. Two monasteries were singled out for attention during Lamprecht's reign: the Cistercian monastery of Langheim and the Augustinian house at Neunkirchen am Brand. The financial condition of the two monasteries was, at least in the beginning, the primary concern. Langheim had long been in serious financial trouble. In 1364 the bishops had acquired the Amt of Teuschnitz from the abbey on mortgage. To alleviate Langheim's debts, Lamprecht purchased the Amt in the years 1381–88. The bishop also bought the monastery's estates near Marktleugast in 1384. The bishops thus acquired the towns of Teuschnitz and Marktleugast, as well as thirty villages and hamlets and fifteen deserted settlements.[73]

The reform of Neunkirchen was conducted along rather different lines. A general reform movement of the Augustinian canons had begun at Raudnitz in Bohemia in the 1370s, and Lamprecht wished to extend the reform to Neunkirchen. On the financial side, the bishop and the general of the order had become concerned about the alienation of the house's estates. Consequently, Neunkirchen's land holdings were consolidated and reorganized.[74] In addition, the canons were required to accept the revised rule devised at Raudnitz. A collection of sermons, prepared at Neunkirchen in the early fifteenth century for the edification of the canons, appears to embody the spiritual side of the reforms.[75]

Not long after his appointment, Lamprecht von Brunn undertook to overhaul the ecclesiastical courts. Prior to his accession, clerical discipline was the province of the cathedral dean. Lamprecht created a new office, that of vicar general, whose court stood over and above that of the dean. Initially an ad hoc position, after 1387 the office became a fixed part of the episcopal administration. The vicar general was independent of the cathedral chapter; consequently the chapter tried to force both Lamprecht and his successor Albrecht von Wertheim to appoint only canons to the post. The canons failed, and throughout the fifteenth and sixteenth centuries, the office of vicar general was a powerful counterweight to the claims of the dean and the chapter.[76]

Bishop Lamprecht convened at least three diocesan synods (1378, 1387, 1394) that were directed toward reform of the parish clergy. The synods were noteworthy for two reasons. Through such meetings with the diocesan clergy, the bishop assumed personal responsibility for the education and discipline of the priesthood. The synods also provided the opportunity for the promulgation of reform ordinances, binding on all of the clergy. The synodal statute of 1378 in particular has been described as providing a "constitution *in spiritualibus* for [the] diocese."[77] The synodal decrees of Lamprecht von Brunn were later reissued (with minor additions) at a synod convened by Albrecht von Wertheim in 1402. The main principles of these synods were codified in the *Directorium pro instructione simplicium presbyterorum,* written by the cathedral vicar Johann von Auerbach sometime after 1430. Auerbach's work circulated widely in manuscript before being printed in the 1460s and remained for many years the handbook for the parish clergy in the diocese of Bamberg.[78]

Despite the political difficulties that plagued his reign, Anton von Rotenhan proved an energetic and effective reformer. With the blessing of the papacy, Anton intervened frequently in the affairs of the monasteries. He ordered the reform of Weissenohe in 1438 and subsequently tried to settle the fiscal problems of the Carmel in Nuremberg.[79] The main focus of Anton's attention was the Benedictine abbey of Michelsberg. Throughout the fourteenth century, the abbey had been in decline. Visitors from Würzburg in 1424 reported that no one followed the rule, celibacy was more an ideal than a reality, and that the monks performed their spiritual duties with little enthusiasm if at all. In 1435 Anton appointed Johannes Fuchs as abbot. When it became clear that Fuchs could neither control the monks nor balance the books, Anton took matters into his own hands. From 1446 to 1450 the bishop administered the monastery directly. The monks were allowed to elect their own abbot in 1450, but Hartung II proved as venal and incompetent as any of his predecessors. Anton deposed Hartung and appointed his suffragan bishop, Johannes Rupp, as provisor in 1453. They abbey remained under Rupp's leadership for another ten years.[80]

Georg I continued the reforming activity of his predecessor, unhindered by any serious opposition from the canons. He reorganized the church courts and sharpened ecclesiastical sanctions against clerics and lay people alike.[81] Nearly every monastery in the diocese was targeted for reform. The Franciscan house was reformed in 1460, followed by the Carmelite and Augustinian monasteries a few years later.[82] The convents received particular attention, although the Dominican convent of St. Theodor was able to resist intrusion.[83]

The abbey of Michelsberg proved a much more difficult nut to crack than in the other monasteries. The suffragan bishop Johann of Rupp continued to serve as provisor until 1463. Thereafter, Bishop Georg appointed Eberhard III von Venlo as abbot. Eberhard came to Bamberg intent on bringing Michelsberg into the Bursfeld Congregation of reform abbeys. The events of the night he arrived revealed just how much work there was to do. Under the leadership of their prior, Nicholas von Rabenstein, the monks broke into the sacristy and made off with a number of treasures, including the abbot's miter and staff. Bishop Georg was furious and sent word to all neighboring bishops to arrest the "God-robbing apostates." Rabenstein berated the bishop, arguing that the monks had only taken what belonged to them. The monastery had been founded by noblemen for the nobility, and the bishop had no right to impose a "foreign abbot" on them. Rabenstein obtained the support of sixty-six Franconian knights, who presented their case to the Benedictine provincial assembly in Würzburg. The abbots were unimpressed and sharply condemned Rabenstein and the renegade monks. By the end of 1465 the rebel monks had all been captured and their noble supporters excommunicated. The abbey was subsequently reformed and joined the Bursfeld Congregation in 1467.[84]

Although the monastic reforms were significant, the farthest-reaching reform efforts were directed toward the secular clergy. Following in the footsteps of Lamprecht von Brunn, Anton von Rotenhan convened a series of reform synods, in part to promulgate the decrees of Constance and Basel, in part to remedy local concerns.[85] The close association between the Hussite War and the Immunities Contest led many of the burghers' opponents to identify them as Bohemian heretics. The Elector of Saxony referred to the burghers as worse than "heathens or Hussites," while the Dominican theologian Johann Nider was convinced that the Bohemian heresy was the font of the burghers' demands.[86] In 1448 the cathedral preacher Heinrich Steinbach was tried before a diocesan synod for preaching "Wycliffite" heresies. Only two canons participated in the synod; the remaining fifteen clerics who took part in the proceedings came from parishes outside the city. In 1451 Nicholas of Cusa presided over a synod intended to resolve disputes between the secular clergy and the mendicant orders.[87] What is notable about these two synods is that the cases in question would normally fall under the jurisdiction of the cathedral dean. Anton von Rotenhan's use of the synod marked a usurpation of the dean's spiritual authority, just as the dean had used the council of regency to usurp the secular authority of the prince-bishop.

Following the publication of decrees from the Council of Basel in 1433, Anton von Rotenhan issued a comprehensive reform statute.[88] It begins with a condemnation of "certain heretical errors," specifically utraquism. The statute roundly condemns certain offensive habits of the clergy as well, including wearing beards, excessive drinking in taverns, participating in tournaments, concubinage, and simony. Although clerics at all levels indulged in most of these vices, the prohibition against jousting would seem to apply only to noble canons. The canons also seem to be the target of a section dealing with "conspiracy." Clerical "conspiracies" and "confederations" had led to "discord" and the collapse of ecclesiastical discipline. Consequently "the good church is dissipated and souls are brought into peril."[89] In the wake of conflicts between the bishop and the chapter and between the chapter and the *civitas,* the reform ordinance placed the blame squarely on the canons.

The next major synod was convened by Bishop Heinrich III Groß von Trockau in 1491. By now the utraquist threat had diminished; hence the portions of the synodal decrees dealing with heresy are of a vastly different character. Much of Title XLV (*De haereticis*) deals with "demonic incantations" and "magical superstitions," not surprising since the *Malleus malificarum* had been composed in Bamberg just five years earlier. Title XXXIII (*De celebratione missarum et sacramente eucharistiae*) was directed primarily against negligent pastors who did not perform the sacrament according to the official rite. No mention is made of giving the wine to the laity during communion. Clerical conspiracies do not appear to have been a concern either. Rather, Title LVIII calls for the excommunication of any lay people who might attempt to revoke the ecclesiastical immunities.[90]

Clearly much had changed since the Council of Basel. The statutes of Bishop Heinrich's synod perceive less of a threat from Bohemian heretics and rebellious canons than from witches and aggressive laymen. Still, the sections on the Eucharist were sharply critical of negligence on the part of some priests. When priests are diligent in the administration of the sacraments, the statutes declared, then faith is served. If they are not, "errors in faith rise up amongst the people."[91] A half century earlier, Johann von Auerbach had stressed the same point: the negligence of the pastors is the surest source of heresy and disorder.[92] In the wave of liturgical printing that began in the 1480s, we can see the bishops taking positive steps to remedy perceived defects in the administration of the Eucharist. Philipp von Henneberg issued the first printed breviary in the Hochstift in 1484. Additional editions appeared in conjunction with the synodal statute of Heinrich III in 1493 and 1498/99. Complete missals were printed in 1490, 1491, 1499, and 1506/1507. Few examples of these early printings survive, but those that do show signs of heavy use.[93] The appearance of missals seems to follow the reforms endorsed by Heinrich III, aimed primarily at improving the quality of the ways in which the mass was celebrated. Beyond that, to ensure the fidelity and orthodoxy of the common people, priests were admonished to preach "in the mother and vulgar tongue."[94]

What was being preached? There are few clues. A manuscript Latin Bible from the Carmel, dated 1384, contains extensive marginal annotations on the text, in particular on the book of Job, which might have served as sermon notes, although this is not entirely clear.[95] Several fifteenth-century priests prepared manuscript copies of sermon collections.[96] A few parish priests also made copies of theological works, including the *ars praedicatoria* of Alanus ab Insulis and works by Nicolas of Lyra, Johann Nider, and Jean Gerson.[97] For the period after 1500 no such manuscripts survive, although it is clear from a handful of wills that some priests did own printed books. Heinrich Fuchs had both a missal and a printed Latin Bible.[98] Laurentius Einwich of Pottenstein had several books at his disposal, including a copy of the 1522 printing of Johannes Tauler's sermons.[99] Overall, wills and inventories point to an expansion of parish libraries in the late fifteenth and early sixteenth centuries.[100] In the sermons and book collections a variety of strains are represented—late scholasticism, the *Devotio moderna,* humanism, Christian Neoplatonism, mysticism—in an orthodox, albeit eclectic, assortment.

One surviving sermon from pre-Reformation Bamberg is the *Oratio ad clerum bambergensem,* preached by Abbot Johannes Trithemius of Sponheim at the Carmel in 1508.[101] The text for the sermon is I Peter 2:11–12a: "Beloved, I beseech you as aliens and exiles to abstain from the passions of the flesh that wage war against your soul. Maintain good conduct among the Gentiles." In good Neoplatonic fashion, Trithemius begins his sermon with a line from Palladas:

> Naked I came to this earth and naked I will return to it.
> And in all for which I vainly strive, I perceive my naked end.[102]

According to Trithemius, when we observe the bones in the grave it is impossible to see "any difference, neither birth nor the prerogatives of office."[103] The reason is clear: in this world we are merely sojourners. So long as we are at home in the body, we remain distant from God.[104] Our spirit is an exile that temporarily dwells in the physical body, but ultimately is at home only with God. Here the abbot quotes Hermes Trismegistus: "In the soul there is the spirit; in the spirit, reason; in reason, the mind; in the mind, God."[105] Humanity's journey is the journey of the mind toward God. Humans are created with an intellect that is divine and immortal. But owing to the fall, our wisdom is imprisoned in an ignorant body. Pure knowledge evades us until our death; in the meantime, that knowledge remains potential rather than active. It is only through the teachings of Christ that we may see how to realize the potential of our divinely created intellect while we still live in this mortal state.

The danger comes from the temptations of the flesh. Rather than seeking out divine knowledge, which our mind naturally desires, our body hunts after entertainments, honors, offices, and all libidinous pleasures. Unless we abstain from carnal desires and constrain the flesh through vigorous penance, our minds will be weakened. Ignorance is the font of sin; we ought rather abandon the contemptible passions of the flesh and follow the "*imperium* of reason."[106] The clergy have a special responsibility in this respect, for when they fail to provide a good example, the laity are likely to have contempt for the doctrines of the church. Ministry requires a pure mind, an unpolluted body, and constant study. "Good conduct among the gentiles" means "living according to Gospel norms" and not transgressing "the sanctions of the fathers of the Church."[107] "You are the light of the world," Trithemius tells his listeners. "[L]et your light so shine before men, that they may see your good works and give glory to your Father who is in heaven."[108] And what does it mean to let your light shine? "The light of life . . . signifies the preaching of the Gospel."[109]

Trithemius's sermon indicates the prospects and perils of ecclesiastical reform in the years before 1500. Improving the morals and habits of the clergy was central to any successful reform; on this point Trithemius and Johann von Auerbach are in complete agreement.[110] Every synod from the time of Lamprecht von Brunn onward demanded a more educated priesthood, better able to provide for parishioners' needs. Ultimately, however, the synods were long on principles but weak on substance, providing general goals but little direction. Although they may have increased the prominence of the bishops in one regard, they did little to relieve the tensions among the bishop, the chapter, and the estates. Moreover, like Trithemius's sermon, the synodal decrees contain a germ of anticlericalism. The reform synods depict failure of clerical discipline as the source of error among the laity. By singling out the canons in particular, the reform synods would seem to be fanning popular anger against the chapter. It could also be charged that the synods raised expectations as to the quality of the clergy that, in the absence of seminaries and other institutions to train priests, were wholly unreasonable. As we have already seen, the impetus for sending clerics to university came not from the episcopal court, but from local communities whose aims might not exactly square with those of the central regime.

Against the various threats to orthodoxy, the synods and sermons of the fifteenth century offered only one concrete remedy: the preaching of the Gospel. Later events suggest that the reformers' simple faith in the efficacy of preaching was, to say the least, misplaced. The idea of the preacher as expressed in sermon texts did not necessarily bode well for the maintenance of stability. For the humanist Trithemius, the preacher was a scholar and philosopher, but the image that we derive from other homiletic texts is rather different. In the sermon collection from Neunkirchen, the preacher is a prophet whose primary task is to challenge the religious and secular authorities. John the Baptist and the protomartyr Stephen, a figure notorious for his assault on the temple priesthood, are presented as models. They are to interrogate (*interogavit*) the temporal and spiritual leaders; they are to display their wisdom in the face of the ignorance of the synagogue; above all, they are to direct their message to the people, who are moved to belief in spite of the ignorance of the "priests and Levites."[111] This same conception seems to underline Johann von Auerbach's understanding of the role of the preacher. He too speaks of the need to interrogate, but here he places special emphasis on the role of secular magistrates. Errors in the faith lead to disobedience among the young, obstinacy among the old, dissolution among the clergy, pride (*superbia*) among the poor, and a general collapse of decency. The result is that "justice is suffocated." Johann contrasts the benefits that come with faith and sobriety with the "terrors" that accompany vice. It is the job of the preacher to "interrogate" the magistrates and compel them to preserve good order in matters of faith, so that they may avert social unrest.[112]

The alliance of pulpit and magistrate against the "priests and Levites" described in the reformist literature of the fifteenth century sounds strangely familiar. It recalls the alliance of nobles and townsmen in the early stages of the communal reformation in the countryside, described in the previous chapter. It also reminds one of the alliance of bishop and estates against Bamberg's cathedral chapter in the 1440s and 1460s. In either case, Auerbach's emphasis on the magistrates points to the fundamental reality of political and religious life: the success or failure of reform tended to depend on the degree of local support. More than that, local authorities, whether noble or common, were expected to play a leading role in the process of religious reform. But herein lies a problem. For Auerbach, the preacher should always stress the redemptive, creative, beneficent ways of God, contrasting divine grace with the various human actions that are offensive to God.[113] Clearly the preacher may reveal God's grace through the witness of holy scripture, but could secular authority do anything except address those activities that were most offensive to God? Auerbach provides no meaningful answer to that question. Instead, he seems to assume that the surest foundation for true religion lies in the close cooperation of preacher and magistrate at the local level. Auerbach's own rhetoric reveals the potential for conflict between the preacher's promise of grace and the magistrate's demand for order.

Chapter 3

"Lord in Our Own House"

The history of the late-medieval reformatio in the lands of the Franconian Hohenzollerns illustrates the tensions inherent in magisterial attempts at religious reform. As in Bamberg, the process of religious reform during the fifteenth century was closely tied to the problem of territorial consolidation. The Hohenzollern domains comprised a series of small lordships strewn across Franconia, stretching from the Swabian Alb in the west to the Bohemian Forest in the east. For administrative purposes, the lands were organized into three regions: the Niederland in middle Franconia, the Unterland in the upper Aisch valley, and the Oberland. The latter, in the highland region of upper Franconia, was poor but strategically vital, lying across the main lines of communication between Bohemia and the Rhineland and between Brandenburg and Bavaria. The Hohenzollerns had sought to capitalize on their relationship with the emperors to consolidate their domains and acquire the Upper Palatinate, but the ambitions of Charles IV and the house of Wittelsbach ultimately frustrated their plans. Although the acquisition of Brandenburg by Margrave Friedrich I certainly raised the dynasty to new heights, in the short term it merely exacerbated the fragmentary nature of the Hohenzollern domains.[1] Friedrich I passed to his son Albrecht Achilles a motley collection of lands with no common identity except the person of their prince.

During his long reign (1440–85) Albrecht Achilles earnestly sought to construct a more or less unified *Land* in Franconia. He had little to work with. The institutions of the princely government were rudimentary at best, and the structure of the Ämter has been described as chaotic.[2] Central to Hohenzollern claims was the Landgericht of Nuremberg, which the Hohenzollerns presided over as burgraves. In their efforts to extend the authority of the court over the rest of Franconia, the Hohenzollerns faced serious competition from the bishops, in particular the bishops of Würzburg. The prince-bishops of Würzburg, like their brethren in Bamberg and Eichstätt, ruled over fairly extensive territory. Unlike their neighbors, however, the bishops of Würzburg had been granted the title of dukes of Franconia by Emperor Frederick Barbarossa in 1168.[3] Where the jurisdiction of the Landgericht of Nuremberg and that of the bishops of Würzburg as dukes ended was a matter of dispute. Both the bishops and the margraves claimed to be the highest authority in Franconia; both claimed to do so as imperial officials. Both could, at times, count on support from the emperor, but neither could ultimately make good on their claims.[4]

In the long run, the goal of creating a unified Hohenzollern duchy in Franconia proved impossible: Brandenburg and the lands to the east ultimately proved far more fertile for nurturing the dynasty's ambitions. In the short term, however, Albrecht Achilles and his successors made a determined effort to consolidate their Franconian territories. In the process, they consciously presented themselves as reformers in both the secular and the religious realms. The end of the Hussite War, the collapse of the Council of Basel, and the accession of the Habsburg emperor Frederick III all seemed to signal the end of the reform movement in the empire. But reform movements, once set into motion, are difficult to stop. The reform of the church and the empire continued after 1440, directed by regional and local powers, in particular the territorial princes.[5] The Hohenzollern state that emerged in the late fifteenth and early sixteenth centuries was, as much as that in the neighboring Hochstift, built around the principle of reform. But although Albrecht Achilles might claim that actions that clearly served dynastic interests were actually undertaken for the greater benefit of church and empire, it remained open to question how far his authority truly extended. For the bishops of Bamberg, the idea that religious reform could provide a foundation for the expansion of princely authority seemed natural. In the case of the Hohenzollerns, the problem was far more complex, and the solutions were bound to be more controversial.

During the first part of the fifteenth century, relations between the Hohenzollerns and the Franconian bishops were generally amicable. Margrave Friedrich I played a key role in the conciliar movement and was eager to maintain the goodwill of the prelates. Friedrich convinced his brother Johann III, then regent in the Oberland, to negotiate a treaty with the bishops of Bamberg and Würzburg in 1415. Among other things, Johann agreed to abandon earlier claims that he had the right to tax the clergy.[6] The outbreak of the Hussite War led to even closer cooperation between the margraves and the bishops. In 1435 Friedrich entered into an alliance with Johann II of Würzburg and Anton von Rotenhan against the Swabian cities.[7] Friedrich's sons Johann the Alchemist and Albrecht Achilles were signatories of a second treaty with the bishops in 1437.[8] After Friedrich's death in 1440, Albrecht and Johann abandoned their father's policy and began to intervene forcibly in the affairs of the prince-bishops.

Albrecht and Johann initially sought to increase their influence in the ecclesiastical states by acting as mediators in domestic disputes. As we have already seen, Johann the Alchemist played a role in negotiations between Anton von Rotenhan and the estates in Bamberg during the constitutional crisis of the 1440s. Albrecht chose to involve himself in the election of the bishop of Würzburg in 1440, triggering a four-way struggle among bishop Siegmund, his brother Elector Friedrich II of Saxony, the Würzburg cathedral chapter, and the city. The conflict was partially resolved when the chapter deposed the bishop and elected Gottfried Schenk von Limpurg as coadjutor.[9] Initially, relations between Albrecht Achilles and Gottfried were cordial, as the coadjutor continued to support Albrecht in his conflicts with the imperial cities. In 1445, however, Gottfried forged an alliance with Nuremberg and the Swabian cities. In return, the cities recognized the bishop as duke of Franconia.[10] War broke out between the margrave and the bishop (each with his assorted allies) in 1448. Neither side was able to gain the upper hand and agreed to a cease fire arranged by Anton von Rotenhahn. In 1454 the feuding parties on all sides agreed to lay aside their differences and uphold the peace.[11]

Gottfried Schenk von Limburg died in 1455, but this did not end the contest between Albrecht and the bishops. In 1457 Albrecht traveled to Mantua to meet with Pope Pius II. The margrave offered to lead a crusade against the Turks; in return, the pope recognized Albrecht as duke of Franconia.[12] After his return, Albrecht formed a league at Mergentheim with Württemberg and the archbishop of Mainz. The Mergentheim league was clearly directed against the house of Wittelsbach, but appeared to threaten the Franconian bishops as well. In response, the bishops Johann III of Würzburg and Georg I von Schaumberg abrogated an earlier agreement with the Hohenzollerns and joined with Bavaria and the Palatinate against Albrecht.[13] The bishops raised an army of twelve thousand men and marched south, meeting up with the duke of Bavaria at Roth in the *Niederland.* Faced with overwhelming odds, Albrecht agreed to a cease-fire. In the *Rother Richtung,* a temporary agreement between the feuding parties, Albrecht agreed to put aside his claims to the duchy of Franconia and his jurisdiction over the clergy in general.[14] Once the troops had departed, Albrecht repudiated the agreement and renewed hostilities, but with little success. Georg Podiebrad of Bohemia arranged for a general peace at Prague in January 1464.[15]

After 1464 Albrecht focused his energies on securing the right to tax and judge the clergy in his own domains. The basis for Albrecht's claims over the church were thirteen papal bulls that Pope Eugene had issued in favor of the Hohenzollerns in 1447. Eugene granted the margraves the right to nominate the bishops of Brandenburg, Havelburg, and Lebus, along with two canons in the collegial churches of Ansbach and Feuchtwangen.[16] The papal privileges amounted to little in Franconia, but this did not stop Albrecht from making use of some of the imprecise language in the bulls to claim extensive rights as "protector" of the church in Franconia.[17] Beyond that, Albrecht sought to exploit the alliance between Frederick III and Pope Pius II. Pius agreed to use the threat of excommunication against the emperor's enemies, including the prince-bishops, "for the preservation of [imperial] authority." Consequently, in his struggles with the bishops, Albrecht presented him as a true ally and supporter of the emperor while painting his adversaries as opponents of the crown.[18]

The first test of this new approach came in 1474 when Emperor Frederick III called on the German princes to support him in a campaign against the duke of Burgundy. In response to the emperor's request, Albrecht demanded that all priests in his domains provide horses and wagons for the Imperial army. Since "one should never flee from his rightful lord when he is in need," anyone who resisted the order would be severely punished.[19] Albrecht had hoped to obtain twenty-eight wagons and eighty-eight horses; in the end only twenty-four of ninety-one priests were willing to comply, and then only in part. All Albrecht could muster was eighteen horses and six wagons. A year later he tried again, this time charging each priest 6 gulden in lieu of a horse. Although Albrecht argued that the clergy were obligated to shoulder the same burdens as any other subjects, the Amtmänner noted widespread resistence to the levy.[20]

In January 1481, Albrecht Achilles made a third attempt to tax the clergy in his realms, this time to finance a war against the Turks. The struggle that resulted has come to be known as the *Pfaffensteuerstreit,* the "priests' tax contest."[21] When Bishop Rudolf II of Würzburg protested the new levy, Albrecht responded that he was doing nothing more than he had in 1474, adding that no one had minded the tax then. (He seems to have conveniently forgotten what had occurred at that time.) The parishes in question were in the margraviate, not the Hochstift. Rudolf subsequently invoked the *Rother Richtung* and threatened to place the Hohenzollern lands under the interdict. Albrecht was unmoved. Rudolf wanted to be both plaintiff and judge in his own case. He argued that the *Rother Richtung* was just one of several agreements. In any event, it had been superseded by the Peace of Prague, and nothing in that treaty prohibited him from taxing the clergy. Brandenburg had five bishops and an archbishop, but none of them had complained. The bishop of Würzburg was the only one preventing his priests from fulfilling their obligations.[22]

Albrecht's officials began collecting the tax in the summer of 1481, beginning in the Niederland.[23] As the tax collectors began to enter parishes within the boundaries of the diocese of Bamberg, Bishop Philipp von Henneberg threatened Albrecht with the ban if he proceeded any further. Albrecht remained adamant, saying that the emperor himself had demanded the funds to fight the infidel. How could any good Christian subject deny the emperor's request? Albrecht was merely doing what he was entitled to do as protector of the church in the Oberland. "We wish to be lord in our own house," Albrecht wrote. "[T]hat we say in good German, so that even you can understand." On September 22, the Hauptmann in Kulmbach sent the Amtmänner a list of prebends subject to assessment and ordered the Amtmänner to begin collecting the tax. The next day the pastor of Kulmbach announced that the city was under the interdict.[24]

Albrecht had clearly miscalculated. Earlier he had told the cathedral dean in Bamberg that he did not believe the Franconian bishops to be "so foolish and hard-headed [as] to bring down the ban."[25] Initially the margrave showed no public concern over the ban. Many other cities and principalities had been placed under the interdict, some for as long as three years, but their rulers had always triumphed in the end. He was in the right: there was no injustice in collecting revenues required by the emperor from ecclesiastical benefices. And if the priests refused to say mass, perform baptisms, or conduct funerals, so be it. But the Amtmänner were instructed to deposit unburied corpses in the churchyard so that the priests could see—and smell—the fruits of their ban. It only took one rotting corpse to convince the clergy of Kulmbach to return to their duties.[26]

Response to the ban was mixed. One Amtmann reported that in his Amt priests were willing to say mass\ but feared the bishop's wrath if they did so. The dean of Schlüsselfeld said that he would be happy to administer the sacraments, but it was ultimately not his decision to make: "I have as much power in this as any common layman or peasant."[27] Resistance was stiffest in parishes within the diocese of Würzburg. The pastor in Höchstadt an der Aisch refused to grant communion or send chaplains to filial chapels.[28] Albrecht's initial response was to withhold the priests' income. Albrecht felt confident that this would bring the matter to a speedy conclusion: "[N]o one can force an ox to drink, but if he's thirsty, he'll drink all by himself."[29] When the clergy still refused to back down, Albrecht threatened to take away their concubines, but even this drastic measure failed to produce the desired results.[30]

After a few weeks, Albrecht began talks with the bishops of Würzburg, Bamberg, Eichstätt, Augsburg, and Regensburg in order to find some sort of mutually acceptable solution. By the end of November, he felt that he had come to terms with everyone except Rudolf II of Würzburg. Rudolf's stubborn refusal to compromise emboldened the other bishops to break off negotiations. Albrecht then turned to his friends in Rome, and with their help, he was able to convince the pope to lift the interdict. In return, however, Albrecht had to agree to back down on the taxation issue.[31] Thereafter he would have to find other means of becoming lord in his own house.

The contest between the Hohenzollerns and the Franconian bishops over the right to tax the clergy proved a watershed in the political history of the Hohenzollern lands. Albrecht's aggressive policies, in particular his conflicts with the bishops, drove the Hohenzollern domains deeper into debt. As in Bamberg in the wake of the Immunities Contest, pressure was building from the estates to enact fiscal reforms. The result, just as in the neighboring Hochstift, was the emergence of the territorial diet and a series of vigorous reforms directed toward the monasteries.

Prior to 1470 there are scant references to meetings of the estates. Friedrich I and Albrecht Achilles do refer to the nobles in a few treaties, suggesting that they had consulted the knights during negotiations. The estates met in 1436 and 1460, but in both cases the assemblies were essentially Landfriede coalitions, made up of nobles and prelates sworn to maintain peace and order in the margraviate.[32] In 1470, on account of acute financial difficulties, Albrecht called a meeting of the estates that is generally considered the first Hohenzollern Landtag. The diet met again in 1486 to approve taxes to support the emperor's campaign against the Turk. After 1488 the diet met fairly regularly as the margraves fell ever deeper into debt.[33]

These early diets can hardly be seen as a manifestation of the *Land.* Among the nobility, only a select group from the Oberland was involved in deliberations, usually those who were also serving as Amtmänner. The towns were invited to all of the early diets, though here again, not all of the towns were represented at every Landtag. In 1508 only Hof, Bayreuth, Kulmbach, and Wunsiedel sent delegates to the diet. In 1509 six delegates were chosen to represent each of the three estates, selected for being the "most excellent (*trefflichsten*)."[34] "Excellence" in this case seemed to refer to the ability and willingness to provide the prince with money. The lion's share of tax revenues came from the towns and countryside, with the towns carrying a disproportionate share of the burden. Administrative centers such as Hof, Kulmbach, and Bayreuth, contributed the most. In 1444 these three towns alone were responsible for a quarter of all taxes collected.[35] Although the nobles were not liable to taxation, the Hohenzollerns came to depend heavily on them for credit. By 1529 some three-quarters of the prince's debts were owed to members of the nobility. Of those nobles who were the margrave's creditors, more than a third held official posts either in the court or provincial administration.[36]

The prelates were conspicuously absent from most early diets. Delegates from the first estate appeared at only two of nine diets held between 1499 and 1507.[37] As the *Pfaffensteuerstreit* indicated, the ecclesiastical estates in the margraviate proved the most severe challenge to Hohenzollern attempts to consolidate their lordship. From the fourteenth century onwards, the Hohenzollerns' efforts regarding the church were directed along two lines. With respect to the secular clergy, the margraves sought to acquire greater patronage rights over parishes in their domains. When it came to the regular clergy, the princes made use of their rights as advocates and protectors (*Schütz- und Schirmvogtei*) of the monasteries and collegial foundations.[38] The margraves possessed the right to nominate pastors in seventy of the 159 parishes in the Oberland. Nobles held thirty-two parishes, while twenty-two were under the control of monasteries within the margraviate. Only eleven parishes were held by patrons from outside the Hohenzollern domains. Albrecht Achilles instituted a requirement that all clerics who received prebends in the margraviate had to swear an oath of allegiance.[39] Albrecht made frequent reference to the oath during the *Pfaffensteuerstreit*–indeed, it provided the legal basis for his order to suspend the incomes of priests who abided by the ban. Albrecht issued ordinances defining the responsibilities of priests, sextons, and other parish officials.[40] The margraves also took some interest in the training of pastors. They endowed a number of preaching chairs, first at the collegial church of St. Gumprecht in Ansbach, later in Kitzingen, Neustadt an der Aisch, and Bayreuth. The clerics who held these chairs were responsible for instructing the canons and other clergy in matters of the faith.[41]

Albrecht Achilles occasionally intervened directly in parochial disputes. In 1466 a chaplain in Creussen was accused of harassing and possibly seducing the daughter of a prominent burgher. The town council and the Stadtvogt conducted the initial investigation and determined that the chaplain had acted improperly. The burghers subsequently demanded that the pastor in Creussen denounce the chaplain from the pulpit and declare the girl's innocence. When the pastor refused, Albrecht called in the deacon of Gesees to help resolve the matter to the burghers' satisfaction.[42] In 1479 Martin Schuss, a chantry priest in Kirchlamitz, complained to the margrave about his pay. Although he was supposed to get 20 gulden from prebends administered by the "entire council and community," he had only received 4 gulden and some change. Likewise, although the peasants owed him tithes in the amount of 6 gulden they had only paid him 35 pence. Schuss had first turned to his spiritual overlord, the bishop of Regensburg. The bishop offered no aid, noting that the endowment Schuss referred to had never been confirmed. Schuss then went to Hans von Redwitz, the *Hauptmann auf dem Gebirg*, in order to collect his income. The officials in Kulmbach examined the matter and decided in favor of the burghers. The burghers had endowed the chantry, hence they had the right to determine just how much the curate received.[43] In both cases, the margraves upheld the burghers' demands against the protests of the local clergy, but with at least the sanction of prominent churchmen.

From 1464 onwards the Hohenzollerns attempted to reform the monasteries in their lands. The first step in the process involved securing formal recognition of their position as advocates and protectors of specific foundations. The margraves could then appeal to their responsibilities as protectors to begin a process of reformation, ultimately allowing them to intervene directly in the monastery's affairs.[44] The first monastery to come under official scrutiny was Münchaurach, subject of a visitation in 1476. The appalling state of the monastery's finance seems to have provoked the reform. Princely officials audited the accounts and then punished tenants and donors who were in arrears.[45] A more extensive visitation was conducted at Himmelkron in 1497 under the supervision of the Hauptmann of Kulmbach, the Abbot of Langheim, and the prior of Heilbronn.[46] In 1502 a new *Klosterordnung* was issued for Hof following a visitation.[47] Other visitations were conducted in Kitzingen, Birkenfeld, Münchsteinach, Münchaurach, and Frauenaurach, all of which were then made to submit to reform ordinances.[48]

The monastic visitations allowed the margraves to increase their control over the territorial church in several ways. The margraves frequently intervened in the election of abbots in the reformed monasteries.[49] Given that the monasteries held patronage rights over twenty percent of the parishes in the Oberland, regulation of monastic estates could provide the basis for expanding the margrave's control over the appointment of the parish clergy.[50] The Hohenzollerns were also keen on ensuring that the monasteries did not provide aid and comfort to their enemies. In 1498 and 1501 Margrave Friedrich the Elder ordered the abbot of Münchsteinach not to allow any knights in the service of the bishop of Würzburg to enter the monastery. In both cases, the abbot agreed, recognizing the margraves right as protector of the monastery to make such demands.[51] Given the possible implications of the visitations, it is not surprising that the bishops frequently opposed them. The bishop of Würzburg complained that if princely officials continued with their reformation of Münchaurach "the monastery would be severely injured," and the monks "would be subjected to disorder."[52] Despite such objections, however, the margraves continued to conduct periodic visitations of monasteries up until the time of the Reformation. In so doing, they effectively asserted their lordship over the monasteries at least with regard to temporal matters.

Certain aspects of Hohenzollern church policy in the later fifteenth century seem to prefigure the formation of the territorial church in the sixteenth century. In his study of the reign of margrave Friedrich the Elder (1486–1515), Reinhard Seyboth noted that "after 1517 the margraves Casimir and Georg [the Pious] instituted in a more radical form . . . what their predecessors had already been practicing."[53] The question remains, however, whether or not the various reformations initiated by Friedrich I, Albrecht Achilles, and Friedrich the Elder had any theological content. The reform ordinances reveal very little, being almost entirely taken up with fiscal concerns. We might find some evidence of radical teachings in the writings of Franconian churchmen, but as noted earlier, such works are few and far between. One figure whom historians of the Reformation have seized on is Theodorich Morung, lauded by eighteenth- and nineteenth-century Lutherans as the "forerunner of the Reformation in Franconia."[54]

Morung's significance for Reformation historians rests largely on his quarrel with Cardinal Peraudi in 1488 over indulgences. In his position as cathedral preacher in Würzburg, Morung had called out for a remedy of the abuses associated with the sale of indulgences. Peraudi subsequently came to Nuremberg and gained the support of Margrave Friedrich the Elder against Morung. Morung was ordered to appear in Nuremberg before Emperor Maximilian I, the margrave, and the cardinal to explain his actions. Although he believed he had come to Nuremberg under safe conduct, Morung was arrested and imprisoned. His case dragged on for nine years before he was finally cleared of the charge of heresy and released. In 1498, perhaps as compensation for his ill treatment, Margrave Friedrich the Elder granted Morung the parish of Hof, the richest prebend in the margraviate. Morung remained in Hof until his death in 1508.[55]

Theodorich Morung's criticism of indulgences aside, little in his biography prior to 1488–or after 1498, for that matter–suggests that he was any sort of "forerunner of the Reformation." Morung was born around 1440 into a prominent burgher family in Hassfurt. After completing studies at the University of Leipzig, he went to Bologna, earning a doctorate in canon law in 1465. Morung received a canonry at St. Stephen's in Bamberg in 1466. Thereafter he amassed a considerable number of prebends in Bamberg, Würzburg, and Freising. In 1476 he assumed a position in the council of Bishop Philipp von Henneberg and was his leading advisor during the *Pfaffensteuerstreit*.[56]

It was in the closing states of that contest that Morung composed a satirical work directed against Albrecht Achilles. The *Passio dominorum* is a parody of the Passion of Christ according to Matthew, casting the margrave in the role of Pontius Pilate. The work appeared anonymously in 1482, first in manuscript, then a few months later in print.[57] Albrecht described the work as "entirely blasphemous, disgraceful and hateful." To his mind it had been composed "under the protection of the devilish Mammon against obedience to authority and Christian love, for the defense of so-called priestly liberty."[58] The passion begins with Albrecht Achilles plotting how to rob the clergy. His advisors warn him to proceed carefully. Were the bishops to impose the interdict on his lands, "there would be sedition and rebellion among the people." Unmoved by their pleas, Albrecht levies a tax on the clergy. When the priests refuse to pay, he tells them that they have no right to refuse to honor the emperor's demand for money. The clerics reply that a host of emperors–Constantine, Julian, Otto I, Frederick Barbarossa, Henry I, Conrad I, and Charles IV–had freed them "from all assessments, demands, and laws of the secular powers."[59]

Faced with this rebuff, Albrecht attempts to collect the tax by force. When the tax collectors come to Steinbach, the chaplain tells them that he has nothing to give. The pastor of Marktschorgast controls the prebends and tithes, and what little he has goes to support the poor. The chaplain is forced to live by begging "door to door, like a mendicant friar." The beadle is unmoved by the chaplain's plight. "You are a scoundrel," he yells, "and only try to delay us and pay with words. Pay up or we will put you in irons!" At that moment a knight intervenes. Taking pity on the chaplain, the knight offers to pay on his behalf. In return, the knight asks the chaplain to say thirty masses for his soul. The chaplain agrees, and much relieved, goes on his way.[60]

Following further similar encounters, the clergy imposes the ban on the margrave's lands. Morung recounts the story of Albrecht's order that unburied corpses be stacked outside the churches until the priests submitted and buried them. Local women took to burying the dead themselves. After a short time the common folk began to cry out against the priests, demanding that they should pay their taxes like everyone else.[61]

Morung declares that Albrecht Achilles' decision to tax the clergy revealed that he "was becoming a heretic and was opposed to the Roman church." He charged that Albrecht was no different than Wyclif and Hus, sharing their ambition to place the church under the control of secular powers.[62] Of the four pillars of the Roman church—that is to say, the four secular Electors—both the king of Bohemia and the margrave of Brandenburg had fallen away from obedience to the church: "Their works say 'blessed are the barren, who have never had children, that they will never see their sons submit to [Albrecht's] sect, tainted with heretical wickedness.'" On account of his apostasy, Albrecht is to be counted with Pharaoh, Senncherib, Eglon, Antiochus IV, Nero, Diocletian, Julian the Apostate, Leo IV, Leo V, Henry IV, and Frederick II as a forerunner of Antichrist.[63]

It is not difficult to understand why Albrecht Achilles was annoyed by Morung's tract. Shortly after its publication, Albrecht asked Dr. Johann Seiler, a monk at Heilbronn and a former professor at the University of Vienna, to compose a reply.[64] Seiler wasted little time, publishing his riposte a few weeks later under the title "The other passion in defense of the honorable Margrave Albrecht, Elector, after St. John's passion, against the bishops and clergy who, having overturned all legality, are liable to taxation." In this "Passion," "Theodorich Iscarioth" betrays Albrecht to "Caiphas," a.k.a. Bishop Philipp von Henneberg.[65]

Seiler's "Passion" opens with the bishops and their advisors plotting against Albrecht Achilles. "What shall we do?" they ask. "[T]his man does many wonderful things; if we leave him in peace, all will believe in him, and then all of the princes of the Empire will come and take away our states and subjects and rule them for themselves." The prelates decide that it would be better "for one man to die for the priests" so that the entire clerical estate might not be lost. They seal their plot by making a mockery of the sacrament. The bishop gives them the cup and says "[D]rink ye all of it, this is the cup of the new league for the destruction of the Margrave. Do this together in conspiracy."[66]

The bishops call Albrecht to appear before them to answer for his "crimes." The "prince of priests" demands to know what Albrecht believes, asking, "Must the priest pay tribute and taxes or give aid to the protector of the Church, that is, the Roman emperor" so that he can defend the prelates "against all the enemies of the Church and of the Empire?" Albrecht responds by saying "render unto Caesar that which is Caesar's." Seiler then points out that according to Saint Jerome, Saint John Chrysostom, Saint Ambrose, and Albertus Magnus, "the emperors, along with the princes of the Empire, fight as advocates for all Christians, and not for their own profit." It was for this reason that Pope Leo IX had given financial support to Otto the Great and his successors.[67]

The bishops reply with the law of Moses: "[W]hat has once been offered to the Lord God may no more be turned to human use." This law freed them from paying taxes. A number of popes, including Innocent III and Alexander III, "have given liberty to the priests so that, under threat of excommunication, no secular power may levy taxes or otherwise injure them." Albrecht's rhetoric now takes on a more radical cast. "The Holy Scriptures are not concerned with external things."[68] He quotes extensively from Matthew 23, where Christ condemns the hypocrisy of the Pharisees. What then follows is perhaps the most striking passage in the entire text:

> Faith is the foundation of our hope and of our entire spiritual life, and faith has two works: one internal, that is, the subordination and obedience of the will to the articles of faith; the second and external work is the public profession of faith. As Paul says in Romans 10[:10], "for man believes with his heart and so is justified, and he confesses with his lips and so is saved."[69]

The importance of these words for Luther's thought is profound, something that ought to make us cautious regarding Seiler's intentions. Still, some aspects of Seiler's argument do seem to point toward the Reformation. Throughout the "Passion," the bishops argue their case on the basis of passages from the Old Testament and the canon law. Albrecht, on the other hand, quotes from the Gospels and Paul's epistles, in particular Romans. Seiler also musters support for Albrecht's position from the writings of the Latin and Greek Fathers. In the choice of authorities, Seiler's passion appears to be in line with the writings of German humanists. Seiler's distinction between external actions and internal matters of faith also seems significant. He condemns the bishops for pursuing a notion of external freedom "that helps them not." With regards to the bishops' wealth, Seiler asks, "[T]o what extent are your prebends, your goods, and your houses endowed to support your expensive courts, your concubines, your children?" Seiler argues that the prebends were endowed by the faithful not "for human ends," but to support only "truly Godly things and the common good." As far as the bishops' political power is concerned, Seiler tells

them to heed the advise of Saint Bernard, who taught that it is unchristian
to exercise dominion over others. Finally, Seiler calls on the bishops to
return to the practices of the early church and live "the form of priestly
life as it was maintained before, from Saint Peter until the time of Constantine and Pope Sylvester." Seiler draws a stark contrast between the "good"
church of the time before Constantine with the "bad" church, represented
in his passion as the time from the Investiture Contest of the eleventh century through the reign of Innocent III down to the present day.[70]

It is unclear to what extent Seiler's statements reflect Albrecht's own theological opinions. Albrecht's religious views appear to have been thoroughly
conventional. And although Seiler's passion contains a none-too-subtle
assault on papal authority, the margrave was keen to maintain good relations with the popes, in particular Pius II.[71] Nevertheless, Seiler was correct
to see the long-term implications of Albrecht's policy. Albrecht had tried to
paint the bishops as opponents of the empire and obstructors of ecclesiastical reform. From the bishops' vantage point, it was Albrecht whose conduct
was indefensible insofar as it marked an assault on the privilege of the clergy.
Any attack on the privileges of the clergy and the authority of the bishops
had theological significance, whether the prince was willing to admit it or
not. In that sense, Morung's portrayal of Albrecht Achilles as a heretic and
enemy of the Roman church might not have been so far fetched after all.

For the moment, the margraves were unwilling to abandon the old church.
Indeed, one of the main goals of Hohenzollern dynastic policy around 1500
was to acquire high church offices for family members. Perhaps the best
known Hohenzollern bishop of the sixteenth century was Albrecht of Mainz,
son of Elector Johann Cicero of Brandenburg and nephew of Friedrich the
Elder.[72] It was the Franconian line of the dynasty, however, that proved a
veritable prelate factory. Friedrich the Elder found vocations in the church
for six of his eight sons. Friedrich the Younger held a canonry in Mainz and
was provost of the cathedral chapter in Würzburg as well as provost of collegial foundations in Ansbach and Wülzburg. Johann Albrecht was appointed
coadjutor of the sees of Halberstadt and Magdeburg by his cousin, Albrecht
of Mainz. Wilhelm went east, becoming archbishop of Riga in 1539; the
youngest brother, Gumprecht, ended his career in Rome as a papal cham-
berlain.[73] Perhaps the most famous of Friedrich the Elder's many sons was
Albrecht, elected grand master of the Teutonic Knights in 1511 and, after
1521, first ruler of the secular—and Lutheran—duchy of Prussia.[74]

Friedrich held out the grandest scheme for his eldest son, Casimir. Casimir held canonries in Würzburg, Bamberg, Augsburg, Cologne, and Mainz.
With the blessing of Emperor Maximilian I, Friedrich the Elder hoped to

secure Casimir's election as Elector-archbishop of Cologne. Casimir was a candidate for the office twice, in 1504 and 1508, but was defeated both times by candidates supported by the Palatine electors. He subsequently resigned his prebends.[75] Although these plans came to naught, it is not inconceivable that on the eve of the Reformation, the house of Brandenburg might have had two Elector-archbishops in the family.

The Hohenzollern pursuit of high church offices in the decades before the Reformation was, in large measure, the logical extension of Albrecht Achilles' goal of being lord in his own house. The secular goals of this policy seem fairly clear; the religious implications are rather murkier. Certainly being a prelate did not necessarily require deep religious feelings. While living in Italy, Johann Albrecht and Gumprecht developed quite a reputation for loose living. In 1520 Casimir was told that if his brothers did not give up their concubines and live "ordinary" lives, they would bring shame and scandal on the entire house of Brandenburg.[76] At the same time, Albrecht and Friedrich the Elder saw to it that their children received a more formal education than had earlier members of the dynasty. The young princes received solid instruction in the classics, both Latin and Greek, and appear to have been well schooled in the Bible. Both Friedrich the Younger and Wilhelm were sent to study at the University of Ingolstadt in 1514. The religious writings of Georg, Albrecht, and their cousin Elector Joachim II of Brandenburg reveal an extensive knowledge of scripture and a good grasp of theology.[77]

The Hohenzollern pursuit of church offices reveals the difficulty in trying to distinguish purely "political" from purely "religious" policies. This ambiguity may also be seen in the margraves' relations with the nobility. The Hohenzollerns actively patronized knightly tournament societies, in particular the Society of the Brooch (*Fürspängergesellschaft*).[78] In the fifteenth century, the Hohenzollerns established their own order of knighthood. In imitation of the dukes of Burgundy, Margrave Friedrich I created the Order of the Swan after returning from a pilgrimage to the Holy Land. The order was open to all "princes, knights and noble persons of both sexes" willing to abide by the rules promulgated in 1443. The badge of the order depicted the Virgin Mary with the infant Jesus standing on a half moon with the words "*ave mundi domina.*" Below that was the image of a swan. The swan, depicted piercing her breast to feed her young with her own blood, was a standard image in the late-medieval Eucharistic cult. The badge hung on a chain over the wearer's heart, as a reminder of the pain the wearer should feel on account of his or her sins and as a call to sorrow, confession, and penance.[79]

The Order of the Swan figured prominently in the dynasty's self-representation. A chapel devoted to the order was established in St. Gumprecht's church in Ansbach. The left wing of the altar depicts the five oldest sons of Margrave Friedrich the Elder, all wearing the badge of the order. In a portrait painted in 1521 by Hans Süss of Kulmbach, Margrave Casimir has the swan embroidered with pearls on his bodice. Albrecht of Prussia was also frequently depicted wearing the badge of the order. The Order of the Swan played a central role in the dynasty's political ambitions. Initially, membership was limited to thirty men and seven women, but those limits were abandoned after Albrecht Achilles extended the order into Franconia in 1459. By 1465, largely on account of Albrecht's efforts at recruitment, the order counted ten princes, fourteen princesses, eighty-three counts, 115 knights, and 104 dames among its members. Most members of the order came from Franconia, but Albrecht was eager to offer membership to princes and nobles in Bavaria, Württemberg, Saxony, and Silesia—all regions he wished to draw into his sphere of influence.[80]

Hohenzollern support for orders of knighthood represented, in part, an effort to strengthen the bonds between the dynasty and the Franconian nobility. Still, we should be careful to avoid downplaying the religious character of these organizations. When we consider them alongside other aspects of Hohenzollern church policy—the efforts to place members of the dynasty in the church and to gain greater patronage rights over parishes and monastic estates—it becomes clear that from the time of Elector Friedrich I onward, the Hohenzollerns increasingly turned to the church as the means to advance their influence and prestige. Their policy did not constitute an attempt to secularize their *Herrschaft,* but exactly the opposite: Hohenzollern territorial and ecclesiastical policies point toward a sacralization of territory. By the end of the fifteenth century, the Hohenzollerns had come to conceive of their *Land* not simply as a collection of feudal estates, but as a sacred society. Monastic visitations, as well as other aspects of Hohenzollern ecclesiastical policy, indicate the extent to which by 1500 the margraves understood religious reform to be a natural and necessary expression of lordship. Significant problems with this idea remained, however, not least of which was the fact that there was no single blueprint for reform. In the absence of strong leadership, either from the emperor or the papacy, the estates were left to interpret the specific content of the reforms on their own. Of course, they tended to couch reform in terms that served their immediate political ends. In this regard, the Hohenzollerns were little different from the prince-bishops. The difference was that according to canon law and tradition, the bishops had the right to enact reforms. It was unclear whether the margraves' feudal rights over church lands in secular matters could be translated to lordship in spiritual matters. The experience of the *Pfaffensteuerstreit* suggested not. *Vogtei* was not *Herrschaft;* the traditional Gelasian division of spiritual and secular power remained at the heart of the fifteenth-century concept of church and state.[81] As Seiler's "Passion" reveals, it remained to be seen whether the Hohenzollern conception of the relationship between the territorial church and the prince could be maintained within the confines of the old faith.

Matched against the ambitions of the dynasty, there seems to have been a growing expectation on the part of their subjects that the margraves would take the lead in reform. Part of this stemmed from a growing distrust of the motives and effectiveness of the bishops among well-meaning churchmen such as Seiler. In both the monasteries and parishes, the intervention of the margraves was usually directed toward fiscal concerns. But their actions went further, touching on matters of clerical discipline and liturgical practice. As in the sermons of Johannes von Auerbach and Johannes Trithemius, the habits of the clergy were a central issue, in particular on account of the potential negative effects that a lack of clerical discipline might have on the spiritual needs of the laity. Whether or not the prince had an objective legal right in this matter was not important. As shown in the debates during the *Pfaffensteuerstreit* and in Seiler's "Passion," the margraves represented themselves as the defenders of the faithful against the priests. By the time Albrecht Achilles died, the estates and subjects of the margraviate had come to expect that the prince, not the bishop, should be the one to correct the offenses of the spiritual estate.

Chapter 4

REFORMATION AND REVOLUTION

In his ecclesiastical history of the town of Selb, Paul Reinel noted that until the year 1517 the gospel of Christ lay buried under papist lies and human teachings. After cataloging the extent and depth of popish errors, he announced how Martin Luther, "the third Elijah and prophet of the German lands," revealed God's true word.[1] Some three hundred pages later, in his chronicle of world affairs, Reinel described two events that occurred in 1517: the birth of Johannes Streitberger, general superintendent of the Lutheran church in the Oberland after 1560, and the misadventures of Jordan Prantner, vicar of Selb, and his mistress. No mention is made of Luther or Wittenberg. The next entry in the chronicle that concerns religion is a brief notice on the peasant "bloodbath" that began in 1524.[2]

Reinel's account of the early years of the Reformation suggests that in his own researches he faced much the same problem as do modern scholars: how to relate the changes in religion on the local level with the larger course of the Lutheran Reformation. For Reinel, two events clearly stand out–Luther's protest of 1517 and the Peasants' War of 1524–25. But although the latter event is easily reconciled with local history, the former seemed to have no appreciable impact. Rather, a careful reading of Reinel's history would suggest that a reformation of the sort that Peter Blickle described was already at work well before 1517 and continued on until the publication of the first reformed church ordinances in the later 1520s.[3] But it is here that problems arise. As we have already noted, there was a distinctive culture of religious reform in upper Franconia in the later Middle Ages. It manifested itself in formal efforts toward reform on the state and diocesan levels as well as locally directed attempts to improve the quality of religious life. In the writings of a number of churchmen– Auerbach, Seiler, and Trithemius–we can see ideas that seem to anticipate the reformations of the sixteenth century. Likewise, the reforms that the Hohenzollerns initiated after 1520 have been described as merely a "more radical form [of] what their predecessors had already been practicing."[4] Some have pointed to the presence of Hussites, particularly among the nobility, in upper Franconia in the later fifteenth century, suggesting a continuity between the Bohemian and the Franconian reformations.[5] But preconditions cannot explain everything. It remains unclear where the domestic reform currents of the fifteenth century might have led. One difficulty is a paucity of evidence. The first decades of the sixteenth century are among the most poorly documented in the archives. Political instability may have played a role, but the ultimate cause is not clear.[6] So although it is an attractive hypothesis that before some nobles in the Oberland were Lutheran, they were Hussites, there is no evidence to support such a claim. What is clear is that with the appearance of Luther, the entire character of the debate shifted. Although we can point to certain threads of continuity and parallels to the fifteenth-century reforms, the vitriolic character of the rhetoric and the extent of violence in the years around 1525 was truly unprecedented. After 1517 the argument over reform would revolve around learned and popular perceptions of the theology of Martin Luther and the reformers who followed in his wake.

Tradition holds that the Reformation in upper Franconia began when Martin Luther preached in Kulmbach on his way to the Diet of Worms in 1521. As nice as this tradition sounds, there is little evidence to substantiate the legend. What is clear is that in the years between 1521 and 1523, Lutheran preachers appeared in a number of towns and villages. Kaspar Löner, a student of Luther, arrived in Hof during this time. Another one of Luther's students, Christoph Hofmann, began preaching in Kitzingen in August 1522. A few months later, Lorenz Hiller of Kleinhaslach and Georg Schmalzing of Bayreuth were arrested for their preaching. Adam Weiss inaugurated the Reformation in Crailsheim. By Easter of 1523 a Lutheran preacher had been installed in Wunsiedel.[7]

In Ansbach, the Reformation began around 1523 in the context of a dispute between the pastor, Johann Rürer, and the canons of the collegial church of St. Gumprecht.[8] Rürer complained that he had received "not more the 43 fl. [gulden] and a few pennies" when 150 gulden per annum was barely adequate for a pastor who required "50 fl. for his own person, for food and drink, 50 for the victuals for the three chaplains, and 50 for the cook, houseboy [*knecht*] and the horse." Only by collecting surplice fees were his chaplains able to pay for food and clothing. Rürer attacked the canons, citing Matthew 10:8: "Freely ye have received, freely give." The canons accused Rürer of preaching contrary to the laws and statutes of the diocese and the chapter, thereby inciting enmity between the laity and the canons. Rürer replied that he was bound by his oath to the margrave to "loudly and plainly preach" the "holy godly word." His critics were responsible for the "unchristian, damnable aggravation" brought about by their "unchristian statutes." The town council, along with the princely officials in Ansbach, agreed with Rürer. They condemned the "erroneous" religious customs of the canons as "heathen fables" and "unchristian, Godless statutes." But the officials went much further than merely to repeat their pastor's concerns. They argued that the bishop of Würzburg was at fault in this matter, because monies that rightfully should have been used for the benefit of the city's churches were being diverted into the hands of the bishop and his cathedral chapter.[9]

In rural parishes, the coming of the Reformation was often linked to disputes between mother parishes and filials. Wendelstein was a filial of the Königspfarrei in Schwabach. Hieronymus Marquard was appointed chaplain of Wendelstein in 1510, but it appears that he made few efforts to attend to his duties. By 1518, Margrave Casimir had grown impatient and demanded to know why Marquard was not fulfilling his responsibilities. Marquard pleaded ill health and resigned in 1520. His replacement, Friedrich Santner, almost immediately found himself opposed by a Lutheran preacher. The village council supported the preacher and in 1524 appointed him as their pastor. According to the parishioners, "the antichrists" had deprived them of true religion. Over the years they had endured "many and diverse abuses . . . unsanctioned by the *gemain* and contrary to its own good." Now they had freed themselves from their "Babylonian captivity." The villagers informed the new pastor that they would not recognize him as lord "but simply as a servant of the parish." Consequently, they ordered him "faithfully to preach . . . the Gospel and the Word of God, pure and clear in accordance with the truth, unsullied and unobscured by human teachings." The parishioners agreed to pay for the pastor's support, but would not tolerate surplice fees or any feudal dues.[10]

In Gefrees and Stammbach, the Reformation grew out of the long-running dispute with the mother parish of Marktschorgast. The peasants of Stammbach began paying a pastor out of their own pockets in the years around 1525.[11] By 1520 the council of Gefrees was again voicing its claims to be able to administer the prebends associated with the chapel.[12] A chantry priest, Johann Gangolf, had begun administering the sacrament *sub utraque species* in his house.[13] In 1527 a number of disputes arose over the status of the prebends as well as the tithes from Gefrees, Berneck, and Wirsberg. The council of Gefrees wrote in January 1528 that the pastor in Marktschorgast was required to "proclaim the holy word of God and administer the Christian sacraments" in their community. The margrave concurred, adding that the residents of Gefrees ought to hear only the "pure word of God" and receive the sacrament "of the body and blood of Christ."[14] The town council was by then administering all of the parish income, although they maintained that they were forced to, seeing that the pastor of Marktschorgast had not provided them with a chaplain willing to administer the sacraments and proclaim the Gospel.[15]

In all of these cases, the Reformation appears to have had its origins in disputes over church finance. The initial conflict seems to have been between chaplains, allied with town or village councils, and the absentee pastors and canons who derived income from the parish. In Ansbach it was Rürer against the canons of St. Gumprecht; in Gefrees it was Gangolf against the pastor of Marktschorgast and the canons of St. James in Bamberg. The question of parish incomes was nothing new—since the fourteenth century communities had attempted through various means to obtain control over local church finance. The support that the margrave gave to towns and villages in their efforts had clear antecedents in the policies of Albrecht Achilles. The novelty here, well articulated in the sources concerning Gefrees and Ansbach, was the division within the ranks of the clergy and the use of the word of God as a weapon against the higher clergy. In administrative towns (Ansbach, Hof, Bayreuth, and Wunsiedel) and villages (Gefrees, Stammbach, Wendelstein, and Selb) we see demands for the purity of the Gospel message, the election of pastors by the community, local control over finance, and statements of the community's authority in deciding disputes over doctrine.[16]

At the Hohenzollern court, the chief secretary, Georg Vogler, had been in correspondence with Luther from 1521 onward. In 1524 Vogler was joined by Johann von Schwarzenberg, formerly chief of staff in Bamberg.[17] Within the Hohenzollern family, opinions were decidedly mixed. At the outbreak of the Reformation, Margrave Friedrich the Younger was provost of the cathedral chapter in Würzburg and of the collegial churches in Ansbach and Wülzburg. Johann Albrecht was appointed coadjutor of the sees of Halberstadt and Magdeburg by his cousin, Cardinal Albrecht of Mainz. Both were outspoken opponents of Luther. On the other side stood Albrecht of Prussia, who had embraced Lutheranism by 1521. Albrecht was joined by his elder brother Georg as one of the first converts to the evangelical faith. Georg had met Luther at the Diet of Worms in 1521 and after 1523 maintained a regular correspondence with Wittenberg.[18]

The religious views of Margrave Casimir are much more difficult to discern. He has been described as "at first indifferent, then Protestant, finally Catholic as he feared political isolation and imperial enmity."[19] Part of the problem was that in the eyes of much of the world, Casimir was a usurper. Friedrich the Elder proved an erratic ruler whose spendthrift ways drew strong criticism from the estates.[20] With the approval of the nobility, Casimir took on ever more responsibility for the day-to-day administration of the margraviate.[21] By 1509 there were reports that the young prince wished to rule on his own.[22] In the end, Friedrich's mental instability provided the justification for a coup d'état. In the early morning of February 13, 1515 Casimir and his brother Johann Albrecht burst into Friedrich's bedroom and forced him to sign a document formalizing his abdication. For the next thirteen years the old margrave remained a prisoner at the Plassenburg, incarcerated under horrific conditions.[23]

The precise reason behind the old margrave's deposition is unclear. It appears that he was delusional and potentially violent—or at least that was the rationale behind the severity of his imprisonment. Several observers, including the cardinal-archbishop of Mainz, agreed that the measure was warranted.[24] Still, Casimir remained in a precarious position. The validity of his claims to rule ultimately rested on the support of the estates. Two weeks after Friedrich's deposition, the estates convened in Baiersdorf and agreed to recognize Casimir and his younger brother Georg as coregents. As regent, rather than sole reigning prince, Casimir exercised his authority at the pleasure of his brothers and the diet.[25] During the debates over the introduction of the new learning, Casimir's political opponents—including at times his younger brothers—did not fail to suggest that he was a usurper. Consequently, it is not surprising that when the question of the Reformation first arose, Casimir left the matter to the estates.

The first steps toward formulating a religious policy in the margraviate arose in the wake of the Reichstag of Nuremberg in April 1524.[26] During a meeting of the secular estates of the Franconian Reichskreis, Casimir perceived that the religious issue offered a means for cementing his leadership over the Franconian nobles and cities.[27] The center point of this policy would be the drafting of a *gravamina* identifying particular religious issues to be discussed at the imperial diet.[28] The articles were organized as theses for debate, with Lutheran propositions set alongside the Catholic counterarguments. The majority of articles dealt with the sacraments, in particular whether "there are not more than two," and ceremonies. Salvation by faith is briefly mentioned in article 14.[29] The last three articles concern the church and the relationship between clerical authority and scripture. In article 21, the evangelicals assert that "popes, bishops or common council decisions and decrees are not founded on the pure word of God." Article 22 continues in this vein, counterposing the notion that the religious dispute could be reasonably resolved by "the clerical estate in the Councils" with the argument that "no human logic or force may stand against the Holy Writ." The articles conclude with a repudiation of papal authority: The "holy common (*gemain*) Christian church" is not ruled by any one state or person, "but exists only in spirit and in faith, and is [the] one body and bride of Christ, and of Christ alone."[30]

The articles were printed and distributed in preparation for a meeting of the Landtag in September 1524. As was to be expected, the prelates found the Lutheran propositions "somewhat controversial."[31] They were willing to accept German baptism, but by and large defended the practices and traditions of the Roman church.[32] The Lutheran position was articulated by Hans Rürer and three other leading reformers: Kaspar Löner, Adam Weiss, and Christoph Hoffmann. Rürer's comments were highly polemical. He called indulgences "dangerous," derisively referred to Extreme Unction as "oil smearing," and decried auricular confession as a recent innovation without scriptural foundation. Adam Weiss, perhaps showing his ties to the Rhenish humanists, used Zwinglian language in his rejection of Catholic teachings, stressing the spirit over the flesh.[33] The Lutherans were joined by a small group of prelates, among them Johann Schopper, the prior of Heilbronn.[34] Casimir felt confident that the "greater part" of the clergy supported the Reformation.[35] Of the other estates, enough of the nobles supported the preaching of the word of God to mollify any concerns the margrave might have had. The towns were unequivocal in their support for the Reformation.

With the support of the estates, Casimir issued a proclamation endorsing the Reformation, albeit in a limited fashion. He ordered that "the Holy Gospel and Godly Word, Old and New Testaments, should be preached clear and pure according to correct and true interpretation and nothing to the contrary, so that the common Christian folk will not be led into aggravation or error." Still, the mandate upheld the division between the secular and spiritual estates, and forbade the discussion of religion in language that was "quarrelsome, angry, or seditious." *Amtmänner* were admonished to put an end to "unsanctioned reforms" and seditious preaching.[36]

Following the diet, the leading Lutheran clergymen recorded their opinions on the twenty-three articles in a detailed little book, published in the fall of 1524.[37] The *Ratschlag* was composed by six unnamed clergymen, although it is generally assumed that the primary authors were Rürer and Weiss. Although fairly conservative on matter of ceremony, the authors present a radical redefinition of the church, in no small measure in order to defend their claims that the church had to be founded on scripture alone.[38] They argued that Catholics claimed that the authority of scripture rests solely on the decisions of "human councils." That simply could not be true, since in the earliest days "Christendom (*gemeinenn Christenhayt*)" comprised a number of churches, of which Rome was but one.[39] The authors cite several passages in defense of their claim that "the Gospel existed before, and is older than the Church," beginning with I Corinthians 3:11: "There is no foundation other than Christ alone." The discussion of the marriage between Christ and his church in Ephesians 5, along with the opening passages of the Epistle of James provided further proof that the apostles "speak of the Church being born of the Gospel."[40]

Against the claims of the papists, the authors provide an alternative interpretation of Matthew 16:18. The "rock" or foundation of the Church is neither Peter nor the popes, but, according to Matthew 7:24 and other passages, the word of God in Christ.[41] In the "holy, *gemayn*, consecrated church," all apostles were equal. If Peter was chosen, it was not "as the most prominent, but as the weakest." Here the authors paraphrase Christ's words: "Look Peter, I perceive the weakness of your faith, and know that you will deny me."[42] How then can the pope, as Peter's successor, claim to be the "physical head" of Christendom? There is only one head of the church, as Paul writes in Ephesians 1:22 and 4:4–6, and that is Christ. "As the physical head directs the members of the body in life, movements, and all works, so too does Christ direct through faith his spiritual body and members in life, faith, love, will, thoughts, words, deeds, and all goodness."[43] Therefore, there is no need for any person to direct the church here on earth. As for councils, the authors compare them with Pharisees, declaring that "the councils are not the *gemain* Christian church."[44]

If the "external" papal church is not the authentic, spiritual Church, then what is? Here the authors consider the derivation of the word *church:*

> Now one finds in the writings of the old and new Testaments, that in Greek [it is called] *Ecclesia,* and sometimes in Latin *concio,* but nowadays the Greek *Ecclesia* is customary, which in our German [is] an assembly, or community. Therefore it follows that in our German language, when we find the word "church" in the Holy Scriptures, we should understand that to mean an assembly or community.[45]

The church constitutes "the common and special council and physical assembly" of the faithful. It is merely the "assembly of the faithful in Christ, unified in the spirit, faith, hope and love." This is the church mentioned in the creed. It is "spiritual and invisible."[46] Within that church the clergy have no special powers, but are merely there "to preach the Word of God, to provide [the people] with baptism and the holy body and blood of Jesus Christ."[47]

The publication of the *Ratschlag* brought to a close the first stage of the Reformation in the margraviate. It represented the views of the leading reformers in the major towns of the Hohenzollern domains, but it remains unclear to what extent Rürer, Weiss, and the others spoke for either the prince or the mass of his subjects. Between 1522 and 1525 several reformations were at work in the margraviate, all of which may be seen as continuations of older struggles: princely attempts to dominate the first estate; attacks on wealthy clergy by well-meaning, well-educated priests who perceived a threat to mens' souls and bodies in the fiscal structure of the church and the teachings that supported it; finally a communal reformation, born out of the ongoing quest of local communities to secure greater autonomy in spiritual and temporal matters. What bound these three distinctive reformations together was Luther's message, received and used in varying degrees by all sides to articulate their position. Luther provided a clear focal point for the discussions between churchmen and statesmen at all levels, but the full implications of his ideas were hardly apparent in the years 1523–24. "Lutheranism" as yet did not exist; what did exist was a debate over Luther and his ideas that ranged throughout Germany, from the imperial diet to the smallest villages. And just when Rürer and his associates presented their *Ratschlag* to their prince, the early consensus began to break down as the varied participants in the debate turned from words to action.

In Bamberg, the first voices in support of the Lutheran revolt were heard within the small cadre of humanists in the bishop's court. In the first decades of the sixteenth century, in large part owing to the good graces of bishops Heinrich III Groß von Trockau and Georg III Schenk von Limpurg, Bamberg showed signs of evolving into an important humanist center.[48] Crotus Rubeanus and Albrecht Dürer both resided in Bamberg in 1517.[49] After Joachim Camerarius left the court to join Luther's inner circle, his brother Hieronymus remained in Bamberg and provided a personal link to Wittenberg in the early years of the Reformation.[50]

Among the first supporters of Luther at court were the brothers Jakob and Andreas Fuchs von Wallburg.[51] In 1523 Jakob published an open letter to the bishop of Würzburg defending clerical marriage.[52] He suggests that it is necessary for men to marry, "otherwise one might sin with unmarried women or against nature." As proof he offers up Paul's advice in I Corinthians: it is better to marry than to burn. As far as the clergy were concerned, Paul was clear in his letters to Titus and Timothy that "a priest should have a wife."[53] Anyone who would try to prevent priests from entering the estate of marriage must "be party to forbidden, extramarital impropriety, and thus be sinning against God's law." Such persons "should die an eternal death and have no inheritance in the kingdom of God."[54]

Another humanist in the episcopal court to embrace Lutheranism was the Hofmeister, Johann von Schwarzenberg. Schwarzenberg is best known for composing the Bamberg criminal code (*Halsgerichtsordnung*), the source for the *Carolina* of Charles V. He also dabbled a bit in theology. Luther was apparently pleased with Schwarzenberg's theological writing.[55] The Franciscan polemicist Kaspar Schatzgeyer was less impressed. He described Schwarzenberg's writings as a "cesspool of all the new errors," comparing the author to a knight who had ridden into a tournament unarmed.[56]

In 1524, Schwarzenberg published an open letter to Bishop Weigand von Redwitz. He recalled how twenty years earlier he had placed his thirteen-year-old daughter in a convent. Since "the Word of God had been suppressed," Schwarzenberg believed at that time that the "perverse, twisted, pharisaical monastic life" was godly. Since then, along with several prominent burghers, Schwarzenberg had discovered that the Dominican monks who controlled the convent "had done certain ungodly things." Even though his daughter was now prioress of the convent, she was unable to defend either herself and the other nuns from the bullying monks. Consequently, Schwarzenberg organized a raiding party that entered the convent and liberated the oppressed nuns. Schwarzenberg and the burghers were concerned that under the "monkish ungodly tyranny" their "innocent daughters" would be unable to hear the word of God. The monks served Baal rather than God, he charged. The convent was a "tyrannical diabolical monkish prison" ruled by the "tyrannical estate of the monks."[57]

Both Schwarzenberg and Fuchs suggest that it was the clergy, either through the prohibition of clerical marriage or through monastic orders, who were bringing the souls of their flocks into peril. If people sinned, it was the fault of preachers who refused to follow the word of God. For both authors the word was a form of law. This was especially true for Fuchs, who consistently referred to the Gospel as *Gebot,* "law" or "decree." Schwarzenberg hinted at the dissatisfaction of prominent burghers with the monks and contrasted the "tyranny" of monkish rules with "the light of the Godly word."

A third figure in the episcopal court to speak out on behalf of the new learning was the bishop's chaplain, Ulrich Burchardi. In 1523 Burchardi composed a *Dialogue on the Faith,* recording a conversation between Credulus (the believer) and Didymus (the doubter). The work is Lutheran in tone, emphasizing salvation by faith alone as well as the centrality of scripture. For Burchardi, true faith was not simply the belief that Jesus Christ lived and was the son of God—even demons knew that—"rather, it must also constitute a trust in the mercy of God in Christ."[58] Romans 10:10 appeared as the central definition of true Christian faith.[59] Works cannot save us, Burchardi believed, for we do them not on account of our own righteousness. Rather, God "has made us holy through the remission of sins and second birth and renewal of the Holy Spirit."[60] But not all who have been baptized can be saved. "Pay no attention to whores, adulterers, thieves, misers, drunks, blasphemers or other criminals" who claim to have faith. Keep mindful of Christ's warning in Matthew 7 that "you will know the faithful by the fruits of their faith."[61] "If a man's inner desires are good, then he can bring forth nothing other than good fruits."[62]

In the preface to the 1525 edition, Burchardi lamented the "sorrow" that had arisen, "disturbing the common good," not only among the common lay people, but even "among the great and learned doubt has replaced confidence" on account of new interpretations of scripture.[63] The fault, according to Burchardi, stemmed in part from preachers "who understand even less their own preaching."[64] Burchardi was also concerned about the impact of the plethora of religious texts that had appeared. Didymus's doubts arose from the books in his "little library . . . the Holy Bible as well as other devotional writings."[65] But there is another source of confusion. Only those who had been "blessed by the Holy Spirit" are able to understand Holy Writ, Burchardi believed.[66] This emphasis on the spirit suggests a streak of radicalism in Burchardi's thought, one that did not go unnoticed. In 1527 the theological faculty at Ingolstadt banned the work as heretical.

The courtiers represented one face of the early Reformation in Bamberg. Meanwhile, a more radical voice was being heard in the streets. One of the main supporters of Luther in the city was the printer Georg Erlinger. His activities attracted the attention of the papal nuncio, Franciscus Chieregati, who sent a series of letters to the town council in Bamberg, demanding that they shut down Erlinger's press. Erlinger printed the letters, adding his own scurrilous comments in the margins. For the papists, he said, "Christ is simply holy, but the pope is the most holy of all." Who had manipulated ordinary Christians through deceit and false words, Luther or the pope? Who lived a "free, unchaste, shameless life, and refused to be subject to any lordship?" Who had insulted and excommunicated kings and princes, "cursing them unto the third, fourth, even the ninth generation"? The work of the popes was nothing but robbery and mischief.[67]

One piece published by Erlinger was *The Courtesan and Prebend-Eater,* a satirical poem that appeared in 1522.[68] In 213 lines of execrable doggerel, the author bewails the state of the church, condemning the wealthy and powerful canons who gobble up prebends while providing nothing for the salvation of the laity. The cover illustration shows a wealthy canon, bedecked in ermine and a fine robe, seated before a church. Around him hover two demons. One demon stuffs a church in the canon's mouth; the second carries two charters marked with the crossed-keys symbol of the papacy. The point of the image is all too clear: wealthy canons were devouring the local church, aided by the devil and the pope. The poet claims to present the grievances of the "peasant and common man" and calls on the "nobility and all government" to find a remedy to the prebend eater's misbehavior.[69]

The poem opens with a description of the means of salvation:

Know you Christians pious and good
How Christ Jesus with his blood
That on the wooden cross he shed
And through his sorrows and bitter death
Has done enough for our sins.

The devil ensured, however, that "this especially good work has been forgotten." With the devil's aid, the prebend eaters and their ilk had corrupted God's teachings, telling the common people to trust in themselves and their own works.[70] As they led the flock astray, the prebend-eaters enriched themselves off the benefices that supported their idle ceremonies. Such priests, "to whom the scriptures are unknown," had little interest in preaching the Word of God.[71] "The grace of God they replace/ with human teachings and make-believe." They claimed that "through singing, chanting, and loud noise" people could be saved "as if Christ Jesus had never come down on earth."[72]

Prebend eaters were mainly concerned with collecting their incomes: "The tithe of corn, and also the wine/ to them all must be consigned." And it was not as if the canons used this money for doing good. Rather, "With labor dues and manorial fees/ they bring to all men misery." The peasant's work fed the canons' "arrogant whores."[73] How different were the poor curates who ministered to the common people! The curates received next to nothing for their labors. They "must eat chaff and tares/and sleep on straw." Only by begging could the poor priest stave off starvation.[74]

The author ends by warning the secular authorities to remedy the situation before matters become worse. The solution seems clear:

> Let no priest be ordained
> Unless he knows and can proclaim
> the Old and New Testament
> That God to us from heaven sent."

Beyond that, the clergy must be disciplined so long as their disgraceful manner gave offense. Otherwise, the common man might be led to "believe the scriptures not aright." The lords had "sworn to punish injustice" and must do so before being called before God's strict court.[75] The author exhorted his readers not to protect the clergy and their privileges, not to protect the monks and nuns; instead, the should care for the good common people by whose "sweat and blood . . . these blasphemers are fed." The poem concludes with a direct warning to the prebend-eaters:

> So says each common wife and man,
> And so say I, all that one can,
> Turn to God, you Courtesan![76]

The injustice of the old system of parochial finance is the central issue in the *Courtesan and Prebend Eater*. There is clear evidence that discontent over the breakdown of the system was brewing in the early sixteenth century. Complaints about surplice fees became increasingly common between 1521 and 1525.[77] In the face of such complaints, unbeneficed curates might well redirect local discontent toward the higher clergy. It seems likely that the author of this miserable little poem was just such a cleric—reasonably well educated but trapped between the demands of his congregation and his superiors. The appeal to the nobles, *Amtmänner,* and town councils—the sorts of people who endowed chantries and prebends—suggests an effort on the part of the author to build a coalition among these individuals and the middling clergy against the cathedral chapter. As for the peasants, the poem carries a vague threat that popular insurrection might result if the canons were not put in their place.

In its detailed catalogue of fiscal and spiritual abuses, *The Courtesan and Prebend Eater* suggests how preachers might mobilize the commons to resist the ecclesiastical hierarchy. Beginning in 1523, several preachers began attracting the attention of the authorities in Bamberg for doing just that.

The Carmel was one of the early centers of the new learning. Eucharius Ott was the first Carmelite to be identified with Lutheranism, although he later recanted.[78] Lukas Arnold, assistant preacher at the Carmel in 1526, was dismissed after openly declaring his support for Luther.[79] Lutheran preachers also appeared in the countryside, in Kronach, Windheim, Hollfeld, Ebersberg, Marktleugast, and Forchheim.[80]

The most important of the early preachers was Johann Schwanhäuser, *custos* of St. Gangolf's Church in Bamberg. Schwanhäuser was the son of a wealthy Bürgermeister from Ebern and had studied at Wittenberg in 1502. By 1522 he had become the most popular preacher in the city, drawing crowds of thousands to his sermons.[81] Two of Schwanhäuser's sermons from the years leading up to the Revolution of 1525 have survived in print. The first was delivered on All Saints' Day, 1523.[82] Schwanhäuser begins with the observation that there are two types of saints: the living and the dead. The former are "all the elect and faithful in Christ who belong to eternal righteousness." These are the "holy *volck* of the Lord God," the "splendid *gemain*," the church of Christ. As for the dead saints, "the scriptures, to the extent that they refer to the saints, do not always speak of the dead ones, but rather do so very seldom."[83] When Paul collected alms for the "saints" of the church in Galatia, who received them?

> The painted idols in the churches? Or the dead saints? Most certainly not! these saints can be none other than the poor! But, God have Mercy! we pay no attention to the living saints, because there are no altars set up before men like we want to set up before the dead.[84]

Anyone who would claim that the Apostle was speaking of the dead saints in any of his letters "clearly does not understand a single word of what Paul says." Still, this had not prevented the people from wasting time and money on elaborate ceremonies and traditions associated with the veneration of saints. The conclusion of Schwanhäuser's sermon leaves few doubts as to his assessment of the situation:

> We foolish people have perverted everything, and want to serve the dead, and forget the living. We bring the dead gold, silver, gems, jewels, cattle, sows, chickens, geese, cheese, bread, salt, and lard. We build them big stone houses. . . . Are we not fools that we give such things to a rock, or a wood carving, or set food in front of them like pagans do? . . . This God has not taught or demanded but forbidden us to do! The poor, on the other hand, for whom such things are necessary, are allowed to remain unhoused, suffering cold, hunger, thirst, sickness, and all other evils. It helps them not that we rob the living and give to the dead.[85]

The defense of the poor appears as well in the second of Schwanhäuser's printed sermons, delivered on the first Sunday in Lent, 1524.[86] The primary theme here is the power of the clergy. "The vineyard," that is, the king-dom of God, "has no other lord but God alone."[87] The clergy are appointed merely to tend the vineyard. Preachers are the "instrument through which God and his Spirit speak."[88] They should be shepherds, tending the flocks that belong to God alone. But "certain Popes, bishops, and priests have criminally proclaimed the sheep to be their property."[89] They "stone, kill and murder, tossing Christ out of the vineyard and setting up themselves in his place, then saying that they are the vicars of Christ."[90]

Insofar as such "highly learned (or so they claim) people insult and slan-der Christ Jesus," Schwanhäuser charged, they reveal themselves not to be preachers of the word of God. Anyone who would teach us not to place all our trust in God is filled with the spirit of Antichrist. The "Pope, the car-dinals and bishops . . . toss God and Christ out of His kingdom, in order to erect [the kingdom] of Antichrist." They place "human teachings, laws, and newly decreed works" over the teachings of Christ.[91] Since they forbid the preaching of God's word, they "are obviously against Christ and right Antichrists."[92] Schwanhäuser consistently stresses the necessity of the word of God for salvation.[93] He also discounts the efficacy of works, declaring in 1523 that all men "are unrighteous and all [their] works useless."[94] It is best to despise the world and its works.[95] In both sermons, Schwanhäuser makes it clear that to trust in our own works is contrary to true faith in God. The popes, bishops and priests who proclaim the doctrine of works are "wolves" and "blind leaders."[96]

All of these points seem to follow Luther's teachings rather closely. At the same time, Schwanhäuser is far more critical of the wealth of the church. "If we were true Christians," he says, "we would sell the monstrances, chalices, and plate and, like the apostles, help ourselves by helping the poor."[97] "God has given to all men a common law, by the sweat of your brow you shall earn your bread."[98] Schwanhäuser's criticisms of "luxury" in the church, whether it be in the unwillingness of the clergy to work or in their love of ceremony, reflects his concerns about the nature of the church and the way it repre-sented itself. Throughout his sermons, Schwanhäuser translates *ecclesia* with the word *gemain,* or "community." So his rendition of Ephesians 5:25 reads, "Husbands love your wives, as Christ has loved his *gemain.*"[99] The church is the assembly of the "common man," whereas the pope, bishops, and cardi-nals preside over the realm of Antichrist. The true church is made up of the elect, chosen by God before time.[100] Schwanhäuser's notion of the church appears to rest on a doctrine, albeit poorly articulated, of predestination. He also sees a much closer correspondence between the church and the secular *Gemeinde.* Schwanhäuser presents the Gospel as a form of law and defines the true church as the body of the elect. Nothing approaching Luther's con-ception of the two kingdoms appears in these early sermons; in that regard, Schwanhäuser's ecclesiology appears closer to that of Zwingli.[101]

By 1524, the debate over reform in Bamberg had changed considerably. What had begun as a dialogue among humanists at court had become the focus of a public debate. Although Jakob Fuchs and Hans von Schwarzenberg were content to take swipes at celibacy and monkish piety, *The Courtesan and Prebend Eater* and Schwanhäuser's sermons reveal a deeper critique of the clergy. Schwanhäuser called for nothing less then the end of the older fiscal system and the clerical hierarchy. Schwanhäuser was certainly far more radical in his theology than Rürer or Weiss in the margraviate. The radicalization of dissent corresponded to a change in the regime. After the Diet of Worms in 1521, Georg III backed down from his initial support for the Lutheran reform.[102] Georg's successor, Weigand von Redwitz (1523–56), proved a vigorous opponent of the new learning. The brothers Fuchs and Schwarzenberg were forced to resign their positions at court. Although Burchardi tried to dedicate his *Dialogue* to Bishop Weigand, that did not help his case. Burchardi was forced to resign from his post as episcopal chaplain. He spent the years 1528–30 in prison and was released on the condition that he never return to the city.[103] With the ouster of the court Lutherans, preachers such as Schwanhäuser emerged as leaders of the reform movement.

Within weeks of Schwanhäuser's Lenten sermon, words gave way to action. Between 1523 and 1524 revolts broke out throughout the Hochstift. The reasons for the risings in Bamberg are complex. Financial difficulties seem to have played an important role. The Hochstift was burdened with a variety of extraordinary taxes in the first decades of the sixteenth century. In 1519 and 1523 a tax was levied to support the Swabian League, followed by a tax to support a campaign against the Turks in 1524. More odious were the consecration taxes (Weihsteuer) collected after the election of the bishops. Consecration taxes had been collected in 1501, 1503, 1505, and 1522.[104] Although the tax records for the period are incomplete, the addition of the Weihsteuer amounted to an increase of at least 25 percent over normal tax burdens.[105] The financial woes brought about by the new taxes were compounded by enclosures and a series of bad harvests in 1502–3, 1505, 1515, and 1517–24.[106]

The Weihsteuer levied by Weigand von Redwitz in 1523 triggered a series of uprisings in the countryside.[107] Opposition to the Weihsteuer quickly developed into resistance to the tithe in towns harboring Lutheran preachers. By the end of 1523, Staffelstein and Heynrieth had refused to pay taxes or tithes. A priest in Zeil began preaching against tithes in early 1524. By the summer of 1524, the tax revolt had spread to eight other towns, all of which had Lutheran preachers by this time.[108]

The cathedral chapter quickly emerged as the target of dissent. At the Landtag in 1521 there were complaints that people had been brought before the dean's court (Dekanatsgericht) in cases in which the dean and chapter had no jurisdiction. Chief among these were cases of debt, "which is better regulated by village authorities."[109] In 1520 the residents of Forchheim had rioted during the Corpus Christi procession, demanding a suspension of tithes paid to the chapter. In 1524 the rebels again identified the cathedral chapter as their primary opponent. They demanded that they should have to deliver the tithe "to no one other than our gracious lord of Bamberg, and not to the cathedral dean." They demanded that the Weihsteuer be abolished and that "all water, birds, and game should be free and common."[110] The revolt spread to Herzogenaurach, but was quickly suppressed by the bishop, with a little help from Margrave Casimir and the city of Nuremberg.[111]

In the wake of the first wave of uprisings, Bishop Weigand and the chapter enacted measures directed against the preachers. In late 1523 or early 1524, a "Mandate Concerning the New Learning" condemned certain manifestations of the new heresy—eating meat on Fridays, blasphemous songs, and Lutheran books. Additional ordinances appeared in early 1524, directed against priests "who preach against brotherly Christian love" thereby inciting their listeners to "ill-will, uproar, and rebellion."[112] Following the revolt in Forchheim, the chapter began taking direct action against the preachers. Jörg Kreuzer of Forchheim was blamed by episcopal officials for the outbreaks of violence, although his actual role remains obscure.[113] A disturbance at St. Gangolf's Church on Easter only increased the chapter's concerns about Johann Schwanhäuser. On July 29 Schwanhäuser was called before the suffragan bishop along with several other preachers and ordered to comply with the Edict of Worms. Schwanhäuser refused, as did Johann Eichhorn of Memmelsdorf. In August both were deprived of their benefices and exiled.[114]

From his exile in Nuremberg, Schwanhäuser composed an open letter, addressed to his former parishioners.[115] Most commentators have noted the extent to which Schwanhäuser's argument echoes Luther's teachings on authority.[116] Still, Schwanhäuser's rhetoric here is far more acerbic than that in Luther's *On Governmental Authority*. According to Schwanhäuser, the kingdoms of this world are those "where the Devil is the one Lord and Prince." Anyone who wishes to dwell in the godly kingdom must "be taken out of the worldly Kingdom" and take part in the creation of the new kingdom of God. This kingdom is the true church, which has Christ as "one spiritual, invisible lord and Prince . . . He is the single head of his spiritual body, the entirety of Christendom, the Christian *gemayn*."[117]

Schwanhäuser cites the primitive church as the ideal form of the Christian community. As for the "modern" Church, he condemns it in strong language. Councils are "devilish." A council had condemned St. Jerome a heretic. Moreover, "Christ was condemned to death and crucified by the *Concilia* of pharisees."[118] Schwanhäuser suggests that when the prelates claim to base their notions of the church on the "Holy Fathers," they mean "Aristotle, Plato, and the other heathen teachers." The true fathers are Augustine, Cyprian, Jerome, and Ambrose. But if they could, the authorities would declare the writings of these saints heretical, along with the teachings of Christ and the apostles.[119] Although Schwanhäuser calls on his flock not to resist in an outward manner, the bulk of his *Trostbrief* sounds very much like a call to action. He undermines the authority of the rulers at every turn, describing them as devilish, heathenish, and tyrannical. It is therefore not surprising that when conflict erupted in Bamberg, Schwanhäuser's followers figured prominently among the rebel leaders.

The catalyst for rebellion was a decree issued by Bishop Weigand on April 4, 1525. Weigand ordered his vassals to assemble their troops in the marketplace in Bamberg on April 11 and join the Swabian League's forces, deployed against the peasants near Rothenburg.[120] On the night of April 10, a group of concerned citizens met in Zinkenwörth to plan their course of action. Schwanhäuser's more radical partisans convinced the assembly that the troops had actually been summoned by the cathedral canons in order to arrest Lutherans in the city. The following morning the burghers went to hear a sermon preached by Eucharius Ott at the Carmel. Following the service they assembled in the market and selected four of Schwanhäuser's followers to express their concerns to the bishop. They demanded that Weigand dismiss his troops and reinstate Schwanhäuser so that "the word of God and the Holy Gospel [could] be loudly and clearly proclaimed." Meanwhile, the burghers seized the gates. Most of the canons fled during the confusion, leaving Weigand with only a few knights to face down the rebels. Cut off from aid, the bishop had little choice but to submit when three thousand rebels marched on his residence.[121]

The burghers presented Weigand with seven articles, calling on him to disband the cathedral chapter and allow for the incorporation of the immunities into the city. To replace the chapter, the burghers set up a thirty-member council, composed of representatives from the city and from the country towns. The nobles and clergy would have to place themselves under communal law. An eighteen-man executive council was established as the centerpiece of the new regime. The bishop was allowed to appoint nine members to the council, while the burghers of Bamberg, the peasants, and the nobles would each name three representatives.[122] The eighteen-man council assumed power on Holy Saturday, 1525. The new regime found itself hard pressed to maintain order. Bands of rebellious burghers and peasants plundered the Altenburg, along with several monasteries and the houses of the canons. Only the cathedral and the Carmel were spared. Amtmänner and their families were attacked despite attempts by the council to protect them.[123] Following several weeks of rising violence, the council agreed to hear complaints from the countryside. The council members ruled that peasants should have the right to fish and hunt around their village.[124]

Such concessions amounted to little, and by May 10 a second, much larger uprising had begun in the countryside.

Peasant bands assembled around Ebermannstadt, Kirchehrenbach, Höchstadt, and Hollfeld. They marched on Bamberg and set up camp in the suburb of Hallstadt. Some two hundred poor burghers, mostly from Zinkenwörth, joined the band. After the council of eighteen failed to mollify the rebels, the peasants seized cannon from Kronach and the Altenburg in Bamberg and began destroying the castles of any nobles who had done injury to them, their fathers, or their grandfathers.[125] Between May 13 and 16, the peasant forces destroyed 197 castles and sacked six monasteries. Damage to nobles' property totaled over 170,000 gulden. Oddly enough, the only persons reported killed during this wave of violence were peasants.[126]

On Ascension Day (May 25) the bishop and the estates opened negotiations with a band of peasants that had assembled in Hallstadt. The towns of Lichtenfels, Staffelstein, Weismain, Burgkunstadt, Stadtsteinach, Teuschnitz and Kronach suggested that the suspension of tax burdens would undercut support for the rebellion. The towns also warned the peasants to take no further action without the approval of the estates.[127] In the end, it was not the stern warning of the third estate but the relentless progress of the army of the Swabian League that brought the rebels to bay. Rumors began to circulate that the princes were planning to sack the city unless it was clear that the revolt had ended.[128] On June 13, the council of eighteen and the estates issued a decree recognizing the rights and sovereignty of their "good, mild, singular prince and lord." The cathedral chapter was recalled from exile and allowed to resume its previous role in the administration.[129]

The Hohenzollern dominions had not remained untouched by rebellion. Margrave Casimir faced two distinct revolts. The rising in the Oberland was the lesser of the two. A few peasant bands formed around Ludstatt, Gesees, Creussen, Kirchenlamitz, and Tiersheim, but they were small and short lived. Plundering was limited to the theft of a cross from the monastery at Himmelkron and wine and beer from inns and parsonages.[130] Although a few individuals in Bayreuth, Kulmbach, and Pegnitz tried to foment a large-scale uprising, they garnered little support.[131] A confession from Wunsiedel suggested that half the residents were involved in the uprising, but even if that were true, the rebels would have numbered one hundred at most.[132]

The rising in the Niederland was a far graver matter. Owing to the influence of preachers from Rothenburg and Würzburg, peasant bands began to form around several towns, including Kitzingen, Schwabach, and Crailsheim. The latter band, numbering around eight thousand men, plundered the abbeys of Anhausen and Heidenheim to the bare walls.[133] In late April 1525, Casimir agreed to hear the peasants' grievances at a meeting of the diet in Ansbach. The peasants made four demands: the right to shoot game outside the forests; the right to name their own pastors; the right to collect wood without charge; and rents payable in silver, not gold. Casimir agreed in part, stating that his peasants could collect wood "necessary for building purposes," but only under the supervision of his forester. Game could be taken, but the peasants could keep only the hides—meat had to be handed over to the Amtmann.[134] On May 7, little more than a week after the close of the diet, Casimir defeated a large peasant army near Ostheim. The remaining peasant bands dispersed, and Casimir began a revenge campaign directed at towns that had participated in the rebellion, extracting ransoms totally nearly 120,000 gulden. He entered Kitzingen on June 5 and had sixty-two rebels blinded. Further executions were carried out in Neustadt an der Aisch, Bayreuth, Kulmbach, and Pegnitz. By the end of Casimir's campaign a total of eighty rebels had lost their heads.[135]

The army of the Swabian League entered Bamberg on Corpus Christi only to find the city at peace and the old regime restored. Margrave Casimir, leader of the league's forces, was unimpressed. "Since [the rebels] themselves have thrown away life and goods," he argued, it was right to "chop their heads off."[136] The canons agreed and demanded that "those persons alone who had clung to the evangelical learning . . . should pay for their excesses with their heads."[137] Twelve rebels were beheaded in the market place in Bamberg. A thirteenth escaped, but was later captured in Nuremberg. Following torture, he too was beheaded. Reprisals continued over the next few months. Five rebels were executed in Hollfeld, four in Kronach. On June 23 a further forty-four rebels were beheaded in Bamberg. The last execution came in June 1526, a full year after the end of the revolt.[138]

After the suppression of the provisional government and the peasant bands, murmurs of dissent could still be heard. Lutheran preachers continued to draw listeners across the border into the margraviate and Coburg. Closer to home, Johann Kraus, a canon in Forchheim, preached in taverns that only once all the priests had been struck on the head could unity be restored in the church.[139] The region around Staffelstein, in particular the parishes belonging to the abbey of Langheim, remained unsettled. A peasant band had sacked the monastery in May 1525, dividing the spoils among the residents of Lichtenfels, Kronach, Burgkunstadt, Weismain, and Staffelstein. The "raging Staffelsteiners" also destroyed the pilgrimage chapel on the Staffelberg.[140] The bands dispersed after the arrival of the Swabian League, but it appears that the region around Staffelstein became a haven for participants in the rebellion. When Hans Hut came to the area in November 1526, he found that he had no reason to be shy about his association with Thomas Müntzer and the revolt.[141]

The Langheim estates proved a fruitful recruiting ground for Hut and other Anabaptist preachers. In 1526 and 1527 several Anabaptist communities appeared, the largest in Ützing. It has been suggested that many of the converts had been involved in the uprising, though no single individual has been linked to both movements. Farther south, the matter is less in doubt. The brothers Hans, Marx, and Michael Maier of Herzogenaurach were directly involved in the uprising of 1525, and all three were later identified as Anabaptists.[142] Officials in Bamberg had no doubt that the Anabaptist movement was connected to the revolt and acted accordingly. In January 1527 a mandate was issued against individuals "who accept a new baptism."[143] Additional mandates were issued over the next several years, calling for the arrest of suspected Anabaptists.[144] By 1535, sixteen persons had been executed. After that point, aside from some isolated notices, the movement as such was effectively dead.[145]

The Anabaptist moment provides a fitting epilogue to the early Reformation in the Hochstift Bamberg. Reformed religion had emerged as an explosive and powerfully disruptive force in the years after 1520. Initially, the movement could count on support from the princely court, but such support ended soon after Luther's excommunication. Although the early Bamberg reformers were regularly described as "Lutheran" by friends and foes alike, there are signs that some of the theological currents in the Hochstift tended toward other directions. The emphasis on godly law found in the writings of Jakob Fuchs, Burchardi's emphasis on the spirit, and above all Schwanhäuser's vehement anticlericalism and communitarian views were, at times, more in tune with the theologies of Zwingli, Carlstadt, or even Müntzer than Luther. This is not to say that the early Bamberg reformers were Zwinglians or Anabaptists. Rather, the diversity of viewpoints shows just how confused the various positions were around 1525. If some of Schwanhäuser's followers later became Anabaptists, to some extent this was because they heard from Hut and his followers a message that seemed to resonate with that of the preacher at St. Gangolf's.[146] At the center of the theology of all the participants of the early Reformation in Bamberg was a belief that the church needed to be thoroughly reformed, and that such reformation needed to begin with the clergy and the structure of the church, in particular the fiscal institutions. On this point no document could have been clearer than the miserable *Courtesan and Prebend Eater:* the poor quality of the clergy and the corruption of the ecclesiastical administration lay at the root of discontent and rebellion.

This sentiment was hardly new. Indeed, it echoes the viewpoint represented in the synodal statutes issued in the wake of the Immunities Contest. There is good reason for this. In many respects, the Revolution of 1525 closely resembles its fifteenth-century predecessor. In both cases, conflicts between the citizens of Bamberg and the cathedral chapter led to armed violence. Likewise, both contests were set against the backdrop of a major crisis in the church—the Hussite War and the Conciliar Movement in the first case, the Peasants' War and Lutheran revolt in the second. One significant difference is that whereas the first revolt seemed to owe little to radical religious sentiment, religion was a fundamental issue in the 1525 uprising. After 1525, tensions between the bishops, chapter, and estates assumed a religious character. Protestantism—here in the most literal sense—quickly emerged as the religion of the estates (including, as we shall see, some of the prelates) and was linked to the defense of privilege in the face of redoubled efforts at reform directed by the bishops. The close cooperation between nobles and village communes that had characterized the formative stages of parish organization in the fourteenth and fifteenth centuries continued through the sixteenth century, albeit with two differences. Although there was a latent competition between the bishop and the estates—nobles, towns, and prelates—over local lordship and patronage in the later Middle Ages, in the wake of the Peasants' War this turned more to passive, and at times open, resistance. Moreover, the contest over local authority now had a more overt theological dimension. As the records of the vicar general's court suggest, after 1525 the pastors appointed by the nobility (and even some appointed by the spirituality) tended to be Lutherans, often educated at Wittenberg and conducting ceremonies according to evangelical practice.

What is striking is that the religion of the protesting estates was not that of Schwanhäuser or the court humanists. There was no broad condemnation of the clerical estate or of the traditional forms of ecclesiastical finance. Indeed, one might argue that in their defense of their patronage rights, the nobles and the prelates were more conservative than the bishops and the chapter. There does not seem to have been any attempt at a thoroughgoing reform of life and morals in local communities. It was the bishops who pressed for more active reform. In this regard, Weigand von Redwitz and his successors followed the model laid down in the fifteenth century: ecclesiastical reform, in particular reform of the life and habits of the clergy, became the principal expression of princely authority. What was true in 1435 was even more true in 1525: if religious conflict was the source of political discord and uproar, then the solution to civil unrest could best be found in a continued reformation of the territorial church in head and members. Although they may have drawn their inspiration from opposite poles of the theological spectrum, Johannes Schwanhäuser and Weigand von Redwitz, far more than their erstwhile friends and opponents among the estates, seem to have shared a common vision: the construction in Bamberg of a Christian community, *"ain herliche gemain."*

Chapter 5

The Limits of Obedience

The full social and political implications of Luther's message unfolded only gradually in the years after 1517. The violent upheavals of the years 1520–25 suggested to many–Catholic and Protestant alike–that the Luther problem could not be remedied simply through minor compromises on matters of ecclesiastical practice and administration. For Catholic rulers as well as for more traditional-minded and conciliatory Lutherans, the new faith posed a distinct threat to the social order. From both the Lutheran and Catholic perspectives, evangelical religion needed to be cleansed of its potential for social and political disruption, if not eradicated altogether.[1]

For Catholics, the matter seemed fairly straightforward. Johann Albrecht of Brandenburg wrote that order could result only from the restoration of religious unity on the basis of the old faith.[2] The next several decades would nevertheless see considerable debate among Catholics about what reforms were required to ensure the health and welfare of the church. For Lutherans, the issue was somewhat more complicated, and the years immediately following the cessation of the Peasants' War saw a concerted effort to forge an authoritative definition of evangelical faith, an effort that would bear fruit in the Augsburg Confession and the church ordinances of the 1530s.

The establishment of doctrinal norms could not be fully divorced from political considerations. At both the imperial and territorial levels, the religious question was closely tied to the struggle between the prince and the estates. In particular, the proper relationship between spiritual and secular authority remained a point of controversy. At the center of the debate stood Charles V, whose conception of power rested heavily on the Constantinian ideal of the universal Christian empire. For Charles, Luther's revolt presented an opportunity to reestablish the empire on the basis of a thoroughgoing reform of the church. Of course, not everyone agreed with Charles on this point, including the pope and a fair number of Catholic princes.[3] Among Lutherans, there was a similar tension between the princes on the one hand and the clergy on the other, each of whom were keen supporters of the evangelical cause but had different ideas about both the content and aims of the reforms. For Lutherans and Catholics alike, political necessity rested

79

uneasily with theological imperatives. The limits of obedience–to God and the prince–would be severely tested.[4]

☙

In the aftermath of the Peasants' War, Casimir reversed his previous policies, both at home and abroad. Although he had been leaning toward an alliance with Hesse and Electoral Saxony, Casimir broke off negotiations with both parties and began to court the Catholic duke Georg of Saxony.[5] At the Diet of Speyer in July, 1526 the ducal Saxon representative wrote that Casimir was now doing better work for the Catholic cause than for the Lutherans.[6] Casimir also renewed ties to the emperor. After Charles V agreed to pay off his debts, Casimir received a commission in the Habsburg army in Hungary.[7] Nevertheless, Casimir's relations with the Catholic powers were strained. The margraviate remained diplomatically isolated and vulnerable.

On the home front, Casimir retreated from his earlier support for the Lutheran reforms. Insofar as "unchristian, irresponsible, mutinous preachers" were to blame for the revolt, a fine of 10 pence was levied on each cleric in the margraviate.[8] A preaching mandate issued in 1525 noted how "the recent rebellion and uprising derived, for the most part, from unlearned and irresponsible preaching."[9] Preachers had discussed Christian freedom in an "entirely seditious manner." Consequently, "the common man has come to believe that Christians are not obliged to follow the temporal dictates of authority, but rather are freed from obedience by Godly Law." Preachers should henceforth explain "with good German words" what true Christian freedom was. The prophets and the apostles all taught that one should be obedient to the authorities.[10] "Christian freedom" did not free one from the duty to pay taxes, rents, or tithes, or to provide labor services. The secular authorities were truly servants of God, charged by God to punish evildoers. As for the rebels, they were merely "seduced" by the "devilish unchristian freedom of the flesh."[11]

On October 10, 1526, Casimir issued a new church ordinance, undoing many of the Lutheran reforms he had sponsored less than two years earlier.[12] The ordinance prohibited "papist, Lutheran or heretical falsehoods, complaints and all other things that serve or give cause for ill will, disunity, uproar or revolt."[13] Theological discussions in taverns were banned.[14] Priests were to sing the mass in Latin until a church council decided otherwise. The Gospel should first be read in Latin, then in German for the benefit of the laity.[15] "Evil devilish heretical" theologians who denied the real presence of Christ in the sacrament were roundly condemned. At the same time, the ordinance was silent on whether the laity could receive the sacrament in both species. Auricular confession was required, but priests were admonished not to ask "aggravating questions."[16] No priest could be appointed without the prince's approval. Secular officials were to administer endowments and prebends.[17] Priests were expected to remain celibate and wear proper vestments, but they still had to pay their taxes just like any other subject.[18]

The reaction of the leading reformers to the ordinance was highly unfavorable. Johann Rürer published an anonymous tract in which he called the mandate an example of "godlessness" and condemned Casimir's apostasy.[19] Princes were owed loyalty in secular matters, Rürer declared, but not if they "order things against God, His Word, and sanctity." Lords were enfeoffed by God with their power, and that power was contingent on their continuing obedience to God and his word.[20] The suppression of the godly word and persecution of the preachers was "a great evil, great blasphemy, and horrible to hear of." The princes were the rebels, because they had "rejected and resisted" Christ, "the eternal Word of the Father, the Truth, and our only Redeemer and Sanctifier."[21] Rürer warned Casimir of the fate that awaited him if he did not return to the faith. Like Pharaoh, Saul, Ahab, and Herod. he would be brought down and destroyed.[22]

Rürer was not alone in his dissent. Georg Vogler wrote that "anyone who says that he supports the ordinance is a duplicitous scoundrel." For his words, Vogler was imprisoned. Georg Schmalzing of Bayreuth and Lorenz Hiller of Kleinhaslach were arrested; Rürer and the remaining Lutheran leaders fled.[23] The most vocal opponent of the new order was Margrave Georg. Writing from Jägerndorf in Silesia, he expressed his concern that things other than the Gospel were being preached in the margraviate. The persecution of Rürer and other evangelical preachers distressed him greatly. Georg rejected the new ordinance as "unchristian" and begged Casimir to place his trust in God. In closing, Georg wrote that "even if every man would be the Devil's own, I will trust in God and not willingly damn my soul. I will be guided by Holy Writ."[24]

Within a year of the publication of the revised church ordinance, Casimir was struck down by illness and lay dead before the walls of Ofen in Hungary. Since his son Albrecht Alcibiades was a small child, the reins of government fell to Casimir's brother Georg, known to posterity as Georg the Pious.[25] Margrave Georg arrived in Ansbach on February 14, 1528, and immediately showed his support for the new faith. He appointed Johann von Schwarzenberg and Georg Vogler as his chief advisors. The Lutheran preacher Adam Weiss, as well as Rürer, returned from exile in Silesia, accompanied by a host of clerics sent from Wittenberg by Luther. Among these were two new court preachers, Georg Heyderer and Andreas Althamer.[26] In order to appease Catholic nobles, Georg appointed Hans von Seckendorf, a partisan of the old faith, as Hofmeister. The rest of the prince's council was heavily stacked against Seckendorf and the Catholic party. The Catholics charged that Casimir's noble advisors had been replaced by Silesians and "new men." Noble families that had once figured prominently in the administration were driven out on account of their religious leanings.[27]

In March 1528 Georg convened the diet to consider, among other things, the religious question. Despite protests from a minority of Catholics, the diet approved measures to restore the "clear and pure preaching of the Gospel."[28] Pastors were to follow the "evangelical" interpretation of scripture and abandon the old ceremonies and customs.[29] They should preach nothing contrary to scripture and remain loyal to the margrave as the "divinely ordained government." Cases concerning marriage or heresy were to be referred to the secular authorities.[30] In May clerical marriage was officially recognized; in June the celebration of Corpus Christi was banned, along with all other "popish vigils and masses for the dead."[31] The estates upheld Casimir's ruling of 1526 that the clergy should be subject to the same obligations as other subjects. Consequently, one-third of the newly approved taxes fell on the first estate.[32]

Shortly after the diet, Georg and his advisors looked to the reformation of the parish clergy. John George of Saxony urged the margrave to undertake a general visitation similar to that orchestrated by Luther and Melanchthon in Electoral Saxony.[33] Acting on his own initiative, Adam Weiss of Crailsheim sent Georg a memorandum containing his own ideas for the visitation. Weiss's proposal received strong support from Johann Schopper (the prior of Heilsbronn), Georg Vogler, and Andreas Althammer. Subsequently Georg ordered Weiss, Althamer, and Schopper to draw up plans for a general visitation.[34] Meanwhile, in Nuremberg, Lazarus Spengler was preparing his own visitation proposal. Spengler approached Johann von Schwarzenberg and suggested that religious officials in the margraviate and the city of Nuremberg coordinate their visitations in a cooperative venture. Given the enduring enmity between the Hohenzollerns and Nuremberg, Spengler's proposal was nothing if not novel. In June delegates from both sides met at Schwabach to resolve some long-standing territorial disputes and then drafted the articles for the visitation.[35] The visitation commenced in August 1528 in the Nieder- and Unterland and was extended to the Oberland in December of that year.[36]

Records for 152 of 327 Niederland parishes survive; of these parishes, priests from ninety-seven parishes either refused to answer the questions or simply did not show up. Priests from eighteen *Ämter* absented themselves, in some cases on orders from the nobility. Seckendorf had warned the prince that the visitation would lead "to great injury and disgrace," hinting at opposition by "the people, both noble and common."[37] The lords of Seckendorf, Castell, and Pappenheim were particularly outspoken in their defiance.[38] In parishes where the priests and nobility agreed to participate, only nineteen priests were classified as being "good" (*bene*). Twelve were mediocre; thirteen were bad; five were beyond hope (*pessime*). Some were a little too cagey to allow for easy classification. Lorenz Volker of Regelsbach "responded, but God only knows where he stands."[39]

Only one visitation report survives from the Oberland, that for the parish of Wunsiedel. Although isolated, the report provides a fairly detailed portrait of the condition of the Oberland clergy at the beginning of the second decade of the Reformation. In 1528 there were twelve priests in Wunsiedel. Adrian von Rabenstein, a Praemonstratensian monk, was the titular pastor. Although Rabenstein agreed to pay the taxes levied by the margraves, he would not collect them from the priests but only from laymen living in his parish.[40] The preacher and administrator of the parish was Nicholas Hiltner, an avid supporter of the Reformation. He told the visitors that for a year he had not celebrated mass because it "has no foundation in scripture; indeed it is blasphemy." On Christmas Day of 1527, Hiltner had begun celebrating the "evangelical Mass, which he praised in his sermons." When asked to define the Catholic mass, Hiltner stated that "he considered it to be a false and damnable human invention."[41] Ägidius Friesner, the *Michelsmesser,* and the deacon, M. Johann Scharnagel, explained that in addition to themselves and Hiltner, the three priests at the hospital–Jakob Rössler, Lorenz Zobel, and Lorenz Winter–read the Gospel in German as well as in Latin. All the others "read it as of old."[42]

Scharnagel expressed some concern about the way in which Hiltner approached the issue of reform. He noted that when Hiltner preached against the mass, he called those who clung to it "thieves, murderers, rogues, swindlers and shitheads." Scharnagel hoped that the authorities would convince Hiltner to tone down his sermons a tad. Hiltner refused to budge. In reply to Scharnagel, Hilter said that "he would cling to his teachings, proven with scripture." The Catholic doctrine of works made "a mockery of Christ, the only Savior." Those who "depend on their own works and trust in them" are "thieves and murderers."[43]

The chaplains were a mix of old and new. Johann Gropp had been the *Frühmesser* for forty-four years; he either died or retired in the wake of the visitation. Wolfgang Müssel, chaplain of St. Anna's in Schirnding, was old and had a wife. Albrecht Rab and Johann Burkert had been appointed to replace an even older priest, Hans Möhr, who had lost one of his fingers in an accident and could no longer celebrate the mass. The three chaplains at the *Spital*–Jakob Rössler, Lorenz Zobel, and Lorenz Winter–were all fairly young and supported the Reformation. Zobel and Winter would later found clerical dynasties. The visitors praised the chaplains–with the exception of Müssel–for not keeping concubines and otherwise leading honorable lives.[44]

The visitors also noted the state of affairs in some of the communities around Wunsiedel. The pastors of Röslau and Bernstein were appointed by the abbot of Waldstetten. Georg Schmiedel of Röslau complained that his church had burned down several years before and had never been repaired. Both he and Paul Tiescher of Bernstein had "cooks" and children, but at least attempted to follow the margrave's decrees. On this point Tiescher stated that since only the church in Wunsiedel had a Bible, it was next to impossible "to preach according to the Gospel."[45] In Marktredwitz, Wolfgang Winkelmann followed the margrave's ordinance, even though his parish lay in an exclave under Bohemian jurisdiction. Winckelmann informed the visitors that in several villages on noble estates the mass was still being performed.[46]

By rough count, half of the priests in Wunsiedel could be classified as Lutherans. The comparison between Hiltner and his colleagues, however, reveals just how flexible that definition could be. Hiltner's language is in line with much of the more vehement pamphlet literature of time. Scharnagel, though clearly Lutheran in sympathy, was far less polemical and appeared unwilling to press for reforms either too far or too quickly. The other priests who were identified as Lutherans had even less to say. Their "Lutheranism" appeared to go no deeper than simple compliance with the most basic parts of the *Kirchenordnung*. The debate between Hiltner and Scharnagel, as well as the confessionally ambiguous position of their junior colleagues, indicates the deep divisions within the Protestant camp in the years immediately following the Peasants' War. The disagreement among the curates in Wunsiedel also points to a paradox. Hiltner was the better Protestant; Scharnagel and the other self-confessed Lutherans were better subjects. They were willing to follow the terms of the *Kirchenordnung* but would not exceed their mandate. In his resort to apocalyptic and scatological language, Hiltner made it clear that he would tolerate nothing but a complete elimination of the old ways. To his mind, the true Christians were the people of God and the children of Christ; his opponents could only be the servants of Antichrist.[47] Hiltner's stubborn refusal to moderate his position in the face of the visitation reveals the survival of a spirit of rebellion among the evangelical clergy of the Oberland.

As was the case in the margraviate, the central administration of the Hochstift Bamberg underwent a transformation in the immediate aftermath of the Peasants' War. The change was most notable in the cathedral chapter. Thirteen new canons were appointed between 1528 and 1531, mostly to replace Lutherans who had either resigned or been driven from office. Some of the new appointees were members of families that had not held seats in the chapter before 1525. Dynasties that had once figured prominently, such as the counts of Henneberg and Heydeck, never again held canonries on account of their confessional loyalties.[48] These changes ensured that Weigand encountered little resistance as he embarked on an ambitious program of reform. The mainspring of these early reforms was the vicar general,

Paul Neydecker. An outspoken opponent of the new learning, Neydecker enjoyed the highest confidence of his bishop and the curia.[49]

A number of edicts concerning heresy were issued between 1527 and 1535. Most of these were directed at clerics and laymen, in particular foreigners, who taught doctrines contrary to the Catholic faith. Offenders were subject to fines and corporal punishment.[50] Even stricter penalties were levied on those who sang anticlerical songs.[51] Weigand and Neydecker also took pains to try to reinvigorate the practices of the old faith, apparently with some success. Although attendance at processions between 1521 and 1526 had been uniformly poor, a procession *pro pace et tranquillitate* in April 1528 proved a great success. Subsequent processions and vigils attracted crowds at least as large as those before the Reformation.[52]

Unlike their counterparts in the margraviate, the ecclesiastical officials in the Hochstift did not undertake any visitations during the sixteenth century. However, several sources provide information similar to that found in the visitation protocols. One of the first sources illustrating the religious situation in the diocese after the Reformation is a list of parishes taken over by the margraves of Brandenburg, dated 1532.[53] The *Register* is a graphic portrayal of the disruption of older parish ties in the border regions. Wirsberg had been emancipated from the mother parish of Marktschorgast in the fifteenth century. Until the Reformation, the hamlets of Cottenau and Höflas had been considered part of the parish of Wirsberg. After 1528, since these communities lay within the secular jurisdiction of the bishops, the incomes from both went to the pastor in Marktschorgast.[54] The villages of Stammbach and Gefrees emerged as independent Lutheran parishes after the Reformation, but in both cases, the incomes that formerly paid for their chaplains were significantly diminished. Half of the peasants who had supported the chapel in Stammbach now lived within the borders of the Hochstift.[55] In the case of Gefrees, most of the church estates lay on the border between the Hochstift and the margraviate in an area that had been the focus of territorial disputes for over two centuries.[56]

The tax registers from 1532 and 1537 and the protocols of the vicar general's court provide some insight into the state of the diocesan clergy in the decade after the Peasants' War. Among other things, the registers from 1532 reveal that 85 percent of priests lived in concubinage and that 41 percent had at least one child. Five years later the situation had improved somewhat: only 78 percent of the priests now had concubines.[57] After 1541, Vicar General Neidecker began more vigorous enforcement of synodal decrees concerning concubinage, drunkenness, and other offenses. Several of the leading clerics in the diocese were certainly guilty of some of these offenses—both Neidecker and his assistant Sebastian Ochs von Gunzendorf lived in concubinage. Ulrich Rasch, who presided over a reform synod during the Augsburg Interim, was prosecuted three times for blasphemy and "great mischief."[58] Still, a large number of priests were brought before the vicar general's court, disciplined, and in some cases dismissed.

The protocols of the vicar general's court indicate that between 1535 and 1554 at least fifty-one priests were brought up on charges ranging from battery and concubinage to heresy.[59] The greatest volume of cases were in the years 1535–39 (fourteen cases) and 1550–54 (sixteen cases). The parishes where priests were subjected to disciplinary action fall into three main areas. The largest concentration of cases arose in the southern part of the Hochstift, in the area between Forchheim, Hersbruck, and Pottenstein. This was the southern frontier of the Hochstift, where the bishop's domains bordered on those of city of Nuremberg and the Hohenzollern lands. The region was also dotted with the estates of imperial knights. In no other area were the frontiers of the Hochstift more confused and less clearly defined; in no other area were there so many long-standing disputes concerning lordship. A large number of cases also came from the northern border of the Hochstift with the Hohenzollern Oberland. Since the fourteenth century, this region also had been the focus of territorial disputes among the bishops, the margraves, and the knights.

It is difficult to tell how many priests were actually Lutheran and how many were simply incompetent. In earlier years, Paul Adelhardt of Poppendorf had been ejected from his parish in Nuremberg for refusing to accept Lutheranism; in 1544 he was forced to resign on account of senility.[60] Heinrich Hübner of Adelsdorf was imprisoned for six days on bread and water on account of the "Lutheran heresy." Johann Koburger of Forchheim was prosecuted for his allegiance to the "*secta Lutherana*"; the eponymous Hans Puhel of Bühl was prosecuted for "*Apostasia*"; Heinrich Tulp of Weismain was guilty of "irregularities."[61] When Paul Puchel of Veldenstein was dismissed in 1549 for heresy, he was described as living in a "Lutheran manner."[62] One of the few priests to respond to his accusers with evangelical language was Heinrich Popp of Isling, imprisoned for mocking the Catholic faith in 1536. After his arrest, Popp wrote to his patron, the abbot of Langheim, that he had only "taught and preached the holy Gospels," telling the whole congregation that "Christ is our only hope and salvation," citing I Corinthians 3:11: "For no foundation can anyone lay than that which is laid, which is Jesus Christ." Such language did not help Popp's case and he was forced from office.[63]

The vigorous prosecution of priests severely disrupted life in the country parishes. Erhard Tailer, pastor of Affalterthal, was imprisoned on April 1 1545 for "*errores*." He was released a few months later after the vicar general received a series of letters complaining about the problems created by his absence. The "entire, poor *gemein*" of Affalterthal wrote to the bishop on June 18 that on account of Tailer's arrest they had been "deprived of God's word" and "robbed of the most worthy Sacrament." It was several miles'

Table 5.1. Vacant Parishes and Ordinations, 1530–36

Vacant Parishes (Total Parishes = 107)			Priests Ordained	
Years	Number	Percent	Years	Number
1535–36	9	8.4	1531–35	25
1540–41	14	13.1	1536–40	38
1544–45	21	19.6	1541–45	62
1548–49	27	25.2	1546–50	109
1553–54	45	42.0		
1555–56	43	40.2	1551–56	99

Source: Zeissner, *Altkirchliche Krafte,* 290–91, 294–98.

walk to the next parish, hence pregnant women, children, and the sick could not attend church services.[64] The residents of Affalterthal noted that for miles around chapels lay empty and desolate. This was not mere hyperbole. Throughout Weigand's regime, the number of vacant parishes increased steadily (see table 5.1). By 1554, 42 percent of the parishes in the Hochstift had no rector despite a concerted effort to train and ordain new priests. The tide was beginning to turn at the very end of Weigand's administration, but it would take several decades to fill all the vacancies.

The shortage of priests was one of the practical limitations on reform. A second was the resistance of the estates. Although the estates made no formal demands to slow the process of reform, many nobles and even some monasteries continued to appoint heterodox pastors to parishes under their control. Weigand von Redwitz's own brother supervised the Reformation in Küps. The abbots of Langheim were particularly notorious for their choice of Lutheran pastors in Isling and Modschiedel.[65] In contrast, only two cases of heresy arose in parishes where the *Gemeinde* had the right to appoint its own pastor, precisely the sort of places where one would expect to find evangelical preachers.

Here it is worth considering the response of the nobles in the Oberland to the first stages of the Reformation. Noblemen—including the lords of Redwitz— were among the most vigorous opponents of the visitation in 1528. Following the visitation, Margrave Georg ordered priests to turn over surplus chalices, patens, and monstrances.[66] Throughout the Oberland, princely officials encountered opposition as they attempted to enforce the margrave's decree. In the Vogtland, the lords of Deulwitz, Döbeneck, Sparneck, Hirschberg, Rabenstein, and Kotzau refused to allow officials access to churches on their domains. In the *Sechsämter,* the nobles in Röslau and Schirnding, Scheinwald, and Brand likewise resisted the order, as did the Guttenberg and Wirsberg families in *Amt* Kulmbach.[67] In some cases opposition arose from religious scruples–the lords of Wirsberg remained Catholic–but for the most part, the nobles who resisted secularization were committed to the Reformation.

Comparison of the sources from the Hochstift and the Oberland reveal a couple of common patterns. The *jus reformandi* was in large measure an expression of territorial sovereignty. This was nothing new–throughout the fifteenth century, the bishops of both Bamberg and the Hohenzollerns had perceived the ties between state building and religious reform. And this connection was not lost on the nobility. They too had sought through their endowments to increase their patronage rights on the local level. Regarding the seizure of church furnishings, what the knights found unacceptable was the intrusion on their estates by princely officials intending to seize objects that were meant as gifts to the communities the knights ruled; the gifts were expressions of generosity and care for their subjects' souls. The chalices and patens were, in this sense, little different from the prebends and chantries endowed by the nobles a century earlier.

The second point is a bit more subtle but no less significant. On both sides of the border, disobedient clerics were generally identified as adherents of the opposing confession. So "bad" priests in the margraviate are represented as Catholics and their noble patrons as followers of the old religion. Likewise, "bad" priests and their patrons in the Hochstift are almost uniformly referred to as "Lutheran" in the *Protokollenbücher*. But are we to accept these judgements at face value? It hardly seems plausible that while the border regions of the Hochstift were infested with Lutherans, only a stone's throw away–literally in some cases–border parishes in the margraviate were occupied by unreconstructed papists. According to the visitors in Wunsiedel, Marktredwitz was a Catholic center, but its lord was credited with the introduction of Lutheranism in two parishes in the Hochstift, Küps and Obristfeld. How could the same nobleman be simultaneously Catholic and Lutheran?

The most reasonable answer would be to say that the lord of Redwitz was neither, or at least not according to the standards of confessional orthodoxy that emerged in the latter part of the century. For the period between 1530 and 1535 it would have been difficult to define "Lutheran" with any precision. Likewise, what passed for Catholic before 1570 was not necessarily what would have been acceptable according to the terms of Tridentine orthodoxy. The visitation of 1528, the *Register* of 1532, and the *Protokollenbücher* reveal the doctrinal uncertainty that prevailed at all levels in the years before 1550.

❧

The question of doctrine cast a long shadow over imperial and territorial politics. Since 1518, both Catholic and Protestant leaders had called for a general council to resolve the growing religious crisis. Weigand von Redwitz had supported the reform congresses of Regensburg and Landau in the 1520s, but neither meeting produced any consensus among or within the disputing parties. Although bishop and chapter agreed with the religious aims—improving the educational standards for the priesthood in particular—the anti-Habsburg overtones of both meetings was not to their taste.[68] In 1533 the papal nuncio Ugo Rangoni visited the German electors to settle on a time and place for a general council. As the leading ecclesiastical prince in the Franconian Reichskreis, Weigand was party to these early negotiations.[69] This first attempt to organize a council failed, largely on account of the Protestants. With the publication of the Augsburg Confession (1530), Lutheran states had broadened the range of theological issues in play and made it clear that they were unwilling to cooperate.[70] Luther advised the Saxon Elector not to be swayed by Rangoni, describing the proposed council as "half angel and half devil."[71] The theologians in the Oberland likewise rejected the council as a "godless mob."[72]

With the arrival of a new nuncio, Pietro Paolo Vergerio, negotiations began that would lead to the Council of Trent.[73] In August 1535, Vergerio tried without success to sell the idea of a council to Margrave Georg. The nuncio found a more sympathetic audience in Bamberg, and Weigand's encouragement convinced the Franconian bishops and prelates to support Mantua as the site of the council.[74] When the proposal was put to the remaining members of the Reichskreise, however, Margrave Georg protested. It was totally unacceptable to Protestants for the council to be held in Italy: the religious question was a German question.[75] Vergerio's successor, Peter van der Vorst, once again tried to woo the Protestants. Van der Vorst went so far as to hear the mass in German at Georg's court, even receiving communion *sub utraque species* from the margrave's chaplain. Despite van der Horst's open-mindedness, Georg remained loth to approve of a Mantuan council. The nuncio returned to Rome empty handed.[76]

The lack of consensus over the council made the cathedral chapter skeptical of the entire business. Even after Trent was chosen as the site of the council, the chapter was hesitant about appointing a representative. In the end, the apparent unwillingness of Protestants to accept what seemed to Catholics as generous concessions led the canons to warm to the idea of the council. Vicar General Neidecker persuaded the canons to send a delegation to the preliminary conference at Hagenau, and their efforts drew strong praise from Rome.[77] When the Council of Trent convened in 1546, Johann Grau, dean of the collegial church of St. Martin in Forchheim, was sent to represent the see.[78] Thereafter, Bamberg tended to side with hard-line Catholics who rejected the slightest whiff of compromise.[79]

Margrave Georg's position was rather more complicated. In the years following 1528, Georg had emerged as a leading figure among the Lutheran princes. When Georg Vogler composed the Protestation of Speyer (1529), the margrave was the first to put his name to the document.[80] After 1530, however, he became far more cautious, refusing to join the Schmalkaldic League and working with his cousin Joachim II of Brandenburg to arrange some sort of bilateral toleration between the feuding confessional parties.[81] At home, Georg found little enough support from his own clergy for a broad Protestant coalition. After the failure of the Marburg Colloquy (1529), theologians from the margraviate, Saxony, Hesse, and Nuremberg met at Schwabach in late October 1529 to seek some common ground in religious matters.[82] Most of the representatives were willing to accept the Saxon articles of faith as a standard for Lutheran orthodoxy, but this proved unacceptable to the upper German cities, led by Strasbourg and Ulm. For their part, the Saxon and Hessian delegates, along with those from the margraviate, condemned the "errors" of the upper Germans.[83]

In Ansbach and Nuremberg, leading churchmen and officials had been groping toward a statement of religious policy. In July 1528, Andreas Osiander and Wenzeslaus Linck prepared a draft church ordinance. The ordinance dealt primarily with the order of worship, but was rather vague on certain key issues, in particular on whether or not the sacrament should be distributed in both species. A revised version, prepared by Georg Heyderer, was sent out in manuscript form to some parishes in the Niederland in October.[84] In February, 1531 a new *Religionsmandat* reflecting the spirit of the Augsburg Confession was issued. All subjects were ordered to attend sermons and "the Godly office of the German evangelical Mass." Although all were admonished to receive "the Holy and most worthy sacrament of the altar" it remained unclear whether this was to be *sub utraque species* or not. The feast days of the evangelists and a few other saints were upheld as days of obligation.[85]

Although the mandate is somewhat equivocal on doctrine, the power of the prince in religious affairs was here more directly articulated than it had been in previous ordinances. A Christian ruler is "earnestly ordered by God" to make his subjects diligent, "not only in temporal matters, but also and primarily [with respect to] the salvation of one's soul." To this end, the prince has "spared neither trouble, energy, or cost" to fill every parish with "pious, Christian, educated pastors, curates, and preachers."[86] Here we can perceive a contrast to earlier official statements: the ordinance presumes that the clerics appointed by the prince are worthy of respect, no different from the Amtleute.[87] Although legislation issued before 1528 tended to be directed against the clergy, who were held accountable for the debacle of 1525, now it was the laity who needed to be disciplined and subjected to "Christian order." According to the new mandate, lay people were guilty of leaving church early, going to taverns, drinking, dancing, gambling, and other sins. Consequently, God sent down "various diseases, above all the most gruesome enemy of Christendom, the Turks."[88]

Between 1531 and 1533, a team of theologians from the margraviate and Nuremberg, led by Johannes Brenz, prepared the final draft of a new church ordinance. Copies began going out to the parishes in March 1533, along with an addendum to clarify certain articles that the margrave found confusing.[89] The Brandenburg-Nuremberg Church Ordinance of 1533 was far more comprehensive than any previous mandate. It was reissued in 1552 and again (slightly revised) in 1591, and remained the official statement of doctrine for the margraviate until the end of the Old Reich.[90] The ordinance was divided into two parts. The first section described the teachings of the church, the significance of the Old and New Testaments, penance, the law, the gospels, the passion and sufferings of Christ, prayer, the doctrine of free will, Christian unity, and the utility of human teachings. The second part contained the order for baptism, the mass, collects, and prayers, and instructions on liturgical music. The 1552 edition, printed in Leipzig, included oversized leaves with the plainchant setting of the Great Thanksgiving. Each parish received a copy of the ordinance, along with a hymnal and a catechism. Pastors were ordered to read the ordinance from the pulpit on the Sunday after it had been received.[91] They were also required to hold catechism classes each Sunday and maintain a baptismal register containing the names of each child, its parents, and godparents.[92]

Although the ordinance was intended to provide religious unity throughout the margrave's domains, there is reason to believe that local traditions remained strong. In particular, it appears that the clergy in the Oberland held a rather different conception of the church and doctrine than did their brethren in Ansbach. The differences between the two are most clearly articulated in the statements submitted by pastors on the eve of the Diet of Augsburg in 1530.[93] The clergy in both halves of the margraviate believed that a higher authority in church affairs was required and that the episcopacy had a clear basis in scripture. This sentiment was echoed in the 1533 *Kirchenordnung*. Rürer and other Ansbach theologians were willing to grant the margraves extensive powers over the church, leading one scholar to describe their position as "caesaro-papism."[94] The Oberland clergy, on the other hand, were of a different mind. Johann Schabel, Ludwig Agricola, Johannes Eck, and other clergymen in Kulmbach held fast to the two-kingdoms theory, placing limits on the rights of secular authorities in spiritual affairs.[95] For them, God ruled "a part of the world, namely the Christians" through the "apostles and preaching office." Worldly authority existed for purely external purposes, to punish evildoers, maintain "the general Landfriede," and protect "our bodies, lives, and goods." Secular rulers could correct ecclesiastical abuses, as these were purely external matters. At the same time, princes who claimed authority in spiritual matters "challenge[d] Christ in his regime." Such rulers were rebels against heaven who "like the Pope" would be laid low.[96] Other Oberland pastors echoed the opinions of their Kulmbacher brethren. Konrad Vensser of Berneck wrote that "only the clergy have the spiritual sword, the word of God."[97] Kaspar Löner of Hof saw the true church as comprising "all the elect, truthful servants of God." It was up to the church, as the "holy, spiritual *Gemeinde* of God" to interpret scripture, teach, and discipline its members.[98] Ulrich von der Grün of Bindlach wrote that "in spiritual things only the clergy are to decide; secular law exist for *Bürgerliche* purposes and secular authorities alone."[99] Johann Groetsch of Birk stated that "princely ordinances should not be the final standard."[100] So although the clergy of the Niederland were generally willing to accept the authority of the prince, almost without exception the pastors in the Oberland opposed the idea that any layman should have dominion over the church.

As fate would have it, the fiercely independent Oberland clergy soon found themselves ruled by a prince of a rather less congenial nature than Georg the Pious. In 1541 Georg turned over the Ober- and Unterland to his nineteen-year-old nephew Albrecht Alcibiades. As we have seen, Albrecht was not yet five when his father died, and might well have ended up in the historical trash can. A family conclave, held in Frankfurt in 1536, dictated that his minority would extend until his twentieth birthday, and even then it remained doubtful whether he would be allowed to claim his inheritance. After Albrecht turned eighteen, Margrave Georg offered the young prince 1,000 gulden per year and the right to set up a small court. Albrecht refused, acting on the advice of Georg Vogler and Wilhelm von Grumbach, one of Albrecht's comrades in arms.[101] With their support, Albrecht convinced the estates to divide the margraviate.[102]

When Georg the Pious died in 1543, Albrecht expected to be named regent for Georg's four-year-old son, Georg Friedrich. This would have allowed him to rule all of the territories that his father had held, including Ansbach and the rich Niederland. When the will was opened, however, it revealed that Georg had named the Electors of Saxony and Brandenburg, along with the landgrave of Hesse, as coregents.[103] Blocked in his efforts to expand his domains and bored with life in the Franconian highlands, Albrecht entered imperial service. In return for a subsidy of 36,178 gulden, Albrecht Alcibiades agreed to support Charles V in his campaign against the Schmalkaldic League. The emperor promised that if victorious, he would award Albrecht the duchy of Saxe-Coburg for his troubles. As it turned out, Albrecht was captured by the Saxon Elector on March 2, 1547 and remained in captivity until after the battle of Mühlberg six weeks later.[104]

One of the consequences of the emperor's victory was the Interim of Augsburg, Charles's attempt to restore religious unity and political order. Execution of the imperial edict proved problematic, however. Several princes who had allied with Charles stood in opposition to the Interim. Even Moritz of Saxony felt that without resort to force, he would be unable to gain his subjects' support for the change.[105] Elector Joachim II of Brandenburg, as regent in the Niederland, sought to work out a compromise, and to that end called together a deputation of nobles and clerics at Heilbronn in October 1548. They determined that fairly minor changes in ceremony would be sufficient to give the appearance of compliance.[106] Joachim had little trouble convincing Albrecht Alcibiades to accept the Interim. Unlike his cousin Joachim in the mark, however, Albrecht was not interested in any sort of compromise. He issued a stern mandate ordering his pastors to return to the practices and teachings of the old religion. In response, eighteen ministers assembled at the Augustinian monastery in Kulmbach and drafted a letter of protest. They would clearly have no truck with Albrecht's decree: "we cannot and will not accept the Interim; no cleverness nor extreme hardship can convince us to, except the Scriptures alone."[107]

After receiving this rebuff from the clergy, Albrecht decided to lay the matter before the diet.[108] Wilhelm von Grumbach, now acting as Albrecht's chancellor, presented a detailed proposal, explaining the reasons why the estates should accept the terms of the Interim. Following the emperor's lead in the matter of religion would not only lead to "common religious peace in our fatherland, the German Nation" but would be "to the honor of God, [and] the unity of his holy Church and our salvation."[109] So far so good, but Albrecht's proposal could have offered little solace to the Protestants. First of all, the ordinance upheld the authority of the pope in all matters: "the Roman bishop has been recognized as the highest bishop since the time of the Apostles, and so the holy fathers and the common Christian church has consequently bestowed upon him the most honorable name 'Pope.'"[110] Papal authority was supported by "the apostolic canons of Dionysius, Clement, Anacletus, Ignatius the disciple of Saint John the Apostle . . . the old councils, namely Laôn, Chalcedon, and the fourth (council) of Carthage . . . [and] all the other old doctors of the church, Cyprian, Ambrose, Augustine, Jerome, and Innocent." The ordinance further declared that apostolic succession was upheld in the writings of Irenaeus and Augustine. The historical episcopacy was indeed a gift of God, "useful and to be well respected."[111] As far as scripture was concerned, "it is a false and pernicious error that nothing ought to be believed or accepted except that which is passed down to us in written form in the Gospels and Apostolic writings."[112]

Regarding the sacrament, the margrave's theologians were willing to make some concessions, admitting that at the time of Cyprian and Augustine it had been administered in both species.[113] Nonetheless, the old ceremonies of the church ought to remain in place "if for no other reason than for the sake of unity." Although there might be room for negotiation on the particular forms of the sacrament, the basic theology and liturgical practices of the old church must be preserved, regardless of what the heretics might dredge up out of scripture. The new German ceremonies and hymns were especially noxious. They were "the songs and psalms of idiots, ordained by plebeians" and unworthy of the Christian church.[114]

The estates were not convinced. The towns and the nobility demanded that "the word of God should be preached purely without the addition of any human teachings or laws." The sacrament should also be performed as it had been during the past few years, though again the articles are rather vague about how that was. In any event, in matters of faith the diet would defer to the judgment of the superintendents, pastors, and ministers. The estates would implement no change in religion that had not been approved by the clergy.[115] Albrecht requested that the estates reconsider, but when the diet reconvened on November 22, he received the same reply.[116]

Albrecht submitted his revised church ordinance to the clergy for their approval. Throughout the night of November 22–23 the pastors framed their response to the Catholic articles. Their concern was not so much with the unity of Christendom, but rather with "building up the Christian community" in the margraviate.[117] They rejected the revised order of service as "contrary to [God's] word and law" since "a *Gottesdienst* that derived from human reason separate from God's word is an insult to God and useless."[118] As Paul writes in II Thessalonians 1:8, "in the time to come Christ our Lord will punish with flaming fire and eternal damnation all those who do not believe in God and obey the Gospel of our Lord Jesus Christ."[119] The pastors then added that they had sworn in their oaths to the margrave to teach "nothing from the pulpit than the pure clear word of God, free from all human additions." Their third objection was even more subtle. Some of the revisions in the *Kirchenordnung* were impractical or hard to understand. Such an ill-conceived document could only lead to sorrow and regret.[120]

In their concluding statements, the pastors stated that they would act against neither God nor their oaths to the margrave. They were willing to undergo any earthly trial "including death" for the sake of "divine righteousness" rather than accept the margrave's ordinance.

> In such cases one is to be more obedient to our God than to men of any estate. . . . If [the master] should order anything contrary to scripture, then [the servant] should be more obedient to his spiritual lord, that is God, than the lord of his flesh.[121]

God would bring about peace and unity, not Albrecht or the emperor. As for Albrecht, the pastors advised him to place himself "in God's gracious care and protection through Christ Jesus, our only comforter and redeemer." If Albrecht would not repent, then he must be prepared "to answer for this pernicious insult to the honor and works of God before God, who is coming to judge the quick and the dead."[122]

Albrecht threatened to send the pastors to answer before the emperor for their "insidious, arrogant and disagreeable" statements, but soon thought better of it. Instead, he asked the superintendents to review the ordinance and suggest revisions. After much consultation, the pastors in the Ämter of Hof and Kulmbach reported that although they would be willing to compromise on some aspects of ceremony, most of the ordinance was unacceptable. Albrecht decided to publish it without their approval.[123] Within two weeks, the pastors of fourteen towns in the Oberland had formally registered their complaints against the statute. In particular, they refused to conduct services in Latin. By the end of January 1549 the clergy in Hof and four other parishes had joined the revolt in defense of "the liberty of the pastoral office."[124] In 1550 Albrecht once again asked the estates to impose the Interim but received no support.[125]

The seemingly endless conflict with the estates and the clergy soured Albrecht on the whole business. Just as Moritz of Saxony understood at the beginning, now, in the wake of negotiations with the diet, Albrecht came to understand that without broad support the Interim would fail.[126] Albrecht began negotiations with his cousin Margrave Johann von Cüstrin to create a princely league in opposition to the newly victorious Charles V. Albrecht's reasons for joining the new league are murky, and his reckless and chaotic campaigns brought more headaches than help to his allies.[127] It is clear that the margrave was angry at not receiving Coburg as promised. Albrecht was also deeply in debt, and neither the estates nor the emperor seemed willing to pay what he felt was his due. On February 2, 1552, Albrecht negotiated a subsidy treaty with King Henry II of France, where the latter agreed to provide funds for a campaign against the emperor. Shortly thereafter, Albrecht joined forces with Moritz of Saxony in a rebellion "to preserve and uphold the liberty of the German Nation."[128]

During the campaign that followed, Wilhelm von Grumbach hatched a plan for the occupation and secularization of the Franconian ecclesiastical states.[129] The Hohenzollern forces invaded the Hochstift Bamberg during the first weeks of May. Forchheim was plundered, as were several other towns.[130] On May 14, 1552, Bishop Weigand was forced to cede twenty Ämter to the margrave.[131] With the conclusion of the Peace of Passau in early August, Charles V annulled the treaty. This allowed Weigand to reconquer most of the occupied *Ämter*. But in November the Charles changed his mind. In return for Hohenzollern military support, Charles reissued the treaty of May 14, recognizing Albrecht's annexation of the twenty Ämter.[132] Throughout the next year Albrecht waged open war against the Franconian bishops. After several unsuccessful attempts to negotiate a cease-fire, an alliance of princes and imperial cities was formed to restrain the wild margrave. In the fall of 1553, a contingent of Bohemian troops, raised by Ferdinand I, invaded the Oberland. Hof, Bayreuth, and Kulmbach were besieged and destroyed. On December 1, 1553 Albrecht Alcibiades was outlawed and driven into exile. His lands were confiscated and placed under an imperial commission. Albrecht died a defeated man at Pfortzheim on January 8, 1557. His own chaplain refused to grant him communion before he died.[133]

Chapter 6

A Plague of Preachers

The two decades following the death of Albrecht Alcibiades were a time of transition and confusion. The year 1555 is generally taken to mark the end of the Reformation and the start of the confessional era.[1] At the same time, when describing the religious situation in the 1560s, it is easier to say what it was not, rather than what it was. The "storm years" of the Reformation were clearly over, but the future trajectory of Lutheranism remained uncertain. On the Catholic side, even after the end of the Council of Trent, the general religious ethos remained largely pre-Tridentine for several decades. This is not to say that the reforms had little impact, but the mood was tentative. The range of religious options had increased rather than narrowed; meanwhile the emergence of Calvinism offered an increasingly viable alternative to either Wittenberg or Rome. Confessional orthodoxies had yet to harden, and in the age of Maximilian II, the possibility for compromise on numerous aspects of doctrine and practice remained open.[2]

On the political side, the 1560s has been identified as the peak of the "crisis of the nobility" in the Holy Roman Empire.[3] Franconia was indeed the arena for what has become one of the symbolic episodes in the crisis, the campaign of Albrecht Alcibiades' former chancellor, Wilhelm von Grumbach. His career is representative of the general character of the crisis. Frustrated in his efforts to rise to the ranks of the territorial nobility, Grumbach became a champion of the lower nobility against the princes. He embodies both the growth and futility of noble opposition to the process of territorial consolidation in the sixteenth century. The declining political fortunes of the lower nobility matched their economic decline and the widening of the gulf between the petty nobles and the great lords.[4]

That Volker Press identified 1564—the closing year of the Council of Trent—as the *"Zuspitzung"* of the crisis in the relations between the princes and the nobility was largely coincidental: the defeat of Wilhelm von Grumbach, not the Tridentine reforms, defines the moment. It is nonetheless clear that in Catholic territories, opposition to princely centralization was often framed in terms of religion. Moreover, the Grumbach affair (*Grumbachschen Händel*) reveals serious tensions beneath the calm that seemed to prevail in the first years after the end of the Schmalkaldic War. And although it would be many generations before the larger aims of princely state building or confessionalization were accomplished (to the extent they *were* accomplished, but that is another matter), Press was correct to see the first decades after 1555 as crucial for the development of the confessional state and the emergence of both confessional consciousness and a revised conception of the role of the estates.

It is difficult to assess the precise impact of Albrecht Alcibiades' invasions on the confessional climate in upper Franconia. Certainly his campaigns were destructive. The Cistercian convent of Schüsselau had barely survived the Peasants' War of 1525; in April 1553 Albrecht burned it to the ground, and it was never rebuilt.[5] In the wake of his 1552 campaign, Albrecht and his officials made halting attempts to introduce Lutheran pastors into the newly acquired Ämter.[6] Most of the Catholic clergy fled during the invasion. Only two priests in the cities of Bamberg and Forchheim are known to have collaborated with the Hohenzollerns.[7] In the countryside, few priests would recognize Albrecht's authority, even if they were devotees of the new learning. Pankratz Degen of Weismein was one of the most vigorous proponents of Lutheranism in the diocese, but he nonetheless refused to swear allegiance to Albrecht.[8] Only two rural pastors appear to have sworn the oath of allegiance to the margrave: Johann Lencker, the chaplain in Burgkunstadt, and Georg Rein of Altenkunstadt. Both were among a group of fifteen priests brought to Bamberg in the fall of 1552 to answer for their apostasy. Lencker recanted and was subsequently appointed pastor of Tschirn. Rein also maintained his innocence and received the parish of Burkersdorf. In 1554 he was accused of heresy yet again. This time, Rein was brought to Bamberg in chains, tried, convicted and exiled.[9] Other priests shared Rein's fate when they were hounded out of office following Albrecht's second offensive in 1553. Albrecht had appointed Johann Beheim pastor of Hausen and Heroldsbach; after eluding capture on several occasions, Beheim was finally caught and exiled in November 1554.[10] Georg Rappolt of Unterleinleiter was likewise exiled for his adherence to "errores et schismata lutherana."[11] Some priests who had proven sympathetic to the new learning were able to avoid prosecution. Georg Adelhardt of Poppendorf was brought to Bamberg with the others in October 1552, but admitted his errors and was absolved. His successor, however, declared that Adelhardt had "*apostatirt*" and regularly preached in a Lutheran manner.[12] Perhaps the most notorious survivor among Albrecht's pastors was Aegidius Schnabrich, the first in a long series of Lutheran preachers in the border town of Presseck. Though called to Bamberg in 1552, Schnabrich refused to submit to the bishop's order and until his death in 1574 remained a thorn in the side of the Catholic authorities.[13]

The case of Schnabrich suggests that the conflicts of 1548–53 were not only as physically destructive as the Peasants' War but, in the long run, proved more disruptive to the fabric of ecclesial life in the Hochstift. The cases before the vicar general's court in the years after 1553 suggest just how fragile the first stage of Catholic renewal was. Thanks to the "wild margrave," thirty years of reform were nearly undone in a few months. The secular and ecclesiastical regimes collapsed under the weight of Albrecht's invasion. Weigand von Redwitz died in 1556, exhausted by the strains of war.[14] His successor, Georg IV Fuchs von Rügheim, found his authority limited by a particularly strict *Wahlkapitulation.*[15] The new bishop was also seriously ill. When the papal nuncio, Zaccaria Delfino, visited Bamberg in February, 1561, Georg was too weak to meet with him. A month later, Georg IV was dead.[16]

The next bishop was Veit II von Würtzburg, provost of the cathedral chapter and a delegate at the Council of Trent.[17] Veit was praised by the cardinal-archbishop of Augsburg, in part because he was a nephew of Weigand von Redwitz, the man "who had prevented all of Germany from becoming Protestant."[18] For his own part, Veit had little use for the curia. He was personally offended that although the archbishops of Mainz, Trier, and Cologne had been allowed to permit the administration of communion *sub utraque species* in their sees, Rome had denied his request to do likewise.[19] Veit also viewed the frequent visits by papal nuncios as a positive annoyance.

The first nuncio to call on Veit, Anton Cauchius, was treated to a special welcome—he was waylaid and robbed by Wilhelm von Grumbach. Cauchius spent most of his visit recounting his travails to anyone who would listen. Eventually he composed himself enough to reject Veit's second request for the right to allow his pastors to administer communion under both species.[20] The next nuncio, Bartholomew Portia, was extremely critical of Veit: "the bishop of Bamberg [is] most negligent and lives a most scandalous life and his diocese is full of heretics."[21] The chapter refused to allow Jesuits in the diocese, fearing "foreign influence." Portia also claimed that the cathedral dean, Marquard von Berg, was a Calvinist. Indeed, the "uncanonical jurisdiction of the cathedral dean . . . and the electoral capitulation of the bishop" were cited as the main obstacles to reform.[22]

Nicolas Elgard was the next nuncio to arrive in Bamberg. Veit patiently listened to Elgard's complaints and assured him that he was doing all he could to enforce the Tridentine decrees. The chapter did less to elicit the nuncio's confidence. They appointed a Lutheran to serve as his interpreter and initially refused to answer any of his questions. Although two canons, among them the future bishop Johann Georg Zobel von Giebelstadt, expressed their genuine support for reform, Elgard was unimpressed.[23] Bishop Veit told Elgard that, despite the papal order to construct a seminary, the diocese just did not have the money. Veit also expressed serious concerns about what the nobility in the Hochstift might do if Catholic reforms were pressed too far, citing the recent rebellion in Fulda as proof of the need for caution.[24]

Elgard's report was not long on praise. Still, neither Elgard nor the previous nuncios had been entirely fair in their assessment. Over the objections of the cathedral chapter, Veit did publish the decrees of the Council of Trent in 1572.[25] Portia and Elgard also failed to note a subtle change in the administration of the Hochstift. In an effort to get around the authority of the chapter, Veit began to turn to a select group of diocesan officials, the spiritual council *(Geistliche Rat)*, established in 1562.[26] Over the next few years, the Geistliche Rat became the spearhead of efforts to reform the parish clergy.[27] Between 1562 and 1577, some two hundred new priests were ordained in the diocese.[28] In the wake of Elgard's visit, the chapter agreed to provide 1,000 gulden to renovate the old Carmel for use as a seminary.[29] Veit also ordered the publication and dissemination of liturgical materials. A new breviary appeared in 1575; a new prayer book was issued the following year.[30] A special edition of Johann Leisentritt's Catholic hymnal was ordered for use in the Hochstift.[31] Official decrees suggest that the hymnal was widely disseminated in manuscript form; one such copy survives from the later part of the century.[32] Elgard's dire portrait notwithstanding, it is clear that under Veit II, Catholic authorities in Bamberg were making an honest effort to restore the old faith.

One of the guiding lights in this dark period was the suffragan bishop Jacob Feucht.[33] Feucht was certain that the major threat to Catholic renewal came from "preachers or fugitive monks."[34] These "seducers and noisome preachers" had wrought much confusion, thereby misleading the "common little people."[35] Feucht used both the pulpit and the press to combat the preachers. One of his favorite targets was Lukas Osiander of Nuremberg, against whom Feucht published a number of polemical works.[36] In Bamberg, Feucht used his position as preacher at St. Martin's parish church to innoculate his parishioners against the calumnies of "godless non-Christians" (Calvinists) and the Lutherans, "who are also wont to call themselves Christians and evangelical."[37]

A central point of Feucht's sermons was that since they could not honestly refute the Catholic faith, Protestants "must turn to untruth, lies and insults." Their sermons contained "nothing learned, nothing authoritative, nothing important nor proper."[38] By unraveling their lies, Feucht demonstrated that Protestant doctrines were hardly different from those of the heretics of old, in particular the Nestorians and Arians.[39] Lutheran teachings on the sacrament, according to Feucht, were Nestorian.[40] Likewise, Lutheran comments about marriage seemed in line with those of Tatian and his successors, Heraclion, Marcion, Mani, the Adamites, Arius, Priscillian, "and now some of the

Anabaptists."[41] Protestant iconoclasm merely recycled heresies condemned by the second council of Nicaea, where three hundred fifty bishops had agreed that "an image is not the same as God, [but] to look upon the image directs one's mind onto what which is depicted therein."[42]

Feucht also argued that admittedly, the "common, unlettered Lutherans" could not help falling into error. Most Lutheran preachers were "shoemakers, tailors, sextons, weavers, and other lower sorts . . . who have not studied, any more than they have gorged themselves on Nuremberger delicacies."[43] They preached things that they did not understand, merely what they were told to preach by the "learned Lutherans." The educated preachers, on the other hand, must know better. If they truly believed the things that they say, they were heretics, either Nestorians or dualists of some variety. "Shameless preachers" such as Osiander were without honor. So was Luther; his repudiation of his vow of celibacy proved that. The "educated" preachers had no respect for scripture, twisting it to suit their whims. Iconoclasm and the refusal of Protestants to venerate the saints showed them for the coarse, disrespectful, and dishonorable rogues that they truly were.[44]

Feucht's sermons reflected the widely held opinion that Catholic renewal required the elimination of the "noisome" preachers and their replacement with good, orthodox priests. As it turned out, removing the preachers and winning the loyalty of their listeners proved no easy feat. In 1558 the chapter had ordered the arrest of anyone who preached in a Lutheran manner, but once one preacher was removed, his followers would simply go find another. Lutherans in Bamberg were willing to walk the 12 kilometers to Walsdorf to hear evangelical preachers appointed by the local noble family.[45] Noble opposition to the Counter-Reformation comes as no great surprise, but resistance to Catholic renewal also emerged in far less likely quarters. On January 22, 1574, Bishop Veit raised a complaint against the abbot of Langheim. In four parishes under the abbey's jurisdiction—Altenkunstadt, Isling, Kirchlein, and Modschiedel—the pastors "had fallen away and *apostitirt* from the Catholic Religion." The abbot was requested to do away with these apostates and appoint good, Catholic priests. Otherwise, the "common man" might be led into perdition.[46]

The village at the heart of the controversy, Modschiedel, lay on the borders of the Hochstift. Included in the parish were five smaller communities, some of which had their own chapels, but all of which were dependent on the pastor of Modschiedel for the sacraments.[47] The residents were of various allegiances. Of some six hundred fifty parishioners, only forty or so were under the direct lordship of the bishops of Bamberg. A few were Hohenzollern subjects, but the vast majority lived under the nobility, in particular the Giechs of Thurnau. Diocesan officials noted that there were only "three and twenty Catholic communicants in the entire parish," scattered among the villages of Modschiedel, Wunkendorf, Neudorf, and Weiden. In

Göra and Seubersdorf there were no Catholics. The residents of Seubersdorf "were of all the most disobedient, not coming to the church all year long, but rather run off to Lutheran preachers in Arzendorf."[48]

It is not clear why the residents of Seubersdorf felt the need to travel so far. For the previous eighteen years the devout Cistercian abbots of Langheim had appointed Lutheran preachers in Modschiedel. The preacher in question in 1574 was Friedrich Hohenberg. Hohenberg had been pastor of Modschiedel for nine years before the issue of his confession came to the attention of episcopal authorities. In April 1574, the bishop had Hohenberg arrested; he then suspended the rights of the abbot for appointing an "aggravating and dishonorable pastor in Modschiedel, [who] from the open pulpit . . . attacked our Christian Catholic religion and clergy with vile calumnies."[49] On account of the abbot's negligence, the parish had been "polluted" by Lutheranism.[50]

After Hohenberg had been taken away to Bamberg, letters of protest streamed into the bishop's court. Hans Branzmann Giech von Thurnau defended Hohenberg, stating that he had served "with true diligence." Branzman demanded to know why "with minimal cause" the pastor had been seized, arrested, and subjected to various indignities. Margrave Georg Friedrich likewise came to Hohenberg's aid. He too demanded to know why his "subjects in Modschiedel" were being so oppressed by the bishop. Perhaps the most interesting argument was presented by the village councils in Modschiedel and the five surrounding communities. "The entire congregation" wanted no other pastor than one who would preach "the Holy Word of God" according to the Augsburg Confession. They further demanded "the holy, most worthy sacrament of the true body and blood of Jesus Christ . . . received in both kinds." For the past twenty years they had been supplied with Lutheran pastors, so according to the terms of the Peace of Augsburg the bishop had no legal right to force the residents to change religion. As Lutherans, all of the parishioners in Modschiedel and the surrounding villages ought to be reckoned as subjects of the margraves of Brandenburg, a Lutheran prince. Whether the residents were in fact Hohenzollern subjects or not made no difference: their religion determined their political allegiance. In effect, the villagers had turned the doctrine of *cius regio, eius religio* on its head. Veit was unimpressed. He answered the villagers "with hateful words" and condemned them as "Lutheran rascals."[51] He ordered that a "legitimate priest, ordained according to the Catholic rite" be appointed in Modschiedel, one who would preach "Catholic and orthodox doctrine, as restored by the Council of Trent."[52]

Of all the preaching centers in the border regions, perhaps none was so notorious as Presseck. The parish of Presseck had its origins in a collection of hamlets and small villages surrounding the castle of Wildenstein.[53] In the early sixteenth century the parish spread out over a broad area, including nineteen settlements. The majority of these, as indicated by their names, were *Rodunge* from the fourteenth century.[54] The records for Presseck suggest that although the bishops held patronage rights over the parish, they had little success in ensuring that it was staffed by a pastor of their choosing. In 1460 and 1525, the lords of Wildenstein claimed patronage rights over the parish.[55] In 1551, Weigand von Redwitz asserted his rights over the parish, but not long thereafter Aegidius Schnabrich, "one of the most zealous agents of Lutheranism in the Frankenwald," was appointed pastor.[56] Despite attempts by Bishop Georg IV to bring Schnabrich around, it was not until 1574 that a concerted effort to remove him from his parish began.[57]

In October 1574, five pastors from surrounding parishes registered their complaints against Schnabrich. Johann Angermann of Stadtsteinach, Konrad Kempf of Kupferberg, Johann Hofmann of Marktweiher, Wolfgang Weber of Grafengehaig, and Johann Prentel of Marktschorgast were all fairly young priests and, at least for the moment, firm in their defense of Catholic doctrine. They complained that Schnabrich intended "to do violence against the Catholic priests and religion."[58] Their parishes were overrun with "sectarians and evangelical preachers" who "from the open pulpit and other places" attacked the mass "most hideously." Catholic priests had to endure endless "blasphemous injuries and insults." To these priests, Schnabrich was, by far, the worst of the preachers. During the celebration of Pentecost, he disrupted the traditional procession from Presseck to Grafengehaig, attacking the participants "with many vile blasphemies," characterizing the Catholic rituals as "inhuman heathen acts."[59]

Despite sincere efforts to discipline or remove Schnabrich, he died in 1576 still in possession of his parish. After Schnabrich's death, Bishop Veit took the opportunity to appoint a Catholic priest in the parish. The new pastor, Nikolaus Beck, soon discovered that remaining a good Catholic in Presseck was no simple task. The lords of Wildenstein treated him abominably.[60] On one occasion they broke into the church and sold a monstrance that the family had donated some years earlier.[61] In 1578, two peasants from the Wildenstein estates in Kützenreuth, Nicolas Kalbskopf and Eberhard Büttner, came to Beck and demanded in the name of "tradition" that the pastor turn over to them a portion of the tithe. More specifically, they were looking for beer. Beck refused. In response "Kalbskopf came from behind and hit him [Beck] hard on the head with his fist." When the pastor tried to get away, Kalbskopf threatened to strike him with an axe.[62] Not surprisingly, Beck resigned his post in 1579.

Again, a staunch Catholic priest was appointed to the vacant parish. Johann Cauda had previously served in Steinwiesen, and no one seemed concerned about his orthodoxy. Until his arrival in Presseck he had always behaved in a "Catholic manner." Nonetheless, within a year of his arrival in Presseck, ostensibly under pressure from the "Jünkherr, being those of

Wildenstein," Cauda began dispensing the sacrament "*sub utraque species* as had the previous pastor."[63] Beck apparently had warned Cauda about this prior to his resignation. According to two witnesses, when Cauda asked how the parishioners wanted the sacrament administered, Beck replied "he had to give it to them in both kinds, since [they] would not be satisfied with anything else."[64]

Among the priests who had raised the hue and cry against the Pressecker preachers was Johannes Prentel of Marktschorgast. His own experience shows just how strong the pressure could be on priests to conform to the wishes of their flocks. Prentel had been appointed priest of Marktschorgast in 1561 on a temporary basis. On January 17, 1571, he was named pastor *in perpetuum*.[65] Only a few months later, in April 1571, the Bürgermeister, council, and Vogt in Marktschorgast leveled a series of profoundly serious accusations against Prentel. According to their report, "he loves his housekeeper like a whore" and further acquiesced to an illicit liaison between his Knecht and maid. Prentel supposedly set aside a room for them in the parsonage, and "thereafter it followed that she gave birth to a child, which was murdered." She had told Prentel that she didn't want a baby, but he assured her that she had her rights as a woman to do as she willed with the child. The Vogt in Kupferberg knew about this as well—he had seen the maid and noted that milk flowed from her breasts. After killing the child, the maid took it "to the wastes in Brandenburg jurisdiction, and laid it in a ditch where it was devoured by wild animals."

In addition to being a murderer and a panderer, the authorities charged, Prentel was a heretic. He administered the sacrament *sub utraque species* and told his parishioners that they should never accept communion from a Catholic priest. He regularly preached against the pope, saying things that no good Catholic priest could bear to hear. On Maundy Thursday and Good Friday he had not celebrated mass, but rather observed the holy days "according to the Margravish ordinance." Prentel sold grain illegally in the margraviate.[66] Finally, he had been ugly to the schoolmaster and refused to let him into the church.[67]

Describing himself as a "poor, persecuted priest," Prentel denied the allegations. He claimed that there was a conspiracy led by the schoolmaster, the Vogt, and the lords of Guttenberg, Wallenrode, and Hirschberg, to eject him because of his efforts to get rid of the Lutheran preachers in Presseck and Grafengehaig. Prentel had also frequently preached against adultery, noting that for years the authorities had tolerated such activity. This clearly angered some people in the parish. During Holy Week, as well as on the last three Sundays in Lent, the schoolmaster was drunk and had not fulfilled his duties as sacristan. On Good Friday the schoolmaster, the Vogt, and members of the council came into the church roaring drunk and so disturbed the service that Prentel could not finish saying mass. They were apparently angered that Prentel had refused to join them drinking "in the robber's chamber," that is, the local tavern. As far as the other allegations were concerned, Prentel stated that they were all a pack of lies and that for years he had tried to ignore the gossip about goings-on in his household.[68]

During the vicar general's investigation, the parishioners were asked about Prentel. Few could get their stories straight. No one said anything about selling grain, although some stated that he had illegally sold manure. Four of those testifying told about the Knecht and maid, but differed on the details. One said that he had heard all about it from the Knecht, who bragged that he had slept with two different maids in the parsonage. Michael Pauer and Hans Nüßlein both said that Prentel had preached against the Catholic faith, saying that it "wasn't right." Nüßlein, however, was a Lutheran from across the border, as were several other people who testified against Prentel. His supporters included members of the Tulp family, which had endowed several masses in years past, and Lorenz Brandtmüller, who had built a mill with Prentel's support. His most vociferous opponents represented a broad coalition, made up of peasants, noblemen, the Vogt, and the village elders. Internal disputes within the community, then, seem to have played a key role in the accusations.[69]

Prentel's problems with the nobility did not end here. Between 1574 and 1580 he was involved in an extended dispute with the lords of Wallenrode over the income from a chantry. For generations, the Wallenrodes had viewed the chantry as a personal fiefdom, to be doled out to various family members as income until they married. Prentel attempted to exercise his rights as pastor to administer the prebends and took over the account books. Accused of fiscal improprieties, the Wallenrodes and their ally, the Vogt, called Prentel a liar, attacking his fiscal and religious sensibilities. Prentel called on the bishop to prevent the Wallenrodes from interfering in parish affairs. He noted that peasants living on Wallenrode estates were allowed to cross the border to Berneck to marry. In the 1571 dispute, Prentel indicated that other parishioners had gone to Neudrossenfeld to marry. The only response that the Vogt could come up with was to claim that Prentel approved of such acts.[70]

It is difficult to get a handle on Prentel. His letters reveal a self-pitying streak, at times bordering on a persecution complex. He also seems to have been prone to violence and was twice investigated for assaulting parishioners.[71] Still, pressed as he was between the demands of the state and resistance from below, we might be able to appreciate, if not sympathize with, Prentel's frustration. He and other priests, the first fruits of the wave of ordinations that followed the wars of Albrecht Alcibiades, were charged with restoring the Catholic faith and defending their flocks against Lutheran preachers. They were asked to rebuild damaged or destroyed churches and consolidate the incomes of parishes that had been torn apart by the Reformation and subjected to looting and burning during the *Markgräflerkrieg*. Neither activity proved terribly popular among either the common folk or the nobility. And priests were generally forced to choose. They could, like Cauda, abandon their faith and enjoy the support and protection of their parishioners and the nobles, or they could, like Prentel, fight against these forces. Either course opened them up to attack from both their superiors and their parishioners.

In the years immediately after 1555, conditions in the Hohenzollern Oberland were hardly better, if not worse, than in the Hochstift. Albrecht Alcibiades died an outlaw, an exile, and intestate. From the fall of 1553 until the summer of 1558, the Oberland remained under the control of an imperial commission. Thereafter, bowing to pressure from the Electors of Saxony and Brandenburg, Ferdinand I agreed to turn over the Oberland to Albrecht's cousin, Georg Friedrich of Brandenburg-Ansbach.[72] Georg Friedrich, the only son of Georg the Pious, has been praised as "a man of unusual political ability [and] of supreme importance for the history of the entire house of Hohenzollern."[73] He inherited his father's lands in Ansbach and Jägerndorf at the tender age of three. In 1556 he was named coregent of Prussia for his mentally disturbed cousin Duke Albrecht Friedrich. In 1578, when it became clear that Albrecht Friedrich would never be competent to rule in his own name, Georg Friedrich was formally recognized as duke of Prussia. A central chancery was established in Ansbach for all four Länder—Ansbach, Kulmbach, Jägerndorf, and Prussia. Territorial governors (Hauptmänner) were appointed for each of the territories.[74] Prussian affairs consumed much of Georg Friedrich's energy. Consequently, for some years after he achieved his majority, the former regents, Margrave Johann of Brandenburg-Cüstrin and Chancellor Wolf von Kötteritz, continued to manage affairs in Ansbach.[75]

Among the first acts of the regents was to reorganize the administration of the church in the Oberland. Superintendents were appointed in the towns of Kulmbach, Bayreuth, Wunsiedel, Hof, Neustadt an der Aisch, and Bayersdorf.[76] The superintendents were a mixed lot. The superintendent of Bayreuth and general superintendent, Justus Bloch, along with his assistant Johann Brückner, were among the pastors who signed the protest against the Interim in 1548.[77] The superintendent in Wunsiedel, Christoph Evander, had been appointed pastor of one of the parishes annexed by Albrecht Alcibiades in 1552/53.[78] His brother-in-law Johannes Streitberger had been appointed head of the *Gymnasium* of Hof by the wild margrave in 1548 and was subsequently named superintendent.[79] Overall, the administration was split between those who had opposed Albrecht Alcibiades and "new men" such as Streitberger who had benefitted from Albrecht's patronage.

There was a widespread belief that during the interregnum (July 1554–
March 1557) ecclesiastical discipline had collapsed. This is not to say that
the Oberland was filled with Catholic preachers. The imperial commission
had made no effort to appoint Catholics priests to vacant parishes.[80] Nonetheless, Bloch and Brückner complained about the quality of the clergy,
especially those appointed during the war. They cited "many and noxious
crimes" among the clergy, and among the laity "common public vice, blasphemy, adultery and other immorality."[81] Something clearly needed to be
done to remedy the "defects and disorder" in the church.[82]

In 1558 the superintendents and the Hauptmänner were ordered to
begin preparations for a general visitation of the Oberland.[83] Between 1561
and 1565 the state of the church in the Oberland was examined in great
detail.[84] Local church finance was one of the primary concerns of the officials. If they were searching for signs of financial impropriety, the visitors
were not disappointed. The visitation revealed that communal officials had
failed to provide funds for the maintenance of churches and schools.[85] The
visitors cited the case of Trebgast as typical. The parish church in Trebgast
had been destroyed during the invasion of the Oberland in 1553 and never
rebuilt. Nonetheless, the town council continued to collect 30 gulden per
annum from parish estates even though there had been no pastor there for
a decade.[86] In the wake of the visitation, officials decided to grant a much-
needed addition to the incomes of pastors and schoolmasters throughout
the Oberland. A total of 2,000 gulden was set aside for this purpose, mostly
drawn from the estates of the monasteries in Kulmbach, Hof, and Himmel-
skron, as well as from a host of moribund chantries in the major towns in
the Oberland. The values of rents in kind were adjusted for inflation, and
special provisions were made to ensure a steady supply of firewood for the
parsonage. Subsequently, funds from the monastic estates were available to
pay for the repair of churches and parsonages.[87] When they examined the
quality of pastoral care, the visitors found a number of causes for concern.
In Bayreuth, a number of "old church customs" were still being practiced.[88]
The Lutheran liturgy for baptism and the Lord's Supper was not being followed according to the terms of the *Kirchenordnung,* and services were held
at unacceptable times and places. The visitors were shocked to find that ele-
vation of the host was widespread, even though it was "contrary to the first
commandment" and mere "blasphemy and sorcery."[89]

To remedy such problems, rural chapters were set up throughout the
margraviate.[90] According to the *Kapitelsordung* of 1565, clerics were required
to attend a chapter meeting each year on the first Sunday after Trinity. The
first session of each meeting would included a discussion of the catechism,
the Augsburg Confession, the *Loci praecipui theologici* of Philip Melanchthon,
the Schmalkaldic Articles, and the *Kirchenordnung.* After supper, the chapter would deal with more immediate problems, such as parish discipline.[91]

Superintendents were ordered to conduct special visitations of parishes in each chapter.[92] Although problems still arose, by 1574 some superintendents questioned whether the special visitations were really necessary. They argued that too much of the pastors' time was taken up preparing the registers required by the visitors. Many pastors simply found the visitations to be an annoyance.[93]

On the surface, it would appear that by the 1570s, officials in the Oberland had erected an effective set of mechanisms to improve the general level of pastoral care. But appearances can be deceiving. Better than a third of the parishes under the jurisdiction of the superintendents of Hof and Kulmbach lay on noble estates.[94] Records from the visitation of 1561/65 suggest that Hohenzollern officials did not have full access to many of these communities. Only one of the sixty-five pastors whose income was adjusted following the visitation had been appointed by the nobility.[95] The situation in the Oberland, then, appears to have been similar to that in the Hochstift. In both places, reform efforts were limited to parishes where the rulers had more or less complete control over patronage. Despite the impressive institutional façade, the territorial church in the Oberland was susceptible to many of the same difficulties that bedeviled reform in the Hochstift. Here too, pastors would find themselves pressed between their flocks and their prince.

In 1560 the residents of Gefrees complained bitterly that the incomes from a mass endowed by local families in times past was being used to pay a minister in Bischofsgrün. In addition, the villagers complained about the seizure of a consecrated bell from their church by Albrecht Alcibiades. Although it seems likely that the bell had long since been melted down and cast into cannon, the residents pled earnestly for its return. In 1593 they were still sending petitions to Kulmbach in the matter.[96] The disputes concerning Gefrees ultimately had their origins in the disruption caused by the wars of Albrecht Alcibiades, as well as in the reorganization of church finances. In 1568, Pastor Nicolaus Sella related the poor condition of the parsonage, damaged during the war. The roof was missing on much of the building, shingles were everywhere missing or rotten. A year later visitors noted the problems, indicating that the schoolmaster's house was likewise in poor condition.[97] The parish desperately needed money to repair buildings damaged during the war and pay officials.

It should have had the money—for a small parish church, Gefrees had been richly endowed in the fifteenth century. But the operating costs of the parish had increased, in large part because now the pastor and his assistants could legally marry. That meant that parish income had to be turned to provide for their wives, children, and widows.[98] Moreover, some of the old incomes were either no longer available or subject to dispute. So although previously the chaplain in Gefrees had received half the tithe from Stammbach, now that village was struggling to support its own Lutheran pastor. A farm in Lützelreuth that had once paid 5 gulden to the Lady Mass in Gefrees was under Catholic jurisdiction. Böseneck, according to a treaty of 1538 part of the margraviate, remained a focus of controversy. Pastor Johann Hofmann noted in 1580 that half the residents of Böseneck were Catholic subjects.[99]

That the community did not have the means to support its own clergy resulted in part from the centralization of church finance. The incomes that Albrecht Alcibiades had turned over the pastor of Bischofsgrün came from a mass endowed by the Roth family of Gefrees along with twenty other members of the community. For many years, the mass had been supported by a local confraternity that had been a primary expression of the village's religious and civic identity. Now the villagers wanted the income to rebuild the schoolhouse and pay the salary of the schoolmaster and the cantor. Wolf von Kötteritz decided that funds should be transferred either from the parish of Hof or from one of the secularized monasteries.[100] The point was clear: the residents of Gefrees now depended on the prince to provide pastoral care. The endowments that the community had made over the years had been absorbed into the general fund or lost with the stiffening of the confessional frontier. Local finance was also complicated by the claims of the nobility. In 1569 a dispute arose over subjects of Peter and Johann von Hirschberg in Zettlitz. The Hirschbergers complained on behalf of four of their subjects concerning the amount of tithe they paid to the church in Gefrees. These were the same farms that, nearly a century earlier, the Hirschbergers had turned over to a chantry administered by the Roth family. Now the lords of Hirschberg were attempting to reclaim the income from these estates.[101]

The conflict between the nobles and parish in Gefrees was not an isolated incident. The lords of Wirsberg had endowed an chantry in Goldkronach, the income from which was supposed to support the pastor and the schoolmaster in Lanzendorf. In 1567 several members of the family, in particular Gottfried von Wirsberg and Anna, the widow of Christoff von Wirsberg, refused to pay their share of income to the parish. As a cathedral canon in Würzburg, Gottfried von Wirsberg could claim religious scruples, but Anna had no such defense.[102] Other members of her immediate family proved no more willing to fulfill their obligations. Christoff Siegmund von Wirsberg was in arrears to the tune of 800 gulden.[103] Such a cavalier attitude on the part of Anna and her children ought not be surprising–her late husband had taken three gold chalices and a monstrance from the parish church in Lanzendorf and sold them for 100 gulden. The parishioners complained about that as well, and in 1570 the family was ordered either to replace the lost items or turn over the 100 gulden.[104] The Wirsbergers, however, seemed immune to threats. In 1586 the widow of the recently deceased pastor, Caspar Giersch, complained bitterly that she and her husband had received no income for nine years. When the new pastor, Conrad Geisler, came to her aid, he was literally hunted down and driven out of the village by the Wirsberg clan.[105]

Pastors in some border communities also encountered another threat to good order. In 1573, following the death of Pastor Leonhard Bauer, the town council of Wirsberg wrote to the superintendent requesting a new pastor. They noted how Bauer "proclaimed the *Evangelia* and the pure word of God, and also administered for us the holy *sacramenta* as it was instituted by our only savior and redeemer Jesus Christ." With Bauer gone they had become fearful because "in this area, in the midst of and largely surrounded by Bamberg *Obrigkeit* there are preachers . . . [who are] pure criminals and ravaging wolves."[106]

Who were these preachers? Catholic priests? Pressecker Lutherans? The sources are silent on this point, but the complaint from Wirsberg suggests that at least in the border regions, the plague of preachers was no less acute in the margraviate than in the Hochstift. Moreover, the same underlying tensions that so bedeviled reform in the Catholic parishes may be detected in Lutheran ones. In the case of Neudrossenfeld, we can see definite parallels between the plight of Johann Prentel and one of his Lutheran contemporaries.

In the fall of 1567 "the poor people" in a number of communities attached to the parish of Neudrossenfeld complained to the officials in Kulmbach about the unwarranted financial demands made by their pastor, Caspar Günther. Günther had been pastor in Neudrossenfeld since 1559, and following a visitation in 1566 requested an addition to his income and the right to gather timber to make needed repairs to the church and parsonage. Specifically, he required six thousand shingles since according to the visitors, there was not a dry room in the parsonage. The consistory approved the request, and gave Günther leave to ask his parishioners for assistance.[107] The villagers responded with a formal protest, claiming that Günther wanted to build a palace, not repair the parsonage, and that he had demanded 12 pence from each peasant "in the devil's name." They further accused him of conducting strange, alchemical experiments in the parsonage.[108]

The authorities in the Oberland were somewhat puzzled. Günther had previously been pastor in Berneck, and no one had heard of any such problems there. Günther's financial expectations might have been out of line— Berneck was an unusually rich parish with "a surfeit" of income, according to officials. Still, Günther had asked for no more than the *Hauptmann und Räthe* were willing to give him.[109] The inquisition that followed revealed a comedy of errors, pitting Günther's quest to craft powerful metaphors against his parishioners' ability to twist his words.

According to Günther, the problems all began when he tried to enforce the full terms of the Brandenburg church ordinance in the surrounding communities. In Waldau, Bechgraben, and Altdrossenfeld, unrepentant persons were living "in open whoredom," had not taken the sacrament in years, and "in other ways beheld themselves rudely." As far as marriage was concerned, he wrote, "[I]t is not that no weddings are held, [but rather] that the groom either did not represent himself properly, or entered in ignorance, and had similarly not complied with the articles and previous instructions." Regarding the accusations that he had invoked the devil, Günther could only surmise that this arose as a result of a sermon he had preached on the twelfth Sunday after Trinity.

> Among other things, I preached what the Gospel brings with it, namely how the devil desires to injure our body and parts, etc., for which reason man should pray for his sins, and ask God for protection. For further contemplation and consideration, I quickly followed by reading with a stern warning the shocking story . . . when the devil, in clear view, seized a woman in the land of Mecklenburg who had been urged by many parishioners to fear and repentance.[110]

Soon after preaching this sermon, word spread that Günther was telling his flock about "shocking miracles" from the chancel to scare the parish into compliance. As for alchemy, Günther replied that he was merely distilling water so it would be safe to drink. From his perspective, the accusations were "pure nullitates and hyperbole."[111]

Günther was wont to use the devil in his sermons on several occasions. His parishioners accused him of preaching a sermon telling them not to pay their taxes. Günther claimed that this was a misrepresentation of his reading of the text "render unto Caesar." All he had tried to say was that whatever one did not give either to God or Caesar one in fact gave to the devil.[112] In 1569 he was accused of striking a pregnant woman so that she became ill and lost the child. He replied that the story was a "conscious, gross, manifest and obvious untruth." What he claimed had actually happened was that during catechism class several students were quarreling, and he struck one of them on the shoulder. The girl then went to the inn and told the story to a few people, and it got all twisted around. But Günther only made matters worse by taking his quarrel to the pulpit. In a sermon following the incident, he compared himself to Christ and some of his parishioners to those who persecuted Christ. Günther then wondered "what the devil thinks he will accomplish through my parishioners."[113]

What indeed. Caspar Günther, like Johann Cauda and Nikolaus Beck in Presseck, discovered that despite his plans to spread true religion, his parishioners had very decided opinions on matters of doctrine and practice. In their demand for pastors who would conduct services and preach in a particular fashion, local communities demonstrated that they already had a clearly definable confessional identity. This is also revealed in the donations made to churches after 1560; Lutherans gave money for Bibles, hymnals, pulpits, and organs; Catholics were more likely to donate vestments and other furnishings appropriate to the mass.[114] Even if peasants may have been coached in their use of particular terms and phrases—we cannot help but feel that the malcontents of Modschiedel who made reference to the doctrine of *cuius regio, eius religio* received some help from Hohenzollern officials—they were keenly aware of which theological issues would attract attention. Indeed, the ability of the parishioners in Neudrossenfeld to manipulate terms and concepts took center stage in the reports from various officials. According to the Amtmann of Neudrossenfeld, if the peasants were displeased with anything Günther said in the pulpit or did not understand his meaning, that was sufficient reason "to turn his words around" and make mischief. And the main point of their complaint was that he preached "that we are not simply instructed and comforted with the Word of God, but punished as well."[115] The Castner saw the parishioners in a more cynical light. He noted that they were willing to pay Günther as much as they thought his sermons were worth, "like an artisan, who should receive his salary or daily wage and nothing more."[116]

The remark about pay points back to a larger issue found in all the cases discussed in this chapter. To a large extent the conflicts at the parish level were about maintenance of local control over church finance and ecclesiastical practice. In that regard, in the disputes of the 1560s and 1570s we can hear echoes of the communal reformation that had begun some two centuries earlier.[117] In both the Hochstift and the margraviate, confessional identity was defined in local terms, in the context of the parish "community" in the sense described in chapter 1, where noble patrons, communal officials, and parishioners cooperated to build and secure the local ecclesiastical *Gemeinde*. And just as confession could define the territorial state, it could just as easily be used to define the community, and often in ways that stressed its distinct character and bolstered claims to local autonomy. Local elites, both noble and burgher, continued to view their role as princely officials in the same light, as a buttress to their own authority and a recognition of their estate. And as in the past, a principal means for displaying estate was through the defense of true faith. The resistance of local elites to the reform programs emanating from the center reflected a fundamental disagreement over both the character of local governance and the connections among ecclesiastical patronage, status, and lordship. The reformations of the sixteenth century did not, then, immediately provide any sort of resolution to the paradox of local governance in the territorial state. Rather, in the identification of a single orthodoxy intended to be binding on all subjects regardless of privilege or rank, the reforms added a new dimension to the age-old contest between the prince and the *Land*.

Chapter 7

ORTHODOXY AND ORDER

Viewed from the perspective of officials in Bamberg and Kulmbach, two issues stood out in the parochial disputes of the 1560s and 1570s. Throughout the second half of the sixteenth century, increasingly greater emphasis was given to replacing the old priesthood with better-trained, orthodox pastors. It was on the shoulders of the new priesthood, men born and raised after the Lutheran Reformation, that the burden of enforcing the new confessional norms was laid. In the confrontations between the new clergy and their flocks, serious questions arose concerning the moral character of the laity. And although a number of peasant failings—superstition, addiction to gossip, drinking, blasphemy, and so on—are recorded by ecclesiastical officials, one particular fault took center stage: sexual immorality. Caspar Günther and Johann Prentel both discovered that of all their duties, the reform of marriage was the most likely to provoke anger and resentment.

The education of pastors and the reform of marriage have often been considered two aspects of the same phenomenon: the formation of the modern state and society.[1] Insofar as the clergy were in a "strategic position," it was important to ensure that clerics were well trained, not simply instructed in orthodox doctrine, but also trained to serve as effective administrators within the confessional state.[2] The transformation of the "peasant clergy" of the Middle Ages into the self-consciously professional clerical order of the eighteenth century is generally understood as an essential stage in the evolution of modern bureaucracies.[3] Likewise, the reform of marriage in the sixteenth century has been seen both as an early expression of absolutist social discipline and a point of origin for the modern family.[4]

Attempts to reform the clergy and marriage are perceived to be reflections of a conscious program to create a unified polity and an orderly society, mediated through a common, orthodox faith.[5] Frequently, this effort is portrayed principally in terms of its negative aspects, "social discipline" and the expansion of police power. But we ought to be careful in assigning entirely political motives to these varied endeavors. As Susan Karant-Nunn has observed:

The religious Reformations of the sixteenth century, and the generations that most immediately felt their weight, were also characterized by utopian fervor. Their pessimistic, neomonastic strands notwithstanding, taken together they constitute one of the most concerted efforts in Western history to make human beings the very best that they could be. In the ways the Reformers behaved, we see their confidence that earthly society could be transformed.[6]

Of course one may question just how effective this transformation was–a rich literature on the question of the "success and failure" of the Reformation attests to that.[7] As we have already seen, the behavior of both clergy and laity in the years immediately after 1550 would have given little comfort to the most ardent reformers of the 1520s. At the same time, it is clear from the language of the disputes that ordinary persons seem to have had a reasonably good sense of the theological issues, enough to be able to frame their dissent in confessionally charged language. To borrow a phrase from Marc Forster, the people of rural Franconia developed a confessional consciousness without being "confessionalized."[8] What this meant on the ground is that although the residents of the territories–here I would include the nobility as well as the commons–were generally willing to accept the revised forms of worship and devotion, and even seemed to have embraced some of the doctrinal positions underlying the reforms, they treated the social-disciplinary aspects of the reforms, however "utopian" they might have been, with suspicion. To put it bluntly, it remains open to question whether or not the prince's subjects wanted to be "the very best that they could be," so long as someone else provided the authoritative definition of "best."

The failure of the Reformation, in this context, lay in official attempts to substitute communal religious discourse with a centrally determined orthodoxy. The salvific function of the religious rituals and their power in defining community was now subverted by an emphasis on discipline. It has been argued that what lies at the heart of the conflict was that although the community desired to hear the Gospel–the word that spoke of grace, salvation, life, and peace with God–what they heard from the pulpit was the Law–words of sin, sickness, death, and enmity against God.[9] Such were the complaints against Günther's sermons. But note that not simply discipline but, as Karant-Nunn observed, a genuine desire to bring about a real spiritual transformation inspired the clergy in their efforts. To be fair to the preachers, there simply are times when parishioners need to hear hard words from the pulpit. The question, then, is not so much a matter of the imposition of some kind of alien and oppressive discipline, but how it might be possible to serve *both* the spiritual needs of the laity *and* the political needs of the secular regime in ways that minimized conflict and secured religious orthodoxy and civil order. This same question lies at the heart of the synods of the fifteenth century and Johann von Auerbach's *Directorium*. And as in the past, the training of pastors and the moral edification of the laity were seen as critical. The difference is that only in the second half of the sixteenth century can we see a coordinated institutional response to the problems that were perceived to threaten the church and society. The education of the clergy constituted a practical response to the problems that the first generation of priests and pastors faced in their efforts to enact reforms. Likewise, the reform of marriage, in particular the creation of consistories and a body of law concerning marital relations, can also be seen as a practical response to the sorts of problems we saw in the previous chapter. Our concern here is not so much with charting the success or failure of either project. Rather, the focus will be on the relationship between the ideals inherent in the reforms and how they played out in reality. In the gulf between ideal and reality we can see the something of the character of the confessional state in the closing years of the sixteenth century and its promise, but also its fundamental limitations.

The Council of Trent called for the foundation of a clerical seminary in each diocese in order to improve the moral and intellectual temper of the secular clergy. The decree envisioned schools in which the students and faculty lived together according to the vita communis. The curriculum combined humanistic studies of language and literature with more formal training in theology–the school would thus be neither a Gymnasium nor a university, but combined elements of both.[10] In Bamberg, plans to erect a seminary emerged in the later years of Bishop Veit's reign. Suffragan Bishop Johann Ertlin (1581–1607) kept the project alive during the short and largely insignificant reigns of Veit's immediate successors, Johann Georg I (1577–80) and Martin von Eyb (1580–83).[11] In August 1583, Martin resigned, allowing the pope to appoint a candidate of his own choosing. Ernst von Mengersdorf was only twenty-nine years old at his accession, but the curia had great hopes that the young man would champion the Tridentine reforms. A nephew of Bishop Veit II and a grandnephew of Weigand von Redwitz, Ernst was the first bishop of Bamberg to have studied under the Jesuits, first in Würzburg, and later at Ingolstadt and Louvain. He proved a keen politician, and between 1584 and 1588 broke the power of the estates in fiscal matters. Unhindered by either a Wahlkapitulation or the estates, Ernst initiated a vigorous campaign to restore the Catholic faith.[12]

The foundation of the seminary, the Collegium Ernestinum, was the first-fruits of Ernst's reform program. The chapter agreed to resurrect plans for the seminary in February 1584.[13] Making those plans a reality, however, required close cooperation among the bishop, chapter, monasteries, and collegial chapters in the diocese–no mean feat considering the less than amicable relations between these parties in the past.[14] It was decided that the Carmel would provide the best location, but it soon became clear that the structure required extensive renovations, costing over 20,000 gulden. The monasteries of Langheim, Banz, and Michelsberg donated funds, as did the bishop, canons, and various nobles. Thanks to the generosity of the donors, all but 2,500 gulden was paid for.[15]

The Ernestinum housed six faculty and thirty-six students. Twelve of these attended on full stipends while the remainder were given half stipends.[16] Of the earliest curriculum, little record survives. An ordinance from 1593 indicates that students studied the catechism, grammar, rhetoric, and philosophy. Students who did not use Latin in their conversations with their peers were subject to penalties. Music also was part of the training from an early date, although some officials felt that it was a distraction. Since priests needed to have some knowledge of worldly and political affairs, once a year the students should stage "a comedy, tragedy, or else a dialogue from sacred or secular, albeit inoffensive, histories."[17]

In the margraviate, clerical education was organized along rather different lines than in Bamberg. After abortive attempts to found a university in Ansbach in the 1520s, funds were directed to provide basic Latin education for students at home and to fund their advanced studies abroad, the best students going to Wittenberg.[18] The most prestigious Latin school in the Oberland was the Gymnasium in Hof. One of Luther's associates, the Hebraist Nicolaus Medler, was appointed to run the school in 1527.[19] In 1543, the school was reorganized by Albrecht Alcibiades, and thereafter carried his name.[20]

Between three and four hundred students attended the Albertinum, the best of these receiving stipends drawn from secularized monastic estates.[21] The curriculum stressed instruction in Christian doctrine and classical languages. Teaching duties were divided among the five faculty, with the cantor and *quartius* given responsibility over the youngest students. In the lower classes, students learned the alphabet and penmanship. In the higher classes, they studied Latin grammar and composition. Latin was the language of instruction, and, as in Bamberg, students were forbidden to use German in class. Discipline was a special concern, and the punishments meted out could be quite inventive:

> Concerning one who is ashamed of nothing or speaks or behaves in an unchristian manner, part of his punishment shall be to recite a scene from the comedies of Terence or several fine little verses from Virgil or Ovid.[22]

Summer term was set aside for musical education. In addition to simple chant, the students were expected to be able to sing motets from parts. The younger students learned notation by copying the parts from motets onto large boards mounted in the choir. Here again the ordinance cites a disciplinary concern. If the notes were too small, then the singers would be able to see "barely three or four notes," leading to "all manner of confusion and annoying dissonance in the church."[23] Two exams were given each year, and students were advanced or held back depending on their performance.[24]

By the 1560s, the Albertinum in Hof housed seven classes of students. In the seventh (lowest) class, the boys were taught the Latin alphabet, the Lord's Prayer, and responses. In the sixth class they were introduced to "the primary points of Christian doctrine," including the Ten Commandments.[25] At that point students began learning Latin vocabulary and were also taught the German alphabet. Instruction in Latin and Christian doctrine continued through the fifth class. The fourth class was devoted almost entirely to Latin grammar. By the end of the third class, students were expected to have memorized the Latin declensions and conjugations. This would prepare them for the second class, where they would begin reading the Gospels in Latin, as well as the letters of Cicero and the works of Philip Melanchthon. In the first class, students learned the rudiments of Greek, a necessary precondition for entrance into the university.[26] After Thomas Blebelius became rector in 1592, Hebrew was added to the curriculum in the first class. Students began to read the Gospels in Greek in the second class, while Paul's letters provided the focus for Greek studies in the first class.[27]

From a purely academic standpoint, the education of pastors in both Bamberg and the Hohenzollern Oberland seems more than satisfactory. The question remains open, however, as to what extent the schools contributed to the professionalization of the clergy. One wonders how useful Hebrew was in dealing with the day-to-day problems of rural parishes. We know very little about first generation of students to attend the Ernestinum in Bamberg. Not until the middle of the seventeenth century is it possible to track the alumni in later careers. On this subject, we are better served by the sources for the Oberland. Fairly complete records survive for the students who received stipends (*Stipendiaten*) at the Albertinum from the 1570s onward. These young scholars were the nascent clerical elite, but their behavior was at times questionable. In 1587 Eberhard Todtschinder lost his stipend on account of some sort of "*Bubenstück*" as well as continued untoward behavior and frequent absences. Four years later another student lost his stipend after "transgressing the sixth commandment" with the mayor's serving girl.[28] What is significant about these examples are the results of the expulsions, as they point to an emerging Protestant elite that would hold sway into the eighteenth century. In the latter case, the rector of the school indicated that currently twenty-three students were awaiting stipends. Todtschinder's stipend was given to Christopher Jordan. What made Jordan worthier of the award than the almost two dozen other candidates was not his scholarly ability—it was his lineage.

For Jordan, as for many other young scholars, kinship proved the single most important factor in securing a stipend. Within two generations after the Reformation, several clerical dynasties had formed, linked by marriage to form a vast kinship network. Among these, such as the Saher and Codomann families, were patriarchal dynasties, some of which continued into the eighteenth century. More common were broad kinship networks based on marriage. Young ministers not infrequently married the daughter or widow of the senior pastor.[29] Such marriage patterns produced what might be considered matriarchal dynasties associated with certain churches. Jordan was selected largely because his father was the assistant to the superintendent of Wunsiedel. Insofar as there were only about half as many stipends as qualified students, such credentials became vital.[30]

Patronage and kinship also figured heavily in the career paths of the students who won scholarships to study at Wittenberg in 1574. The scholarship competition consisted of three parts: Latin prose composition, Latin verse composition, and Greek verse composition. Enoch Widmann, Samuel Codomann, and Wolfgang Reinhard were awarded stipends for their essays, which reveal a good working knowledge of both languages.[31] The results of the exams were not, however, the only factors in the decision to grant stipends in 1574. The consistory also hoped to find money for Johann Evander, the son of Christoph Evander, formerly the inspector of the Gymnasium and the superintendent in Wunsiedel. Even though the young Evander had not done terribly well on his exam, the officials felt they owed him some financial support on account of his father's service to the church. Two years later, the same issue arose concerning Johann's younger brother, who received a stipend even though he too had done poorly on the exam. General Superintendent Johannes Streitberger made no secret of his reasoning. Both boys deserved special consideration as the sons of a minister, his own stepgrandsons, and grandsons of Nicolaus Medler. From Streitberger's point of view, such a pedigree guaranteed that the young Evanders would not be "infected" with Calvinist doctrines taught by "some professors of theology at Wittenberg."[32]

The careers of the other three Stipendiaten from 1574 illustrate the pitfalls facing individuals seeking positions in the church. Samuel Codomann was the son of the rector of the Albertinum and a nephew of the rector of the Lycaeum in Kulmbach. He clearly had the best connections of the group, but died young in 1586.[33] Enoch Widmann was the son of a clothier in Hof. He emerged from Wittenberg as a Magister in 1578. In 1581 he was appointed as the Cantor in the Albertinum, the lowest faculty position. The following year he advanced to the rank of Tertius and was named corector in 1591. From 1596 until his death in 1615, he served as rector. For most of his career, he taught only the highest classes, offering courses on the Pauline epistles in Greek and Virgil's *Georgics*. In 1592 he composed a history of Hof, a work that most certainly ensured his appointment as rector. He also founded a *Convivium Musicum* that gave regular performances of instrumental works and staged operatic treatments of liturgical dramas. The crowning achievement of his career was the publication in 1614 of what became the official hymnal in the margraviate.[34]

The last of the three Stipendiaten was Wolfgang Reinhard of Kulmbach. Apparently a good student, he had two major liabilities. He was not from Hof as were most of the leading clergymen. He also appears to have been rather abrasive. The rectorate in Kulmbach was generally given to men who had received stipends to study at Wittenberg, not as a reward, but as a means of making up their obligation to the prince. Reinhard's predecessors, Johann Gallus and Johann Codomann, had also been Stipendiaten. After a few years' service in Kulmbach, both were able to find more prestigious positions. Gallus ended his career as the chief pastor in Hof, while Codomann served as rector of the princely academy at Heilbronn and later became president of the Consistory.[35] If Reinhard hoped for similar success, he was most certainly disappointed.

The Lycæum in Kulmbach proved a hornets' nest rather than a community of scholars. Reinhard and his associates squabbled constantly.[36] When Reinhard arrived in Kulmbach, the Tertius was Hieronymus Muggenhöfer, an organist from Nuremberg. Muggenhöfer was lured to Kulmbach in 1574 with the promise that he would become the music director of the chief parish church. Fourteen years later Muggenhöfer was still teaching the rudiments of Latin grammar to the lowest classes.[37] When Muggenhöfer finally left in 1588, he was replaced by Eberhard Todtschinder, who, as we have seen, had had his stipend revoked the previous year for misconduct. A profoundly dissatisfied Tertius, then, was replaced by one whom his rector described as a "coarse rascal" and a "loose scoundrel" in front of the students. For his part, Reinhard apparently became a drunk whom Todtschinder berated for his inability to keep his mouth shut when in the bottle.

Throughout his stay in Kulmbach, Reinhard continued to seek a parish. His quarrels with his associates, however, convinced the consistory that he ought not be given a pastoral position. In 1595 Reinhard requested the parish of Bindlach on account of his poor health and sixteen years of service in Kulmbach. His request was turned down.[38] Wolfgang Reinhard died the following spring, leaving behind a pregnant wife and several children. Todtschinder remained in Kulmbach until 1603, when he was turned out for spreading scandalous rumors about the new rector.[39]

For men such as Reinhard, who lacked the connections and social skills necessary to obtain a parish; overqualified misfits such as Muggenhöfer; or juvenile delinquents such as Todtschinder, the Latin schools became a dead end. For some this occurred even earlier in their careers. Michael Egglofen was denied the opportunity to take part in the stipend competition until he had fulfilled his duties teaching school in Teusching, a wide spot in the road in a more desolate part of Franconia.[40] Many young clerics found that rectors saw them as little more than janitors. Georg Breutla of Selb compared his rector unfavorably with Pontius Pilate.[41] And as the sixteenth century came to a close, the consistory became increasingly reluctant to move men out of teaching positions too quickly. The continual "mutation" of the faculty in Hof and resultant lack of consistent pedagogical style had left students "bewildered," according to one report.[42] So temporary teaching positions became permanent, and eager young ministers became reluctant, if not belligerent, Latin teachers. The only way to escape such a fate was to have been born a minister's son, preferably the son of a well-respected member of the clerical elite.

Reviewing recent research on the Protestant clergy, Luise Schorn-Schütte concludes that "one can only speak of 'professionalization' in the sense of modernization theory only towards the end of the eighteenth century." Social networks, in particular family ties, ultimately proved "decisive for the bestowal of offices and prebends."[43] The evidence from the Oberland clearly supports this view. Kinship and other social ties were more significant for the development of the clerical estate than education or any sort of "professional" ethos. As the case of Wolfgang Reinhard and his classmates indicates, ties to the leading clergy were essential for receiving stipends, university scholarships, and parishes. This can most graphically be seen in the case of the parish of Kirchenlamitz. Members of the Ölmann, Winter, and Evander families held the pastorate there as a hereditary possession. Christoph Evander acceded to the post previously held by his maternal grandfather, Fabian Ölmann. When Evander died in 1568, a conflict arose over who should receive the vacant parish. The most obvious candidate was the associate pastor, Johann Frischmann. Frischmann was passed over, however, in favor of Samuel Winter, Evander's father-in-law and Fabian Ölmann's son-in-law. Winter's mother and sister-in-law successfully lobbied the consistory to appoint Winter, arguing that it was only just that a relative of Evander get the job.[44]

Patronage played an even more significant role on the other side of the confessional frontier. Although the social origins of early sixteenth-century Catholic clergy are notoriously difficult to trace, evidence from the Hochstift suggests that towards the end of the century, the older paradigm whereby fathers might be succeeded by their sons was breaking down. What replaced it was a system based in part on nepotism, in part on patronage networks forged in the seminaries.[45] The patronage networks in Bamberg were more centrally controlled than in the Oberland. The seminary was placed under the direct supervision of the suffragan bishop, who also oversaw the ordination and placement of priests. The best seminarians were regularly sent off to the Collegium Germanicum in Rome, where they forged ties with the international patronage network of the Counter-Reformation.[46]

With respect both to kinship patterns and the formation of broad patronage networks, the structure of the parish priesthood in seventeenth-century Bamberg more closely approximates the cathedral chapters of the fifteenth and sixteenth centuries than modern bureaucracies. What is striking here is the extent to which the kinship networks in the Hohenzollern Oberland ended up taking much the same form. The educational reforms of the later sixteenth century in both territories contributed less to the formation of a professional, bureaucratized clergy than to the creation of a self-contained, self-perpetuating clerical estate.[47] The clergy in the margraviate, though not necessarily a homogeneous group, retained a consciousness of their special status and role. They were not–nor would have themselves become–mere agents of the state or representatives of "princely" religion.

In the Hochstift the matter is rather more complex. Although priests were unquestionably subject to the prince-bishop in matters of religion, the relations between the secular and spiritual sides of the regime remained strained, particularly on the local level. And over the course of the Counter-Reformation, as the bishops turned more and more to the secular arm to enforce their decrees, tensions among the priests, their patrons, their flocks, and the prince only intensified. Ultimately, no amount of education could solve the problems the clergy faced as they attempted to administer their office. In Bamberg, as elsewhere, the loyalty of parishioners to the old faith, along with their support of their parish priests were, at least in the short term, more important to the success of the Counter-Reformation.[48] In the long run, the creation of the seminary had a decisive impact on securing the success of the Counter-Reformation. The question remained, however, whether the authorities would have sufficient patience to let educational reform–and time–do their work.[49]

Far more than the education of the clergy, the reform of marriage in the later sixteenth century has been made to carry the burden of modernization. The reform of marriage had deep roots. Arguably, we can trace many of the theological and legal ideas that informed early modern approaches to marriage back to the Gregorian reform of the eleventh and twelfth century.[50] In Bamberg, many of the sixteenth-century reforms derived from the marital decrees issued by the Council of Basel.[51] Johann von Auerbach comments extensively on the pastor's responsibilities as overseers of the sacrament of holy matrimony.[52] In the Hohenzollern territories, the sumptuary legislation concerning weddings was based on ordinances issued in Ansbach in 1387 and 1430.[53] Nonetheless, it was not until after 1560 that we can see officials in either the Hochstift or the margraviate taking concrete steps to reform marriage. The result was the development of new institutions and the publication of a broad range of legislation touching nearly every aspect of family life.

Bishop Veit II issued several ordinances regulating the conduct of weddings. The first, published in 1561, limited the size of wedding parties and required couples to hear mass "according to Christian *ordnung*."[54] A mandate from 1566 states that "one may wish to have a piper and fiddler [to accompany the bridal party] to and from the churching and as far as the house of the wedding, but with all propriety and modesty and beyond that nothing. . . . Certain dances, as noted, with drums and pipes and stringed instruments, will not be tolerated."[55] A 1574 mandate also prohibited lewd dancing and forbade uninvited guests to participate in the festivities. "Frivolous dances," in which women would spin around until their skirts flew up, were considered particularly offensive.[56] Excessive drinking and provocative dances also seemed to lead to all sorts of trouble. A contemporary ordinance from Würzburg noted that many young women had been dishonored following wedding feasts.[57]

Initially, officials merely attempted to regulate, rather than eliminate, traditional communal activities that surrounded weddings. The marriage ordinance of Ernst von Mengersdorf of 1587 aimed at a more thorough reform. Marriage was a sacrament of the church, the ordinance declared, but on account of the influence of "our common opponent, and holy matrimony's particular enemy," many of the "poor people" have been led "into heavy sins and aggravation." Consequently, "marriages in the home, hidden secret marriages, and other improper couplings" were forbidden, since "they are nothing other than heavy sins, shameful mischief, great evil, and wicked damnable abuses of Holy Matrimony." Marriages could be performed only by an ordained priest in the presence of two or three witnesses according to "the recently held Christian Council of Trent."[58]

The reform of marriage in Bamberg did not go unopposed. Both Veit II and Johann Georg I had complained that marriage cases were not being brought before the consistory, but rather being resolved in the secular courts.[59] And although both princes recognized the authority of the cathedral dean in such matters, the jurisdiction of the dean became a point of conflict under Ernst von Mengersdorf. The cathedral dean, Johann Heinrich von Nanckenreuth, allowed a prominent merchant, Hans Burkhard, to be married at the Upper Parish Church in Bamberg. There was only one hitch: Burkhard had been excommunicated by the bishop. Priests at St. Martin's parish church and the cathedral had refused to perform the ceremony for that reason, but Nanckenreuth claimed the right to issue a dispensation in the bishop's name. Ernst retorted that only he and Suffragan Bishop Ertlin had the power to grant dispensations. If the chapter now wished to seize the spiritual sword from the bishop's hand, he would use his secular authority to resolve the matter. The dean and chapter refused to back down, arguing that Ernst's attempts to reform the clergy had failed and that his spendthrift ways were driving the Hochstift into the ground. Given his incompetence, the chapter had the responsibility to take matters into its own hands. Nanckenreuth claimed that Ernst's opposition to his handling of the Burkhard case was personal; Ernst replied that he had nothing against Nanckenreuth, only against his claims to jurisdiction. The conflict was brought to a close with

Nanckenreuth's death in May 1590, but the question of jurisdiction was never fully resolved.[60]

The reform of marriage in the Oberland was no less contentious. There too, secular courts continued to hear marriage cases after 1556, much to the chagrin of the spiritual authorities. In 1563 the visitors in the Oberland argued that a "Christian consistory" ought to be established to decide such cases.[61] They complained that marriage cases "should be taken out of the princely Hofgericht and heard by the general superintendent along with two of his associates."[62] A marriage court, or *consistorium,* was established in Kulmbach in 1567, following the publication of a marriage ordinance.[63] In 1584, however, General Superintendent Streitberger and other clergymen threatened to resign after the secular courts had taken to hearing all cases concerning marriage. In 1589 Streitberger complained again that "for some time" the secular representative on the consistory had not attended meetings.[64] In response to these and other complaints, a revised consistorial constitution was issued in 1594.[65] Ten infractions fell under the jurisdiction of the consistory: bigamy, marrying without parental approval, fornication, pregnancy before marriage, adultery, desertion, illegally marrying abroad, deflowering a virgin, incest, and rape. Prison was the standard punishment, the length of sentence depending on the severity of the offense. If the woman was pregnant, her sentence would not be carried out until after the birth of the child. Adulterers faced exile or corporal punishment; the authors of rape and incest might pay with their lives.[66]

Church law was only part of the total body of law governing marital relations. Serious infractions, such as incest, adultery, bigamy, and fornication, were also dealt by the criminal courts. Both the Hochstift Bamberg and the Hohenzollern margraviate used the same criminal code, the Bamberg *Halsgerichtsordnung,* composed by Johann von Schwarzenberg at the beginning of the sixteenth century.[67] The penalties listed in the code are quite severe. Men who committed adultery or incest were to be punished with the sword (§§ 145, 149); fornicators could have their ears cut off or their eyes gouged out (§ 142). The punishments described for women in these cases were less extreme. No specific penalty was assigned to adultery. Bigamy could be punished by death, although at the discretion of the judges (§ 146). In fact, such extreme measures were rarely employed.[68] In cases where individuals received capital punishment, it was because of gravity of the offense. Heinz Grör of Nanckenreuth was sentenced to die by the sword on August 25, 1620 on a charge of "*duplex adulteria et incest*" by the Bamberg courts after abducting his stepdaughter. His sentence was ordered on account of his having committed three capital offenses: adultery, rape, and incest.[69]

Fines and imprisonment were the most common forms of punishment. The fines could be rather severe. In a case from Stadtsteinach in 1599, a man was fined 30 gulden for committing adultery with a serving girl.[70] Two years later, a member of the Kupferberg town council was fined 100 gulden for impregnating a woman from the margraviate.[71] Court records from Bamberg show that if an adulterous liaison resulted in the birth of a child, the offender might be required to pay to support his offspring. The Brandenburg ordinance of 1567 made similar provisions. Friedrich Fuchs of Entmannsreuth was charged with committing adultery with Catharina Stieglerin in 1598. Fuchs was sentenced to eight days' imprisonment on bread and water, fined 50 gulden, and required to pay the Castner of Berneck an indeterminate sum for maintenance of Stieglerin and the child.[72]

Fornication and its ritualized counterpart, *Fenster,* were serious concerns of the upper Franconian courts.[73] Women accused of having engaged in premarital sex frequently claimed that they had slept with the man following a promise of marriage, and, in some cases, what they thought was the conclusion of a valid marriage. Margarethe Prallin of Wallenfels was involved in several cases of this sort. In 1598 she took in earnest the promise of marriage of one Endres Schübel, commonly known as "Strudel," and slept with him. After she became pregnant, she sued Strudel for breach of contract, and he was required to pay her child support. On account of her "weakened, pregnant state," Margarethe was spared any punishment. In 1602 she ran into the same problem, this time with Michael Schwarz, who had given her a gold piece worth 2 gulden to seal the spousal. She assumed that the gift and her submission constituted a legal marriage. Both were declared at fault in this case, but the judge suggested that Prellin was unusually gullible, and her punishment was again slight.[74]

The exchange of gifts in the latter case created problems for the court. It was common practice to conclude a spousal by giving the intended bride some sort of small gift to seal the contract. In many cases, the parties considered this a binding marriage and proceeded no further. Pregnancy and the birth of a child finalized the marriage.[75] The decisions of the courts in these cases varied. Endres Premser of Rugendorf had given the daughter of an innkeeper some coins and a towel. She claimed that these were tokens intended to seal the marriage contract. Premser called her a whore and said that he had merely paid for services rendered. Because the case involved the criminal courts and consistories in both the Hochstift and the margraviate, the matter was never fully settled.[76] In the case of Hans Erhard of Gössendorf and Katharina Frosch, the exchange of gifts, followed by sex and pregnancy, was taken as a sign of a valid marriage.[77] In the case of fornication between Hans Röd and a woman in Kupferberg, the court was primarily interested in whether the two had intended to marry or not.[78]

The response of the authorities to the problem of premarital sex was to enact punitive measures. The Brandenburg *Warnungsartikel* of 1573 ordered that in cases of "fleshly mixing and cohabitation" the groom would be imprisoned on bread and water, while the bride would not be allowed to wear a flower garland. Music and dancing were forbidden at such weddings.[79] A mandate issued by Ernst von Mengersdorf in 1589 renewed an earlier statute requiring "fallen bridal couples" to wear distinctive headgear—straw braids for women and a straw hat for men—during the wedding. If the priest and local magistrates did not participate in this form of humiliation, they were subject to fines and even imprisonment.[80] A similar ordinance was issued in the margraviate in 1602.[81] In that same year, in a case of "almost sodomitical wantonness," the consistory in Kulmbach allowed for public penance with a special sermon directed against the malefactors.[82] Corporal punishment, as prescribed in the Bamberg *Halsgerichtsordnung,* appears to have been applied in extreme cases, but it was often difficult to prove accusations of sex before marriage unless pregnancy followed. In 1597, the Kulmbach consistory dismissed a suit charging Balthasar Hermann of Seubelsdorf with *Fenster.* Although it was common knowledge that Hermann had slept with Margarethe Behre after getting her drunk, the charge could not be proven to the court's satisfaction because there had been no issue from the union.[83] To avoid prosecution, men might demand that the woman obtain an abortion.[84] In a few cases, children born out of wedlock or from adultery were killed by their parents to eliminate the evidence, although the evidence suggests that infanticide was exceedingly rare.[85]

Catholic and Lutheran marriage reforms created a host of contradictions. Sumptuary and moral legislation regarding the conduct of weddings lay at the heart of the reforms.[86] On the one hand, the policies conformed to the demands of parents to exercise greater control over the lives of their children. Greater parental control over marriage provided a defense against marriages deemed socially inappropriate or potentially injurious to upward mobility.[87] That was theory: in reality, the new regulations neither eliminated old problems nor gave parents "total control" over their children.[88] Police ordinances concerning marriage were generally intended to limit social mobility—precisely what parents hoped to achieve in the choice of marriage partners for their offspring. By limiting the number of guests, the number of courses that could be served a feasts, and the range of entertainments, the laws prevented celebrants from including all members of the community in the wedding celebrations. This did not mean that such laws were always followed. Although the Brandenburg ordinance limited the number of guests to thirty, 114 people had been invited to a wedding in Muggendorf in 1573.[89] People who felt they had been snubbed by being left off the guest list placed curses on the wedded couple or their parents and tried to disrupt the festivities.[90] The wedding feast itself could provide a forum for dissent. The pastor of Arnstein complained that during a wedding celebration one of the guests dressed up in an alb and took part in a dance. This led to "numerous insults against the Catholic Religion."[91]

Considering the course of marriage reform in upper Franconia, it is difficult to avoid the conclusion that the process aroused no small amount of ambivalence, from "above" as well as from "below." Because marriage law cut across the spiritual-secular divide, it was fertile ground for conflict between secular and ecclesiastical officials. There was little agreement among high-ranking officials in either Bamberg or Kulmbach on either the form of the laws or their execution. In any event, neither Catholic nor Lutheran officials shared a common blueprint for reform.[92] This makes it all the more difficult to view the role of either Catholic or Protestant subjects as one of "reactive acceptance or rejection of 'new' marriage teachings."[93] It also remains open to question how "new" the reforms really were. Well before the Reformation, the monastic *ordo* had permeated town life in the structure of guilds and confraternities. The notion that peasants had to be compelled, either through magisterial force or propaganda, to conform to a monastic temperament of "ascetic self-discipline" in the later sixteenth century does not seem tenable.[94]

The real issue was not that an alien culture was imposed on a largely passive and unwilling population, but rather that local communities appeared to be rejecting "urban" cultural forms that for some two hundred years they had actively emulated. What was being resisted were not the cultural values *per se,* but administrative impulses that threatened the communal church, and, by extension, the communal social order. Sixteenth-century states were still far too weak to overcome the stubborn refusal of communities and families to conform to the new standards. Where reforms were welcomed, it was because they were perceived as useful by individuals and communities for their own ends.[95] The problem with the new orders was that they offered reforms that simultaneously supported and undercut many of the fundamental structures of society. Religion had not, to use Blickle's phrase, been "shorn of its power to create social and political disruption."[96] Rather, it was the state, through its newly proclaimed dominance in matters of faith and morality, that wielded the disruptive power inherent in the reform of religion. Perhaps the best way to view the supposed objects of Lutheran and Catholic social reforms is as individuals frustrated by the oftentimes insoluble contradiction between the promise of reform and the cost.

A key to understanding the meaning of the contradictions surrounding religious reform in the later sixteenth century may perhaps be found in the reaction of officials to a set of fairly minor local disputes in the Oberland in the years around 1600. In 1593 Solomon Thümser, the deacon in Berneck, leveled a series of accusations against the senior pastor, Thomas Rühr. Thümser complained of low pay but also called into question the rector's orthodoxy.

Rühr did not require private confession, as was stipulated in the Kirchenordnung. He conducted baptisms at unsanctioned times and frequently changed the order of the services. Thümser was particularly critical of the way Rühr administered the Eucharist. To these complaints Rühr responded that, with regard to pay, Thümser received exactly what he was supposed to get. In any event, Thümser was lazy and prone to shady financial dealings. As far as the services went, he had merely conformed to the wishes of his parishioners. The changes he had made were in any event insignificant. The consistory agreed, ordering Thümser to show more patience with the "entirely human, tolerable, and unaggravating idiosyncracies" of Rühr, "a beloved old man." Thümser was admonished to maintain "Christian brotherly unity" with his superior, "since upon this more than anything else is the church constructed."[97]

In 1602 there were two high profile cases of adultery in the Oberland. On March 3, Erhard Egerers was brought to trial for having eloped with his fourteen-year-old stepdaughter. On June 10, Apollonia Crato, widow of the pastor of Schauenstein, was arrested for having committed adultery with at least five different men over a period of ten years. Erhard was sentenced to die by the sword for having committed three capital offenses: adultery, incest, and rape.[98] Apollonia and her chief paramour, Heinrich Depser, pastor of the church in Selbitz, were likewise condemned to death. Depser was able to escape. Apollonia was not so lucky and went to the scaffold on November 16.[99] It seems significant that both trials coincided with the publication of a new, very rigorous decree concerning adultery. The mandate specifically noted that it would be a good idea to make examples of malefactors to promote chastity and good morals.[100] Further decrees appeared during the year, proclaiming the severe penalties that might result from transgression of the marriage ordinances. The last, dated November 2, cautioned couples against "marital relations" during the penitential season of Advent.[101] Given the timing of the arrests and the fact that Erhard Egerers and Apollonia Crato appear to have been the only adulterers executed between 1550 and 1619, their special treatment seems more than a coincidence.

What is most striking about these cases is how little the punishment (or lack thereof) seems to have had to do with the crime. Rühr was plainly guilty, but the officials had no interest in pursuing the matter. In his long career, Rühr had never made any trouble. Nor had his parishioners. Consequently, the consistory was willing to overlook obvious irregularities in Rühr's administration of an important parish. Thümser, on the other had, had committed the sin of creating trouble where there had been none previously—for that he was censured by the authorities. Apollonia Crato was certainly guilty of the crime of adultery, but her punishment seemed to owe as much to timing and the desire of officials to make an example of her than to the gravity of the offense. To be sure, her status as a minister's wife almost certainly had an impact on the severity of her punishment.[102] But the fact remains that the application of the death penalty in this case was truly extraordinary. Here we see an essential aspect of local governance in the confessional era. What made the confessional state so onerous was not that it was uniformly oppressive, but that its effects often seemed random and arbitrary. The authorities simply could not impose effective discipline on either the clergy or rural communities.[103] The central regime intervened in local affairs only when it was called on to do so or when the problem was too big to be ignored. The responses tended to constitute a series of ad hoc measures that derived not from an established body of law, such as the *Halsgerichtsordnung* or the consistorial ordinances, but from a dimly perceived vision of what society should look like. As a result, it is not law, but an "essential lawlessness," that seems most to have characterized the effort to create an orderly society.[104]

The determinant factor in these cases—as in many of the others described throughout this chapter—was confessional orthodoxy. There was a tendency, one that becomes more noticeable over time, to think of problems in terms of their confessional implications. To some extent this was a result of the state's practice of shifting "the burden of religious conflict downward" by making communal authorities and heads of households responsible for ensuring compliance with the ordinances.[105] There was nothing new about this—since the fourteenth century there had been a tendency to pass responsibility for the maintenance of the peace downward, through the institution of the Landfriede. "Shifting the burden" was an essential and accepted part of late medieval political practice. In this regard, we can say that securing confessional orthodoxy did not require the creation of new social and political institutions, but was accomplished through the "traditional repertoire" of local governance.[106] That said, the practice of late-sixteenth-century local administration parted with tradition in two fundamental ways. First of all, local elites could not so easily use the reforms to pursue their own ends; the demand to enforce confessional orthodoxy seemed to undermine, rather than bolster, the claims of the estates. Second, officials in the later sixteenth century tended to view every conflict through a confessional lens, investing even the most trivial matters with confessional significance. Hence it was not "society" that was confessionalized but the objects of ordinary people's daily concerns.

The confessionalization of politics reflects the broader currents of political culture in the late sixteenth century in other ways. One side of late Renaissance political theory is well known: the social disciplinary ideas associated with the Neostoics, in particular Justus Lipsius.[107] But another side is revealed in the writings of upper Franconian churchmen in the second half of the sixteenth century. The universal principle, embodied in the older imperial ideal, had not diminished. If anything, under the influence of confessional conflict and Neoplatonic speculation, the tendency to examine current events in terms of their broader historical—if not cosmological—significance was amplified.

This universal tendency can be seen in the sermons of Jakob Feucht, who insists on the continuity between Protestantism and the heresies of the third and fourth centuries. It can also be seen in the increasingly elaborate curriculum at the Albertinum, culminating in Blebelius's program combining Hebraic studies with astronomy and mathematics. There is something cabalistic about the approach adopted by Blebelius in this regard.[108] The utopian fervor that drove the reformers was itself a reflection of an "ambitious mentality" that manifested itself in a "programme of global evangelism," a plan of religious reform "conceived *sub specie universi.*"[109] The tendency to view local events in terms of their world-historical significance, or to combine religious education with mystical or cosmological speculation, marks the introduction of an irrational and potentially destabilizing element into local discourse.[110]

If we look at conditions from the perspective of the subjects, we can see a growing resentment, not so much toward the state as toward those community members who did not conform to the new orders. The manifest inequities and inconsistencies that marked the patterns of local administration legitimized resistance to some extent as it became clear that not all bore the same stigma or suffered the same penalty for disobedience. "Resistance" in this context could just as well be seen as the defense of a particular vision of the state, accompanied by a demand that the confessional state actually live up to its promises while preserving law and the traditional constitution.[111] The complaints of Solomon Thümser reflect just this sentiment. His rebuff, however, could only have increased his resentment and frustration. Once again, the character of early modern governance intensified social tensions through resort to ad hoc and symbolic measures. Meanwhile, the idea of reform seems to have drifted further into the realm of metaphysical speculation, widening the gap between ruler and subjects, between ideals and reality.[112]

Chapter 8

THE CHRISTIAN COMMUNE

The religious history of upper Franconia during the first decades of the confessional era presents a complex and often contradictory set of images. Events in both the Hochstift Bamberg and the Hohenzollern Oberland make it difficult to perceive a clear alliance between ecclesiastical and state interests either at court or in the villages. The reform of marriage and the formation of the clerical estate both reveal deep fissures within the ecclesiastical regime and between secular and spiritual officials. The experience of pastors at the local level argues against an alliance of "pulpit and administration *(Kanzel und Amtshaus)* that engendered social control."[1] Reforms took place within a matrix containing a variety of powers and interests: the prince, secular officials, ecclesiastical officials, communal officials, nobles, families, and foreign powers, to name a few. At the center of the matrix stood the parish clergy, constantly pulled by the shifting and contradictory demands of the various powers. Pastors could not simply spread the "orders" of the central regime down to its subjects so long as local officials, patrons, nobles, and the parish community refused to cooperate. And, as we have seen, the central regime did not always hold a consistent vision of the "proper order." Local conditions were hardly conducive to the imposition of alien religious and social norms; divisions within the regime prevented the articulation of an unambiguous definition of norms in the first place.

The difficulties attendant on the early phases of reform produced differing responses. Though keenly aware of the problems that limited reform, Protestant officials in the Hohenzollern Oberland generally seemed satisfied with their efforts. Consequently, they made few administrative changes after 1570. The original *Kirchenordnung* was reissued in 1592; a slightly revised consistorial ordinance appeared three years later. Thereafter, we can note few significant changes either in liturgical practice or administration until the eighteenth century. In Bamberg, the situation was rather different. The bishops were extremely dissatisfied with the apparent failure of early reform efforts. The pace of reform intensified after 1590, partly in reaction to local conditions, partly in association with the larger phenomenon of the German Counter-Reformation.

In historical discourse, the Catholic or Counter-Reformation constitutes a distinctive form of confessionalization. Wolfgang Reinhard has given it the paradoxical title "conservative reform."[2] In recent years a number of studies of the Counter-Reformation in the empire have appeared, including Marc Forster's books on Speyer and the German southwest, and a series of works dealing with the Counter-Reformation in Austria.[3] In the regions Forster examined, weak episcopal authority and weak princely authority limited the possibilities for reform "from above." The situation was rather different in the Hochstift Bamberg, where a very strong central authority was united with princely and ecclesiastical authority in the hands of the prince-bishop. In this respect, the political dynamics of reform are much more like those in the Austrian case, but here again there are fundamental differences. The crucial dynamic in Austria appears to have been the struggle between the archdukes and the estates, in particular the nobility. The Protestant nobles had received fairly extensive privileges, effectively giving them the right to determine the religion of their subjects. The Habsburgs fought long and hard to overcome noble resistance, on several occasions being faced with the prospect of armed insurrection. Although the bishops of Bamberg certainly had to deal with noble opposition, there was never any serious danger of armed rebellion. Moreover, there was never a question of revoking privileges—the subject nobility *(Landsässige)* never were given the right to appoint Lutheran pastors, and the lands of the imperial knights were, strictly speaking, not under the secular jurisdiction of the bishops. It is this latter issue—the rights of privileges of the imperial knights—that was the major stumbling block, although ultimately the bishops found a way to resolve the issue without requiring a military victory. In large part, the opportunities for political advancement in the service of the church provided the means of defusing tensions between the nobility and the bishops.[4] The bishops never had to deal with the sort of broad-based, organized opposition that confronted the Habsburgs; the disputes were generally highly localized, involve only one or two noble families at any one time. The cathedral chapter, rather than the diet, remained the primary seat of action, though after 1600 opposition withing the chapter ebbed away. It should also be noted that, unlike in the German southwest and in the Habsburg lands, the regular clergy played no meaningful role in the Counter-Reformation in Bamberg until the arrival of the Jesuits in 1611.

In Bamberg, the Counter-Reformation began in the last years of the reign of Bishop Veit II von Würtzburg and intensified with the accession of Ernst von Mengersdorf.[5] The construction of the seminary—a project begun by Veit II and completed by Ernst—and the publication of the marriage ordinance mark the first serious attempts to enforce the decrees of the Council of Trent. We might also see the spirit of Trent reflected in the flurry of moral legislation issued by the two bishops. Musicians, street singing, mummery, swearing, and all variety of blasphemies committed during Carnival were banned.[6] According to several edicts, on account of "blasphemy, swearing, cursing and excessive drunkenness," God had visited a number of punishments on the world, most notably inflation and the Turk.[7] Ernst's edicts likewise enumerate the consequences of "gluttony and blasphemy" as well as other "heathen customs." God's anger was clearly manifest in the ever-present "inflation, war, hail, thunderstorms and floods."[8]

On account of the Turk, "worldly celebration and dancing with drums, pipes, and string instruments . . . ought to be entirely done away with." Fines and corporal punishments would be levied against people who continued to behave so shamelessly.[9] Pipers faced imprisonment for their crimes, as did innkeepers whose inebriated patrons disrupted the peace.[10] A fine of 10 gulden–no paltry sum–was levied on individuals who remained in taverns after nine o'clock.[11] More significant than punishment, however, were the frequent calls for public demonstrations of piety. Veit's mandate of 1566 against swearing and blaspheming was accompanied by one calling for "processions and pilgrimages" throughout the diocese to counteract the Turkish threat.[12] Additional procession mandates were issued in 1567, 1571, 1573, and 1574.[13] From at least 1584 onward, printed litanies were issued to participants in processions.[14]

A procession mandate from 1586 reflects the care and planning that went into these public observances. The pope graciously granted an indulgence to all who took part in a three-day cycle of processions and masses and prayed for an end to "heresy, dissension, schism, and disunity in the Christian church." On Wednesday, August 14, and the following Friday and Saturday, the citizens of Bamberg took part in processions, each of which culminated in a sermon given by the suffragan bishop. On the first day, the procession led to the upper parish church on the Kaulberg; on the following days they ended at the Michelsberg and St. Martin's parish church. Following the sermon, the faithful were invited to confession and communion. Participants were ordered to fast beforehand. One member of each household was obliged to attend.[15]

The seminary project and the use of processions indicate an essentially passive approach to the problem of Catholic renewal, what has been called an "administrative-patriarchal Counter-Reformation."[16] After 1591, Bishop Neithard von Thüngen instituted a much more aggressive policy, one that would be carried through the 1630s. Religious and civil disobedience were coupled in the wording of ordinances and dealt with through use of the secular arm. Intolerance and antagonism now defined the attitude toward the "repugnant religion" of the Augsburg Confession. The new policy in Bamberg followed closely the model of reform put forward by Julius Echter in Würzburg. The aggressive posture of the reformers reflected dissatisfaction with the pace of reform as well as growing frustration with the tenacity of Protestant resistance at home and abroad.[17] It remained to be seen, however, whether or not the new measures and attitudes could overcome the obstacles to reform within the central regime and at the local level.

⁓

When Ernst von Mengersdorf died in October, 1591 he was just thirty-seven years old. His successor, Neithard von Thüngen, was forty-six, sickly, and of a profoundly different disposition than his predecessor. He viewed Protestantism as the "loathsome religion," and its pastors as false preachers, agitators, and wolves, lumping them together with the Turks as the chief enemies of faith.[18] One of his first mandates ordered that anyone caught eating meat during Lent should be flogged.[19] On the political side, Neithard recognized that the papal and imperial mandates calling on him to carry through with the reformation of his diocese provided the justification to increase his own authority at the expense of the cathedral chapter.[20]

Neithard's hard policies immediately led to conflicts with the cathedral dean, Johann Philipp von Gebsattel. In December 1592, Neithard ordered the arrest of the pastor of Pottenstein for fiscal misconduct. As Pottenstein lay in one of the Ämter under the jurisdiction of the chapter, Gebsattel viewed the action as a challenge. He complained that the bishop wished to suspend all the rights and privileges of the canons and the nobility. Gesbattel charged that Neithard was an oathbreaker, a man who persecuted clerics, nobles, and commons alike. He dismissed skilled and noble councilors and depended on advisors who were base born and inexperienced. Neithard merely shot back that if opposed, he was not afraid to take either "great bears" or Gebsattel by the neck.[21]

Neithard's interminable quarrels with the dean and chapter did not prevent him from issuing reams of legislation in the first years of his reign. Eleven mandates concerning religion appeared between July 1592 and February 1594.[22] A revised marriage ordinance was published in 1592, followed by a second two years later, requiring all those who had been married since the first ordinance either to accept the Catholic faith or to leave the Hochstift.[23] In that same year, a *Religionsmandat,* based on one issued by bishop Julius Echter of Würzburg in 1589, was presented to the chapter. Each subject was required to receive communion "according to the old custom" on Easter. Whoever refused faced not only fines but corporal punishment.[24] Gebsattel warned that in Würzburg, the ordinance had "embittered the nobles and made them distrustful." Neithard went ahead and published the decree.[25] Neithard issued a second communion ordinance in May 1595, noting that it was his obligation as bishop "to herd the erring sheep back into the right stall." Neithard would gladly allow his flock another chance to redeem itself, but warned that recusancy was no small matter.[26]

Between 1594 and 1596, processions and vigils were used to identify the faithful in the city of Bamberg. By 1596 the number of processions was staggering. Between July 4 and November 11 of that year, eighteen processions were held.[27] Participants were to petition God to save them from the Turk and all "division, schism, and misunderstandings in our Christian religion."[28] From 1595 onward, a "Turk's bell" would be sounded at various times. All the citizens of Bamberg were required to stop their work and pray for the defeat of the enemies of Christendom. Those who did not would be "severely punished." A special prayer was drawn up for use on such occasions, carefully worded so that no Protestant could recite it.[29] Following the practice of his predecessor, Neithard ordered that at least one member of each household take part in the processions.[30] An ordinance from March 1595 ordered the Hauptmänner and their deputies to go door to door on the morning of a festival and accompany the residents of their borough to the church.[31]

By May of 1597, Neithard seemed confident enough in the success of these measures to issue a proclamation declaring the victory of Catholicism over heresy in his see.[32] When Suffragan Bishop Ertlin made a tour of the diocese in August of that same year, he absolved 1,066 former heretics.[33] Still, it is not entirely clear whether or not the new converts remained true to the faith. Closer examination of religious life in the diocese in the first years of Neithard's reign suggests that the victory was far from complete. In Teuschnitz, Neukenroth, Graitz, Zeuln, Maineck, and Mainroth, Catholic priests met with scorn.[34] The parishioners in Steinwiesen responded to the marriage ordinance of 1594 with their feet, preferring to be married elsewhere.[35] In Weismain, Rattelsdorf, Bechhofen, Höchstadt, Stadtsteinach, and other communities, women were among the most intransigent heretics. Simon Leyn of Lichtenfels reported that his mother, an eighty-year-old widow, would not convert to Catholicism but clung to the Augsburg Confession regardless of official threats.[36] The wives of officials in Stadtsteinach and Kupferberg resisted conversion so strongly that they were threatened with "particularly severe" tortures.[37]

Although it was possible to get rid of heretical preachers, keeping them from coming back was a different matter. The Lutheran pastor in Neukenroth was dismissed in 1595; a year later he was still preaching there with the support of the nobles.[38] In Presseck, complaints about Johann Cauda continued throughout the early 1590s. By 1596, the list of his offenses had grown rather lengthy. He was negligent in his duties, still refused to use the new calendar, administered the sacrament *sub utraque species,* and generally "had erected good Lutheran order" in the parish.[39] His morals were also subject to considerable question: not only did he have a wife, but he had seduced his serving girl. Cauda sent his son to study in "Lutheran places" with money derived from the parish. The lords of Wildenstein finally agreed to arrest Cauda in the spring of 1597 and placed him in irons.[40]

When the question of appointing Cauda's successor came up, officials in Kupferberg and Stadtsteinach both requested that since the parishioners in Presseck had long enjoyed receiving the sacrament after the fashion of the Augsburg Confession, they should be able to continue doing so. They placed themselves under the protection of the Religious peace, and demanded that they be freed from tithes and the recently levied *Türkensteuer*.[41] Cauda's immediate successor, Johann Zell, did not last the year, being dismissed for living "an aggravating life."[42] The next pastor, Martin Hollach, was, from the Catholic perspective, hardly an improvement. The Wildensteiners praised him as "an honorable and well-educated man" who had been examined by the Kulmbach Consistory and found to be a true adherent of the Augsburg Confession.[43] Since "the majority of parishioners have gone over to the Augsburg Confession from the Catholic faith," appointing a Lutheran pastor seemed the proper thing to do.[44]

In 1597 the pastors of Oberailsfeldt and Poppendorf both complained about the nefarious influence of preachers from Kirchahorn, appointed by the lords of Rabenstein. Since 1569 Veit Dockler of Poppendorf had been fighting a rear-guard action against the preachers and their supporters, many of whom were Hohenzollern subjects. These apostates refused to attend services, Dockler charged. The preacher distributed the sacrament to Protestants in his house, and not a few of the bishop's subjects took part in these services and refused to pay their tithes. The sacristan of the filial chapel in Kirchahorn stole four chalices, four candlesticks, three missals and various other church furnishings and sold them.[45] Dockler noted that here too women were among the most vigorous opponents of the Catholic faith.[46]

In 1594, Craft von Crailsheim complained to Neithard that for some time the pastor of Adelsdorf and Aisch, Friedrich Bernhard, had been preaching "insults" against him and his chaplain in Grub.[47] In fact, the chaplain in Grub was a Protestant. Since the 1580s the pastors of Adelsdorf and Zentbechhofen had demanded the expulsion of the Grub preachers. Ernst von Mengersdorf had ordered Crailheim to dismiss the "wicked, evil, annoying people" he had appointed as chaplains, but to no avail.[48] Part of the problem facing Friedrich Bernhard was that many of his parishioners were subjects of the Stiebers of Buttenheim, who demanded that their tenants go to Grub for Sunday services, weddings, baptisms, and burials.[49]

Friedrich Bernhard was a curious character. He was an avid Catholic, and after a prophetic dream endowed a chapel in Willersdorf with estates he inherited from his father. Bernhard was also married, but his children were legitimized in 1595 by Bishop Neithard on account of their father's deep devotion to the old faith.[50] Neithard offered what support he could to Bernhard. On several occasions he demanded that Crailsheim do away with his preacher.[51] Nonetheless, by 1596 preachers could be found in Grub, Röttenbach, and Heroldsbach.[52] The Vogt appointed by the Stiebers was also working to undermine Bernhard's authority. In 1598 Bernhard wrote that the Vogt "had almost entirely destroyed the parish and church." He had turned over ten prebends to the nobility. Peasants in Weppendorf and Uttstet reported that the Vogt had run his sheep through their fields, knocking over fences and causing 50 gulden worth of damage. He gave out estates that had formerly belonged to the convent at Schüsselau to Jews. Monstrances in the chapel in Aisch had been stolen and sold "to the heretics." The innkeeper in Aisch "preached many lies during the fasts in Holy Week." The Vogt refused to allow Stieber tenants to be buried by the parish priest, but had them interred in a common field. When Bernhard expressed his concerns about his parishioners being buried on unconsecrated ground, the Vogt merely insulted him.[53]

Notwithstanding all of Neithard's varied efforts, the conflicts surrounding the preachers in Presseck, Kirchahorn, and Grub show that there was little that the prince-bishop could do against the privileges of the nobility. The Stiebers, Wildensteiners, Rabensteiners and Crailsheimers had all, at various points, made reference to the religious peace in defense of their rights. Of course the question as to whether the formula *cius regio eius religio* actually applied to the imperial knights and territorial nobility remained open. The Peace of Augsburg stated that imperial knights "in matters concerning the two Religions should not be threatened, pressured or persecuted by anyone."[54] By the beginning of the seventeenth century, the bishops, supported by the imperial aulic council (*Reichshofrat*), viewed this protection as applying to the knights themselves, not to their subjects. Nonetheless, the knights viewed the *jus reformandi* as an expression of their estate. If anything, the changes in the regime only stiffened the resolve of the nobility. Robbed of the opportunity to influence policy directly through the diet or princely council and denied offices on account of their confession, only on their estates could they exhibit their status through the traditional means of ecclesiastical patronage.[55]

Resistance in the Landstädte and villages was also strong. The residents of Lettenreuth and Michelau in the parish of Lichtenfels claimed to understand Tridentine Catholicism to be the "new learning" so despised by the authorities.[56] Teuschnitz, Graitz, Zeuln, Maineck, and Mainroth vigorously resisted attempts at recatholicization. The burghers of Neukenroth went so far as to take their case against the bishop before the imperial chamber court (*Reichskammergericht*). The court found in the town's favor, and in very strong language condemned the bishop for violating the religious peace.[57] The residents of Kronach resisted the new calendar, and many refused to accept the Catholic faith. Margrave Georg Friedrich wrote on their behalf, asking Neithard not to press his reforms too far. In Forchheim opposition to the calendar was particularly strong, even though the majority of the inhabitants were Catholics.[58]

In the city of Bamberg the situation was somewhat more complex. Figures from 1596 indicate that of 2,018 adults in the city, 288 (14 percent) were Lutherans. Of these, women were in the majority—182 women versus 106 men. Of twenty-seven council members in 1595, at least ten were Lutherans. Most of these were driven out of the council in the following years, with the last Lutheran Ratsherr converting to Catholicism in 1597. In addition, eighteen of twenty-eight Hauptmänner were Lutherans in 1597. The Lutherans were a mixed social group. A large number of Lutherans could still be found in Zinkenwörth (58), the poor neighborhood that had been moved to rebellion by the sermons of Johannes Schwannhäuser in 1525. But the majority of Lutherans lived in the more prosperous wards. If we consider that nearly a third of the Ratsherrn and more than half of the Hauptmänner were Lutherans, then it would appear that the Protestant minority in Bamberg was over-represented in positions of authority.[59]

In 1596, many of the communities and nobles who felt that the bishop's policies were compromising their rights began looking to the chapter for intercession.[60] On June 6, 1596, the chapter formally presented its grievances to the bishop. It declared that through his reforms of schools, appointment of orthodox clergy, and prohibition of marriage outside the Catholic faith, the bishop had already laid the foundations for Catholic renewal. As the older generation died out, their children and grandchildren could be brought up and educated in the true faith. It was therefore unnecessary to use force, and in any event, forced conversions were of little value. Neithard's attempts to speed up the process of reform might, in the long run, do more damage than good. Instead, it would be better to avoid confrontation and use more peaceful means of conversion, in particular, education.[61] Neithard, however, was supported in his policy by the Geistliche Räte and, perhaps more important, by Pope Clement VIII. The pope demanded that the chapter relent and allow the bishop full jurisdiction over the work of recatholicization.[62] For the moment, the chapter could do little but submit to the pope's request.

By this time Neithard's hard-line policies were drawing fire from beyond the borders of the Hochstift. Both Georg Friedrich and the Palatine Elector Friedrich IV protested Neithard's actions.[63] In May 1597, the "Electors, Princes and Estates" of the Upper Saxon Reichskreis condemned Neithard von Thüngen's "unprecedented inquisition" as "contrary to the religious peace," and threatened to protect Lutherans in border areas with arms if the bishop continued oppressing adherents to "the true Christian Religion of the Augsburg Confession."[64] Despite such warnings, Neithard went ahead and published a mandate in October requiring all residents of the Hochstift either to convert to Catholicism or leave the territory within eight days.[65]

On March 5, 1598 Neithard called the deans of the collegial churches to his court and ordered all canons, vicars, and choristers to give up their concubines by Easter. If they refused, they would be deprived of their benefices. Neithard had finally gone too far. Gebsattel declared the mandate to be in direct violation of the bishop's oath.[66] Within a month, Neithard was threatening resignation as the chapter resumed jurisdiction over the immunities in defiance. The pope was able to convince Neithard not to resign, but it was clear that the bishop had lost the battle. The chapter remained adamant in its opposition to his hard-line policies.

By all accounts, Neithard von Thüngen was a broken man when he died the day after Christmas, 1598. The cathedral dean Johann Philipp von Gebsattel was elected as Neithard's successor. According to a contemporary verse chronicle, after Gebsattel's election "every neighborhood rejoiced."[67] Later historiography has been rather less enthusiastic about Johann Philipp von Gebsattel. His reign is usually portrayed as the low point in the history of the Counter-Reformation in Bamberg.[68] As cathedral dean under Neithard, Gebsattel is cast as the primary opponent to the work of recatholicization, a man whose villainy in statecraft was only matched by his moral decadence. Such views are more a caricature than an accurate picture. Although it is true that he lived in concubinage and fathered at least seven children, Johann Philipp von Gebsattel was in fact a competent administrator and a studious diplomat. After Neithard's death, Johann Philipp took a number of books from his library. Among these were twenty-three works on geography and contemporary political affairs, in particular the conflict in the Netherlands. In addition, he took all the art books, including a treatise by Palladius and an old manuscript with the title "The Art of the Field Commander" *(Kunst des Feldmeisters).*[69]

It would appear that through the election of Gebsattel, the canons hoped to combat the rising influence of foreigners–in particular Bishop Julius Echter of Würzburg–in the Hochstift. For their part, Echter and Maximilian of Bavaria greeted Gebsattel's election with horror.[70] Several members of the Geistliche Rat were likewise concerned. Pankraz Moschenbach and Johannes Wolf, both prominent members of the old bishop's council, sent letters to Rome describing Gebsattel as a heretic. Wolf went so far as to write that "he wished he could stab Gebsattel in the heart." Unfortunately for Moschenbach and Wolf, the letters were intercepted and both men were imprisoned immediately after Gebsattel's election.[71]

Papal confirmation of the new bishop's election was contingent on completion of an inquisition into his morals, character, training, and orthodoxy.[72] Johann Philipp knew that he had few friends in Rome. His supporters in the cathedral chapter hoped to forestall the curia by undertaking their own examination and then telling Rome that a separate report by the papal commission would be superfluous. The commission consisted of Suffragan

Bishop Johann Ertlin, the abbot of Michelsberg, and four canons. Among these was Bernhard von Giech, whose family had installed a Lutheran pastor within walking distance of the city. Although the commission described Gebsattel as an honest and virtuous man, "conspicuous" in his adherence to the Catholic faith, the canons' efforts came to naught. The curia sent Hieronymus Portia to Bamberg to conduct an official inquiry.[73]

Among the witnesses Portia interviewed was Johann Schöner. Schöner was among the first students to attend the seminary in Bamberg. He later went to Rome to study at the Collegium Germanicum, where he remained from 1589 to 1595. Schöner left Italy with a wide network of personal acquaintances. His contacts with cardinals, nuncios, and other officials of the curia may well have aided him during Portia's visit. Schöner defended the bishop, repeating the findings of the earlier commission, apparently to Portia's satisfaction. And the bishop was not ungrateful. Schöner received the prebends confiscated from Wolf and Moschenbach. Three years later he was named vicar general and soon became Gebsattel's most trusted advisor.[74]

During the early years of Gebsattel's reign, the reformers had cause to remain optimistic about the restoration of the old faith. The legislation that Gebsattel promulgated indicated no vast gulf between his religious policy and that of Neithard von Thüngen. Johann Philipp continued to require his subjects to take part in processions and receive communion by Easter. The high fines for eating meat on Fridays and holy days were upheld in mandates unchanged from those of Bishop Neithard. The confession and communion mandates still required priests to maintain registers of communicants and return them to the episcopal authorities within fourteen days of Easter. One distinction from the earlier decrees is that recusants were given a month, as opposed to eight days, to leave the Hochstift.[75] This last change reflects one of the guiding principles of Gebsattel's regime. Whereas he was more than willing to use force against his political opponents, he abandoned the hard policies of his predecessor toward the parish clergy and the common people. Many priests who had suffered under Neithard von Thüngen were pardoned and able to return to their former vocation. Johannes Cauda, the former Pressecker preacher, became one of Johann Schöner's advisors. Nonetheless, many of the older problems persisted, and the new methods offered no remedies.

In 1603, the chaplain in Kirchehrenbach complained about his rector, Michael Steib. Steib had been among the married priests whom Neithard had chased out of the diocese, but under Gebsattel, he was allowed to return. Now he was accused of conducting a funeral for a man who had died after refusing to follow the mandates concerning confession and communion.[76] Three years later, a longer list of Steib's "excesses" was brought before the authorities. He had agreed to perform a wedding for a soldier without following the proper procedures. The soldier had not received permission from his priest to be married in Kirchehrenbach; moreover, he and others ate meat on Friday. In fact, Steib regularly conducted weddings at forbidden times or in other ways contrary to the ordinances. Once he performed a wedding for a man who was a notorious bigamist. He was frequently to be found drinking in Pretzfeld when he ought to have be in the church hearing confessions. On one occasion, he made people come to his house to confess. He gambled incessantly and cursed "worse than a soldier." When he was drinking or gaming, he often failed to administer the sacrament. He struck a peasant, splitting his nose and drawing blood; later he beat an eighty-year-old woman. During one drinking bout, he denied that the Zentrichter and Schultheiss in Forchheim were his lords. Worse, "neither is my gracious prince and lord of Bamberg." According to the complaint, Steib declared, "I am my own lord. The bishop of Bamberg is nothing more than he who administers the gallows, the wheel, and the sword."[77]

Steib responded to the various accusations, always protesting his innocence. There was nothing wrong with the way he conducted weddings. The soldier was leaving to fight in Hungary; it only seemed fair to conduct the wedding immediately. And no one ate meat that he knew of. As for the case of the bigamist, Steib had proclaimed the banns three times, and no one had indicated any impediment. He did not spend his time in taverns when he was supposed to be hearing confessions. Yes, he had gone home once because it was cold in the church. If anyone wanted to confess, he wasn't hard to find. In any event, his parishioners rarely if ever came to confession. As to the beatings, his opponents were telling less than the truth. He never said those things about the officials and the bishop. And if anyone claimed he was a gambler, let them prove it: "I have never ever gambled."[78]

Aside from the chaplain, Steib's main accusers were the officials in Forchheim who had orchestrated his removal years before. As it turned out, they had been less than earnest in the cause of Catholic renewal. For some years a Lutheran preacher had been active in the castle at Regensbach. People from Kirchehrenbach and Leutenbach had regularly attended his sermons. Although Neithard von Thüngen ordered the officials to remove him, the preacher became even bolder, coming to Kirchehrenbach itself to preach and later traveling to communities throughout the parish. By 1599 he had virtually created his own parish, drawing followers and, worst of all, tithes from the seven villages. Another preacher had later appeared in Weichenstein.[79] What had the officials done about these? Moreover, although the bishop had agreed to provide 200 gulden to repair the church in Kirchehrenbach, Steib had received only 40 gulden. The rest, he claimed, disappeared into the hands of officials in Forchheim. If the officials attacked Steib, it was perhaps because they had something to hide.

For the moment, Steib was found guilty of drunkenness and gambling and fined 30 gulden.[80] By the time the sentence was handed down, Steib had been transferred to Adelsdorf. The problems there with the Crailsheimers and Stiebers had yet to be resolved: indeed, the situation appears to have worsened. The Stiebers sold off properties that belonged to the parish and prohibited peasants from Lauff, Uttsett, and Weppersdorf from being buried in Adelsdorf. Instead they were interred in "an unconsecrated field." The Crailsheimers seized tithes from Weppersdorf and Lauff and turned them over to the church in Walsdorf, where they had appointed a Protestant preacher.[81] As he attempted to resolve these issues, Steib once again found himself accused of "unpriestly habits" and was reprimanded several times before finally being deprived of his post in December 1608. As before, the charges that led to his dismissal were drunkenness and gambling.[82]

Michael Steib may well have had a weakness for dice and the bottle, but ultimately he was undone by collusion between corrupt episcopal officials and rebellious nobles. His disputes with the Stiebers revolved around a number of estates that had belonged to the now defunct convent at Schlüsselau. The last abbess of Schlüsselau had been Birgitta Stieber; after her death the family took possession of the convent's lands as if they were her inheritance.[83] For all intents and purposes, the Stiebers and Crailsheimers were playing the role of Protestant Landesherr. They had secularized monastic lands and now, just as the margraves had done, were using the income from the prebends to support Lutheran clergyman on their estates.[84] The Stiebers went so far as to order the composition of a German metrical psalter, ordered according to the Protestant numbering of the Psalms, for use in churches on the estates.[85] Under such circumstances, Michael Steib was asked to restore the Catholic religion. Instead of help, he received nothing from the regime but fines and sanctions. If Steib did claim to be his own lord, it is hard not to sympathize.

∾

Johann Philipp Gebsattel's inability to resolve disputes such as those in Aisch and Adelsdorf did not go unnoticed. The papal nuncio reported in February 1602 that "all is asleep, the enthusiasm for Catholic reform has diminished as well as that for the reform of clerical discipline." He complained that Gebsattel had not yet been ordained a priest, much less consecrated a bishop, and that he had no spiritual councilors. Gebsattel responded that these were idle rumors, told by "enemies of the church," and sent his trusted vicar general, Johann Schöner, to Rome in hopes that he could convince the curia that the nuncio was in error.[86]

It would be no simple mission to convince Pope Clement VIII and the curia of Gebsattel's good faith, and after the visit was over Schöner told the bishop that he would have preferred if the job had been given to someone else.[87] Schöner's instructions contained detailed examples of how Johann

Philipp had successfully combated heresy in his see. Gebsattel had proclaimed publicly that all Lutheran heretics must convert to the true Catholic faith or pay 100 gulden. He had ensured that the decrees of the Council of Trent concerning marriage were "strictly observed." He had succeeded where Neithard von Thüngen had failed in exiling the Lutheran preacher of Teuschnitz. At the same time, efforts at reform were hampered by the fact that most of the nobles in the Hochstift were Lutherans.[88]

Schöner soon discovered that the pope was better informed about the goings-on in Bamberg than anyone had anticipated. The list of complaints against Gebsattel proved much longer than Schöner was prepared to answer for.[89] Nonetheless, in his second audience with the pope, Schöner must have scored some important points for his bishop, for his letter describing that meeting suggested that victory was at hand.[90] By the end of January 1603, Schöner had succeeding in raising doubts in the pope's mind about the accusations.[91] He convinced the pope not to send another nuncio to Bamberg. Although Gebsattel had nothing to fear if Portia were to come to Bamberg, such a visitation might prove prejudicial to the reform party and the Counter-Reformation in Germany in general. The nuncio's visit would imply that the pope did not trust his bishops. Clement was impressed by Schöner's argument; the visitation never took place.[92]

Johann Schöner's visit to Rome had succeeded on several counts. When he came to Rome, many "evil people" held "sinister opinions" about the bishop. Now, through Schöner's efforts, Gebsattel had won the sympathy of several cardinals.[93] Schöner reaped generous rewards for his service, being elevated to the post of suffragan bishop in 1607. Schöner's confirmation in this office, however, did not proceed without difficulties. His most outspoken critic was Friedrich Förner, a member of Neithard von Thüngen's inner circle, his confessor, and perhaps his closest friend. Förner's relations with the leaders of the new regime were less amicable. He detested Johann Philipp von Gebsattel. In 1600, Förner declared that the "Religious Reformation" begun by Neithard von Thüngen had "for the most part ended" on account of Gebsattel's incompetence.[94] When Schöner discovered that someone had sent damning letters about his character to the curia, he immediately accused Förner. Förner responded that he had written nothing about the suffragan elect in his letters. This was in fact true, but the curia had other sources of information. The papal nuncio reported that Schöner took the advice of Calvinists and was generally cold in matters of religion.[95] Schöner's chief patron in Rome, Cardinal Ottavio Paravicini, was not terribly optimistic about his chances for papal confirmation and recommended that Gebsattel find another candidate.[96]

Pope Paul V charged Cardinal Antonio Caetani, nuncio to the imperial court, with the task of examining the candidate. But Caetani was unable to leave Prague. The curia then considered sending Julius Echter. Caetani felt this was not an option: Echter's personal dislike for the bishop of Bamberg might impede his objectivity. Bishop Wolfgang II of Regensburg was selected instead. The witnesses called by Bishop Wolfgang were among Gebsattel's severest critics, among them Johann Gottfried von Aschhausen and Friedrich Förner. Schöner's only hope lay in impeaching the witnesses. Aschhausen was a nephew of Julius Echter; any reservations the nuncio had about the bishop of Würzburg must be applied to his creature. As for Förner, Schöner declared that he had always been his greatest enemy.[97] Schöner ultimately succeeded in convincing Bishop Wolfgang that the opposition to him was personal. Schöner was confirmed in his office in November 1608.[98]

Johann Philipp von Gebsattel and Johann Schöner followed up their victory by ostracizing Förner from the Geistliche Rat. Förner was charged with a variety of offenses, including concubinage, and declared a traitor by Gebsattel during a meeting of the chapter. Förner still had numerous friends in the chapter, however, including Johann Gottfried von Aschhausen and Johann Christoph Neustetter-Stürmer. Förner also had two very important supporters abroad: Julius Echter of Würzburg and Duke Maximilian of Bavaria.[99] Maximilian in particular feared that were Bamberg to fall to the Protestants, the Catholic states of southern Germany would be divided by a Lutheran block stretching from Swabia to the Baltic. In 1608, Echter and Maximilian used their combined influence to begin impeachment proceedings against Gebsattel "*propter turpitudinem vitae*" and hindrance of Catholic reform.[100]

Schöner returned to Rome to orchestrate Gebsattel's defense, certain that Förner had been instrumental in preparing the case against the bishop.[101] Once hearings began in Rome, Förner was threatened with imprisonment.[102] In the end, Friedrich Förner was spared owing to an accident of history. Johann Philipp von Gebsattel died on June 26, 1608. To Förner, Gebsattel's final illness was nothing less than a sign of God's anger.[103] Now Schöner found himself on the defensive. Maximilian informed the pope that Schöner was an "imposter" who "had practiced nothing good in Rome." He was stripped of the offices of vicar general and dean of the college. Schöner's last official act came on July 21, 1609, when he presided over the election of Johann Gottfried von Aschhausen as bishop of Bamberg.

Johann Gottfried von Aschhausen owed his election in good measure to Julius Echter and Maximilian of Bavaria. Both had openly campaigned for Aschhausen's election from the fall of 1608 onward.[104] Echter's role in the election was cause for concern among the more moderate members of the clergy. Suspicion of Echter's plans appeared to have led to the results of the first ballot. Aschhausen lost by a vote of seven to five. Luckily for Echter and his confederates, the victor, the cathedral dean Christoph Neustetter-Stürmer, refused the honor. With Neustetter's support, Aschhausen was elected bishop without dissent on the second ballot. Although generally favorable to Aschhausen's cause, the canons were not willing to allow themselves to be led by either Würzburg or Bavaria.[105]

Johann Gottfried's first act was to appoint Friedrich Förner vicar-general.[106] Förner immediately went to Rome and confirmed every rumor about Gebsattel's regime that had made its way to the curia. He admitted that heresy was rampant and that nothing in the way of reform had been accomplished in the past ten years.[107] A panygeric composed on Johann Gottfried's accession provided an occasion to point out his predecessor's failures. It charged that all members had fallen into slumber; the spirit of Lethe had fallen on the commonwealth.[108] Even Gebsatttel's tomb was used to discredit him. Gebsattel is shown kneeling before a now lost crucifix. The symbols of episcopal authority—miter, crozier, and processional cross—are laid to the side. That the miter is on the ground is of no concern, as it was the common symbol for bishops who were never consecrated. More significant is that the staff and cross—the two primary symbols of a bishop's office—are stripped from his hands, something unprecedented in the iconography of Bamberg bishops. Behind the bishop, the image of God appears from the clouds, conferring his blessing on Gebsattel. The imagery conspires to show a bishop stripped of all dignity, forgiven by God after his death for having assumed an office for which he was manifestly unworthy.[109]

Aschhausen opened the diocese to the Jesuits. He turned over control of the seminary to members of the order, granting them 3,000 gulden from the scholarship fund, and founded a Jesuit college.[110] Such actions did little but add credence to rumors that the Jesuits had poisoned Gebsattel to make way for Aschhausen.[111]

During the first year of his reign, Aschhausen issued a series of ordinances that closely followed those of Neithard von Thüngen. A forty-hour vigil was ordered a week after his election. The Hauptmänner were to make sure that at least one member of each household in their districts took part. Aschhausen took active measures to ensure that the mandate would be observed in the countryside as well as in the city.[112] A second mandate was sent to the rural parishes on September 6, 1609, requiring priests to report the names of all "stubborn adherents of the repugnant religion" in their parishes by the end of the month.[113] In March of 1610 and 1611 Aschhausen decreed that all individuals who refused to return to the Catholic faith had to leave the territory.[114] In November 1611 some two hundred troops were sent to enforce the edicts in Graiz and Zeuln. Lutherans were arrested in several other communities as well and sent to Bamberg for trial.[115]

The use of force on this scale was unprecedented. According to one dissident, even Echter, "the treacherous old fox," was not so cruel, preferring to use "sweet words and cunning." Aschhausen, however, used "coercion with all manner of force." A naked woman was ripped from her bath in Burgstahl; a sacristan's child in Langheim was tortured.[116] In some regions, the nobility were initially able to defend their priests and parishioners. The pastor of Altenkunstadt was cited for concubinage in 1609 and 1610 but was sheltered by "rebellious nobles."[117] Pankratz Volk of Adelshofen noted in 1610 that the houses of "the nobles and other Lutheran lords" served as meeting houses for Lutherans in his parish. Although sixteen Lutherans from Etzelkirch had converted to Catholicism, it was only a few weeks before they began attending Lutheran services on noble estates. Among other things, they found the new calendar confusing. Ultimately, Volk blamed "cold Catholic officials" for refusing to support priests in their efforts to keep converts in the fold.[118]

In April 1611 Aschhausen ordered Förner to organize a general visitation of the diocese.[119] At the conclusion of the visitation, Förner composed a summary of the commission's findings and presented it to the bishop. The visitors had uncovered "enormous errors and detestable defects" throughout the diocese. Most priests were ignorant of the rudiments of Catholic doctrine. Few had missals, and even among those who did, there was great "confusion" over the conduct of the mass. German and Latin songs were used interchangeably and were often taken from Lutheran hymnals. Large portions of the see were "infected" with concubinage. Priests failed to teach catechism classes, rarely heard confessions, and hardly ever maintained registers. Weddings were conducted according to "fantastic" rituals; Extreme Unction had not been performed in living memory. Among the laity things were no better. Few people knew how or when to make the sign of the cross or genuflect. The festivals of the Virgin Mary and other saints were not observed outside the city of Bamberg. Sex before marriage was the norm, bigamy was common, discretion unheard of. The Sabbath was frequently profaned: in Weismain and Kupferberg, markets were held during mass. Churches stood in ruins, altars remained unconsecrated, heretical preachers were everywhere. The countryside was full of soothsayers, magicians, and witches.[120]

Förner's summary report presented the image of a diocese that was Catholic in name only. But was that an accurate representation? Close examination of the surviving protocols from the archidiaconate of Kronach reveal a much more subtly shaded picture than Förner painted. Complete protocols remain for twenty-one parishes in the archidiaconate.[121] In most parishes, only about half the residents were communicants. In Altenkunstadt, only one person in eight had recently taken communion. These numbers, however, were somewhat misleading. Better than half of the eight hundred people listed as living in the parish of Marktschorgast were, in fact, Hohenzollern subjects. Confessed Catholics did make the sign of the cross frequently but were "ignorant and rude" on other matters of Catholic doctrine and practice. In Stadtsteinach and Marktschorgast, the priests had made earnest efforts to instruct their parishioners, but to little effect.

The visitors were extremely dissatisfied with the habits of the clergy in the archidiaconate. All but five of the twenty-two priests they interviewed had concubines. All but two drank to excess. Several priests had children and in some cases considered them legitimate. At the same time, there was evidence of improvement. The median age of priests who lived in concubinage was fifty-seven; the median age of celibate priests was thirty-nine. The older priests had been ordained during the early phase of the Counter-Reformation, before the opening of the seminary, when there was a severe shortage of priests. No priest under the age of forty had a concubine, suggesting that the practice was dying out as graduates of the seminary received parishes.[122] The only place where the pastor openly conducted Lutheran services was Presseck. All the rest appear to have said mass in a Catholic manner. Few if any priests administered all the sacraments or did so according to accepted practice, but they at least made an effort to do so. Reports from the pastors in Ützing and Zeyern, written about the same time as the visitation, suggested that parishioners were fairly selective when it came to obeying the various religious mandates. Most would confess and receive communion, but resisted attending Friday services. Banns were proclaimed, but weddings were still conducted at home, according to tradition.[123] Ultimately, examination of the visitation reports suggests that the confessional mood of the diocese was overwhelmingly Catholic, despite numerous irregularities among both clergy and laity. Förner's report glossed over the positive side of the visitation, painting a far darker picture than was accurate. His *Extractus Generalis* is a melancholy reflection of what he perceived to be the complete collapse of the Counter-Reformation in the diocese.

The mood of pessimism that prevailed in the *Extractus Generalis* stands in marked contrast with the tone of Förner's writings from the beginning of the century. In his *Defense and Exoneration of the Catholic Religion,* written in 1600, he presents the familiar case that the doctrines of the Catholic church had been passed down from Christ to the apostles. Since the days of the apostles, the bishop of Rome had always been "the ruling head on Earth" of the church. Thirty years earlier, in about 1570, Jakob Feucht had said the same thing. But in his *Defense,* Förner added something. Recent times had seen a phenomenal expansion of the church:

> In Oriental and Occidental India, even to the New World, in Japan, in the Antipodes where they stand with their feet opposite ours—daily many thousands of souls are baptized into the Catholic faith by the Fathers of the Society of Jesus.[124]

As for Luther, his "groundless confession" had only been around for eighty years at most. Luther merely recycled the "mouse turds" of such heretics as Valdes, John Wyclif, and Jan Hus, trying to pass off their lies as gospel truths. Luther was like a merchant who "sells mouse turds for Calcutta pepper."[125] Not only that, but who could tell from day to day what Lutheran doctrine was? The Saxons had their version; the Württembergers had theirs. Lutheran "untheologians" couldn't decide what they believed. And whereas the Catholic faith waxed stronger, Lutheranism daily grew old: "it has already lost its teeth, it has gone bald, all its hair has fallen out."[126]

We might be tempted to dismiss Lutheranism as a dying creed, Förner argued, but ultimately something more sinister lurked in its shadow. The Augsburg Confession was merely a ploy, a cover for the "bloodthirsty Calvinists" who exploited the legal protections granted Lutherans to infiltrate the empire. Now they were free to rob churches, rip down monasteries and convents, smash altars, and fill their bellies with the spoil. There could be no question but that they are agents of "the archenemy of all goodness," Satan, who raised these heretics up in order to destroy of the church of God. It was Satan who raised up Valdes; it was Satan who raised up Wyclif; it was Satan who raised up Luther. And now that Lutheranism had foundered on "the Rock of the Catholic Church," Satan had raised up Calvinism.[127]

In 1600, when Förner penned these words, he seemed confident that pious administrators could overcome the Satanic threat without much difficulty. Good rulers, such as Neithard von Thüngen, would lead those trapped in the darkness of error into the light of the knowledge of truth and ensure the salvation of the "Christian commune of this Fatherland."[128] Two decades later he seemed less sure. The misery of Germany in the Thirty Years' War had been brought on by the "Calvino-Lutherans" and their "apostate vomit," the Augsburg Confession. The "feces of Calvinism" lay at the root of all sedition and rebellion. Protestants were vermin, and God demanded that the emperor exterminate them.[129]

It has been said that one of the most intriguing features of the Counter-Reformation was its "nice blend of insecurity and confidence."[130] Friedrich Förner's writings reveal just such a blend. In his youth he was supremely confident, but his travail during the reign of Johann Philipp von Gebsattel had left him angry and bitter. The longer he remained locked in the struggle to advance the Catholic faith, the more apocalyptic his rhetoric became. Catholicism would win in the end, since only the Catholic faithful were allowed access to the wonder-working God, the *Thaumaturgus Emmanuel*.[131] The perception of the miraculous in the struggle, however, points to a crisis in confidence in the old political system. Förner's experiences suggested to him that it was not possible to create a Catholic society within the older constitutional framework. In his advice to Ferdinand II on the Edict of Restitution, Förner concluded that the suppression of Protestantism could have no foundation in civil law. Förner reminded Ferdinand II of the fates that befell

Frederick Barbarossa, Otto IV, and Frederick II, emperors who refused to obey God. Forget the Peace of Passau; ignore the Peace of Augsburg–this was not a matter of law or politics, but a matter of faith.[132] Viewed through the lens of confessional conflict, traditional privileges–whether they applied to the canons, nobles, towns, officials, or patrons–appeared as bulwarks for the enemies of Catholicism. What in the past had been disputes over the extent and limits of *Herrschaft* were now recast as part of the cosmic struggle between the forces of God and the devil.

Chapter 9

Cuius Regio?

About the same time that Friedrich Förner penned his visitation report, Paul Reinel, a Lutheran deacon in the town of Selb, sat down to record his thoughts on the course of religious reform. His reflections took the form of the Annotationes, a manuscript history of Selb from earliest times down to the present.[1] A basic theme of Reinel's history was that his village had always been Christian. In ancient times, "all of Germany was corrupted with heathen superstition and idol worship." Consequently, one might think that Reinel's ancestors were pagans and polytheists as well. Reinel argues that this was not true, since "at the time of the Apostles this place was an utter wilderness and wasteland." Christianity came to Selb from Regensburg in the person of Lucius Cyrenaus, a figure mentioned in Acts 13. Lucius established a mission in Regensburg, one that was later taken over by Saint Emmeram. According to Reinel, by A.D. 700, Christianity had a firm footing in the Danube valley, and it was only after that time that Christian settlers came from Regensburg to Selb. But even though "our forefathers in this place were not heathens but Christians," Reinel admits that their religion "was not entirely pure." The reason was simple: "[U]ntil the year 1517, Christ was much betrayed, and soiled and buried under popish human doctrines."[2] Priests were more concerned with ceremonial objects than Gospel truths. For them, "Christ in Christianity was like a fifth wheel on a wagon."[3] Only with the coming of Martin Luther, "surely the Third Elijah and Prophet of the German Lands," was the truth revealed.[4]

The central themes of Reinel's history were repeated five years later in an ordinance composed by General Superintendent Christoph Schleupner to mark the centenary of the Reformation.[5] At the beginning, Schleupner notes that Christ had foretold how "in the last days false christs and false prophets will rise up and accomplish many great signs and wonders," leading many into error. This great darkness had come into the world "with the kingdom of the antichrist in Rome." The love of truth diminished; people were led to "take pleasure in unrighteousness." But God had also promised that just before the end of the world, the Gospel would be preached again. To that end God "had not chosen princes and potentates, nor jurists, nor clever orators to set against the Pope, but rather used *Herr D. Martinum* Luther as his chosen weapon." Through Luther, God would bring down not only "the great prelate of Rome" but "Spain as well."[6]

Reinel's *Annotationes* and Schleupner's ordinance are replete with apocalyptic imagery. Reinel presents all of history as a struggle between the forces of Christ and Antichrist. This apocalyptic strain underlies both authors' chronology. Schleupner notes that Christian truth had been suppressed for nine centuries before the coming of Luther.[7] Reinel is more precise, identifying the reign of the emperor Phocas (602–10) as the moment when "the Devil brought forth the two antichrists, Mohamet and the Pope of Rome."[8] For the next thousand years, the people of Selb had remained true to the teachings of the apostles as they had received them from Lucius Cyrenaeus. The timing would seem propitious: both Reinel and Schleupner saw the year 1617 as the end of the thousand-year reign of Antichrist.[9]

The signs of Antichrist's defeat were all around them. Although Protestantism appeared to be on the defensive, Schleupner was adamant that this was a false perception. Evangelical teaching "is so strong in its progress that it has made the pope tired with all the effort he must expend to dampen it just a little."[10] Still, both authors perceived the continued threat from "lying spirits" who would obscure divine truth. Schleupner clearly identified Spain among the chief enemies of the Gospel. But both also saw the Calvinists as agents of Antichrist. Even more striking is the skepticism that both Reinel and Schleupner expressed concerning the princes. According to Schleupner, God intended to "put the wise to shame: He has chosen what is weak in this world; He puts down what is powerful." In this spirit he chose a simple man—Luther—to do his work, rather than a prince.[11] Although Reinel credited Margrave Georg the Pious with legalizing the reforms, his narrative makes it clear that the good people of Selb had begun the work of purifying the church according to the Gospel message.[12] For Reinel, the Reformation was deeply rooted in the traditional structure of communal society, and, by extension, the territorial constitution.

Reinel's thesis is revealing, for at the time he composed his history the Oberland and the empire were both in the throes of constitutional crisis. On the imperial stage, Protestant states fought for the recognition of their rights in the face of an increasingly vocal Catholic majority in the Reichstag. On the local level, the estates fought to maintain their influence against the centralizing efforts of a new prince with uncomfortably close ties to international Calvinism. Reinel's and Schleupner's histories of the Reformation portray the Oberland as a steadfastly Lutheran community simultaneously threatened by Catholic foes and Calvinist "friends." In that regard, the antiphon for the centennial celebration of the Reformation could also be read as the question that the clergy and estates posed to their prince on the eve of the Thirty Years' War:

Wilt thou have anything to do with the stool of wickedness;
which imagineth mischief as a law?[13]

Viewed from the perspective of the margrave and his advisors, the previous
decades had seen no shortage of either wickedness or mischief. Although
nominally at peace, the Protestant and Catholic estates of the Franconian
Kreis eyed one another warily throughout the 1560s.[14] When the Kreistag
discussed preparations for a Turkish war in 1566, the Protestants expressed
their fears that the emperor intended to use the troops against those "estates
who adhere to the Augsburg Confession."[15] Tensions between Catholics and
Protestants in Franconia sharpened following the election of Julius Echter
von Mespelbrunn as bishop of Würzburg in 1573. Echter's invasion of Fulda
in 1576 and his involvement in the war in Cologne in 1583 provoked an
angry response from Lutheran rulers. Protestant delegates in the Kreistag
chastised Echter for "hunting down their poor evangelical subjects," comparing his policies with the atrocities inflicted on the Dutch by the Spanish
general, the duke of Parma, a decade earlier. In Würzburg, Strasbourg, and
other places "adherents of both religions—princes, counts, and noble lords—
had charitably tolerated one another" for forty years. Now Catholics were
attempting to extend the power of the papacy through force of arms. Protestants pointed to France and the Netherlands as warnings of what was to
come if the papists continued to violate the Religious Peace of Augsburg.[16]

Throughout the 1560s and 1570s, Protestant leaders sought to establish
some sort of defensive alliance. Margrave Georg Friedrich played a leading
role in negotiations among the Palatine Elector, the Elector of Saxony, and
the landgrave of Hesse.[17] As had their predecessors half a century earlier,
theologians in the margraviate wrestled with the confessional implications
of a Protestant union. They feared the pope's "so-called religion," branding
it "heathen superstition, blind and counterfeit." The "anti-Christian council"
of Trent and the first rumblings of the Counter-Reformation revealed the
threat of Catholic tyranny. At the same time, Superintendent Georg Karg
of Bayreuth recognized that within the Protestant camp there was "no concord." The original unity of the Lutheran reform had been "obliterated" by
disagreements among "sacramentarians, Calvinists and Zwinglians."[18] Ultimately, the theological discussions pointed toward the impossibility of rec-
onciling the clergy of the margraviate with either their Catholic foes or their
erstwhile Calvinist allies.[19]

The events of the 1590s gave the Protestant camp little cause for optimism. The collapse of imperial justice under Rudolf II was one source of
concern. The expulsion of Protestants from Aachen in 1598 and subsequent appointment by the emperor of a Catholic mayor and council, set

a dangerous precedent. By issuing his judgment against Aachen through the Reichshofrat, rather than through the Reichskammergericht, Rudolf II bypassed the usual legal channels. Since the Protestants had no representative or advocate in the Reichshofrat, the emperor's decision to establish that body as the supreme court of the empire appeared to threaten the rights of all Protestants, especially their rights over secularized ecclesiastical lands.[20] Georg Friedrich maintained that a defensive alliance was "urgently needed," but mistrust between Lutherans and Calvinists precluded any sort of agreement.[21] Meetings in Oehringen and Heidelberg produced nothing more than vague protests against the "persecution of the evangelical religion" and Catholic assaults on the "privileges and ancient liberties" of the Protestant princes.[22]

Georg Friedrich died on May 6, 1603. He left no heirs, and by the terms of the Treaty of Gera (1599) his domains reverted to the Electoral line. The disposition of Georg Friedrich's estates presented an opportunity to his cousin, Elector Joachim Friedrich of Brandenburg. Since 1596 Joachim Friedrich had been engaged in a dispute with his half brothers Joachim Ernst and Christian over their inheritance. Christian demanded the division of the mark so that he and Joachim Ernst could have their own states. Christian set his eyes on the Neumark, which under Hans von Küstrin had taken on the character of an independent principality. Joachim Friedrich refused, citing the Golden Bull and the will of Albrecht Achilles as precedents.[23] The death of Georg Friedrich offered a means to resolve the dispute. Joachim Friedrich agreed to turn over Ansbach and Kulmbach to his younger brothers. Joachim Ernst received the Niederland, while Christian took up residence in Kulmbach as ruler of the Oberland.[24]

The Treaty of Gera stipulated that the estates should be summoned immediately following the death of Georg Friedrich. They had not met since 1583 and now took full advantage of the situation by presenting Christian and Joachim Ernst with a detailed *gravamina*. The princes had to promise to uphold the Augsburg Confession and stop all interference by the secular powers in religious affairs, as stipulated in the Consistorial Ordinance of 1592. The estates also demanded the expulsion of the Jews, whom they condemned as "harmful, blasphemous people and notorious usurers." Elimination of the excise was the third demand, followed by articles calling for the princes to moderate servile dues and refrain from hunting on communal land. The princes agreed to all but the elimination of the excise tax.[25]

Shortly after the end of the Landtag, Joachim Ernst and Christian were approached by the Palatine Elector in hopes that they would assume Georg Friedrich's role as intermediaries of the Protestant estates.[26] Joachim Ernst was more than willing to assume his predecessor's mantle. The revolt of Protestant nobles in Hungary offered the young margrave his first opportunity to try a hand at organizing Protestant opposition.[27] Christian was uncomfortable with such a policy. Rudolf II had yet to recognize the succession, and Christian warned against taking any action until both he and his brother were secure in their inheritance.[28] The Bavarian occupation of Donauwörth in 1608, however, removed any doubts about the need for a Protestant alliance.[29] So long as the "Jesuits" intended to do to all Protestant states what they had done to Donauwörth, a "new Schmalkaldic League" was desperately needed.[30] The religious inclinations of the heir presumptive, Archduke Ferdinand of Styria, were also a cause for concern. The chancellor of Brandenburg feared that Ferdinand might well "pick up where Charles V left off and make some [of the Protestants] shorter by a head."[31] Margrave Christian abandoned his earlier caution and joined his brother in helping to finalize the formation of the Protestant Union at Auhausen in May 1608.[32]

With the foundation of the Union, the Protestant states were confronted with a new set of questions. The members were unsure whether or not they should make common cause with Protestant nobles in the Habsburg lands.[33] Closer to home, the allies wondered whether it would be possible or useful to pull the Franconian lower nobility, including Protestant knights in Würzburg and Bamberg, into the Union.[34] Union intervention in the Hochstift went even further. In 1611, the Union agreed to take up the case of peasants in Graitz and Zeuln against the bishop of Bamberg, declaring that members of the Union would not abandon their coreligionists to oppression.[35]

Shortly after the establishment of the Union, Christian asked the estates for additional funds to support the Protestant alliance. Initially, the estates offered no resistance, but news that the diet in Ansbach had balked at a similar request strengthened their resolve. The delegates in Ansbach pointed out that Joachim Ernst and Christian had failed to remedy the concerns raised in the *gravamina* of 1603, in particular with respect to the Jews.[36] In Kulmbach, the estates demanded a more active role in government. They asked that representation in the diet be broadened to include peasants, so that "the poverty and hourly decline of the poor Landvolck may be heard and considered." The inclusion of peasants certainly spiced up the debate. One official described the protests against the margrave as "coarse, offensive, insulting, and treasonous, peppered through and through with obscenities." Embarrassed by their rustic colleagues, the urban deputies offered a compromise. When the deputies suggested a reduction in the tax, the prince's representatives simply responded that the peasants would have to be satisfied with drinking two mugs less beer than they would have liked.[37]

The deputies responded with a new *gravamina,* demanding that the prince remedy certain defects in religion. Christian's newly appointed court preacher, Vitus Albinus, provoked controversy by suggesting that exorcism be removed from the baptismal liturgy. Nicolaus Senft, a member of the consistory and deacon in Kulmbach, smelled something. To his fervently Lutheran nostrils, Albinus's proposal reeked of Calvinism.[38] Senft took his concerns to the pulpit: ultimately the matter ended up before the diet. The *gravamina* of 1608 included a demand to maintain exorcism in the form outlined in the 1533 *Kirchenordnung*. To preserve the purity of evangelical doctrine, all Calvinist ministers and schoolmasters had to be dismissed. The estates reminded Christian of his duty to uphold the Augsburg Confession and the Formula of Concord. If he would not, there was no room for further discussion. When the diet adjourned for Christmas, the prince and estates were at an impasse.[39]

Throughout the spring, the estates met on their own to plan strategy. When the diet reconvened in June, however, the threat of war in Bohemia weakened the estates' resolve. After nineteen months of debate, the deputies demurred to the prince's demands after he agreed to some fairly minor concessions.[40] The estates renewed the excise in 1612 and 1614, effectively recognizing it as a permanent institution. In the meantime, the diet of 1608 revealed the possibility that the prince could negotiate with small groups of deputies. This opened the way for the creation in 1614 of the Directorium, a committee of princely officials and representatives from the Landschaft charged with administering the excise tax.[41]

Not long after the creation of the Directorium, Margrave Christian was able to secure the submission of the knights in the Vogtland through an agreement subsequently known as the Vogtland Recess. After 1560, the knights in the region around Hof had entered the imperial knights' canton of Gebirg.[42] They soon began to chafe at the financial demands that the emperor imposed on them. Between 1570 and 1576, the knights of the Vogtland attended the canton's diet sporadically; after 1576 they ceased to appear at all. Consequently, Maximilian II issued a penal mandate against the knights.[43] In 1614, as a means to resolve the issue, Christian and the knights opened negotiations over a submission treaty. The knights agreed to pay a portion of their older levies to the prince; in return, he would shield them from the imperial mandate, as well as from the bishop of Bamberg and the elector of Saxony.[44] The agreement was finalized in the fall of 1615, along with a similar treaty with the nobles around Wunsiedel. Not long thereafter Christian levied a property tax on the knights' subjects, the first collected from those estates since the Hohenzollerns purchased the Vogtland in the fourteenth century.[45]

Seen alongside the creation of the Directorium, the subjugation of the Vogtland knights would seem to be a victory over the estates. It is worth considering, however, why Christian sought such a treaty in the first place. The financial strains of the Protestant Union were, from the margrave's perspective, the driving force behind the treaty. In their complaint against the emperor, the knights argued that their poverty (real enough, it would seem) prevented them from paying the full subsidy to the canton. Christian was satisfied with rather less—one-fifth of the original levy—but was glad for the additional revenue. The agreement with the knights of the Vogtland was symptomatic of the prince's fiscal weakness more than anything.[46]

The agreement had significant limits. The knights were willing to recognize the authority of the prince only to the extent that it had been defined in the charters that confirmed the Hohenzollern purchase of the Vogtland in 1373. In that sense, the recess of 1615 merely constituted the formal recognition of legal claims that the Hohenzollerns had been entitled to make for over two centuries.[47] The knights maintained the right to present the prince with a *gravamina*. They echoed the third estate in their demand that the prince grant "free exercise of the Augsburg Religion" on the noble estates.[48] What this meant in practice was the freedom of the knights' subjects from the consistory in Kulmbach. Only in 1626 did the knights agree to recognize the jurisdiction of the consistory, and then only after obtaining a number of concessions from the margrave.[49] Among other things, the knights secured the right to form associations with nobles in other parts of the Oberland. Hence rather than leading to the full subjugation of the knights in the Vogtland, the treaty of 1615 provided the foundation for the creation of a self-conscious, well-organized noble *corpus* in the Oberland.[50] During the Thirty Years' War the influence of the nobles increased as the prince was forced to turn to them for support. By 1622 the financial situation had become critical, forcing Christian to dissolve the *Directorium* and recall the diet, once again made up of representatives from all three estates.[51]

The struggle between Christian and the estates, like that surrounding the formation of the Protestant Union, displayed both the strengths and weaknesses of Lutheranism in the early seventeenth century. The defiance of the Protestant estates at the Diet of Regensburg in 1608 could not mask the internal divisions that ensured the Union's demise a dozen years later. In the narrower confines of the Oberland, weakness and defiance also seem best to describe the position of prince and estates. Neither side could dominate the other, but the growing threat of war, followed by its reality, demanded compromise on fiscal matters. No one party was strong enough simply to impose its own political or religious agenda.[52]

Behind this weakness, however, lay the immense strength of the Lutheran Reformation in the Oberland. The diets of 1608 and 1622 show certain similarities to those of 1524 and 1548. In each of the four cases, a coalition of nobles and towns supported the vision of Protestantism put forward by the leading Lutheran clerics. The strength of Lutheranism rested on the cooperation of the parish clergy, nobles, townspeople, and villagers. That in and of itself should come as no surprise. What the diets of the sixteenth and early seventeenth centuries demonstrate, however, is that this cooperation seems to have derived not from the organizing power of the prince but in direct opposition to various aspects of princely policy. In times of duress the clergy, with the support of the second and third estates, voiced their claim to ownership of the Reformation. Schleupner and Reinel insist that it was not the prince but the common preachers who had brought about the revival of the Gospel. Likewise, the position of the towns in the diet as well as the language of the Vogtland Recess make it clear that the estates perceived themselves as the primary defenders of the Lutheran Reformation against princes–Christian among them–with suspicious religious leanings. In the rhetoric of the clergy and estates, we may thus discern a curious twist on the principle *cuius regio, eius religio:* the religion of the territory is not that of its prince, but of the estates.

There were no comparable constitutional conflicts in early seventeenth-century Bamberg, in large part because by 1600 the estates had ceased to play any meaningful role in the administration of the Hochstift. At a Landtag in 1588, Ernst von Mengersdorf painted a dim picture of the see's finances and asked the estates to approve a excise tax on beer and wine as well as a 0.5 percent property tax. The estates replied with a gravamina, listing mostly traditional grievances about the immunity of clerics and nobles from taxation. They also demanded stricter measures against the Jews and protection from foreign merchants and brewers.[53] After receiving some rather vague guarantees from the bishop, the estates agreed to grant both taxes for twelve years. They also agreed to the establishment of an Obereinnahme- or Landschaftskollegium, similar to the Directorium in Kulmbach, to oversee the collection and distribution of revenues.[54] By the reign of Bishop Johann Gottfried von Aschhausen, the tax had effectively become permanent, and he renewed it without even pretending to consult the estates.[55]

Meanwhile, the pace of religious reform quickened. The visitation of 1611 provided Aschhausen and Förner with ample ammunition against the old regime. With papal approval, Johann Schöner was stripped of his benefices and exiled, clearing the path for Friedrich Förner's ordination as suffragan bishop.[56] Förner made great use of his combined authority as suffragan bishop and vicar general to execute a host of decrees issued in the wake of the visitation. The first assault was against concubinage. Although priests had been ordered to give up their concubines and lead "exemplary lives" in 1609 and 1611, few chose to obey.[57] A new ordinance appeared in January 1613. This time the bishop sent troops to enforce his decree, leading to the arrest of concubines in twelve parishes.[58]

The visitation also led to a complete reorganization of the administration of the diocese, in particular the archidiaconates.[59] Förner kept in close contact with the archdeacons, who conducted regular visitations in the same manner as the superintendents in the Hohenzollern Oberland. Each priest had to attend yearly synods and swear to uphold the statutes. Those who demurred faced harsh fines and the loss of their benefices. At the parish level, local consistories (Sendgerichten) were set up. The Sendgerichten were staffed by the priests and chaplains, along with communal and princely officials from each village in the parish. These local consistories maintained clerical discipline and provided the archdeacons with more detailed information on parish life than had been available before the visitation of 1611.[60]

The local consistories played a central role in the visitation of 1613. Pastors interviewed local officials and parishioners, then passed the information back to the suffragan bishop.[61] In Stadtsteinach, the pastor heard reports from the Schultheissen in Vordern and Römershaidt about the activities of Lutherans in those villages. The pastor of Kupferberg only knew of a few heretics, "namely, the Stadtknecht, his wife and sister, the miller from Ludwigschorgast with his wife, servant and maid, and several women in the parish." Local officials were required to arrest all those who did not confess and take communion at Easter and either fine them 10 gulden or put them behind bars.[62] But it appears that this rarely happened. The pastor of Teuschnitz reported that "secular authorities" would do nothing to support the reforms. Consequently, the ordinances concerning catechism classes, baptism, and weddings were "completely ignored."[63] Secular officials were not alone in their unwillingness to support the full range of reforms. In the newly reconstituted archidiaconates of Hollfeld and Eggolsheim, many priests refused to abide by the new statutes, claiming that the suffragan bishop had no right to impose such "novelties" on them. Förner replied that he would use force if necessary to compel priests to attend the synods and obey the revised statutes.[64] Any priest who refused to execute decrees requiring the exile of recusants faced fines of up to 10 gulden. Secular officials who similarly failed in their duties were subject to fines and imprisonment. Ordinances of 1615, 1616, 1617, 1618, and 1621 required priests to inform the authorities about Amtmänner who failed to prosecute recusants and heretics.[65]

The sharp policies of Johann Gottfried von Aschhausen began to meet with protests from the chapter. The most egregious case involved the Dominican convent of the Holy Supulcher. Although the convent was not under episcopal jurisdiction, Aschhausen ordered the arrest of the prior and confiscation of the account books. In 1615 the nuns asked the cathedral dean to intercede on their behalf. Förner was called before the chapter to answer a series of charges brought against him and the bishop by the nuns. Förner dismissed the accusations as idle rumors and refused to answer.[66] Over the next few years, the chapter lodged further complaints against the bishop. Despite raising taxes, Aschhausen had failed to reduce the growing budget deficit; he had impinged in the rights of the chapter and other immunities; he attempted to tax the clergy in violation of his oath. Aschhausen was dismissive of these and other charges.[67] Then, in 1617, Aschhausen was elected to succeed his mentor, Julius Echter, as bishop of Würzburg. The pope voided his *Wahlkapitulation,* allowing him to issue legislation without the chapter's approval.[68] After 1617, the chapter, continually identified by the curia as the greatest stumbling block to Tridentine reforms, saw its authority dissipate.

In the reign of Johann Gottfried von Aschhausen we may see an example of the phenomenon described by R. J. W. Evans.[69] The reaction against the more aggressive form of Counter-Reformation, manifested in the election of Johann Philipp von Gebsattel, proved to have no long-term significance. Catholics in the mold of Aschhausen and Förner, Echter and Maximilian I, Ferdinand II and William Lamormaini retained control. Under Gebsattel they had been in the minority in Bamberg, but they retained sufficient influence to isolate their religious and political enemies. By 1617 it seemed as if Aschhausen and Förner could either ignore or eliminate all those who stood in the way of their vision of a thoroughly Catholic state.

Johann Gottfried von Aschhausen died in Regensburg in December, 1622. In his funeral sermon, Friedrich Förner praised the late bishop as "the firmest pillar of the Roman Empire."[70] He notes that Aschhausen's accession coincided with the rebellion of the Bohemian nobles against Rudolf II. The Letter of Majesty, issued by Rudolf to the Protestant nobles in Bohemia in 1608, like the Augsburg Confession earlier, was merely a cover under which Calvinists were able to undermine the good order of the realm. The result of their treachery was the defenestration of Prague in 1618 and the outbreak of war.[71] In the years immediately after 1618, heresy had been rampant and all of Germany had been exposed to the "violent machinations" of not only Calvinists, but witches and sorcerers.[72] In the midst of the danger, though, like a star shining through the clouds, stood Johann Gottfried. Förner likens the bishop to Moses, leading the Catholics away from danger—here he compares the Calvinists with the Egyptians. Although the virtues of Ferdinand II and Maximilian of Bavaria rank them among such heroes as Hector and Achilles, how could anyone doubt that it was Johann Gottfried von Aschhausen who had saved the empire from perdition?[73]

There is something curious in the way Förner frames this last question. First of all, he compares Ferdinand II with Hector and Maximilian of Bavaria with Achilles. Were these two not enemies? Was not Achilles the greater of the two heroes? Given that earlier he laid much of the blame for the outbreak of war at the feet of Rudolf II, it would seem that Förner's comments contain a subtle criticism of the house of Habsburg. This critique runs like a thread through the works Förner dedicated to the emperor in the early years of the Thirty Years' War. In *Palma Triumphalis Miraculorum Ecclesiae Catholicae,* Förner called on Ferdinand to have faith. Many times in the past emperors had won miraculous victories over the infidels and barbarians with the aid of the Blessed Virgin Mary: such a victory could not be far off for the Catholic emperor and his allies. Meanwhile, the spread of "that most pestiferous dragon, Calvinism" seems to have derived, in part, from the presence of alchemists and Rosicrucians in the imperial court in the days of Rudolf II.[74] In his edition of Lupold of Bebenburg's *De Zelo Catholicae Religionis* (1624), Förner congratulates Ferdinand on his victory over the Calvinists, reminding him of his earlier assurances in *Palma Triumphalis,* all the while pointing out that Tilly and the armies of the Catholic League won the victory for him.[75] In any event, the true course of Catholic renewal would be plotted by the bishops, not the emperor. If the empire was to be saved, it would be through the theological virtues and prophetic powers of men such as Johann Gottfried von Aschhausen.[76]

The election of Johann Georg II Fuchs von Dornheim brought no immediate change in the administration of the Hochstift. Friedrich Förner continued as the chief advisor to the new bishop.[77] At the same time, we can see a radicalization of reform, arising from both zeal and frustration over the practical limits of Catholic renewal.[78] Reports from the local consistories in 1624 and 1625 would have given little comfort to the new bishop.[79] In Burgkunstadt the burghers were almost all Catholic, but noble subjects living in the parish were mostly Lutheran. In both Burgkunstadt and Altenkunstadt, the Lutherans showed "contempt" for the new calendar and attended Protestant services in Stressendorf.[80] In the village of Triebenreuth, "no more than a fifth" of the parishioners were Catholic. The remainder were Lutherans and subjects of the lords of Wirsberg and Guttenberg. Lutheran preachers could still be found in Mugendorff, Presseck, Lehenthal, and Guttenberg.[81] Some of the reports were contradictory. In his Easter communion registers for 1624, the pastor of Posseck proudly announced that "his parish was completely and entirely Catholic, having no Lutherans any more." That same year the pastor of Wallenfels counted 457 Catholic communicants and only seven Lutherans in his parish.[82] A year later, the archdeacon in Kronach reported that in both parishes the new calendar was not being followed. Some of the residents of Posseck were going to Lutheran services. The pastor of Wallenfels was found to have a library full of heretical books.[83]

In response to these dire reports, Johann Georg II made efforts to tighten discipline. A new synodal statute of 1623 sharpened considerably the sanctions that could be imposed by the local consistories, leading to a wave of denunciations in the 1620s and 1630s.[84] Although the confession and communion mandates from 1623 and 1626 are almost identical in wording to Aschhausen's ordinances, after 1628 we can see a change. Earlier mandates stipulated either fines or jail as punishments; later ones included a provision that all persons who failed to confess at Easter would have to attend the children's catechism classes.[85] Catechism classes also figure prominently in a rather eclectic *Polizeiordnung* from 1624. All children had been required to attend catechism classes since the 1590s, but the ordinance noted that many parents still refused to send their children for instruction.[86] Therefore, pastors were ordered not to conduct weddings for anyone "whether they be men or women, young or old" unless they had been "suitably instructed in the most important articles of the Christian faith." If the bride and groom failed to give the correct answers to the pastor's questions, the wedding would be postponed until they had learned the articles of faith. This also applied to godparents: no one could sponsor a child at baptism who could not pass an examination on the catechism.[87]

The archdeacon of Kronach argued that such measures were of no help. The real problem was the nobility.[88] The registers from the 1620s reveal that the vast majority of those who refused to embrace the Catholic faith lived on noble estates. In the archidiaconate of Hollfeld, 9,693 persons had confessed before Easter 1627. Of 566 persons identified as Lutherans, 525 were subjects of the knights.[89] Preachers remained active in Pressack, Grafengehaig, and Grub, and Johann Georg II had no more success silencing them than had any of his predecessors. In Aisch and Bechhofen, the parishioners claimed to be willing to confess and receive communion in a Catholic fashion, but were prohibited from doing so by the Stieber Vogt. When the new pastor arrived in 1631, he did not find a single Catholic communicant.[90] In October 1624, the bishop had decided to take measures to remove finally the preachers in Presseck, Fischbach, Grafengehaig, Guttenberg, and Rugendorf. He ordered the lords of Guttenberg and Wildenstein to appoint Catholic pastors; when the lords refused, the Castner of Stadtsteinach was ordered to remove the preachers and install Catholic priests. The Wildensteiners responded by stripping the churches of all the plate and furniture. They destroyed grain stores and ordered their subjects to have nothing to do with the new priest. When the bishop complained to Margrave Christian about the activities of the Wildensteiners, Christian was less then sympathetic and claimed that the Johann Georg's actions in Presseck and Grafengehaig constituted "excessive provocation."[91]

Johann Georg's attempts to restore Catholicism in Presseck and Grafengehaig proved merely a foretaste of things to come. In March 1629, Ferdinand II issued the Edict of Restitution, ordering the return to the church of lands secularized since 1552.[92] Johann Georg was named head of the commission to oversee execution of the edict in the Franconian Reichskreis.[93] Friedrich Förner played a leading role in attempting to gain imperial support for his rather ambitious plans to restore Catholicism in Nuremberg, as well as in the Hohenzollern territories and those of the imperial knights. Ultimately all of Förner's plans remained simply that—plans on paper. In the case of the knights, although Ferdinand II was willing to allow the bishops to use whatever means were necessary to remove Protestant preachers, these measures could not be applied to the Reichunmittelbar estates of the imperial knights.[94]

Of the Protestant states in Franconia, it was Nuremberg that most attracted Förner's attention. In 1630 he traveled to Regensburg to plead with Ferdinand II to take a stronger hand against the city.[95] In his private meetings with the emperor, Förner reiterated the positions he had laid out in print a year earlier. In the books *Norimbergae in Flora* and *Relatio Historico-Parenetica*, Förner described how the major churches of the city had been established by Emperor Charles IV. Charles chose Nuremberg as the place to meet with Margrave Ludwig of Brandenburg to secure the imperial regalia. Later, on account of the Hussite threat, Wenceslas and Sigismund had decided to transfer the imperial regalia, in particular the Holy Lance, to Nuremberg for safekeeping.[96] For the next hundred years, all could see "with what zeal for the Catholic religion" the citizens of Nuremberg defended the sacred relics of empire. But then a "rancid, married Augustinian" named Wolfgang Ruprecht had seduced the good people of Nuremberg into the Lutheran apostasy. As a result, the churches and monasteries of the city were taken over by the city, secularized, and profaned.[97]

Förner was quick to point out that the secularization had occurred between 1557 and 1596—after the Peace of Passau, in other words. Ultimately, however, Förner had no interest in legal arguments. The most sacred relics of the empire had been hounded out of Bohemia into Nuremberg by Hussites in the fifteenth century; now they were in the hands of Lutherans and even viler Calvinists. The so-called liberties of the city merely allowed the burghers to foment rebellion in the spirit of their coreligionists in Geneva and the Netherlands. The heretics had driven the republic onto the rocks of sedition and tumult. God Himself demanded that Ferdinand reclaim the relics and restore the fortunes of the church.[98]

In the margraviate, the initial focus of the commission's inquiry was the convent of Himmelkron, which had been secularized after 1541.[99] But ultimately the commission pushed the matter further. According to Johann Georg, the Religious Peace of Augsburg only applied to states that had maintained the religion of the Augsburg Confession as it had been presented to Charles V in 1530. This ensured that no Calvinist princes could claim protection under the peace. Johann Georg also interpreted the wording of the Edict of Restitution to mean that any state that had accepted the Interim of 1548 was likewise not under the protection of the religious peace. States that had accepted the Interim had, *de facto* and *de jure*, returned to the Catholic fold. Any attempt to restore Protestantism in any form after 1552 constituted a violation of the religious peace.[100] If the church in the Oberland had returned to the old faith in 1548, then potentially all church lands might be returned to the Catholic church.[101]

Margrave Christian ordered a search of archives and records in order to determine precisely what had happened in 1548. Eventually the superintendent of Wunsiedel reported that he had found the required documentation.

The collected documents recorded the resistance of the clergy to Albrecht Alcibiades in November 1548 and the resulting decision of the estates rejecting the Interim. There could be no doubt: the clergy, nobles, and towns of the Oberland had refused to accept the Interim of Augsburg. Consequently, the margrave could proclaim that "in this land and principality from 1531 until now, for nearly one hundred years a single Church Order has been followed."[102]

The officials in the margraviate published their findings at the beginning of June 1630. The timing appears to have been carefully calculated: exactly one hundred years had passed since that Saturday in June 1530 when the Lutherans presented their confession to Charles V in Augsburg. A few weeks after the findings were published, Margrave Christian invited several leading Lutheran princes to Selb for a hunt. Between chases, the princes sought to plan a strategy to block execution of the edict, hoping that the emperor could be persuaded to abandon his chosen course.[103] They presented their grievances to the emperor at Regensburg in September 1630. Among other things, the Protestants argued that 1620, rather than 1552, should be established as the base year for determining the status of ecclesiastical estates. They were particularly outspoken about monastic estates. Since the "authority to alter religion" rested on "the *iurisdictionem territorialem*," it was not right that monasteries lying within a Lutheran *territorio* should be under the authority of a Catholic ruler. That would amount to the introduction of one religion into another's state, contrary to the terms of the religious peace.[104]

The Catholic Electors were not convinced by the Protestant arguments.[105] Friedrich Förner and others—most notably William Lamormaini and Adam Contzen—maintained that the emperor should be unwilling to make even the most minor concessions to the heretics. Lamormaini advised the emperor not to fear "the giants, the sons of Enoch, or the Goliaths." Rather, "with God's aid we will devour them."[106] Förner compares the "Luthero-Calvinists" with the biblical plagues, describing them as "vermin, vomit, lice, and even locusts" who must be "exterminated and annihilated root and branch."[107] Not all Catholics agreed with this sort of rhetoric, dismissing both the Old Testament language and apocalyptic tone. Following the Thomist position, they argued that prudence and reason were better guides in this context. Compromise was not only permissible but would be more effective in the long run. But although even some Catholic princes opposed strict execution of the edict, Ferdinand would not relent. Although he did agree to allow for further discussion of the implementation of the edict, he refused to negotiate on its substance.[108]

On July 4, 1630, only a few weeks after the meeting in Selb and two weeks into the Regensburg Conference, Gustavus Adolphus of Sweden landed in Germany. His arrival did not immediately have much impact on the political or confessional climate in Franconia. Förner remained in Regensburg until the middle of November, pushing for full execution of the Edict of Restitution.[109] The Catholic Electors remained confident that even as the military threat to the empire had increased, it might yet be possible to come to terms with the Protestants. To that end, a conference was to be held in Frankfurt to seek some agreement on the enforcement of the Edict.[110]

Shortly after the Frankfurt conference was announced, the pope admonished the German bishops to make no concessions to the Protestants.[111] That was also the charge given to Dr. Anton Winter, Friedrich Förner's replacement as Bamberg's representative in Frankfurt. To the main Protestant argument–that the restitution of monastic estates constituted a violation of territorial sovereignty–Winter offered a novel counterargument. The terms used in the Religious Peace–"*Landsobrigkeit*" and "*regium ius territorii*"–were not customary in Franconia. In Franconia, there was no such thing as territorial sovereignty, but rather six distinct forms of lordship. There was the *ius diocesanum,* the rights held by the bishops from the emperors that ensured that "so far as the see's land and estates are concerned, they cannot be subject to any other lordship." Second was criminal jurisdiction–*Zent*–held by nobles over their estates. Third was *Vogtei,* or "civil authority," including the right to taxation and matters of *Polizei.* Fourth was authority over forests, hunting rights, and rights of passage (*Geleit*). Fifth was feudal authority, the right to grant and receive fiefs. Sixth and last was lordship over towns and villages.[112]

Winter argued that, with the exception of the *ius diocesanum,* none of these forms of lordship carried with them the right to alter religion. Clearly "chasing deer and boars has nothing to do with religion." Lordship over towns and villages was a confused mess, since the residents of any given community could be subject to any number of different lords. It was generally recognized that Vogtei represented princely authority, whereas Zent represented the authority of local landlords. Consequently,

> if one follows the law, then one ought to acknowledge the superiority of the Prince over the Zent or Fraisch: "who judges me, that is my lord." And therefore all of the Imperial Hochstift Bamberg's vassals, servants, and subjects are specifically exempt from all other imperial or princely courts.[113]

Winter explained that according to this standard, the bishop of Bamberg held Vogtei over any of the subjects of his vassals. As an example he cited the abbots of Langheim, noting that insofar as the abbot was a vassal of the bishop, any estates belonging to the monastery, even if they lay within the borders of the margraviate, were under the civil jurisdiction of the bishop as suzerain and supreme Vogt.[114]

For Winter, there was only lordship over communities, defined in terms of a hierarchy of rights and privileges, all of which derived from the emperor as supreme suzerain. Of course, his claim that one could have supreme authority without holding criminal jurisdiction was absurd, but it did not diminish his central proposition. Although the Hohenzollerns had gained more rights and added more hundreds to their estates, their landholdings remained distinct legal entities. The margraviate was not a territory, but an assemblage of local jurisdictions—*Ortschaften*—over which the margraves held limited rights as landlords rather than as princes.[115] To some degree, this was essentially the argument that the estates in the Oberland had raised in their protest against Margrave Christian. Reinel's perception of the Reformation as a local event found an echo in the claims of the estates to ownership of the Reformation: it was not the prince who determined the confession of his subjects, but rather the prince who had to accept the confession agreed on by the estates, here representing those various local jurisdictions. Of course, Winter had something very different in mind when he presented his interpretation of the *Ortliche Prinzip*. With this bizarre argument, Winter was, in effect, suggesting that territorial state did not exist.[116] From his perspective, the central question of the confessional era—*cuius regio?*—was moot.

Winter put his argument on paper on September 1, 1631. The Swedish victory at Breitenfeld fifteen days later effectively ended the discussion. Within two weeks of the defeat of the Imperial Army under the command of Count Tilly, remnants of the defeated Catholic armies began entering the Hochstift on their retreat south. By the first week of November, it became clear that nothing could be done to prevent the Swedes from occupying the Hochstift. Everywhere troops were in flight, and government collapsed. Visitations ceased as priests and ecclesiastical officials fled.[117] Johann Georg sought aid from Count Tilly and Maximilian of Bavaria, but neither were willing to offer much help. The bishop then turned to Christian, hoping that the margrave would be able to convince his nephew Gustavus Adolphus to spare the Hochstift.[118] Ultimately, however, Johann Georg's missives were a case of too little, too late. With the collapse of the regime, a wave of reaction against the bishop's policies swept across the Hochstift. As the Swedes approached, the imperial knights rose to greet them, offering their services to the Swedish king and voting him a generous subsidy.[119] Swedish troops, accompanied by local nobles, began raiding the center of the Hochstift in early January 1632, the main body of the Protestant forces trailing not far behind. On February 10, Bishop Johann Georg II abandoned the Hochstift. The next day the Swedish army entered Bamberg.[120]

Chapter 10

THE STOOL OF WICKEDNESS

When the Swedes entered Bamberg in February, 1632, they encountered a scene of horror. For two decades the Hochstift had been the scene of one of the most ferocious witch-hunts in history, one that claimed perhaps as many as a thousand lives.[1] Our treatment of the witch-hunts in Bamberg must here be brief, but at the outset several points of clarification are in order. The phenomenon of witchcraft per se is not our concern here. Few of those accused seem to have had any genuine interest in the magical arts. The records in Bamberg reveal very little about any sort of "magic folk culture" other than the widespread assumption among people at all levels of society that there was such a thing as magic and that it could be efficacious. The trials were largely the product of a system of inquisitorial justice, in which the indiscriminate use of torture and unquestioned acceptance of denunciations obtained on the rack and in the lye bath drove the process forward. Our concern here will be with the ideological and institutional implications of the trials and what the "witch-craze" in upper Franconia can tell us about the larger questions of reformation and the development of the state.[2]

In his survey of the witch trials in southeastern Germany, Wolfgang Behringer noted certain patterns that seem common to the region.[3] The major trials occurred within a very narrow time frame, lasting from roughly 1560 to 1630. Within that period, trials remained rare and episodic, coinciding with short-term agrarian crises. The intensity of persecution seems to follow the price curve, but here we should be cautious.[4] Economic causes were not enough; witch-hunting only occurred under "extraordinary circumstances."[5] One thing that was required was an agreement between the authorities and their subjects. Only with at least the tacit consent of the state could the trials move forward to their conclusion. The trials also assumed an increasingly ideological dimension, especially after 1600, when the polarization of Catholics and Protestants was accompanied by an increasingly aggressive denunciation of witchcraft. Behringer characterizes the conflict between the opponents of witch-hunting and the persecuting authorities as one of "common sense" and "reason of state" versus "ideology."[6] The ideology was a byproduct of the "new piety," which stressed the responsibility of both the state authorities and individuals for the spiritual and temporal well-being of the state. God would punish a sinful people with his wrath; to prevent this, both the state and the individual were obligated to find and punish all that was offensive to God.[7] Behringer describes a "hardening" of mental attitudes in the wake of the late-sixteenth-century political and economic crisis. With the onset of a short-term agrarian crisis, pessimistic attitudes combined with apocalyptic sentiments to produce "national panic," leading to persecution.[8] But here again, the conjuncture of political, ideological, and economic factors was insufficient to cause the persecutions. A strong personality on the order of a James VI and I, a Maximilian of Bavaria, or a Julius Echter was required. The classic "ideologues of witch persecution" were above all "intransigent champions of internal and external religious reform." And the first name to appear Behringer's list of archetypal ideologues is one that should by now be familiar: Friedrich Förner.[9]

Much of Behringer's characterization of the trials may be applied to Bamberg. But questions remain, particularly about the specific aspects of the "new piety" that led to witch-hunting. We need not accept the cynical view that "the witch-hunt was the pursuit of ideological crime in the process of legitimizing new regimes."[10] In her recent book *Witch-Craze*, Lyndal Roper links the belief in malevolent witchcraft and the persecutions to the premodern demographic regime.[11] Witches represented an inversion of natural fertility—they engaged in lascivious sex with the devil, but "their sexual congress was barren." They haunted the birthing room; they caused men to be impotent and women to be sterile; they were old and infertile women "who heartlessly murder[ed] little children, babies and pregnant women." They also killed livestock and destroyed crops. Witches attacked life on all fronts, threatening the fecundity of people, beasts, and the earth itself.[12] Such beliefs created fear but on their own were insufficient to produce persecution. Here the authorities played a key role. As we have seen, the confessional state took great pains to control and regulate marriage. Sex outside of marriage was punished, sometimes with extreme penalties, as shown by the fate of Apollonia Crato. The aim of the authorities was to create a godly society. That end could only be accomplished through the imposition of a godly mode of reproduction, one that would ensure not only the survival of the species but also the perpetuation of the social order. In this light, the persecution of witches takes on a particular meaning: it marks the conjuncture of popular fears with the aims of social discipline and the organization of reproduction. But this conjuncture could only last so long as the older demographic regime remained in force and so long as the state saw organizing reproduction as one of its tasks. By the eighteenth century, both conditions had ceased to exist. Thereafter, tales of witches became the subject of nursery rhymes rather than of the courtroom.[13]

Roper's approach has much to recommend it, but can it be applied to the trials in upper Franconia? In some ways, the events preceding the witch-hunts do seem to conform to image she describes. From the 1570s onward, authorities in the Hochstift and the Oberland had made extensive efforts to regulate marriage. In Bamberg, these efforts intensified in the 1620s, just before the beginning of the last, most violent wave of witch-hunts. It would also seem significant that on the eve of the witch-hunts, the bishops undertook a campaign to eradicate concubinage. The second wave of trials in Bamberg began with an accusation of infanticide. But ultimately too many exceptions arise. As we have noted, the prosecution of adulterers and fornicators was a spotty affair; punishments rarely rose to the levels prescribed by law. In any event, prosecution remained haphazard, in part on account of conflicts within the regime.[14] The witch trials themselves do at times reveal concerns with reproduction, but rarely is that the central issue.[15] Details that Roper would read as symbols of fertility can also be read in other ways. The discourse on witchcraft in Bamberg in particular bears striking resemblance to the mid- to late-sixteenth-century discourse on heresy.[16] What seems to have attracted the attention of authorities initially was fortune-telling and divination. In the Habsburg lands, divination, prophecy, and rebellion were closely linked.[17] In Bamberg, the witch-hunts coincided with the most aggressive phase of the Counter-Reformation and the outbreak of the Thirty Years' War. Social and political unrest, rather than reproduction, figures most prominently in the sources on witchcraft from Bamberg.

The first witch trials in upper Franconia occurred in the Hohenzollern Oberland. In 1563, a single execution was carried out in Bayreuth.[18] Six years later there was a "cry" (Geschrei) out of Creussen concerning Katharina, the wife of Bastien Höfer, schoolmaster and sexton in Birk.[19] According to the pastor of Birk, Katharina used a crystal to tell fortunes. She also was able to cure sick cattle by having them drink out of a hollowed-out skull.[20] Although she confessed to assorted dealings with the devil, Katharina late retracted her confession, claiming that it was only on account of torture that she had said such things.[21] Ultimately, she was sentenced to do penance, with the warning that if she returned to her earlier practices she faced exile.[22] In 1587, Barbara von Lichtenstein, her maid Margaretha Höflein, and Else Vischer—known as "Bath Els"—were arrested on charges of sorcery. The charges derived from Höflein's use of coffin nails as talismans against theft and to find lost objects.[23] In 1595, Regina Streitberger of Kulmbach was arrested for theft and sorcery.[24] In 1603 Margaretha Vießmann was investigated for using a crystal to tell fortunes. The last case pointed back to an earlier series of accusations concerning a wisewoman (or two wisewomen) in Baiersgrün who attracted visitors from a number of towns and villages along the western edge of the Oberland. Vießmann supposedly was given the crystal by her aunt, who had received it directly from the wise-woman of Baiersgrün.[25]

The famous soothsayer, such as the woman (or women) of Baiersgrün, is a familiar character in the annals of witchcraft. After a cattle plague in 1602, the Stadtvogt in Kulmbach complained about the prevalence of witches in his Amt. In particular, he heaped scorn on a certain "Vettel" in Kupferberg, reporting that people flocked to have her "bewitch" judges into giving favorable decisions.[26] The villages mentioned in these accounts lay on the border of the Hochstift Bamberg and the Oberland—precisely the same region that in the 1560s had harbored preachers. Given the supposed notoriety of the witches in Baiersgrün and Kupferberg, we might expect that firm action was taken against them. In fact it was not. Even at the peak of the Bamberg witch-hunts, no one from Kupferberg was arrested.[27] Likewise, despite their supposed notoriety, the alleged witches of Baiersgrün were able to practice their art unmolested.

The circumstances surrounding the handful of trials in the Oberland indicate several general characteristics of witch-hunting in the later sixteenth and seventeenth centuries. The earliest trials coincided with the first wave of witch-hunts in southern Germany in the 1560s. Heightened concern over witchcraft is manifest not only in the interrogation of Katharina Höfer, but also in the investigation surrounding complaints against Simon Günther in Neudrossenfeld.[28] Although Günther tried to deny it, he did have an interest in alchemy. This interest, combined with the references to demonic possession in his sermons, set off alarms among his parishioners and the officials in Kulmbach. It has been noted that the printing press and the pulpit were essential for the dissemination of the theory of demonic witchcraft in sixteenth-century Germany.[29] In Günther's case we can see both: he drew examples from printed *Hexenzeitungen* and used these in his sermons.

The first trials also coincided with the establishment of regular visitations and the consistory in the Oberland. Communities were expected to oversee matters of *Polizei* and report on the actions of parishioners and, if need be, pastors, should their actions appear serious enough to warrant an official inquiry. The *Geschrei* in Creussen and the other cases had their origins in the complaints of either village officials or the rector. Here, though, note the distinction between the Oberland and the Niederland. In the former, the consistory was far less concerned with witchcraft than with other irregularities, in particular Calvinism. In the Niederland, witch trials were conducted on a fairly large scale in the 1590s. Two factors led to the persecution: proximity to states that advocated witch-hunts and the presence on the governing council of a passionate and vocal supporter of trials—Adam Francisci, the titular abbot of Heilsbronn. The importance of foreign influence was obvious. The "General Instructions Concerning Witches," the code governing the trials, was based on a set of instructions prepared in the Bavarian district of Landshut.[30] The judges were nearly all foreigners, summoned from Oettingen and Eichstätt. The presence of Catholic inquisitors unquestionably soured many officials on the whole business. In 1591, the town council of Ansbach refused to recognize the decision of a judge from Oettingen.[31]

In the Oberland, no singular advocate for witch-hunting emerged. Although Ansbach and Kulmbach were both ruled by the same prince, each had its own governing council. Since Prussia remained the primary focus of Georg Friedrich's energies, each Land was pretty much left to its own devices. Officials in the Oberland viewed witch-hunting as a peculiarly Catholic practice, one they had no wish to emulate. Despite the tocsin raised by such local officials as the Oberschultheiss of Kulmbach, the council would not call in the foreign "specialists" whose presence proved essential to the expansion of trials in the Niederland. Although the foundational institutions and attitudes were present, the officials in Kulmbach were unprepared to move to the next step.[32] After 1563, no witches were burned in the Oberland.[33] Ultimately, Bamberg alone would see the expansion of witch trials to truly horrific proportion.

∽

Bamberg remained largely untouched by the wave of witch trials that swept across southern Germany in the 1590s. There are records for four trials during the reign of Neithard von Thüngen. Kunigund Weissin was arrested and examined on the charge of witchcraft sometime before 1595, but the circumstances surrounding the case are obscure.[34] Margarethe Pemmerin (Böhmerin) was charged with witchcraft in 1595. In the course of her examination she admitted to having sexual relations with the devil over a period of some ten years. Margarethe was sentenced to be burned at the stake, but Bishop Neithard allowed her to be executed by the sword.[35] In 1598, two women were prosecuted for harmful magic in Erbesbühl and Neufang.[36] In neither of these cases does it appear that the accused were condemned.

Only one witch trial is known for the reign of Johann Philipp von Gebsattel. In August 1601, a diarymaid named Anna Böhmerin was examined by secular authorities on the charge of putting mouse feces in butter and bread in order to poison one of her patrons. A few days later she was released.[37] Other signs, however, point to increased concern over demonic activity in the Hochstift. In 1607, a new mandate against swearing forbade the use of the devil's name in curses, listing several that were deemed particularly odious. Some of the offending phrases included "the devil take you," "the devil take you in body and soul," "may a thousand devils take you," and "thanks to the devil." In order to stress the seriousness of the matter, the mandate included two cautionary tales. In Eggolsheim, a man swore at cards that if he could win, "in body and soul he would be the devil's own." Shortly thereafter, the "evil spirit made himself visible in the form of an unknown tall black man." The figure recalled the man's vow and began to beat him. The injured man was brought to the rectory, where the priest attempted to convince him to confess his sin. Before the victim could do so, a loud noise caused the priest to leave the room. At that point the black man returned and thrust a rusty knife into his victim's neck. He died three days later without being able to confess. In another case, a young man said to his father, "The devil take you." Immediately he was seized by an evil spirit who made him murder his father. The ordinance made it clear that even casual use of the devil's name was sufficient to conjure evil spirits, including the devil himself.[38]

It was under Johann Gottfried von Aschhausen that witch-hunting began in earnest. In 1610 a new ordinance concerning witchcraft was issued. According to the mandate "certain sorcerers and so-called fortune-tellers" were active in the Hochstift, contrary to the decrees of almighty God and the laws of the empire. As a result, the "anger and vengeance of the Almighty" weighed heavily on the land, leading to all manner of discord. In order to ensure the "maintenance of the common good and the propagation of Christian life and manners," secular officials were ordered to begin a careful investigation of the territory. Anyone those found practicing "forbidden arts, fortune-telling, or whatever it may be called" would be "severely punished."[39]

The visitation of 1611 revealed a wide range of "horrendous blasphemies," including fortune-telling and spell casting.[40] "Sages and fortune-tellers" were found in twelve of twenty-two parishes in the archidiaconate of Kronach, although the visitation reports are a little vague on details.[41] In Altenkunstadt, Burgkunstadt, Kupferberg, Zeyern, Wallenfels, and Nordhalm, magicians and sages were found in abundance; in other towns, the visitors noted that there were "not a few" fortune-tellers. A pagan shrine, popularly known as the "Old School Temple," supposedly attracted visitors from Nordhalm, where all sorts of prohibited "morbid incantations" were held.[42] A visitation in 1617 likewise reported the existence of a magic mountain near Stadtsteinach.[43] In several villages, parishioners sought to have water and salt blessed by the priest as a means of warding off spells and "demonic infestation."[44] But despite the parishioners' concerns, diocesan officials could discover the name of only one magician, Johannes Zipfel, a blacksmith in Posseck.[45] In other places, reports of magicians appeared to have been little more than rumors.[46]

The visitation of 1611 failed to produce enough evidence of witchcraft to warrant any serious investigation. Then, on September 27, 1612, officials in Kronach informed the Privy Council that they had arrested Lena Panzerin, an elderly widow, who had been accused of witchcraft by her daughter and son-in-law. Pantzerin had allegedly tried to poison her son-in-law by serving him soup with three spiders in it.[47] Other accusations followed. Wolf Hübner claimed that Pantzerin had made him ill because she believed he had stolen some plums from her. Pantzerin, it appears, was well known for her magical cures, in particular for charms intended to protect people from thieves or secure the return of lost or stolen objects.[48]

A special commissioner, Dr. Steiner, was sent out to conduct the inquiry, assisted by the Hauptmann of Kronach. No one seemed to know how to examine a witch, so the commissioners sent to Coburg for assistance. A master named Trill was brought in to interrogate the witnesses. His initial efforts to extract a confession failed, so Steiner called in another torture master, Ott Heinrich Wahl from Meiningen.[49] Pantzerin eventually identified four other people as witches: Sibilla Schmidin, Anna Krauch, Jakob Krauch, and Kunigund Schrepferin. Following her last torture session, the officials noted that Pantzerin was extremely weak. She died in early December 1612 and her body was subsequently burned.[50]

Sibilla Schmidin and Kunigund Schrepferin were examined by the Scharfrichter from Bamberg not long after Lena Pantzerin's death. Schmidin had been Pantzerin's neighbor for more than thirty-seven years and was also known as a practitioner of magic. She confessed that her devil provided her with an enchanted butter churn that she used to milk several cows to death. Schmidin had also taken the consecrated host to make grease for the pitchfork she used to ride to the witches' dance. Schmidin gave the names of four other witches, including old Pantzerin, Pantzerin's daughter, Anna Krauch, and Jakob Krauch.[51] Schrepferin, a widow from Steinwiesen, admitted to having engaged in "*Unzucht*" with the devil. She too had a magic churn and had stolen milk from several people in town. She had also made one woman lame and two others sick.[52] Both women were executed on February 17, 1613. In contrast with later victims, both were allowed to confess and receive communion before the sentence was carried out.[53]

By now, the investigations had yielded the names of nine other alleged witches, six from Kronach and three from Steinwiesen. By the end of January 1613, all were in custody. Although the houses of several suspects had been searched for incriminating evidence, no pitchforks, salves, or herbs could be found.[54] The suspects in Steinwiesen included Anna Helgothin, her daughter Margarethe (known as Maigel), and her daughter-in-law Katharina Helgothin. Like the others, Anna admitted to stealing milk and desecrating the host. Under torture, she accused fourteen others of witchcraft.[55] Maigel was also tortured but steadfastly denied being a witch. Rather, she blamed everything on Hans Schnabrich. Schnabrich was something of a ne'er-do-well who had fathered an illegitimate child on Maigel years before. Maigel claimed that Schnabrich had introduced her to his devil and tried to get her involved in witchcraft. Although she initially admitted to stealing milk and desecrating the host, Maigel recanted and was eventually released.[56] Katharina Helgothin was likewise released following a fairly brief examination. Schnabrich was not so lucky. He appears at the center of most of the tales told by the women of the Helgoth family and became the special focus of the inquisition in Steinwiesen. On April 24, 1613, Schnabrich and Anna Helgothin were both burned at the stake.[57] The last offering of this first wave of trials was Anna Krauch of Kronach, executed on June 10, 1613.[58]

The trials in Kronach and Steinwiesen reveal several patterns. Neither town was mentioned in the 1611 visitation as harboring sages, fortune-tellers, or anyone else practicing prohibited arts.[59] This seems rather striking given the fact that three of the primary victims—Lena Pantzerin, Sibilla Schmidin, and Kunigund Schrepferin—were supposedly well known for their skills. At the same time, both communities were considered of wavering orthodoxy, in particular Steinwiesen. Anna Helgothin stated that she would remove the host from her mouth before drinking from the chalice, indicating that she received communion *sub utraque species*.[60] The most significant issue appears to have been kinship. The investigations were largely restricted to the members of three families, the Pantzerins, the Krauchs (including Sibilla Schmidin), and, in Steinwiesen, the Helgoths (including Schnabrich). In the latter case, although Anna Helgothin named fourteen others as suspects, the only name of interest to the officials was that of Hans Schnabrich. Schnabrich quickly emerged as the central figure in the investigation, and with his death, the trials in Steinwiesen came to an end.[61]

For three years after the execution of Anna Krauch, there are no records of any witch trials.[62] Then, in January 1616, a series of witch-hunts began in Ellwangen. The panic quickly spread to the dioceses of Würzburg, Eichstätt, and Bamberg, as well as to the Electorate of Mainz.[63] Johann Langhans, Ratsbürger in Zeil, noted in his diary that the summers of 1615 and 1616 had been marked by serious drought. In addition, there had been hard freezes in both years, damaging the wine crop. Langhans reported on June 22, 1616 that several people in Zeil had been stricken with fever. Two days later, Elizabeth Buckel was arrested. On November 26, nine women from Zell were burned in Zeil, the first mass burning in the Hochstift. Elizabeth Buckel remained in captivity until June 1617, when she too went to the stake.[64]

In Bamberg, the first arrest came in July 1616. Dorothea Böhmerin, possibly the daughter of the woman executed in 1595, was taken into custody.[65] Shortly thereafter, a special commission was assembled.[66] In August, three women were arrested. Katharine Rüglein (Reubler), Magareth Schmidtin, and her serving girl, Gertraud Bicklin, were charged with infanticide and witchcraft.[67] Schmidtin named a further woman, known only as Seilerin, who was pregnant. The officials in Bamberg thought it best simply to keep her under house arrest, but Johann Gottfried von Aschhausen, writing from Julius Echter's deathbed in Würzburg, disagreed. According to his reasoning, "the foetus would suffer more outside (the prison) than within."[68] Bicklin, Riglein, and Schmidtin all confessed to being witches under torture and were condemned to death. Bicklin was convicted not only of practicing witchcraft but of "murdering her own flesh and blood." For the crime of infanticide she was sentenced to be burned alive after being pinched with white-hot tongs.[69] In the end, the bishop allowed her to be strangled before being burned. Both Schmidtin and Riglein were beheaded.[70] The witch-hunt of 1616 also yielded a young boy from Zell who was turned over to the Jesuits and, following an exorcism, put into a trade.[71]

The scope of the trials increased dramatically in 1617. By the end of 1619, some 155 people were charged with witchcraft. At least ninety-six went to the stake or died in prison.[72] These figures may be low: according to the yearbook of the Jesuit College in Bamberg, in 1617 alone 102 persons were executed.[73]

The expansion of the trials has been linked to the influence of Friedrich Förner. In addition to his role as senior administrator in the diocese, Förner was a noted demonologist. In 1602 he published an account of his encounter with a demon in Kronach, renowned for only attacking Protestants, Calvinists especially.[74] Förner's most famous and influential work was *Panoplia Armaturae Dei,* a collection of thirty-five sermons published in 1626.[75] *Panoplia* draws on a wide range of authorities, including Peter Binsfeld, Nicolas Rémy, Jean Bodin, Justus Lipsius, and, above all, Martin Del Rio. Förner was also clearly influenced by key figures in Bavaria, in particular Adam Contzen, Gregory of Valentia, and Andreas Fachinieus.[76] Förner also cites examples from the trials held in Bamberg between 1616 and 1619. In his collection of this mass of data, Förner was determined to provide the people of Bamberg with "spiritual medicine" against the demonic threat by giving them a comprehensive theory of witchcraft.[77]

Friedrich Förner praised Johann Gottfried von Aschhausen for his great zeal in rooting out devil worship.[78] In truth, Johann Gottfried remained somewhat dubious about the whole endeavor. The trials were stepped up only after his departure for Würzburg in 1616. In Bamberg, the witch-hunt of 1616–19 had no shortage of critics. At the very outset, the cathedral chapter disputed the right of episcopal officials to prosecute suspected witches in the immunities in Bamberg.[79] Later on, officials in Zeil, Hallstadt, and Staffelstein complained that the costs of the trials had become unbearable. The Malefizkommission (Witchcraft Commission) in each town was sorely understaffed, and officers of the court complained of long hours and fatigue.[80] Conrad Örter, an innkeeper and the mayor of Zeil, demanded that the court reimburse him for the cost of feeding and housing suspects and officials.[81]

By 1619 an opposition party had formed in the princely Hofrat. The provost of the cathedral chapter, Johann Christoph Neustetter-Stürmer, and the cathedral dean, Hektor von Kotzau, were both outspoken opponents of witch-hunting.[82] The soul of the opposition was the chancellor, Dr. Georg Haan, a close associate of Johann Philipp von Gebsattel and Johann Schöner and leader of the moderates in the council. Under his leadership, the opposition party was able to bring the trials to an end. The main argument was financial: with the outbreak of war in neighboring Bohemia, the prince could ill afford the luxury of chasing phantoms.[83]

The election of Johann Georg II Fuchs von Dornheim effectively removed opposition to witch-hunting. After a few isolated trials in the years 1623 and 1625, mass trials resumed in 1626. The immediate cause of the new wave of denunciations was a terrible freeze that destroyed the wine crop.[84] Zeil, within the diocese of Würzburg but under the secular authority of the bishops of Bamberg, was the center of the trials. By the end of the year, fifty-nine persons in Zeil had been charged with witchcraft, of whom at least thirty-nine were burned or died in prison. In 1627, 130 persons were called before the court. In 1628, the trials spread to the city of Bamberg. Altogether, from the accession of Johann Georg II until 1631, no fewer than 642 individuals were brought to trial for witchcraft. Forty-five were either released or able to escape. The rest—nearly six hundred people—went to their deaths.[85]

Who were the victims? During the second wave of trials, between 1616 and 1622, women made up 81.1 percent of the victims. Likewise, women made up 72.7 percent of those brought to trial from 1623 to 1631.[86] These figures are broadly comparable with those for other parts of Germany. At the same time, closer examination of the evidence shows that few victims fit the stereotype of the witch as old and poor. In Zeil, the epicenter of the trials in the 1620s, the number of elderly women sent to the scaffold was remarkably small—seven. Only two of the victims were identified as "wisewomen."[87] The vast majority of the women brought to trial were either married or single but of marriageable age. The number of spinsters and widows is negligible. Of some three hundred women whose ages can be accurately gauged, the average was 33.5 years. In other words, women of childbearing age, not barren crones, were the most likely targets of persecution.

Examination of cases where several family members were executed suggests that the reason female witches outnumber male witches two to one is not that women were the special focus of the trials. In a number of cases, we can see a pattern in which the father was executed along with his wife and daughter. The episcopal chancellor Georg Haan was arrested and tried for witchcraft following the conviction and execution of his wife and an unmarried daughter. The chancellor was under suspicion, in no small measure because he had petitioned the Reichskammergericht to intervene on the side of certain "injured" (*beschuldigten*) women in Bamberg. Haan's wife and daughter were arrested and burned while he was in Speyer. Ultimately, the execution of his wife and daughter proved necessary steps to convince others of his guilt. The condemnation of his son, daughter, and daughter-in-law followed after they protested the treatment of their parents. In other words, the various members of the Haan family—in particular the women—were burned principally on account of their relationship to the chancellor.[88]

Perhaps the most extreme example of guilt by heredity is provided by the leading families in Zeil. The Ratsherr Conrad Merklein and the Bürgermeister Conrad Örter of Zeil were both executed on November 10, 1626. Within two months, Örter's wife, Ottilia, and his daughter Katharina had also been arrested. On April 9, 1627 Christina Morhaupt, née Merklein, was arrested for witchcraft. Four days later, her sister Anna Han, wife of the Schultheiß of Steinbach, and her brother Hans Merklein, husband of Kunigunt Örter and son-in-law of Conrad Örter, were taken into custody. Anna was executed on May 10; later that same day her brother Paulus was arrested. Paulus went to the stake in June; his sister Christina Morhaupt followed him six weeks later. Both of Christina's sons were arrested along with two serving girls from her house in Bamberg. The younger son was about ten; the eldest, Hans, was fourteen when he was arrested. Hans claimed that he had been seduced into witchcraft by one of the serving girls who was Lucifer and a succubus. Not long after his fifteenth birthday, he too was burned.[89] The fates of the younger son and the two serving girls, along with that of Hans Merklein, are unknown. By 1629, all three families—the Örters, the Merkleins, and the Morhaupts—had been almost completely exterminated.[90]

Beyond kinship, victims were often neighbors. Along the Lange Gasse in Bamberg, seventeen households, including those of the Morhaupts and Haans, were affected by the trials.[91] The Lange Gasse was no peasants' lane. It was the main street through the center of Bamberg, housing many of the city's most prominent residents. This points to an additional pattern that becomes evident during the last wave of trials. A central theme in complaints against the witch-hunts was that the authorities resorted to practices that were violent and had no foundation in either imperial or territorial law, and that they paid no attention to social status or merit. The latter tendency— so it seemed to contemporaries—led to the persecution of "good people."[92]

The leading citizens of Zeil suffered mightily at the hands of the Malifizkommission. Three of seven members of the town council, both Bürgermeister and three of six Viertelmeister were burned. At least twenty other relatives of members of the town council were condemned. On February 27, 1627 the Malifizkommission found before it seven women, all of whom were either wives, daughters, or sisters of members of the town council. All were executed. Even the judges were not safe—the wives of two members of the Malifizkommission were arrested in 1627. Dorothea Schäll was executed, even though her husband was the chief financial officer of the Malifizkommission. The Schultheiß of Ziegelanger, along with the wives of the Schultheißen in Steinbach and Schmachtenberg, were also executed. In all, perhaps as many as half the victims in Zeil were either local officials or their relatives.[93]

In *Panoplia Armaturae Dei,* Förner declared that it is a known fact that witches are impotent against divinely ordained magistrates. "Experience shows" that witches are unable to use their powers either to escape or to confuse their captors.[94] So why were so many officials in Bamberg and Zeil accused of witchcraft? Most of the officials who were executed were opponents of the trials who, like Georg Haan, had dared to speak out. This august company included the mayors of Bamberg and Zeil as well as Georg Eder, the son of a prominent Catholic reformer at the Habsburg court.[95] Eder could not fathom how a dedicated supporter of the Counter-Reformation could be accused of witchcraft. From Förner's perspective, however, this may not have been surprising at all. In their opposition to the trials, the officials were aiding the devil in his work. Officials who did not persecute witches effectively demonstrated that they had not been given their power "by God."

The belief that officials who opposed the trials were themselves witches was widely held. It formed the basis for the accusations against the episcopal chancellor and his family. Haan's trial went forward without any denunciations; he was indicted for sorcery solely on the basis of his dissent. This idea appears as well in an anonymous dialogue found under the door of a chancery official in Bamberg in September 1629. In the dialogue, two laborers express their concern over the number of witches in the town of Forchheim. When one wonders why the bishop has yet to take action, his companion replies, "[M]any folk say that the bishop just doesn't have the heart to fight with the Ratsherrn. . . . [I]n all of Forchheim there are only two honorable officials, the rest are all witches." The dialogue ended with a plea to the bishop to act immediately lest Forchheim be destroyed like Sodom and Gomorrah. It claimed that the city government was a "sin and a scandal"; the council chamber was filled with "witches, thieves, and scoundrels." Meanwhile, little children learned sorcery on the street.[96]

If Friedrich Förner did not inspire the dialogue, it is certainly consistent with his views. While discussing the origins of witchcraft, Förner noted that man's disobedience was the source of sin, idolatry, and witchcraft.[97] Conversely, obedience to the divine Will was the source of faith, true religion, and order. In the historical struggle between God and the devil, the latter preyed on man's natural disobedience to offer up a range of false gods and doctrines. These had proceeded in a sequence from the days of the pharaohs down to the present. Each false religion had failed, but the devil always responded by raising another, more dangerous heresy or superstition.[98] The closer one drew to the final defeat of the devil, the more violent the means the devil resorted to. In recent times, the devil had brought forth Calvinism, leading to the revolt in Bohemia and the outbreak of the Thirty Years' War.

And whereas Calvinists attacked the *Respublica* from the outside, the devil had raised up witches to destroy it from within.[99] According to Förner, one should have expected to find more witches in Catholic territories than in Protestant states: the devil did not need to use force against those who willingly embraced his lies. It seemed noteworthy that more witches had been tried and executed after the military defeat of the Protestants. The devil was clearly losing, and his resort to this sort of terror was a sign of desperation. For Förner, the presence of witches was to be taken as a sign of the success of the Counter-Reformation.[100]

Despite Förner's contention that the trials be taken as a positive sign, by 1627 concerns were mounting over the nature of the witch-hunts. Complaints about innocent people being condemned for witchcraft began to flow into both the episcopal and imperial courts. In July 1627, Johann Georg II issued a mandate against "dangerous and evil people, who either out of envy and hatred, or on account of an evil disposition . . . shamelessly accused many honorable men and women of high and low estate, young and old, on the basis of entirely fictitious and false testimony." Those guilty of giving false testimony should be flogged. A new whipping post was set up for just this purpose. The mandate was renewed in 1628, as "malicious and frivolous accusations of witchcraft" had not ceased.[101] Several such cases did appear in the years leading up to the publication of the mandates.[102] What appears to have provoked the legislation was a series of accusations directed against members of the regime. In November 1628, the bishop informed Adam Contzen and William Lamormaini that Friedrich Förner and Johann Christoff Neustetter-Stürmer had both been slandered. Johann Georg was perplexed that such "pillars of the church" who "had greatly assisted in the work of exposing and extirpating sorcery" could be accused of such crimes.[103] Contzen and Lamormaini both recorded their shock over the accusations, calling those directed against Förner in particular "most malignant fables."[104]

Meanwhile the scope of the investigations expanded. Secular officials took to examining parish registers, reporting individuals who failed for one reason or another to receive communion at Easter to the Malifizkommission.[105] Individuals who feared being arrested resorted to flight. Albert Pfersmann, whose wife, mother-in-law, and sister-in-law had all been burned, sought protection in Hungary. The brothers Johann and Georg Kauwer, both of whose parents had been executed, traveled throughout Europe seeking aid, ending up in Rome, where they found willing ears to hear their complaints against the bishop. Margarethe Weltzin of Zeil had seen her mother, her sister, and most of her friends burned. She fled to Vienna in 1629 and appealed to the imperial court.[106]

Well before 1629, Ferdinand II had found his own reasons to protest the bishops' actions. The emperor was deeply troubled by the judicial murder of Dr. Haan and his family. On October 28, 1628, Ferdinand wrote the bishop, expressing his concern over manifold irregularities in the trials in Bamberg, in particular the excessive use of torture and the strict confinement of suspects. He demanded that the trial documents of those currently in custody be sent on to the imperial court for review. In the meantime, the bishop was ordered to stop the "irregular inquisition" and release the prisoners or, at worst, fine them.[107]

One trial more than any other appears to have led the emperor to step up pressure to stop the witch-hunts in Bamberg. On December 16, 1629, Dorothea Flöckhin, the pregnant wife of a prominent council member in Bamberg, was arrested on a charge of witchcraft.[108] Dorothea, née Hofmann, was from a well-respected Nuremberg family and had recently married a member of the Bamberg city council, Georg Heinrich Flockh. Georg Heinrich's first wife had been burned alive a little more than a year earlier after being accused of desecrating the Host.[109] After Dorothea's arrest, Georg Heinrich found it prudent to flee to his wife's family in Nuremberg for protection.[110]

In a letter to Bishop Johann Georg II, Flockh argued that his wife's treatment was contrary to all law and humanity. The only explanation of the thirteen denunciations produced to indict Dorothea was that they were the work of Satan, "the father of lies." Dorothea's relatives in Nuremberg sought aid from other quarters. In January 1630, "the entire Hoffman'schen kindred" asked Friedrich Förner to intercede with the bishop on Dorothea's behalf.[111] Dorothea's sister Magdalena turned to the Capuchin monks in Nuremberg and Würzburg for support. One of the Capuchins, Father Paris van Griepen, wrote a long letter to the bishop on behalf "of the young Nuremberg lady" in custody in Bamberg. Father Paris explained that Dorothea's arrest had inflamed public opinion in Nuremberg against the Catholic faith. When so much suffering was known, "one could easily say 'in Bamberg no one is redeemed.'" Consequently, many "who had finally disposed themselves to accept our Catholic faith" had shied away. How could they, in good faith, seek entry into a church that treated a pregnant woman this way? Given the severity of her treatment, it was not surprising that "well-intentioned people assert that God Almighty had punished this imprisoned woman with so great a penalty because she became a Catholic."[112]

Johann Georg was not so easily persuaded. Consequently Dorothea's family sent letters to the emperor and several imperial officials, including Hofrat von Popp, Cardinal Khlesl, and Count von Fürstenberg, president of the imperial Hofrat. In early April 1630, Ferdinand II was moved to issue a mandate directed against the prince-bishop, calling on him to release Dorothea and bring the trials to a close.[113] In response to the imperial mandate, the bishop claimed that Dorothea's confinement had already been relaxed.

She had just delivered a daughter—mother and baby were doing just fine. As for the form of the trials, the bishop was merely following the standards set down in Bavaria, Würzburg, Eichstätt, Augsburg, Constance, and other prince-bishoprics. In any event, Georg Heinrich Flockh was less than honest in his representation of the facts. The emperor should ignore his complaints and allow the trials to go forward. "I have only instituted such trials," the bishop wrote, "to increase and further the honor of God and for the salvation of many imperiled souls."[114]

On April 28, 1630, proceedings began anew against Dorothea Flöckhin. Her relatives again turned to the emperor and the pope for help. Ferdinand II and the pope both demanded that Johann Georg stop the trial. All documents were to be turned over to the imperial Hofrat for review. In the meantime, on pain of punishment, the bishop was to proceed no further.[115] Hearing that letters were on the way from Vienna and Rome, Johann Georg pushed the trial to its conclusion. On May 14, Dorothea was condemned "on account of her evil deeds, done with sorcery, wherein she first denied almighty God and the all-holy Trinity in a shocking and unchristian manner, then gave herself bodily to Satan, and did much other evil, in particular, desecrated the most holy Host and gave herself to Satan as a lover." She was sentenced be burned alive after being pinched with white-hot tongs. In the end, Johann Georg graciously permitted her to be beheaded before burning. Contrary to standard practice, the sentence was carried out in secret at 6:00 A.M. on the morning of May 17. The last thing Dorothea Flöckhin saw before her death was the executioner tearing her six-week-old daughter from her breast.[116]

Dorothea's execution provoked a storm of protest. Her relatives sent a long, bitter letter to Ferdinand II, charging that Dorothea's trial and execution were inhuman and illegal, running contrary to both the laws of Charles V and canon law, in particular "the canon *Episcopi*." The trials were conducted in secret, and no one was allowed contact with the accused. The victim had no advocate to review or question the testimony of her accusers. Although the *Carolina,* the criminal code issued by Emperor Charles V, required the judges to establish the credibility of witnesses, the very nature of the proceedings made it impossible to determine if those who had identified Dorothea as a witch were trustworthy "and unpartisan folk" or "mischievous rascals." According to the *Carolina,* forced confessions should not be "taken for pure gospel" but had to be supported by other evidence.[117] It was as if the commissioners "had forgotten their Christian education, and had allowed themselves to be seduced . . . through illusions [brought on] by the devil and wicked people."[118]

The sad case of Dorothea Flöckhin attracted a great deal of attention at the imperial court. On July 5, Johann Murmann, Bishop Johann Georg's man in Vienna, informed the bishop that "Georg Heinrich Flockh, whose wife was recently condemned, as well as two people who had escaped from the Malfizhaus in Bamberg along with some others" had brought their complaints directly before the emperor and the Electors and princes at court. Murmann said that he could not entrust any more specific information to the pen, but would explain the details after his return to Bamberg. Meanwhile, Johann Georg should take immediate action "to frustrate the intrigues of his enemies, if his reputation is not to suffer irrevocable damage."[119] To that end, the bishop sent two of the witch commissioners to the Diet of Regensburg to defend the trials. Drs. Harsee and Schwartzkonz made contact with three individuals who they hoped would be sympathetic. Father Joachim Hamann, S.J. had been rector of the Jesuit college in Bamberg; surely he could be trusted. Hamann agreed to take the bishop's case to William Lamormaini and Count von Fürstenberg. Eventually, Harsee and Schwartzkonz were able to meet with both men, along with other members of the Reichshofrat, and present their case. Although they felt the audience had gone well, both commissioners were somewhat disturbed that Fürstenberg had not yet indicated whether he supported their petition or not.[120]

Harsee and Schwartzkonz had reason to be concerned. Neither Lamormaini nor Fürstenberg was well disposed to the witch-hunts in Bamberg. The latter had been in contact with Dorothea Flöckhin's relatives for over a year and had already expressed concern over the bishop's cavalier attitude when human lives were in the balance. Lamormaini had formed an adverse opinion of the trials years after hearing of the accusations against Förner. Lamormaini's concern was in part political–Johann Georg's conduct only encouraged mistrust of the emperor and Catholics in general. Both the election of Ferdinand's son as king of the Romans and the execution of the Edict of Restitution might be jeopardized if Ferdinand were to tolerate the persecutions.[121]

It was at this moment that Dr. Anton Winter arrived in Regensburg to explain the bishop's position on the Edict of Restitution.[122] As it turned out, Ferdinand had other plans for the inventive jurist. In a letter to Bishop Franz von Hatzfeld of Würzburg, Winter noted that the emperor, along with members of his privy council and the Reichshofrat, found the trials "odious."[123] Winter confirmed the testimonies of Flockh and the others who had petitioned the emperor on behalf of the victims. On August 15, 1630, Ferdinand II chastised Johann Georg for continuing the trials in defiance of the earlier mandates. In addition to the case of Dorothea Flöckhin, the emperor complained about the treatment of Barbara Schwartzin, who had escaped the "Hexenhaus," a special prison built for holding and examining accused witches, and fled to Vienna. Ferdinand declared Schwartzin to be under his protection and ordered the bishop and commissioners to send the original trial documents for review.[124]

On September 20, 1630, after reviewing the trial documents, Ferdinand II issued a third, sharply worded mandate directed against Johann Georg.

Ferdinand lamented how, "completely contrary to imperial orders, the princely commissioners had been far too zealous in their use of torture." Ferdinand was particularly concerned that such measures "have also been used against women, in particular the frequently mentioned Frau Flockh." Ferdinand invoked his authority as supreme suzerain, noting that insofar as Johann Georg had received the Hochstift from his hand, he was obligated to respect imperial decrees.[125] Of course, this was essentially the argument Winter had presented at Regensburg against the Hohenzollerns; now it had been turned back on the bishop.

Johann Georg was again ordered to turn over all trial documents to imperial Hofrat von Popp. When they arrived, Popp discovered that he had received copies and demanded to see the originals.[126] The bishop refused. Instead, "true verbatim transcripts" were sent, whose authenticity was attested to by the members of the Malifizkommssion. Included with the transcripts was a letter from the commissioners. The charges against the bishop had been raised by "infamous confederates, strongly indicted for witchcraft, who had taken flight out of fear of punishment and their own evil nature." As "slaves of the devil," these men sought to hinder the work of bringing to justice the sorcerers who worked "so many sacrileges, sodomies, and other serious crimes." Nevertheless, in obedience to the emperor's will, no one had been arrested for witchcraft since June 1630. Meanwhile, the children in the street were learning sorcery, and their seducers remained unpunished. For the sake of the children, the trials had to go forward.[127]

The commissioners' letter proved to be a tissue of lies. In March 1631 Ferdinand was informed that at least twenty-five more people had been arrested for witchcraft in Bamberg and Zeil since publication of the imperial mandate.[128] The relatives of victims from Zeil claimed that the number of people there who had been executed or had died *in carcere* "was nearly 400—a terrifying number." It was well known that "no one who had been arrested for witchcraft ever came out again." Rather than suffer continued pain, the tortured prisoners "would confess to anything, even if they had never ever done it." The cost of the trials was crippling the town. The commissioners, meanwhile, had grown rich through the confiscation of the victims' goods. The relatives claimed that the bishops' subjects had been reduced to penury, so that they "can barely provide daily bread for their wives and children." Only the innkeeper had profited by this business.[129]

The most damning indictment of the trials was written by Georg Wilhelm Dümler, the former administrator of St. Martin's Church in Bamberg. For over three years, the burghers of Bamberg had suffered under the most woeful circumstances. Many people had been brought to "the unprecedented Hexenhaus and other prisons" and had suffered "torture, with all sorts of terrifying newly discovered *Instrumentum*."[130] As a result, "several hundred prominent and respectable people had suffered in body and life, honor and estate, goods and blood." The bishop had given over his subjects to "two foreigners, entirely unknown, along with many cursed, merciless tyrannical associates" who were pure idiots. Much of the blame was laid at the feet of Dr. Ernst Vasoldt, the head of the Malifizkommission. He and the commissioners paid no heed to "quality, good name, estate, or wealth" in their accusations. Rather, on the basis of "false imputations" they subjected their victims to all sorts of new tortures. Many had died in prison; others were executed, sometimes six or eight at a time, without any sufficient proof of their guilt and without being allowed any opportunity to defend themselves.[131] Dümler had personal experience with such treatment. In August 1628, his pregnant wife had been plucked out of the doorway of their house and taken to the Hexenhaus. She was tortured, and in the course of her suffering she miscarried. Not long afterward she was executed. Now he was accused of witchcraft, despite the fact that from his youth he had been raised a Catholic and had been educated by *"patribus Societatis Jesu"* in both Würzburg and Bamberg.[132]

From Dümler's perspective, the trials were illegal. Both the *Carolina* and its predecessor, the Bamberg *Halsgerichtsordnung,* permitted the accused an advocate before the court. Evidence obtained solely through torture was inadmissable. Such cases should be heard by the civil courts (Zentgericht), but in Bamberg they were conducted in secret by the commissioners, none of whom were subjects of the Hochstift.[133] It was clear what guided these foreigners: "carnal desire, unrestrained audacity, hatred, calumny, cruelty and reckless haste, insatiable greed and rapacity, and vileness." Dümler called on Ferdinand to come to the aid of his long-suffering subjects and bring the bloodbath to an end.[134]

Dümler's hopes were not disappointed. On June 12, 1631, Ferdinand announced that he had no choice but to "punish the frightful mischief which had occurred in Bamberg on account of the witch-trials under prince-bishop Johann Georg." In order to bring the situation under control, Ferdinand appointed Dr. Anton Winter president of the Malefizkommission. Henceforth, all trials had to be conducted according to the strict letter of the *Carolina.* The accused would not simply be given over to torture. Rather, the accusation, along with all evidence and damning testimony, would have to be subjected to the greatest scrutiny before anyone could be taken into custody. Confiscation of goods, a major source of complaint, was strictly forbidden.[135]

Johann Georg proved none too eager to abandon the witch-hunts. Winter found little support from either the bishop or the other commissioners in his efforts to bring some measure of restraint to the trials. When Johann Georg finally responded to the imperial mandate, he merely restated his earlier position that the accusations brought against him were made by criminals who had fled to avoid justice. The emperor was responding to calumnies and rumors.[136] Even though Johann Georg was now under much closer scrutiny, he made no effort to release those remaining in custody. Only as he fled the advancing Swedes were the prisoners in Bamberg freed. Dr. Anton Winter–Johann Georg's reluctant representative at Regensburg and the man charged by Ferdinand II with ending the terror–negotiated the city's surrender.[137]

In the space remaining it is hardly possible to explain the causes and significance of the Bamberg witch-hunts in full, but we can indicate some general characteristics and suggest possible avenues for interpretation. First of all, personalities played a vital role in the instigation and expansion of the trials. More than any other single individual, Friedrich Förner must bear the onus in this regard. Behringer's description of the suffragan bishop as "spiritus rector" of the trials is fitting.[138] Still, Förner did not act alone. Without the consent of Johann Gottfried von Aschhausen, the first wave of trials in Bamberg would never have gone forward. The passion that the Hexenbischof Johann Georg II threw into the witch-hunts ensured the expansion of the trials to truly horrific proportions. Besides the rulers, a cast of lesser actors played key supporting roles. The members of the Malifizkommission, in particular Dr. Vasolt, along with the torture masters, were indispensable for moving the witch-hunts from policy to practice. Without these professionals, most of whom were from outside the Hochstift, the trials would likely not have been carried out with such vehemence. What made this group so especially dangerous was that they were able to operate outside of the ordinary structures of the territorial judiciary. Instead of the "experts" being held accountable to established principles of law and judicial practice, it was the judges and other officials who were beholden to the professional witch-hunters. As a consequence, any sort of judicial restraint was waived, in large part because of the high esteem in which the leading officials of the Hochstift held the professional witch-hunters.[139]

Somewhat more difficult to chart is the role of local and communal authorities in the trials. In Zeil in particular, members of the town council, as well as other local officials, appeared prominently in the witch-hunts as both judges and victims. It seems clear that the mayor and the council members in Zeil were reluctant members of the courts and proved to be among the most outspoken opponents of the trials. In the city of Bamberg, the victims included a number of high officials. If we keep in mind that a generation earlier, a large proportion of officials in Bamberg and other communities was Protestant, it becomes possible to understand some of the dynamics surrounding both their role in the trials and the accusations leveled against them. The communal and district officials in many cases were either converts or first-generation Catholics. This was true of both Johann Schöner and Friedrich Förner. The witch-hunts provided the first chance for many of these new Catholics to prove their loyalty to the faith and to the regime. In that sense, we might see the trials as a "test" of the officials' obedience and effectiveness.[140] As Förner pointed out in *Panoplia Armaturae Dei,* if the officials failed in their duty to convict accused witches, it would demonstrate that they were not godly magistrates. The anonymous dialogue from Forchheim expressed just such a concern: the Ratsherrn's reluctance to prosecute witches proved that they were themselves witches.

From the beginning, the mass trials displayed a markedly political character. There is evidence to suggest that the trials in Kronach and Steinwiesen may have been orchestrated to demonstrate the failures of the regime of Johann Philipp von Gebsattel. Several sources point to the presence of "Calvinist" preachers in Kronach and the environs, as well as an increase in "demonic" activity during Gebsattel's reign.[141] More obvious is the connection between the prosecution of witchcraft and the Edict of Restitution. It was no accident that the last and most intense phase of the witch-hunts coincided with the attempts to enforce the edict. As Förner suggests in both *Panoplia Armaturae Dei* and his treatises on Nuremberg, the rulers had both the opportunity and the obligation to act now to exterminate the two demonic threats of heresy and sorcery, "root and branch." It is on this point that perhaps the most radical aspect of the witch-hunts becomes clear. By the end, the bishop was willing to defy even the emperor in his pursuit of final justice. Here it is worth recalling Förner's comments in the funeral sermon for Johann Gottfried von Aschhausen. The text contains a subtle criticism of the house of Habsburg, laying the blame for the outbreak of the Thirty Years' War on the emperors' willingness to compromise with the Protestants. The same charge appears again in a slightly different form in the *Relatio Historico Paranetica* of 1629. In both cases, the suggestion was that the emperor should obey God first and use his divinely appointed authority to secure the faith, even if it meant going against the law of the empire. In 1631, Ferdinand II found himself at odds with the bishop of Bamberg on two points—execution of the Edict of Restitution and continuation of the witch-hunts. In the first case, the emperor seems to have failed to take advantage of his strength and allowed the Protestants to achieve through negotiation what could not be won on the battlefield.[142] In the latter case, the emperor's support of such malcontents as Georg Heinrich Flockh and the subsequent appointment of Anton Winter to bring the witch trials to a close was allowing the devil to continue his assault on the Hochstift unchecked. In either case, the bodies and souls of the bishop's subjects were in jeopardy. By the logic that Friedrich Förner laid out in *Panoplia Armaturae Dei,* the emperor, like any other magistrate, had effectively proven that his power was illegitimate in his opposition to the witch-hunts and his willingness to treat with heretics. Although Johann George II never said as much, his conduct in the face of numerous imperial edicts in 1630–32 strongly suggests that he no longer felt that, in this matter at least, he had any reason to obey the emperor. Here Behringer's characterization of resistance to the trials as a contest between ideology and reason of state seems valid.[143]

The witch-hunts may thus be seen as the culmination of the process of territorial state building that had begun long before. In the aftermath of the Peasants' War, the older structures of the political order in the Hochstift—the cathedral chapter, the estates, and local officialdom—were gradually neutralized or placed under the direct control of the central regime. From the time of Johann Gottfried von Aschhausen onward, there appeared to be no effective organized opposition to confessional absolutism. By the middle of the 1620s, officials in at least parts of the Hochstift no longer represented local interests, but now acted solely as representatives of the state. But note that throughout this process, the expansion of state power was never the rationale for the increasingly strenuous methods employed. The aims were religious and utopian. The results were rather different, but the trials seem to have affected only portions of the Hochstift, in particular the towns of Zeil and Bamberg. Forchheim was spared, despite the pleas of some of its residents. In the hinterland, the records of criminal courts (Zentgericht) show that throughout the 1620s isolated trials continued to be heard by the local courts rather than by the centralized Malifizkommission.[144] Except for those in the years 1612–13, the large-scale witch-hunts did not touch the highland regions, the home of the wandering preachers and the location of the major conflicts between the bishops and the nobility. In these latter regions, coercive force was directed against Protestants and other malfeasants, not witches. The mass witch-hunts, in other words, were one option, and an option that seemed workable only in areas where the bishop's authority was effectively unquestioned and where the residents were nominally Catholic.[145] The trials appear to have been one particular consequence of the consolidation of the princely regime and the success, at least in some regions of the Hochstift, of the Counter-Reformation.[146]

CONCLUSION

As we take stock of the three centuries that preceded the Swedish invasion, two themes predominate. In the first case, the dominant principle of government in upper Franconia was that governance was local (örtlich). In the administration of their domains, the princes followed the pattern of the Hohenstaufen emperors, delegating authority to the level below them; meanwhile, local elites sought to transform delegated powers into expressions of their own status and lordship. If anything, this tendency intensified over time. In the fourteenth century, execution of the Landfriede was delegated to the princes; in the fifteenth and sixteenth centuries, resolution of religious crises was, first unofficially, then officially, passed down to the territories. The downward shift of the burden of religious reform to communities and householders, evident from the 1570s onward, was an extension of what had been the common practice of governance in the empire from the time of the Hohenstaufen. It is in this deeply ingrained habit of passing the responsibility for the execution of policy downward that the formative—and disruptive—power of the princes and the emperors becomes most visible. On account of this practice, all officials were to a degree "princely," owing their powers and privileges to the prince. At the same time, officials tended to view their offices as recognition of their status and estate. This set into motion one of the principle dynamics of state formation; the tension between the prince and those entrusted with the task of governance. As it turned out, the two had decidedly different opinions on the significance and uses of delegated authority.

Political authority was inexorably bound to religion. The noble Amtmann was often the patron of the local church; the members of the village council were also the most prominent members of the local Corpus Christi brotherhood. In both cases, officeholding and ecclesiastical patronage were complementary, if not inseparable, representations of estate. From the late Middle Ages onward the actions of the emperors, the princes, and the local elites were bound up in a general idea of political and religious reform. Winfried Eberhard's observations concerning Bohemia seem relevant to Franconia in this regard: the formation of the estates (*Ständebildung*) and the process of confessional formation (*Konfessionsbildung*) were closely linked.[1] "Reform," however, was not a static concept with universally accepted content. In the thirteenth and fourteenth centuries, "reform" was understood in the most literal sense to refer to the reconstruction of the empire in the aftermath of the collapse of the Hohenstaufen state. Under the emperors Louis the Bavarian and Charles IV, the question of reform centered on the proper relationship between the emperor and the papacy and between the emperor and the princes. By the end of the fourteenth century, "reform" had taken on a rather different meaning. Charles IV introduced a number of religious reforms in Bohemia. Certain aspects of the Bohemian reforms, in particular those dealing with church finance and the monasteries, spilled over into Franconia. Following the Schism and the Hussite War, Sigismund embarked on a much more ambitious policy of political and religious reform. In theory, the goal of reforming the church in head and members ought to have had a direct impact on local religious life. As it was, despite the high-sounding rhetoric of the conciliar decrees, the aims of the fifteenth-century reform movements were fairly limited. After 1440, the emperors abandoned the idea of reform, allowing by default the impetus of religious and political reform to fall to the princes. It was in their hands that we can see a gradual intensification as the principles of reforming church and society were connected to the consolidation of both the territorial regime and local lordship. Meanwhile, throughout the later fourteenth and fifteenth centuries, we can see a process of reform "from below" in the towns and villages. "Confessionalization" simply marks the last phase of a process that had been going on for at least two centuries before 1550, the nominal starting point for the "confessional era."

The idea that the reforms of the sixteenth and early seventeenth centuries were connected to the late-medieval *reformatio* was central to the historical conception of Friedrich Förner. Förner drew explicit parallels among the Hussite War, the Peasants' War, and the Thirty Years' War, seeing in all three cases a definite link between heresy and rebellion. The defeat of heresy in each case had led in a genetic fashion to the elaboration of a more virulent and mendacious heresy and its counterpart, a more aggressive form of Catholic renewal. In his treatises from 1600, Förner identifies the proclamation of the papal jubilee by Boniface VIII as the response to the spread of Waldensianism; in *Panoplia Armaturae Dei,* the witch-hunts were the "reform" directed against the latest incarnation of the lying spirit. For Förner, the fundamental dynamic of regional history was the dialectical relationship between heresy and reform. The process of reform, involving cooperation between the bishops of Bamberg and the emperors, had begun in the fourteenth century and had continued over the next three centuries. A comparable idea can be gleaned from the work of Förner's contemporary Paul Reinel. He too draws parallels between the restoration of the village church in his own day and the "communal reformation" of the late fifteenth and early sixteenth centuries. But note that Reinel approaches the history of the church from an entirely communalist perspective. Reinel consistently emphasizes the local character of religious reform and its roots in the ecclesiastical history of the *Gemeinde.*

The juxtaposition of Reinel's and Förner's historical writings suggests that the various reform movements–late medieval *reformatio,* the communal and magisterial reformations, Lutheran and Catholic confessionalization–are all reflections of a larger, long-term process. But although certain continuities bind together the reformations of the late-medieval and early modern eras, the process of reform was not linear, nor did all its strands lead in the same direction. It was punctuated by a series of crises, each of which had a profound impact on the direction and focus of the reforms. The ecclesiastical reforms of Lamprecht von Brunn were clearly influenced by the policies of Charles IV in Bohemia, but also by the violent confrontations between cities and princes in Franconia. The synodal statutes of Anton von Rotenhan, though repeating many themes found in the statutes issued by his immediate predecessors, reflected both the decrees of the Council of Basel and his own experiences in the Immunities Contest. What distinguishes the reforms of the period after 1520 was the closer identification of "reform" with specific theological and ecclesiopolitical systems–what later might be termed "confessions." At each step in the process of reform, the stakes in the conflict between confessional groups, whether on the international stage or at home, were heightened. Jakob Feucht and Paul Reinel both tended speak of the conflicts between true Christians and heretics in world-historical terms. For Friedrich Förner, events such as the Thirty Years' War and the witch-hunts were conceived of not simply in their historical context, but in terms of their cosmological significance. The ideas of these authors were not matters of idle speculation. Feucht, Reinel, and Förner were practical men whose thoughts had immediate implications for public policy. In that sense, their writings are of a kind with the sermons of Johannes Schwannhäuser: they are programs for social and political action. But when the perspective of reform broadened, the rhetoric of the reformers became more extreme as they called for stricter measures to combat heterodoxy and heresy at home and abroad.

Leaving aside for the moment the political implications of the argument over reform, if we consider the religious questions that occupied the minds of churchmen and lay people from the fourteenth century onward, the dominant issue was the care of souls. Religious communalism, popular anticlericalism, and institutional and educational reforms were all responses to questions of pastoral theology. Under the pressure of political and religious conflicts, pastoral theology was transformed into a political ideology. But the transformation was not, nor could be, complete. Pastoral concerns remained at the heart of resistance from below as well as from within the ecclesiopolitical edifice. The evidence simply cannot support the view "that cynical public men stabilized the commune by encouraging private delusions."[2] Even the witch-hunts were justified in terms of the salvation of mens' souls–on this point there seems no reason to doubt that Friedrich Förner and Johann Georg II were deadly serious in their understanding of the problem. Whatever the secular political implications of the reforms, their explicit goals had to do with religion, and, more narrowly, with eternal salvation.[3] Perhaps the most significant difference between the discourse on reform before and after the beginnings of the confessional era had to do with assigning responsibility for reform. Before 1530, the blame for poor pastoral care was consistently laid on the clergy; after that point, reforms were increasingly directed toward the laity, who were held more accountable for their own beliefs and actions. We might see such a shift as marking the emergence of the modern notion of the individual; as a manifestation of the Neostoic conception of self-discipline; as a decline of paternalism and (in the Hegelian sense) a foundation of liberty; as a "bureacratization" of the household; or as a form of oppression, but the fact remains that the explicit end of this accountability was redemption.

The experience of the witch-hunts reveals the difficulties attending to the concept of reform. Förner certainly saw himself as a reformer, but so did Georg Wilhelm Dümler, a man who despite his Jesuit education and impeccable Tridentine Catholic credentials found himself accused of sorcery. Johannes Schwannhäuser, Johann Rürer, Nicholas Hiltner, Johann Scharnagel, and Aegidius Schnabrich might all be identified as "Lutheran reformers," but we can readily point to significant differences among their views on doctrine and church governance. The "reformers" constituted a loose and incomplete alliance of clerics and laymen from various levels of society. What bound them together was participation in the argument rather than uniformity of vision. Part of the problem was that they tended to define their program in negative terms. Beyond that, the clear lack of consensus reveals that people at various levels of society—villages, towns, and Ortschaften; imperial, princely, and noble courts; bishop, chapter, and regular and secular clergy—understood confessional norms in different ways and could modify those norms to suit their own particular ends. The age-old rhetoric of the the church notwithstanding, there was always a multiplicity of churches, both in the sense of the body of the faithful and the clerical corporation, each with their own theological viewpoints. The ideas of the reformers were highly individualized responses to the demands of the religious life. Drawing on a common stock of theological, rhetorical, and philosophical traditions, men such as Schwanhäuser, Rürer, and others constructed their own distinctive understanding of the relationship between Christian belief and social life. But their personal views often stood in tension with the more generalized confessional norms. "Confessionalization" did not fundamentally alter this situation; it merely problematized the diversity of religious life, which previously had gone largely unremarked, without being able to provide an effective remedy.

At this stage we could legitimately argue that reform was not so much the goal as conformity. Princely regimes, as we are told, sought to discipline an unruly society and enforce religious and social conformity on their subjects. The aim was on the one hand restorative, an attempt to reestablish the proper order in the face of various forces–religious, political, and economic–that threatened traditional society.[4] On the other hand, the reforms often had a strong missionary, if not utopian, character about them, embodying an effort to shape the behavior of ordinary people. Despite the forceful rhetoric of the ordinances, however, the state did not have the means at its disposal to enforce compliance, much less bring about radical changes in society or popular beliefs. Local powers were too well entrenched to be attacked directly.[5] The success of reforms (or of securing conformity) rested on cooperation and at least the tacit consent of local powers. On this point, R. J. W. Evans's remarks about the formation of the Habsburg state ring true for the territories of upper Franconia: although the rulers "pressed fairly consistently for stronger central control, conformity grew more out of consent, the fruit of a process not necessarily understood by those who participated in it, certainly not imposed by any single group." The "combative" confessional ideology could not provide unity unless it was also "sustained by the logic of domestic political relations."[6]

For much of the period between 1525 and 1632, the confessional ideologies often did stand in sharp tension with the logic of domestic political relations. This phenomenon is generally thought of in terms of local politics, the day-to-day practice of *Herrschaft,* but let us pause to consider the matter on the level of the empire. Confessional politics seemed to require that local religious identities be suppressed, or at least downplayed, in the interest of forming larger confederations of states defined in terms of their allegiance to one or another orthodoxy. Whether it was membership in a Lutheran Schmalkaldic League, a largely Calvinist Protestant Union, or a Bavarian-led Catholic League, there were immense pressures on the territorial states to conform to the confessional views of the parties, just as subjects found themselves pressured to conform to the confessional views of their prince. The pressures of confessional conformity on the regional and imperial levels ultimately strained the logic of domestic relations to the breaking point. We can see these strains in the constitutional conflicts in Kulmbach in 1608; we can see them in the controversy surrounding the regime of Johann Philipp von Gebsattel; we can see them in the judicial murders of Apollonia Crato and Dorothea Flockhin. Förner's conspiracy theories about Rosicrucians in the imperial court reflect the triumph of political irrationalism. Paradoxically, confessionalization appears here not as the support of the territorial state, a source of stability and order, but as a threat to these things, a force at odds with the territorial state as a politically and morally autonomous entity. But the territorial state proved immensely resilient. Despite the fiery and at times apocalyptic rhetoric of the reformers, for the most part reforms were carried out in an atmosphere of mutual restraint. To some degree restraint was the consequence of the practical limits of state power, but it also reflected a habit of mind. The fundamental political ethos of the premodern world was conservative, hence neither rulers nor subjects were interested in upsetting the political order. This spirit of restraint seems to have informed the treatment of Thomas Rühr, whose confessional irregularities could be ignored because of the good-will between him and his flock. If the locals created no problems, the officials would not go searching for them. But mutual restraint was not foolproof. It failed in 1525 and again in 1548. It failed most spectacularly in the years between 1616 and 1632, when nearly a thousand people perished in Bamberg.

The failure of restraint derived from two fundamental and interrelated causes. First of all, governance always rested on a certain measure of tacit consent, the willingness of the population to accept the orders of those in positions of authority. Occasional acts of repression were tolerable so long as they did not involve waiving consent. The widespread deportations of Lutherans in Bamberg in the 1590s and 1610s clearly did just that, requiring active submission to an intrusive alien authority. The use of troops to arrest concubines and evict tenants after 1610 must have made it seem to all that the regime had declared war on its own subjects—a fear evinced in 1525 but now made a reality. Given the scope of repression, whenever anyone was spared it appeared somehow unjust: the irregular character of early modern governance became particularly unacceptable once force replaced tacit consent as the norm. This leads to the second cause. The increasingly utopian and apocalyptic tenor of reformist ideology set goals that could never be met. Here it matters not whether we are referring to the official doctrines or to those enunciated by preachers such as Johannes Schwannhäuser. "Official" and "popular" reforms had the same goal in mind: the spiritual and material transformation of earthly society according to Christian teachings. The result was an ever increasing gulf between expectations and realities. The perception of that gulf, in turn, only increased tensions while appearing to justify ever more extreme measures. On this point, Friedrich Förner and the *Hexenbischof* Johann Georg II understood all too well the logic of their own world view.

In their demand for action and the transformation of society, Friedrich Förner and Johannes Schwanhäuser had much in common, even though externally at least, they represented opposite ends of the confessional spectrum. For both authors, the apocalyptic vision provided the basis for their demands for action. We have already noted the tension between the restorative and the utopian elements of Christian thought; to these we add a third element—the catastrophic nature of final redemption in the apocalypse. In the mainstream of Christian thought, redemption is presented as something that occurs in the heart of the individual believer through the communication of grace. Whether it is through the sacraments, faith, election, or some combination thereof, the cosmic drama of redemption is played out in this world in the believer's life. The apocalyptic thinker, in contrast, focuses attention on the role of catastrophe in the process of redemption. Catastrophe is not only necessary, but in the mind of the visionary is simultaneously terrible and desirable. Men such as Schwanhäuser and Förner had a profoundly pessimistic world view. For them, the only path to redemption was through the catastrophic destruction that they believed would accompany the coming of Christ: "their optimism, their hope, is not directed to what history will bring forth, but to that which will arise in its ruin, free at last and undisguised."[7] Both authors link the romance of catastrophe to the revolutionary act by which humanity can hasten the redemption of the world. Schwanhäuser's most dedicated followers were those who not only organized the revolution of 1525 but also refused to accept half measures, pressing on the heels of each success for more radical action. That the survivors ended up as Anabaptists reflects merely the final step in their spiritual journey, a renunciation of the imperfect world of history. For Förner, the revolutionary actors were the bishops and secular princes, such as Maximilian of Bavaria and—he hoped—the emperor. The differing social status of their chosen agents, however, should not distract us from their common vision and their shared belief in the redemptive power of destruction.

The tensions of the confessional era, in other words, menaced not only the external shell of the state, but threatened to consume it from within. Here, though, we must note that the Hochstift Bamberg proved more vulnerable in this regard than the neighboring margraviate. Aside from a few random acts of symbolic violence, the margraviate was never touched by the sort of large-scale religious and social upheavals that plagued Catholic Bamberg. Paul Reinel and Christoph Schleupner also viewed the coming of the Thirty Years' War in apocalyptic terms—in many ways far more explicitly than did Förner—but neither chose to emphasize the catastrophic element and, consequently, never demanded any sort of actions, violent or otherwise, that might hasten the end. Antichrist would be defeated in short order, but by God's edict, not by humanity's actions. In any event, redemption, for them, was something that had already occurred within the community of the faithful—their community, in other words. The question then naturally arises whether the differences between the two states can be explained in terms of confession. Perhaps: Lutheranism, and by extension religious reform generally in the margraviate, was consistently articulated with an eye toward local conditions. The Oberland clergy provided their own distinctive definition of confessional orthodoxy. They did so, moreover, against the more cosmopolitan definitions favored by their prince. Reinel's history demonstrates the ways in which seventeenth-century Protestants might reinterpret Lutheran orthodoxy so as to make it conform to their own conception of their community. In the diets of 1548 and 1608 we can see the same tendency at the territorial level—Lutheranism appears as the authentic religion of the Land, rooted in its history and in the traditional constitution of the estates.[8] Catholic reform in Bamberg, however, was in comparison always far more ambitious, as we can see from even the most cursory comparison of the fifteenth-century synodal decrees and monastic reforms issued by the bishops of Bamberg with the comparable efforts of their Hohenzollern neighbors. In the aftermath of the Peasants' War, and even more so after the Council of Trent, the reform programs in Bamberg increasingly were conceived in terms of the broader context of the Counter-Reformation and imperial politics. Consequently—and paradoxically—Catholic "renewal" in Bamberg appears far more disruptive and fundamentally at odds with traditional religion than the Lutheran "reform" across the border. In harnessing the power of the state to an overly ambitious, if not utopian, program of religious conversion, Catholic officials in Bamberg wrought untold havoc. At least in Bamberg, "the search for Catholic identity seems to have had sorry consequences,"[9] but note here that it was a particular version of Catholic identity, characterized by an obsession with the catastrophic, that was at issue.

The tensions of the age of reform, then, were rooted in divergent understandings of the Christian calling and derive naturally out of Christianity itself. They also reflected different understandings of politics, a disagreement about the highest authority—that of the emperor. Certainly the empire showed the strains of confessional conflict throughout the sixteenth and seventeenth centuries. The forceful policies of Charles V and Ferdinand II contributed to the heightening of tensions in the 1540s and 1620s, in no small measure because their actions threatened the liberties of the princes—not simply Protestants, but Catholics as well. What the princes ultimately wanted from the emperors was a legal bulwark for the territorial state. In that regard, the desire of the princes and nobles was the same in the 1620s as it had been in the 1320s. When Anton Winter was sent back to Bamberg in 1631, his commission was to assert imperial authority through the restoration of the territorial constitution, the old logic of domestic politics. Admittedly, Winter faced an impossible task, but his mission is instructive. The empire was a prerequisite for the existence of such middling states as Bamberg and Kulmbach. Consequently, the princes had a stake in the health and welfare of the empire, something that the experiences of the Reformation only confirmed. On the local level, the overarching legal controls vested in the imperial constitution remained, as Winter pointed out in his treatise on territorial law, the last defense of local privilege against the pretensions of grasping princes and foreign despots. Only in the Reich could the sort of wide-ranging religious and social transformations associated with the reformations of the fifteenth and sixteenth centuries be carried out. Simply put, no Reich, no *Territorium;* no *Territorium,* no reformation. Although the religious and political movements of the fourteenth through the seventeenth centuries may indeed have laid the foundations for the modern world, the religious reformations were also a consequence of the restoration of the *sacri romani imperium.*

Notes

Introduction

1.   Heiko Oberman, "The Present Profile and Future Face of Reformation History: A Review Article," *SCJ* 28 (1997): 170–71.

2.   Luise Schorn-Schütte, "Ernst Troeltschs 'soziallehrn' und die gegenwärtige Frühneuzeitforschung. Zur Disckussion um die Bedeutung von Luthertum und Calvinismus für die Entstehung der Modernen Welt," in *Ernst Troeltschs Soziallehren. Studien zu ihrer Interpretation,* ed. Friedrich Wilhelm Graf and Trutz Rendtorff, 137–40 (Gütersloh: G. Mohn, 1993). Schorn-Schütte identifies two scholars in particular whose work may be considered in this context, namely Natalie Zemon Davis and Patrick Collinson. Davis, "City Women and Religious Change" and "The Rites of Violence," in *Society and Culture in Early Modern France* (Stanford, 1975); Collinson, *The Elizabethan Protestant Movement* (London: Cape, 1967); Collinson, *The Religion of Protestants: The Church in English Society, 1559–1625* (Oxford: Clarendon, 1982); Stephen Foster, *The Long Argument: English Puritanism and the Shaping of New England Culture, 1570–1700* (Chapel Hill: University of North Carolina Press, 1991), ix–xv. On the larger issue of religion in early modern scholarship, see Mack Holt, "Putting Religion Back into the Wars of Religion," *French Historical Studies* 18 (1993): 524–51.

3.   Heinz Schilling, "Die Konfessionalisierung von Kirche, Staat und Gesellschaft–Profil, Leistung, Defizite und Perspektiven eines geschichtwissenschaftlichen Paradigmas," in *Die Katholische Konfessionalisierung,* ed. Wolfgang Reinhard and Heinz Schilling, 1–49 (Münster: Aschendorff, 1995); Schilling, "Die Konfessionalisierung im Reich. Religiöser und gesellschaftlicher Wandel in Deutschland zwischen 1555 und 1620," *HZ* 246 (1988): 1–45; Schilling, "The Reformation and The Rise of the Early Modern State," in *Luther and the Modern State in Germany,* ed. James D. Tracy, 21–30 (Kirksville, MO: Sixteenth Century Journal Publishers, 1986); Wolfgang Reinhard, "Was ist Katholische Konfessionalisierung?" in Reinhard and Schilling, *Katholische Konfessionalisierung,* 419–52; Reinhard, "Reformation, Counter-Reformation, and the Early Modern State: A Reassessment," *Catholic Historical Review* 75 (1989): 383–404; Reinhard, "Zwang zur Konfessionalisierung? Prologomena zu einer Theorie des konfessionellen Zeitalters," *ZHF* 10 (1983): 257–98; Reinhard, "Gegenreformation als Modernisierung? Prologomena zu einer Theorie des konfessionellen Zeitalters," *ARG* 68 (1977): 226–51; Harm Klueting, *Das Konfessionelle Zeitalter 1525–1648* (Stuttgart: Steiner, 1989); Karlheinz Blaschke, "The Reformation and the Rise of the Territorial State," in Tracy, 61–75; Joel F. Harrington and Helmut Walser Smith, "Confessionalization, Community, and State Building in Germany, 1555–1870," *JMH* 69 (1997): 77–101. On the issue of religion and modernization generally, see John Bossy, *Christianity in the West, 1400–1700* (Oxford: Oxford University Press, 1987);

Jean Delumeau, *Catholicism between Luther and Voltaire: A New View of the Counter-Reformation* (London: Burns and Oates, 1978).

4.   Gerhard Oestreich, "Strukturprobleme des europäischen Absolutismus," in *Geist und Gestalt des frühmodernen Staates. Ausgewählte Aufsätze,* 179–97 (Berlin: Duncker and Humblot, 1969); Ernst Walther Zeeden, *Konfessionsbildung. Studien zur Reformation, Gegenreformation, und katholischen Reform* (Stuttgart: Klett-Cotta, 1985); Zeeden, *Die Entstehung der Konfessionen. Grundlagen und Formen der Konfessionsbildung* (Munich: Oldenbourg, 1965); R. Po-Chia Hsia, *Social Discipline in the Reformation: Central Europe 1550–1750* (New York: Routledge, 1989); Schilling, "Konfessionalisierung von Kirche, Staat und Gesellschaft," 5–6; Reinhard, "Katholische Konfessionalisirung," 420–21; Reinhard, "Zwang zur Konfessionalisierung?" 268–69.

5.   Schilling, "Konfessionalisierung von Kirche, Staat, und Gesellschaft," 3; Reinhard, "Was ist Katholische Konfessionalisierung?" 421–22; Schorn-Schütte, "Ernst Troeltschs 'sozliallehren,'" 133–52; cf. Herman Rebel, *Peasant Classes: The Bureaucratization of Property and Family Relations under Eaerly Habsburg Absolutism, 1511–1636* (Princeton, NJ: Princeton University Press, 1983), 10–20, 137–42.

6.   Schilling, "The Reformation and the Rise of the Early Modern State," 22.

7.   To their credit, the authors of the thesis have duly acknowledged its limitations. Schilling, "Konfessionalisierung von Kirche, Staat, und Gesellschaft"; Schilling, "Konfessionaliserung im Reich"; Reinhard, "Katholische Konfessionalisierung?"

8.   Reinhard Blänkner, "'Absolutismus' und 'frühmoderner Staat.' Probleme und Perspektiven der Forschung," in *Frühe Neuzeit–Frühe Moderne? Forschungen zur Vielgeschichtigkeit von Übergangsprozessen,* ed. Rudolf Vierhaus, 45–74 (Göttingen: Vandenhoeck and Ruprecht, 1992); cf. Schilling, "Konfessionalisierung von Kirche, Staat und Gesellschaft," 29–31.

9.   Reinhard, "Reformation," 397, 403; Reinhard, "Gegenreformation als Modernisierung," 234–35, 239; Rebel, *Peasant Classes,* 17–20.

10.   Renzo Sereno, *The Rulers* (New York: Praeger, 1968), 117, 161–66. Sereno suggests that the creation of bureaucratic structures should be taken as a sign of the state's failure, indicating the inability of rulers to address real social problems.

11.   James Allen Vann III, *The Making of a State: Würteemberg 1590–1790* (Ithaca, NY: Cornell University Press, 1984) 17; cf. Reinhard, "Katholische Konfessionalisierung," 424–34.

12.   James Allen Vann III, "New Directions for Study of the Old Reich," *JMH* 58, Supplement (1986): S7–S8; Thomas A. Brady, Jr., *The Politics of the Reformation in Germany: Jacob Sturm (1489–1553) of Strasbourg* (Atlantic Highlands, NJ: Humanities Press, 1997), 8.

13.   Regina Pörtner, *The Counter-Reformation in Central Europe: Styria 1580–1630* (Oxford: Clarendon Press, 2001); Karin J. MacHardy, "Der Einfluss von Status, Konfession und Besitz auf das Politische Verhalten des Niederösterreichischen Ritterstandes 1580–1620," in *Spezialforschung und "Gesamtgeschichte,"* ed. Grete Klingenstein and Heinrich Lutz, 56–83 (Vienna: Verlag für Geschichte und Politik, 1981); MacHardy, *War, Religion and Court Patronage in Habsburg Austria* (New York: Palgrave, 2003). See also Winfried Eberhard, *Konfessionsbildung und Stände in Böhmen, 1478–1530* (Munich: Oldenbourg, 1981).

14.   Blänkner, "Absolutismus"; Horst Kraemer, *Der deutsche Kleinstaat des 17. Jahrhunderts im Spiegel von Seckendorffs "Teutschem Fürstenstaat"* (Darmstadt: Wissenschaftliche

Buchgesellschaft, 1974); cf. Reinhard, "Katholische Konfessionalisierung," 422. For a late medieval perspective, see Howard Kaminsky, "Estates, Nobility, and the Explanation of Estate in the Late Middle Ages," *Speculum* 68 (1993): 684–709.

15. Harvey C. Mansfield, "Machiavelli's *Stato* and the Impersonal Modern State," in *Machiavelli's Virtue*, 281–94 (Chicago: University of Chicago Press, 1966).

16. Schilling, "Konfessionalisirung von Kirche, Staat und Gesellschaft," 4–5, 7–8; Schilling, "Die 'Zweite Reformation' als Kategorien der Geschichtswissenschaft," in *Die reformierte Konfessionsbildung in Deutschland–Das Problem der "Zweiten Reformation"* (Gütersloh: G. Mohn, 1986), 401–11; Walter Ziegler, "Territorium und Reformation," *Historisches Jahrbuch* 110 (1990): 52–75; Zeeden, *Konfessionsbildung,* 60–66.

17. Marc Forster, *The Counter-Reformation in the Villages: Religion and Reform in the Bishopric of Speyer, 1560–1720* (Ithaca, NY: Cornell University Press, 1992), 5; Forster, *Catholic Revival in the Age of the Baroque: Religious Identity in Southwest Germany, 1550–1750* (Cambridge: Cambridge University Press, 2001), 2–3; Philip M. Soergel, *Wondrous in His Saints: Counter-Reformation Propaganda in Bavaria* (Berkeley: University of California Press, 1993).

18. Harm Klueting, *Reformatio vitae. Johann Jakob Fabricius (1618/20–1673). Ein Beitrag zu Konfessionalisierung und Sozialdisziplinierung im Luthertum des 17. Jahrhunderts* (Münster: Aschendorff, 2003); John Stroup, *The Struggle for Identity in the Clerical Estate* (Leiden: Brill, 1984); Forster, *Counter-Reformation,* 5–7; Luise Schorn-Schütte, "Priest, Preacher, Pastor: Research on Clerical Office in Early Modern Europe," *CEH* 33 (2000): 1–40; Charles Trinkaus, "Humanism, Religion, Society: Concepts and Motivations of Some Recent Studies," *Renaissance Quarterly* 29 (1976): 676–91.

19. Oberman, "The Present Profile," 171.

20. Schilling, "Reformation von Kirche, Staat und Gesellschaft," 7–8; Ziegler, "Territorium und Reformation," 55–56; Thomas Kaufmann, *Universität und lutherische Konfessionalisierung* (Gütersloh: G. Mohn, 1997), 29–30.

21. R. Scott Dixon, *The Reformation and Rural Society: The Parishes of Brandenburg Ansbach-Kulmbach 1528–1603* (Cambridge: Cambridge University Press, 1996); Klueting, *Konfessionellen Zeitalter,* 21–24; R. W. Scribner, "Communalism: Universal Category or Ideological Construct? A Debate in the Historiography of Early Modern Germany and Switzerland," *Historical Journal* 37 (1994): 199–207; R. Po-Chia Hsia, "The Myth of the Commune: Recent Historiography on City and Reformation in Germany," *CEH* 20 (1987): 203–15.

22. Bernd Hamm, "Von der spätmittelalterlichen reformatio zur Reformation: der Prozeß normativer Zentrierung von Religion und Gesellschaft in Deutschland," *ARG* 84 (1993): 7–81; Schilling, "Konfessionalisierung von Kirche, Staat und Gesellschaft," 32–35. To a large extent, the notion of continuity underlies Peter Blickle's theory of the "communal Reformation." Blickle, "Communal Reformation and Peasant Piety: The Peasant Reformation in its Late Medieval Origins." *CEH* 20 (1987): 216–28; Blickle, *From the Communal Reformation to the Revolution of the Common Man,* trans. Beat Kümin (Leiden: Brill, 1998). R. W. Scribner ("Communalism," 200) noted the conceptual similarities between Blickle's conception of "communalism" and Schilling's understanding of early modern politics. Both viewpoints, according to Scribner, proceeded from the "self-consciously 'emancipatory' history favoured by the post-1968 generation of historians, who looked for alternative paths to modernity . . . in the corporatist, federalist modes of politics that characterized the early

modern Holy Roman Empire." From Scribner's perspective, this approach begins "to resemble a neo-Whig interpretation of German history," insofar as the political model presented by Blickle and Schilling "look[s] strangely like the Federal Republic of Germany."

23.   Brady, *The Politics of the Reformation,* 5.

24.   Moeller, *Reichstadt und Reformation* (Gütersloh: G. Mohn, 1962); Steven Ozment, *The Reformation in the Cities* (New Haven, CT: Yale University Press, 1975); Thomas A. Brady, Jr., "From the Sacral Community to the Common Man: Reflections on German Reformation Studies," *CEH* 20 (1987): 230–45.

25.   Susan Rosa and Dale Van Kley describe theology as "the great bugaboo of the social historians." Rosa and Van Kley, "Religion and the Historical Discipline: A Reply to Mack Holt and Henry Heller," *French Historical Studies* 21 (1998): 628–29; Thomas Kselman, "Ambivalence and Assumption in the Concept of Popular Religion," in Daniel H. Levine, ed., *Religion and Political Conflict in Latin America,* 37–41 (Chapel Hill: University of North Carolina Press, 1986); Richard C. Trexler, "Florentine Religious Experience: The Sacred Image," *Studies in the Renaissance* 19 (1972): 7–41, esp. 33–40.

26.   Trexler, "Florentine Religious Experience," 8–10; Kselman, "Ambivalence and Assumption," 28–33.

27.   Kaufmann, *Universität und Konfessionalisierung,* 26–27, *contra* Schilling, "Das 'Zweite Reformation,'" 412; Zeeden, *Konfessionsbildung,* 67.

28.   Collinson, *The Elizabethan Puritan Movement,* 25.

29.   David Myers, *Poor, Sinning Folk: Confession and Conscience in Counter-Reformation Germany* (Ithaca, NY: Cornell University Press, 1996); Trevor Johnson, "'Everyone Should Be Like the People': Elite and Popular Religion and the Counter Reformation," in *Elite and Popular Religion,* ed. Kate Cooper and Jeremy Gregory, 206–24 (Woodbridge, Suffolk: Boydell & Brewer, 2006); William Christian, *Local Religion in Sixteenth-Century Spain* (Princeton, NJ: Princeton University Press, 1981); Kselman, "Ambivalence and Assumption."

30.   Otto Hintze, "Staatenbildung und Verfassungsentwicklung," in *Staat und Verfassung. Gesammelte Abhandlungen zur Allgemeinen Verfassungsgeschichte* (Göttingen: Vandenhoeck and Ruprecht, 1962), 34–51; Volker Press, "Das römisch-deutsche Reich–ein politisches System in verfassungs- und sozialgeschichtlicher Fragestellung," in Klingenstein and Lutz, *Spezialforschung und "Gesamtgeschichte,"* 221–42.

31.   Mack Walker, *German Home Towns: Community, State, and General Estate 1648-1871* (Ithaca, NY: Cornell University Press, 1971); Vann, "New Directions," S8–S10; Thomas A. Brady, Jr., "Some Peculiarities of German Histories in the Early Modern Era," in *Germania Ilustrata,* ed. Andrew C. Fix and Susan C. Karant-Nunn, 197–216 (Kirksville, MO: Sixteenth Century Journal Publishers, 1992) 6.

32.   Vann, *Making of a State,* 18–20.

33.   John Elliott, *Richelieu and Olivares* (Cambridge: Cambridge University Press, 1984), 6.

34.   I have borrowed this particular usage from Stephen Foster, *The Long Argument,* 287–88; cf. David Sabean, *Power in the Blood* (Cambridge: Cambridge University Press, 1984).

35.   AEB, Rep. I, 327–38.

36.   Friedrich Förner, *Relatio Historico-paranetica. De Sacrosanctis, Sacri Romani Imperii, Reliquiis, et Ornamentis* (1629); Förner, *Norimberga in Flora Avitae Romano-Catholicae Religionis* (1629): Förner, *Palma Triumphalis Miraculorum Ecclesiae Catolicae* (Ingolstadt: Wilhelm Eder, 1620); Lothar Bauer, "Die Bamberger Weihbischöfe Johann Schöner und Friedrich Förner," *BHVB* 101 (1965): 306–528; William Bradford Smith, "Friedrich Förner, the Catholic Reformation, and Witch Hunting in Bamberg," *SCJ* 36 (2005): 115–28.

37.   StAB, A 245/I, 40/I, *Annotationes Domini M. Pauli Reinelii Diaconis Selbensis Anno 1612*.

38.   John O'Malley, S.J., *Trent and All That: Renaming Catholicism in the Early Modern Era* (Cambridge, MA: Harvard University Press, 2000), 119–43; Ernst Schubert, "Gegenreformation in Franken," *JFFL* 28 (1968): 275–76.

39.   Heinz Angermeier, *Die Reichsreform Die Staatsproblematik in Deutschland zwischen Mittelalter und Gegenwart 1410–1555* (Munich: Beck, 1984); Giles Constable, *The Reformation of the Twelfth Century* (Cambridge: Cambridge University Press, 1996), 3.

40.   Constable, *The Reformation of the Twelfth Century,* 13.

41.   Constable, *The Reformation of the Twelfth Century,* 86–87.

42.   Heiko Oberman, "*Gelehrten die verkerhrten.* Popular responses to Learned Culture in the Renaissance and the Reformation," in *Religion and Culture in the Renaissance and Reformation,* ed. Steven Ozment, 42 (Kirksville, MO: Sixteenth Century Journal Publishers, 1989).

Chapter 1

1.   AEB, Rep. I, 327–38; see Hans Patze, "Neue Typen des Geschäftsschriftgutes im 14. Jahrhundert," in *Der deutsche Territorialstaat im 14. Jahrhundert* (Sigmaringen: Jan Thorbecke, 1970), I, 9–64; cf. Heinrich Lutz, "Normen und Gesellschaftlicher Wandel zwischen Renaissance und Revolution–Differenzierung und Säkularisierung," in *Politik, Kultur under Religion im Werdeprozeß der frühen Neuzeit* (Klagenfurt: Universitätsverlag Carinthia, 1982), 279–80.

2.   Hermann Heimpel, "Das deutsche Spätmittelalter. Charakter einer Zeit," *HZ* 158 (1938): 230; Helmo Hesslinger, *Die Anfänge des Schwäbischen Bundes* (Ulm and Stuttgart: W. Kohlhammer, 1970), 13–14; Karl Siegfried Bader, *Der deutsche Südwesten in seiner territorialstaatlichen Entwicklung* (Sigmaringen: Jan Thorbecke, 1978).

3.   The most famous proponent of this view was James Bryce, *The Holy Roman Empire* (New York, Macmillan, 1904).

4.   Jan Dhondt, *Etudes sur la naissance des principautés territoriales en France (IXe.–Xe. siècles)* (Bruges: de Tempel, 1948); Otto Brunner, *Land and Lordship: Structures of Governance in Medieval Austria,* trans. Howard Kaminsky and James Van Horn Melton (Philadelphia: University of Pennsylvania Press, 1992), 161; Hillay Zmora, *State and Nobility in Early Modern Germany* (Cambridge: Cambridge University Press, 1997), 1–11; Heide Wunder, "Die ländliche Gemeinde as Strukturprinzip der spätmittelalterlich-frühneuzeitlichen Geschichte Mitteleuropas," in *Landgemeinde und Stadtgemeinde in Mitteleuropa,* ed. Peter Blickle, 396 (Munich: Beck, 1991).

5.   Angermeier, *Die Reichsreform*, 13–16, 20–21; cf. the electoral decree of Louis the Bavarian (1338) and the Golden Bull of Charles IV (1356); Zeumer, doc. 127, 156–57; 130, 160–61.

6.   Lupold of Bebenburg, *Tractatus de iuribus regni et imperii Romani* (1340), in Matthias Flaccius Illyricus, *De translatione Imperii Romani ad Germanos*, II, 51–62, 101–2 (Basel: Petrum Pernam, 1566); Smith, *Kessler*, IV, 1437; Werner Goez, *Translatio Imperii* (Tübingen: Mohr, 1958), 228–32; Erich Freiherr von Guttenberg, *Das Bistum Bamberg* (Berlin: De Gruyter, 1937), 216–18.

7.   *RTA*, ältere Reihe, III, 204, 254–60.

8.   AEB, Rep I, 327, fols. 82–103; 330, fols. 128–140v; Förner, *Norimbergae*, 7–36.

9.   Angermeier, *Die Reichsreform*, 15.

10.   Zeumer, 130, 159; Lupold of Bebenburg, *Tractatus de iuribus*, 63–71.

11.   Kraemer, *Deutsche Kleinstaat*, 17.

12.   Heinz Angermeier, *Königtum und Landfriede in deutschen Spätmittelalter* (Munich: Beck, 1966), 5.

13.   *MGH* Const. II, 73, 171, 196, 196a, 204; Angermeier, *Königtum und Landfriede*, 8.

14.   StAB, B 52, 900, fols. 7–18v; Hans-Jürgen Schmitt, "Die Geistliche und Weltliche Verwaltung der Diözese und des Hochstifts Bamberg zur Zeit des Bischofs Weigand von Redwitz (1522–1556)," *BHVB* 106 (1970): 120–21, 130–39; Erich Freiherr von Guttenberg, *Die Territorienbildung am Obermain* (Bamberg: Historischer Verein, 1966), 181–82, 236, 250, 298.

15.   Helmut Maurer, *Der Herzog von Schwaben* (Sigsmaringen: Jan Thorbecke, 1978), 281ff.; Maurer's views are summarized (albeit without references) in his article "Das Herzogtum Schwaben in staufischer Zeit," in *Zeit der Staufer*, ed. Rainer Haussherr, V, 91–106 (Stuttgart: Württembergisches Landesmuseum, 1977); Klaus Schreiner, "Die Staufer als Herzöge von Schwaben," in Haussherr, *Zeit der Staufer*, III, 8; Bader, *Der deutsche Südwesten*, 31–32.

16.   Guttenberg, *Bistum Bamberg*, 28–60; Guttenberg, *Territorienbildung*, 181–82, 236, 298; Wilhelm Neukam, "Territorium und Staat der Bischöfe von Bamberg und seine Außenbehörden," *BHVB* 89 (1948/1949): 11–14.

17.   Otto Hintze, *Die Hohenzollern und ihr Werk* (Berlin: P. Parey, 1910); Christian Mayer, *Geschichte der Burggrafschaft Nürnberg* (Tübingen: Laupp, 1908); Günther Schuhmann, *Die Markgrafen von Brandenburg-Ansbach: Eine Bilddokumentation zur Geschichte der Hohenzollern in Franken* (Ansbach: Historischer Verein für Mittelfranken, 1980); Reinhard Seyboth, *Die Markgraftümer Ansbach und Kulmbach unter der Regierung Markgraf Friedrich des Ältern (1485–1515)* (Göttingen: Vandenhoeck and Ruprecht, 1985).

18.   *MZ*, III, 15, 51, 52, 78.

19.   The "Berg" in question was the hill in Nuremberg. Hans Hubert Hofmann, "Territorienbildung in Franken im 14. Jahrhundert," in Patze, *Der Deutsche Territorialstaat*, II, 266–67.

20.   Ferdinand Seibt, *Karl IV. Ein Kaiser in Europa 1326 bis 1378* (Munich: Süddeutsche Verlag, 1994), 271–76.

21.   *MZ*, III, 319, 320; IV, 68, 206, 207, 220; Klaus Peter Dietrich, *Territorial Entwicklung, Verfassung und Gerichtswesen im Gebiet um Beyreuth bis 1603* (Kallmünz: Lassleben, 1958), 62–67; Guttenberg, *Territorienbildung*, 387ff.; Gerhard Pfeiffer, "*Comicia*

burcgravie in Nuremberg," *JFFL* 11/12 (1953): 45–52; Hans Hubert Hoffmann, "Territorienbildung," 266–67; Götz Landwehr, "Mobilisierung und Konsolidierung der Herrschaftsordnung im 14. Jahrhundert," in Patze, *Der Deutsche* Territorialstaat, I, 495–96.

22. Brunner, *Land and Lordship*, 162–63; cf. Gerhard Pfeiffer's comments on the applicability of Brunner's thesis to the Hohenzollern domains, "Fürst und Land. Betrachtungen zur Bayreuther Geschichte," *AO* 57/58 (1978): 7–20; Angermeier, *Die Reichsreform*, 16–20; Bader, *Dorfgenossenschaft*, 35, 266; Hofmann, "Territorienbildung," 262; Landwehr, "Mobilisierung und Konsolidierung," 498–99. Otto Brunner viewed the "*Land*" as comprising both the territory and its historical inhabitants. In that sense, the *Land* was not merely a geographical or political entity, but a cultural one as well. The unity of the territorial state rested, in large measure on the cultural unity of the *Landgemeinde* (*Land*-community). See Howard Kaminsky and James Van Horn Melton, "Introduction," in Brunner, *Land and Lordship*, xxvii–xxix.

23. Theodore Mayer, "Die Ausbildung der Grundlagen des modernen deutschen Staates im hohen Mittelalter," *HZ* 159 (1939): 457–87; cf. Hofmann, "Territorienbildung," 265–69; Landwehr, "Mobilisierung und Konsolidierung," 498–99.

24. Michel Hofmann, "Cuius regio? Ein Beitrag zum historischen Staatsrecht Frankens," *JFFL* 11/12 (1953): 352.

25. StAB, B 52, 905; Schmitt, "Geistliche und weltliche Verwaltung," 84–85.

26. Angermeier, *Königtum und Landfriede*, 222.

27. Angermeier, *Die Reichsreform*, 331; Patze, "Herrschaft und Territorium," 49.

28. Benjamin Arnold, *Count and Bishop in Medieval Germany* (Philadelphia: University of Pennsylvania Press, 1991), 176.

29. Angermeier, *Die Reichsreform*, 17–20; Angermeier, *Königtum und Landfriede*, 5–6, 20; Hans Patze, "Herrschaft und Territorium," in Haussherr, *Zeit der Staufer*, III, 37–38; Howard Kaminsky, "Estate, Nobility, and the Exhibition of Estate in the Later Middle Ages," *Speculum* 68 (1993): 684–709.

30. This distinction first appears in the early thirteenth century. The *Reichslandfriede* of 1235 identifies two distinct groups, the old nobility and the knights (*milites* and *ministeriales*). Members of the first group were characterized as *virum libere conditionis* in Latin, and as *fursten* and *hohe lieute* in the German text. The *milites* are described as *ministeriales vero et serviles conditionis homines* or, in German, simply as *Dienstmann*. The Bavarian *Landfriede* of 1244 and 1258 likewise notes a division between counts and dukes and their knights, the latter identified as a distinct group. *MGH*, Const. II, 196, § 3, 4, 18, 28; *MGH* Const. II, 427, § 85; Hofmann, "Adel in Franken," 102–7; Fleckenstein, "Die Entstehung des niederen Adels," 31–35; Heinrich Mitteis, *Lehnsrecht und Staatsgewalt* (Weimar: Böhlau, 1958), 225ff.; Kaminsky, "Estate," 695.

31. A fourteenth-century *Landbuch* from Bayreuth describes these peasants as "Erbarer," meaning those who possess heritable (*Erbe*) allodial land (*Eigengut*). Guttenberg, *Territorienbildung*, 428ff.

32. Guttenberg, *Territorienbildung*, 60–65; 298–300; 308–24; Guttenberg, *Bistum Bamberg*, 60, 190–99; Siegfried Bachmann, "Die Landstände des Hochstifts Bamberg," *BHVB* 98 (1962): 42–50; Landwehr, "Mobilisierung und Konsolidierung," 498–99; Ernst Schubert, *Landständische Verfassung des Hochstifts Würzburg* (Würzburg: Schöningh, 1967), 27–34; cf. Kaminsky, "Estate," 636.

33. Guttenberg, *Territorienbildung*, 305–6; Hillay Zmora, "Princely State-making and the 'Crisis of the Aristocracy' in Late-medieval Germany," *P&P* 153 (1996): 39–44; Landwehr, "Mobilisierung und Konsolidierung," 493. Cf. Walter Schlesinger, "Zur Geschichte der Landesherrschaft in den Marken Brandenburg und Meissen während des 14. Jahrhunderts," in Patze, *Der Deutsche Territorialstaat*, II, 111–17; Werner Rösener, "Ministerialität, Vasallität und niederadelige Ritterschaft im Herrschaftsbereich der Markgrafen von Baden vom 11. bis zum 14. Jahrhundert," in *Herrschaft und Stand*, ed. Josef Fleckenstein, 84 (Göttingen: Vandenhoek and Ruprecht, 1979).

34. The Franconian *Landfriede* from 1340 to the end of the fourteenth century all make direct reference to princely officials, sometimes including communal officials, as sworn members of the *Landfriede* coalition. Pfeiffer, *Quellen*, 1, §§ 2, 30; 15, §§ 14, 26; 24, § 2; 62, §§ 1, 2, 30; 71; 73, §§ 1–2; Angermeier, *Königtum und Landfriede*, 107–15, 157; Landwehr, "Mobilisierung und Konsolidierung," 502–3; Patze, "Neue Typen des Geschäftsschriftgutes," 15–16, 26.

35. Urbar A, 135–36; Fritz Schnelbögl, "Siedlungsbewegungen im Veldener Forst," *JFFL*, 11/12 (1953): 221–22; Hofmann, "Adel in Franken," 99; Dieter Rödel, "Grundherrschaft und Landesausbau im Hochmittelalter am Beispiel Mainfrankens," in *Grundherrschaft und bäuerliche Gesellschaft im Hochmittelalter*, ed. Werner Rösener, 294–319 (Göttingen: Vandenhoeck and Ruprecht, 1995); Phillipe Dollinger, *Der bayerische Bauernstand vom 9. bis zum 13. Jahrhundert*, trans. Ursula Irsigler (Munich: Beck, 1982), 84–88, 105–6; Patze, "Herrschaft und Territorium," 45.

36. Schnelbögl, "Siedlungsbewegungen," 223–25; Werner Rösener, *Peasants in the Middle Ages*, trans. Alexander Stützer (Urbana: University of Illinois Press, 1992), 35–37; Guttenberg, *Territorienbildung*, 324; Hofmann, "Territorienbildung," 265–69; Landwehr, "Mobilisierung und Konsolidierung," 498–99.

37. Gerhard Philipp Wolf and Walter Tausenpfund, "Obrigkeit und jüdische Untertan in der Fränkischen Schweiz," in *Jüdische Leben in der Fränkischen Schweiz* (Erlangen: Palm and Enke, 1997), 82–83; A. Eckstein, *Geschichte der Juden im ehemaligen Fürstbistum Bamberg* (Bamberg: Handelsdruckerei, 1886), 4–15, 47–51; Guttenberg, *Territorienbildung*, 324.

38. Goez, "Karl IV," 57; Wolf and Tausendpfund, "Jüdische Untertan," 82–83; Patze, "Herrschaft und Territorium," 46.

39. Guttenberg-Wendehorst, 216, 259–61; cf. Johannes M. Klassen, "Ownership of Church Patronage and the Czech Nobility's Support for Hussitism," *ARG* 66 (1975): 36–49.

40. Guttenberg, *Territorienbildung*, 323–24, 392; Michel Hofmann, "Die Außenbehörden," I, 87.

41. Pfeiffer, *Quellen*, 148A, 418C.

42. Guttenberg-Wendehorst, 177–78, 183.

43. Oestreich, *Geist und Gestalt*, 278–81; Hamm, "Reformatio zu Reformation," 13–18; Kaminsky, "Estate," 698.

44. Dollinger, *Bayerische Bauernstand*, 112–39; Stefan Nöth, *Urbare und Wirtschaftsordnungen des Domstifts zu Bamberg*, II Teil (Neustadt a. d. Aisch: Degener, 1986), 1–5, 153–56; Roger Sablonier, "Das Dorf im Übergang vom Hoch- zum Spätmittelalter: Untersuchungen zum Wandel ländliche Gemeinschaftsformen in ostschweizerischen Raum," in *Institutionen, Kultur, und Gesellschaft im Mittelalter: Festschrift für Josef Fleckenstein*, eds. Lutz Fenske, Werner Rösener, and Thoman Zotz, 727–45 (Sigmaringen:

Jan Thorbecke, 1984); Peter Blickle, "Communalism as an Organizational Principle Between Medieval and Modern Times," in Blickle, *From the Communal Reformation to the Revolution of the Common Man,* trans. Beat Kümin, 2–3 (Leiden: Brill, 1998); Blickle, *Communal Reformation,* 155–56; Peter Blickle, "Communal Reformation and Peasant Piety: The Peasant Reformation in its Late-medieval Origins," *CEH* 20 (1987): 221–22; Rösener, *Peasants,* 50–57.

45. Nöth, *Urbare und Wirtschaftsordnungen,* II, 3; cf. 48, note 199; Guttenberg-Wendehorst, 327–28.

46. Urbar B, 224–25; cf. Nöth, *Urbare und Wirtschaftsordnungen,* 28, note 78.

47. The *urbarium* of 1468 lists three full, fifteen half, and twenty-four quarter *mansi* along with a number of smaller properties. These cannot be considered to represent individual households, insofar as a number of properties lay in land abandoned after a flood of the river Pegnitz and subsequently turned to pasture. Nöth argues that it is nearly impossible to determine the precise numbers of households from such lists of *mansi,* although they can give us a general sense of the relative sizes of communities. Erich Freiherr von Guttenberg, *Urbare und Wirtschaftsordnungen des Domstifts zu Bamberg,* I Teil (Würzburg: Schöningh, 1969), 108–10; cf. 10, 20–31; Nöth, *Urbare und Wirtschafsordnungen,* II, 28, 168–70; Nöth, "'Item darnach sol man fragen . . .' Weistümer in Urbaren der Bamberger Dompropstei aus dem 15. Jahrhundert," *JFFL* 44 (1984): 53–54; Dollinger, 106–12, 127–33; Ferdinand Geldner, ed., *Das älteste Urbar des Cistercienserklosters Langheim (um 1390)* (Würzburg: Schöningh, 1952), 36*–39*.

48. For example, Neuhof, Stammenreuth, Langenreuth, and Moritzreuth; Guttenberg-Wendehorst, 329.

49. Schnelbögl, "Siedlungsbewegungen," 223–35; Karl-Siegfried Bader, *Dorfgenossenschaft und Dorfgemeinde* (Weimar: Böhlau, 1968), 62–90, 105–14; Rösener, *Peasants,* 26, 39; Rödel, "Grundherrschaft," 315–18; cf. Blickle, "Communalism," 7.

50. *MGH* Const., V, 374, 375, §§ 6–7; Guttenberg, *Territorienbildung,* 305–10; Gerhard Pfeiffer, *Quellen,* 1, § 20; cf. Pfeiffer, "Die königliche Landfriedenseinungen in Franken," 230.

51. Dollinger, *Bayerische Bauernstand,* 133–35.

52. *MGH,* Dip. Reg., 152; Nöth, *Urbare und Wirtschaftsordnungen,* II, 4–5.

53. Urbar A, 141–52; Guttenberg, *Territorienbildung,* 264, 377–87; Neukam, "Territorium und Staat," 11–18; Michel Hofmann, "Die Außenbehörden des Hochstifts Bamberg und der Markgrafschaft Bayreuth, *JFFL* 3 (1937): 52–96; 4 (1938): 53–103; Schmitt, "Geistliche und weltliche Verwaltung," 144–49; cf. Dollinger, *Bayerische Bauernstand,* 135.

54. Guttenberg, *Bistum Bamberg,* 60–61; Guttenberg, *Territorienbildung,* 306; Endres, "Stadt und Landgemeinde," 109–10.

55. StBB, Msc. Misc. 67/41; Schmitt, "Geistliche und Weltliche Verwaltung," 165–67; M. Hofmann, "Dorfverfassung am Obermain," 140–96; Nöth, "'Item darnach sol man fragen . . .'" 53–64; cf. Bader, *Dorfgenossenschaft,* 291–304; Blaschke, "Landgemeinde und Stadtgemeinde," 122–23.

56. Pfeiffer, *Quellen,* 418 c, d, 419.

57. Michel Hofmann, "Studien zur fränkischen Bauern-Weistümer I," 102–5; Nöth, *Urbare und Wirtschaftsordnungen,* 73–73, 103, cf. 59ff; Schmitt, "Geistliche und weltliche Verwaltung," 150.

58. Schmitt, "Geistliche und weltliche Verwaltung," 144, 149, 167; Bader, *Dorfgenossenschaft*, 298–303. The title *Vogt*, as a specific designation for a judicial official of burgher origins, received official status in Bamberg in 1503, but had been used unofficially from the late fourteenth century onward. Scholars refer to this new office as the "*neuere Vogtei*" to distinguish it from the older (thirteenth- and early fourteenth-century) usage, where the terms *Vogt* and *Amtmann* were used more or less interchangeably.

59. M. Hofmann, "Dorfverfassung," 154–56; Hanns Hubert Hofmann, "Freibauern, Freidörfer, Schutz und Schirm im Fürstentum Ansbach," *ZBLG* 23 (1960): 264–65.

60. Wilhelm Störmer, "Die Gründung von Kleinstädten als Mittel herrschaftlichen Territorienaufbaus, gezeigt auf fränkischen Beispielen," *ZBLG* 36 (1973): 563–85; Blaschke, "Landgemeinde," 129–30; Patze, "Herrschaft und Territorium."

61. Günter Dippold, "Die Städtegründungen der Andechs-Meranier in Franken," in *Die Andechs-Meranier in Franken*, 183–96; Richard Winkler, "Weismain und die Andechs-Meranier," *BHVB* 136 (2000): 33–45.

62. *MZ*, III, 319; IV, 67, 301; IV, 362; VII, 237–38.

63. Johannes Merz, "Die Landstadt im Geistlichen Territorium," *Archiv für Mittelrheinische Kirchengeschichte* 46 (1994): 55–82.

64. Störmer, "Die Gründung von Kleinstädten," 576–79.

65. Reinel, *Annotationes*, 86–87.

66. Urbar A *passim;* Störmer, "Die Gründung von Kleinstädten," 582–85.

67. Urbar A, 93, 97–100; Störmer, "Die Gründung von Kleinstädten," 579–81.

68. StAB, A 221/XIII, 5380, fols. 1–3v.

69. Rudolf Endres, "Stadt- und Landgemeinde in Franken," in Blickle, *Landgemeinde und Stadtgemeinde*, 101–2.

70. StAB, A 231/I, 6951, 8800; Schmitt, "Geistliche und Weltliche Verwaltung," 148.

71. M. Hofmann, "Dorfverfassung im Obermaingebiet," 152, 188–89; Bader, *Dorfgenossenschaft*, 278–79. Note that this was not so much the case in the village of the Hohenzollern Niederland; cf. Karl-Siegmund Kramer, *Volksleben im Fürstentum Ansbach und seinen Nachbargebieten (1500–1800)* (Würzburg: Schöningh, 1961).

72. See descriptions and inventories of village churches; StAB, A 221[xiii], 5420 (Stadtsteinach), 5525 (Westheim); B 49, 115 (Marktschorgast); Reinel, *Annotationes*, 177–307 (Selb); Karl-Siegmund Kramer, *Volksleben im* Hochstift *Bamberg und im Fürstentum Coburg (1500–1800)* (Würzburg: Schöningh, 1967), 255–57; idem, *Fürstentum Ansbach*, 32–34; Bader, *Dorfgenossenschaft*, 195–98, cf. 182ff.

73. StAB, A 221, 5155; B 49, 22/I; one suspects they may have been exaggerating for effect.

74. Guttenberg-Wendehorst, *Bistum Bamberg, passim;* Fritz Schnelbögl, "Zur Siedlungsgeschichte des Raumes Erlangen-Forchheim-Gräfenberg," *JFFL* 14 (1954): 141–51.

75. Bader, *Dorfgenossenschaft*, 200.

76. Guttenberg-Wendehorst, *passim*. Similar patterns have been observed in the Swiss Thurgau, the Palatinate, Ulm, and the Lahngau; Blickle, "Communal Reformation," 224–26; Theodore Brodek, "Society and Politics of Late-medieval Ulm" (PhD diss., Columbia University, 1970); Brodek, "Lay Community and Church Institutions of the Lahngau in the Late Middle Ages," *CEH* 2 (1969): 27ff. On endowments generally, Bader, *Dorfgenossenschaft*, 186–94; Lionel Rothkrug, *Religious Practices and Collective Perceptions: Hidden Homologies in the Renaissance and Reformation* (Waterloo, ON: Department of History, University of Waterloo, 1980), 50, 171.

77. StAB, C 2, 2018, *Register über das Gotshauß zu Gefrees* (1530); StBB, Msc. Misc, 67/41; Bader, *Dorfgenossenschaft,* 207–9.

78. StAB, A 221[xiii], 5180, fols. 8–13v.

79. StAB, A 221[xiii], 5380; B 49, 176, fasc. 1; Guttenberg-Wendehorst, 135–36; Guttenberg, *Territorienbildung,* 280–81.

80. There is scant evidence of heresy in upper Franconia prior to the outbreak of the Hussite War. A handful of people in neighboring Würzburg and Eichstätt were condemned as adherents of the heresy of the Free Spirit in the later fourteenth century, though it remains open to question whether any such heresy ever existed in the first place. Nuremberg and Würzburg both appear to have been home to Waldensian communities. In Nuremberg, there were trials in 1332/1333, 1354, and 1378/79, although the total number of people indicted is a matter of debate. The last wave of prosecutions seems to have been an extension of attempts to stamp out the heresy in Bohemia. Matthias Simon, *Evangelische Kirchengeschichte Bayerns* (Munich: Paul Müller, 1942), 114–17; Franz Machilek, "Hus und die Hussiten in Franken," *JFFL,* 51 (1991): 22; Gordon Leff, *Heresy in the Later Middle Ages* (Manchester: University of Manchester Press, 1967), 379, 478–79; Malcolm Lambert, *Medieval Heresy* (Oxford: Basil Blackwell, 1992), 158.

81. Franz Xaver Haimerl, *Das Prozessionswesen des Bistum Bamberg im Mittelalter* (Munich, 1937), 60–61.

82. Ludwig Remling, *Bruderschaften in Franken: Kirchen- und Sozialgeschichtlich Untersuchungen zur spämittelalterlichen und frühneuzeitlichen Bruderschaftswesen* (Würzburg: Schöningh, 1986), 22–23.

83. AEB, Rep. I, 337, fols. 635–640.

84. The spread of the Eucharistic cult involving the adoration of the *corporis Christi* has been much studied. In Franconia the cult had its origins in local traditions concerning Eucharistic miracles. The more cosmopolitan form of the cult first appears in Bamberg in 1390. It generally focused around sacramental procession held each Thursday. These were often called Angel Masses (*Engel-Messe*) on account of the hymn *Ecce panis angelorum,* which was sung during the procession. Haimerl, *Prozessionswesen,* 32–43; Werner Scharrer, "Laienbruderschaften in der Stadt Bamberg von Mittelalter bis zum Ende des Alten Reiches," *BHVB* 126 (1990): 82–84; Remling, *Bruderschaften,* 215–16.

85. Bamberg, Forchheim, Kronach, Hersbruck, Kasendorf, Hollfeld, Scheßlitz, Bayreuth, Creußen, Lichtenfels, Hof, Waischenfeld, Ebermannstadt, Ebensfeld, Baiersdorf, Münchberg, Gefrees, Weismain, and Wirsberg (diocese of Bamberg); also Selb and Vilseck (diocese of Regensburg). Haimerl, *Prozessionswesen,* 60–61.

86. Reinel, *Annotationes,* 163–70, 430; AEB, Rep. I, 341, fols. 29–34, 166.

87. Alexander Prechtl, "Bayreuths religiose Bruderschaften des ausgehenden Mittelalters," *AO* 79 (1999): 101–4.

88. Remling, *Bruderschaften,* 20, 132–85.

89. AEB, Rep. I, Urkunde, 331; Rep. I, 332, fols. 1–5; Georg Kanzler, "Die Landkapitel im Bistum Bamberg," *BHVB* 83/84 (1931/1934): I, 11–30; II, 20–21, 31–33; 99–103; Schmitt, "Geistliche und Weltliche Verwaltung," 62–65. Haimerl, *Prozessionswesen,* 32–43; William Bradford Smith, "Some Territorial Implications of Rural Confraternities in Upper Franconia," *Confraternitas* 6 (1995): 13–18.

90. Haimerl, *Prozessionswesen,* 64–65.

91.   Kanzler, "Landkapitel," II, 32–33.

92.   Johannes Kist, *Klerus und Wissenschaft im spätmittelalterlichen Bistum Bamberg* (Bamberg: Philosophische-Theologische Hochschule, 1964), 18; Herman Jordan, *Reformation und gelehrte Bildung in der Markgrafschaft Ansbach-Bayreuth* (Leipzig: Deichert, 1917), 38–42.

93.   Franz Pietsch, *Geschichte der gelehrten Bildung in Kulmbach* (Kulmbach: Freunde der Plassenburg, 1974), 280–83. On the social origins of late-medieval German students, cf. Rainer C. Schwinges, "Karrieremuster: Zur sozialen Rolle der Gelehrten im Reich des 14. bis 16. Jahrhunderts. Eine Einführung," in *Gelehrte im Reich. Zur Sozial- und Wirkungsgeschichte akademischer Eliten des 14. bis 16. Jahrhunderts,* ed. Rainer Schwinges (Berlin: Duncker and Humblot, 1996), 11–22; Michael H. Shank, *"Unless You Believe, You Shall Not Understand": Logic, University and Society in Late-medieval Vienna* (Princeton, NJ: Princeton University Press, 1988), 23–24.

94.   Kist, *Matrikel,* 177, 524, 1166, 3320, 5128.

95.   Kist, *Matrikel,* 5865; Pietsch, *Gelehrte Bildung,* 47–50.

96.   Schwinges, "Karrieremuster," 18–19; Oberman, "Gelehrten," 47–48.

97.   Oberman, "Gelehrten," 46; Jürgen Mietke, "Karrierechancen eines Theologiestudiums im späteren Mittelalter," in Schwinge, *Gelehrten im Reich,* 202–9; Schwinges, "Karrieremuster," 13.

98.   According to Heiko Oberman, the evidence "points to a dialectical movement" whereby the common person acquired ever more first-hand knowledge of higher culture. In response to these encounters, peasants and burghers "developed an impatient thirst for information which . . . came to yield its own broad-based intellectual sense and sensibility." Oberman, "Gelehrten," 62.

99.   Mietke, "Karrierechancen," 189. The expansion of confraternities and schools and the surge in endowments in the second half of the fifteenth century would seem to argue against the "decline" of the peasantry in upper Franconia in the half-century preceding the Protestant Reformation. Cf. Karlheinz Blaschke, "Dorfgemeinde und Stadtgemeinde in Sachsen," 131–35.

100.   StAB, A 170, 1174; *MZ,* III: 78; IV: 67; L III, 112; L IV, 1009; Fuchs, *Marktschorgast. Pfarrei, Amt und Markt* (Bamberg, 1959), 8–11; Guttenberg-Wendehorst, 199–202; Helmut Beisbart, "Marktschorgast–Ein Stadt Kämpft um ihre Rechte. Ein Beitrag zur oberfränkische Stadtgeschichte," *GO* 21 (1997/98): 27–28.

101.   L III, 184–85.

102.   AEB, Rep. I, 341, fols. 12–13; StAB, A 170, Lade 624, 1174; *MZ,* IV, 67; L III, 312; L IV, 1009–10; Guttenberg-Wendehorst, 199–201.

103.   StAB, A 95, Lade 297, 1310; L III, 315; Wachter, 10235.

104.   *MZ,* IV, 345; L IV, 75–78.

105.   L IV, 79; Fuchs, *Marktschorgast,* 24. The names of their first three hamlets suggest that they were *Rodunge;* cf. M. Hofmann, "Dorfverfassung," 191–92.

106.   L IV, 92, 225–26; Fuchs, *Markschorgast,* 24–25; Beisbart, "Marktschorgast," 28–32. By the burghers' reckoning, the *Amt* of Marktschorgast now included over twenty villages and hamlets–substantially more than the eight mentioned in the *urbarium* of 1323/28.

107.   StAB, A 170, Lade 619, 350, 352, 353; AEB, Rep I, 341, fol. 55v; L IV, 906–7; Guttenberg-Wendehorst, 202–3.

108. StAB, A 170, Lade 619, 355, 363, 364; L IV, 907; Guttenberg-Wendehorst, 203.

109. StAB, A 95[ii], Lade 267, 1330; Guttenberg-Wendehorst, 202–3; Fuchs, *Marktschorgast*, 30; Kist, *Matrikel*, 1869.

110. L IV, 908; Guttenberg-Wendehorst, 203.

111. AEB, Rep. I, 341, fol. 54v.

112. StAB, A 170, Lade 619, 365; C 3, 8, fols. 8v–9; AEB, Rep. I, 341, fol. 55; L IV, 908; Guttenberg-Wendehorst, 203; Haimerl, *Prozessionswesen*, 60–61.

113. Kist, *Matrikel*, 1773, 6177, 5216.

114. Kist, *Matrikel*, 1166.

115. Kist, *Matrikel*, 6489, 6491.

116. Kist, *Matrikel*, 1984, 5215, 6331.

117. Jordan, *Reformation und Bildung*," 38–42.

118. Selb, Kirchenlamitz, and Lanzendorf, all towns of comparable size, sent five, six, and three students respectively to universities during the same period.

119. Blickle, "Communal Reformation," 220.

120. StAB, A 170, Lade 619, 365; Kist, *Matrikel*, 2287; L IV, 908.

121. Kist, *Matrikel*, 1918; L IV, 909.

122. Eberhard, *Konfessionsbildung*, 30–36; Kaminsky, "Estate," *passim*.

Chapter 2

1. Ernst Schubert, "Franken als Königsnahe Landschaft unter Karl IV," *BDLG* 114 (1978): 865–90; Ranier Dotterweich, "Die Rolle Bischofs Lambert von Brunn in der Reichspolitik unter Kaiser Karl IV. und König Wenzel," *BHVH* 118 (1982/83): 31–82; Peter Johanek, "Zur kirchlichen Reformtätigkeit Bischof Lamprechts von Brunn," *BHVB* 102 (1966): 235–56; Ivan Hlaváček, *Das Urkunden- und Kanzleiwesen des böhmischen und römischen Königs Wenzel (IV.) 1376–1419* (Stuttgart: Hiersemann, 1970), 181–83; Guttenberg, *Bistum Bamberg*, 228–40; Angermeier, *Königtum und Landfriede*, 205–10, 263–66.

2. Angermeier, *Die Reichsreform*, 35, 51–55.

3. *MGH, Dipl. Reg*, III, 143, 151–53; Bernhard Schimmelpfennig, *Bamberg im Mittelalter. Siedelgebiete und Bevölkerung bis 1370* (Lübeck/Hamburg: Mathiesen, 1964), 10–20.

4. Guttenberg, *Bistum Bamberg*, 61; Kist, *Domkapitel*, 33–40; Georg Weigel, *Die Wahlkapitulationen der Bamberger Bischöfe 1328–1693* (Bamberg: Schmidt, 1909), 6–9, 19; Bachmann, "Landstände," 35–36; Günther Christ, "Selbstverständnis und Rolle der Domkapitel in der Geistlichen Territorien des alten Deutschen Reiches in der Frühneuzeit," *ZHF* 16 (1989): 257–328.

5. Although the free election of bishops was stipulated by the Concordat of Worms (1122), it was not until the early thirteenth century that the practice became accepted. The Fourth Lateran Council decreed that bishops ought to be elected by *maior et senior pars capituli*. This principle had already found its way into imperial law through legislation of Otto IV in 1209 and the Golden Bull of Eger, issued by

Frederick II in 1213. Kist, *Domkapitel,* 4–8; Bachmann, "Landstände," 34–38; Christ, "Selbstverständnis," 259–60.

6. Weigel, *Wahlkapitulationen,* 22–30; 35–36; Bachmann, "Landstände," 37–38.

7. Heinrich Joachim Jäck, *Bambergische Jahrbücher vom Jahre 741 bis 1829* (Bamberg: Selbstverlag, 1829), 178; Chroust, I, xxvi.

8. Albrecht von Eyb, a fifteenth-century canon and early humanist, claimed that walls "represented extensive freedom" for the burghers, and thus posed a threat to the ecclesiastical regime. Isolde Maierhöfer, "Bambergs Verfassungstopograpische Entwicklung vom 15. bis zum 18. Jahrhundert," in *Bischofs- und Kathedralstädte des Mittelalters und der frühen Neuzeit,* ed. Franz Petri, 155 (Cologne: Böhlau Verlag, 1976).

9. Wilhelm Neukam, "Immunitäten und Civitas in Bamberg von der Gründung des Bistums 1007 bis zum Ausgang des Immunitätenstreit 1440," *BHVB* 78 (1922/23/24): 189–367; Alwin Reindl, "Die Vier Immunitäten des Domkapitels zu Bamberg," *BHVB* 105 (1969): 232–33; Maierhöfer, 146–62.

10. Jäck, *Bambergische Jahrbücher,* 227.

11. *Das Bamberger Stadtrecht,* ed. Harald Parigger (Würzburg: Schöningh, 1983), 5; Maierhöfer, "Verfassungstopograpische Entwicklung," 146–50; Reindl, "Immunitäten des Domkapitels," 232–33; Neukam, "Immunitäten und Civitas," 195–99, 230, 254–55.

12. *Stadtrecht,* §§ 376–83; *Rechtsbuch* (1348), 19–21; Chroust, I, xxix–xxx, 176–80; Weigel, *Wahlkapitulationen,* 130–31; Maierhöfer, "Verfassungstopograpische Entwicklung," 151; Reindl, "Immunitäten des Domkapitels," 236–37.

13. *Rechtsbuch* (1348), 23–28; L III, 120–21; Bachmann, "Landstände," 65.

14. Pfeiffer, *Quellen,* 1; Angermeier, *Königtum und Landfriede,* 169.

15. *RI,* VIII, 2188.

16. Schubert, "Franken als Königsnahe Landschaft," 872; Guttenberg, *Bistum Bamberg,* 225, 228–29; Dotterweich, "Lambert von Brunn," *BHVH* 118 (1982/83): 38–39; Gerhard Losher, *Königtum und Kirche zur Zeit Karls IV* (Munich: Oldenbourg, 1985).

17. *RTA,* ältere Reihe, I, 35; Angermeier, *Königtum und Landfriede,* 255–58.

18. *RI,* VIII, 5711, 5715, 5717, 5718; Chroust, I, xxxiv; L III, 410; Guttenberg, *Bistum Bamberg,* 236.

19. Pfeiffer, *Quellen,* 5.

20. Jäck, *Jahrbücher,* 150–59; L, III, 352; Joseph Würdinger, *Kriegsgeschichte von Bayern, Franken, Pfalz, und Schwaben 1347–1506* (Munich: Literarisch-Artistische Anstalt, 1868), I, 101; Guttenberg, *Bistum Bamberg,* 236–37.

21. Chroust, I, 39.

22. Pfeiffer, *Quellen,* 360–62.

23. L III, 472; Jäck, *Jahrbücher,* 167–69; Guttenberg, *Bistum Bamberg,* 237; Neukam, "Immunitäten und Civitas," 239; Chroust, I, xxxiv–xxxv, 2–3; *Stadtrecht,* 6–9.

24. M. Martin Hoffmann, *Vrbs Bamberga et Abbates Montis Monachorum* (1585), in J. P. Ludewig, *Scriptores rerum Episcopatus Bambergensis,* 211 (Frankfurt/Leipzig: Ludewig, 1718); Johanek, 237–38.

25. StAB, B 86, 295; AEB, Rep. 1, 9; L IV, 170–86; Weigel, *Wahlkapitulationen,* 51; Bachmann, "Landstände," 38–41; Guttenberg, *Bistum Bamberg,* 246–47.

26. In 1372, the city of Würzburg rose in rebellion, ejecting the bishop and putting its own candidate on the episcopal throne. In 1397, nine towns in the Hochstift

Würzburg formed a league to protest, among other things, an excise tax on wine. Pfeiffer, *Quellen,* 360–62, 369–70; Wendehorst, *Bistum Würzburg,* Teil 2, 98–99, 102–3, 120–23; Scherzer, "Hochstift Würzburg," 45–50; Würdinger, I, 99–100, 249.

27. Matthias Thumser, *Das Konflikt um die Wahlkapitulation zwischen dem Bamberger Domkapitel und Bischof Philip von Henneberg* (Bamberg: Historischer Verein, 1990), 8–10.

28. Between 1392 and 1409, the canons were locked in a bitter dispute with the cathedral provost, Johann von Heideck, over the latter's alleged financial misdealing. When a commission appointed by Heideck failed to resolve the matter, both sides resorted to violence. A truce was negotiated by Lamprecht von Brunn and Burgrave Friedrich in 1394, but it was not until 1418 that the question of finance was finally settled. Guttenberg, *Urbare und Wirtschaftsordnungen,* I, 39, 44–48; Nöth, *Urbare und Witschaftsordnungen,* II, 1–10; Kist, *Matrikel,* 2489.

29. StAB, B 86, 236; Scharrer, "Laienbruderschaften," 61–63.

30. Guttenberg-Wendehorst, *passim.*

31. Scharrer, "Laienbruderschaften," 65–66.

32. John Van Engen, "Late Medieval Anticlericalism: The Case of the New Devout," in *Anticlericalism in Late Medieval and Early Modern Europe,* ed. Peter Dykema and Heiko Oberman, 31–32 (Leiden: Brill, 1993); Bob Scribner, "Anticerlicalism and the Cities," in Dykema and Oberman, 131–42; Geoffrey Dipple, *Antifraternalism and Anticlericalism in the German Reformation* (Aldershot: Ashgate, 1996), 4. Dipple notes that Carmelites are "conspiciuously absent" from studies of the German Reformation. In Bamberg, they appear to have played an important role in the early evangelical movement up to and including the Peasants' War.

33. Guttenberg, *Bistum Bamberg,* 244; L IV, 92ff.

34. *RTA,* ältere Reihe, IX, 9–10, 206, 209; L IV, 174–214; Maierhöfer, "Verfassungstopograpische Entwicklung," 156; Guttenberg, *Bistum Bamberg,* 250.

35. StAB C 3, 1971; Gerhard Schlesinger, *Die Hussiten in Franken* (Kulmbach: Stadtarchiv, 1974), 31–81; František Palacký, *Dějiny Národu Českého* (Prague: Mazač, 1937), III, 395–97, 403–4, 422–23; Franz Machilek, "Hus und die Hussiten in Franken," *JFFL* 51 (1991): 15ff.; L IV, 203–16.

36. Chroust, I, 2–5; Palacký, *Dějiny Národu Českého,* III, 423–24. The amount of the ransom is the subject of debate.

37. Chroust, I, 6–16.

38. Chroust, I, 18–28.

39. Chroust, I, 29–50; *RTA,* ältere Reihe, IX, 301.

40. *RTA,* ältere Reihe, X, 129, 136, 137.

41. Chroust, I, 51–59.

42. Chroust, I, 60–61; L, IV, 218–24; Guttenberg, *Bistum Bamberg,* 252–54; Neukam, "Immunitäten und Civitas," 230; Reindl, "Immunitäten des Domkapitels," 237.

43. Chroust, I, 83–87. This was the standard punishment for failure to pay taxes.

44. Chroust, I, 97–100.

45. *RTA,* ältere Reihe, X, 362; XI, xx; Chroust, lvi–lvii, 73–86; Guttenberg, *Bistum Bamberg,* 254–55.

46. Chroust, I, 101–7; see also 92–94.

47. AEB, Rep. I, 1, prod. 4; *RTA,* ältere Reihe, XI, 224, 230; Chroust, I, lx, 113–37; Guttenberg, *Bistum Bamberg,* 255.

48.   *RTA, ältere Reihe,* VI, 248, 251b; Chroust, I, 139ff.

49.   Chroust, I, 157–58, 160–61, 168–69.

50.   Bernhard Pfändter, "Die Belagerung Bamberg im Jahre 1435: Ein Zeitgenössische Gedicht, Eingeleitet und Kommentiert," *BHVB* 118 (1982): 83–86; Chroust, I, lxii; L IV, 232–33; Johannes Kist, "Hieronymus von Reitzenstein, O. Cist., Weihbischof von Bamberg (1474–1503)," *BHVB* 90 (1951): 324.

51.   *RTA,* ältere Reihe, XII, 140; Chroust, I, 169; Guttenberg, *Bistum Bamberg,* 256.

52.   Chroust, I, lxiii–lxvi; Caroline Göldel, "Zur Entwicklung der Bamberger Stadtverfassung im 15. Jahrhundert im Spannungsfeld Rat-Gemeine-Klerus," *BHVB* 135 (1999): 14–21; L IV, 237–41; Maierhöfer, "Verfassungstopographische Entwicklung,"158.

53.   Bachmann, "Landstände," Beilage 1, 198.

54.   L IV, 236, 249–50, 265–66, 272.

55.   Bachmann, "Landstände," Beilage 1, 198–203.

56.   StAB, A 29, Lade 30, 41; A 85, Lade 341, 1361; Lade 344, 1482, 1483; Bachmann, "Landstände," 87, Beilage 3–4, 207–12; Reinhard Seyboth, "Markgraf Johann der Alchemist von Brandenburg (1406–1464)," *JFFL,* 51 (1991): 39–65; L IV, 252–53.

57.   StAB, A 85, Lade 341, 1362; Bachmann, "Landstände," 88–90, Beilage 7, 214–20; L IV, 254–57; Guttenberg, *Bistum Bamberg,* 259. The events in Bamberg parallel similar developments in Würzburg. On four occasions between 1408 and 1432, a deputation of knights was called to mediate between the bishop and chapter. According to the terms of the *Runder Vertrag* of January 18, 1435, a council of regency was set up, comprising nobles, prelates, and canons. A third of the canons in Bamberg were also members of the chapter in Würzburg, including Johann Gottfried Schenk von Limpurg. Consequently, it seems likely that the proposed settlement in Bamberg was based, at least in part, on reforms in Würzburg. Schubert, "Landstände," 77–85; Scherzer, "Hochstift Würzburg," 51–59.

58.   Chroust, I, 149–50.

59.   Bachmann, "Landstände," 90.

60.   Bachmann, "Landstände," Beilage 9, 220.

61.   Weigel, *Wahlkapitulationen,* 60–63.

62.   L IV, 309, 312, 329, 332, 335; Guttenberg, *Bistum Bamberg,* 266.

63.   Bachmann, "Landstände," Beilage 10, 221–25.

64.   Bachmann, "Landstände," 237, Beilage 11, 225–27, doc. 17, 235–38; Guttenberg, *Bistum Bamberg,* 263–64.

65.   Ludwig Unger, *Die Reform des Benediktiner Klosters St. Michael bei Bamberg in der 2. Hälfte des 15. Jahrhunderts* (Bamberg: Historischer Verein, 1987), 26.

66.   StAB, B 86, 217, fols. 80v–92; Thumser, *Philipp von Henneberg,* 12–14.

67.   Weigel, *Wahlkapitulationen,* 66, appendix II, 132–35.

68.   Weigel, *Wahlkapitulationen,* appendix III, 136–37.

69.   Thumser, *Philipp von Henneberg,* Beilage 87–91; Weigel, *Wahlkapitulationen,* 67–70.

70.   StAB, B 82, 7a, fols. 52–76v; Bachmann, "Landstände," Beilage 20–23, 239–47; Weigel, *Wahlkapitulationen,* 69–71.

71.   Weigel, *Wahlkapitulationen,* 71–73.

72.   Pfändter, "Belagerung Bamberg," 94.

73.   Geldner, *Langheim,* 69–74; Geldner, *Urbar,* 29*–35*; Guttenberg, *Bistum Bamberg,* 234–35, 238.

74.   StAB, B 113, 10; Johanek, "Reformtätigkeit," 245–47; Guttenberg, *Bistum Bamberg,* 245; L IV, 41.

75.   StBB, Theol. Msc. 37. The manuscript is dated 1437 (fol. 173) but the actual date and provenance are uncertain.

76.   Johanek, "Reformtätigkeit," 240–44; Schmitt, "Geistliche und weltliche Verwaltung," 50–54; Guttenberg, *Bistum Bamberg,* 238.

77.   Johanek, 247–52; Schmitt, "Die bamberger Synoden," 25–26; Guttenberg, *Bistum Bamberg,* 238. A fourth synod, held in 1390, dealt specifically with the reform of the monastery at Neuenkirchen.

78.   StBB, Theol. Msc. 38, fols. 260–299; 211, fols. 99–188; 226, fols. 106–150 (autograph); Kist, *Matrikel,* 3010; Johanek, "Reformtätigkeit," 249–51; Guttenberg, *Bistum Bamberg,* 245.

79.   StAB, B 23, 71; L, IV, 243; Guttenberg, *Bistum Bamberg,* 260.

80.   Andreas Lahner, "Die ehemalige Benediktiner-Abtei Michelsberg zu Bamberg," *BHVB* 51 (1889): 139–74; Unger, *Reform St. Michael,* 9–25; Hoffmann, *Vrbs Bamberga,* 918.

81.   StAB, A 23, Lade 23, 40; L IV, 310, 360.

82.   Hans Paschke, "Das Franziskanerkloster an der Schranne zu Bamberg," *BHVB* 110 (1974): 171.

83.   Schmitt, "Bamberger Synoden," 88–91; Deckart, "Karmalitenkloster," 47–148; Lahner, "Benediktiner-Abtei," 177–79; L, IV, 336; Guttenberg, *Bistum Bamberg,* 265.

84.   Lahner, "Benediktiner-Abtei," 180–98; Unger, *Reform St. Michael,* 33–61; Guttenberg, *Bistum Bamberg,* 265.

85.   Hermann Josef Sieben, *Die Partikularsynode: Studien zur Geschichte der Konzilsidee* (Frankfurt: Josef Knecht, 1990); Joachim W. Stieber, *Pope Eugenius IV, the Council of Basel, and the Secular and Ecclesiastical Authorities of the Empire* (Leiden: Brill, 1978), 170.

86.   Chroust, I, 106; *RTA,* ältere Reihe, X, 238.

87.   Schmitt, "Die Bamberger Synoden," 26–28; L, IV, 280–81; Kist, *Matrikel,* 6041; Machilek, "Hus und die Hussiten," 34.

88.   StBB, Theol. Msc. 226, fols. 169–179; Schmitt, "Die Bamberger Synoden," 48–85; L IV, 280; Guttenberg, *Bistum Bamberg,* 260. Schmitt assigned the date 1431 to the document, following the date that appears in pencil in the original MS. Looshorn dismissed the statute entirely, whereas Guttenberg was convinced of its authenticity. The manuscript itself was prepared by one "Johannes Koppischt de Aurbach," presumably Johann von Auerbach, in 1462 (fol. 179) and appears in a collection that includes, among other things, the *Directorium pro instructione simplicium presbyterorum,* a summary overview of the Bible (fols. 165v–168v), and various other treatises. In context, it appears that the codex was meant as a compilation of materials related to the reforms initiated by Anton von Rotenhan.

89.   Schmitt, "Die Bamberger Synoden," 72; Hamm, "Reformation zur Reformation," 14–15.

90.   Schmitt, "Die Bamberger Synoden," 91–184; Guttenberg, *Bistum Bamberg,* 276.

91.   Schmitt, "Die Bamberger Synoden," 92.

92.   StBB, Theol. Msc., 38, fol. 270v.

93.   Wilhelm Schonath, "Die Liturgische Drucke des Bistums und späteren Erzbistums Bamberg," *BHVB* 103 (1967): 387–89, 394–95.

94.   Schmitt, "Die Bamberger Synoden," 92.

95.   StBB, Msc. Bibl. 17; cf. Kist, *Klerus und Wissenschaft,* 4–5.

96.   StBB, Theologische Mss. 4, fols. 266v–272 (1432); 22, fols. 239v–248 (1456); 142, fols. 139–217 (1431); 143, fols. 1–55, 74–80v, 235v–244 (1458); 153, fols. 1–196 (1458).

97.   StBB, Theologische Mss. 28, fols. 183–228 (1458); 58, fols. 1–341 (1462); 91, fols. 49–70 (1438); 211, fols. 71–80, 93–92 (1454).

98.   StAB, A 50, Lade 902, 202.

99.   StAB, A 50, Lade 901, 154.

100.   AEB, Rep. I, 331, fol. 72v; 336, fol. 252; StAB, A 221[xiii], 5525; B 49, 115.

101.   Klaus Arnold, "Johannes Trithemius und Bamberg: '*Oratio ad clerum Bambergensem*'" *BHVB* 107 (1971): 178–86; Arnold, *Johannes Trithemius* (Würzburg, 1971), 34.

102.   *Oratio ad clerum,* 179.

103.   *Oratio ad clerum,* 180.

104.   II Corinthians 5:6; Hebrews 13:14.

105.   *Oratio ad clerum,* 181.

106.   *Oratio,* 183–84.

107.   *Oratio,* 184–85.

108.   Matthew 5:13, 16.

109.   *Oratio ad clerum,* 185.

110.   StBB, Theol. Msc. 38, fols. 261v–262.

111.   StBB, Msc. Theol. 37, fols. 15v–17v, 27v–28.

112.   StBB, Msc. Theol. 38, fols. 260ff.; 226, fol. 108ff.

113.   StBB, Msc. Theol. 38, fols. 260v, 266v.

Chapter 3

1.   *RTA, ältere Reihe,* I, 205; XIII, 223; Zeumer, 143; Sabine Wefers, *Das politische System Kaiser Sigismunds* (Stuttgart: Steiner, 1989), 5–7, 29–30; Fritz Hartung, *Geschichte des Fränkischen Kreises* (Aalen: Scientia, 1961), 18–24; Angermeier, *Königtum und Landfriede,* 270–82, 381–91.

2.   Seyboth, *Die Markgraftümer,* 341–67; Hofmann, "Die Außenbehörden," 55–56; Karl Heinrich Lang, *Neuere Geschichte des Fürstenthums Baireuth* (Göttingen: J. C. D. Schneider, 1798) I, 4, 34–35.

3.   Friedrich Merzbacher, *Iudicium provinciale ducatus Franconiae: Das Kaiserliche Landgericht des Herzogtums Franken-Würzburg im Spätmittelalter* (Munich: Beck, 1965); Seyboth, *Die Markgraftümer,* 21, 102–5.

4.   Seyboth, *Die Markgraftümer,* 106–7.

5.   Angermeier, *Die Reichsreform,* 100–101, 104–13.

6.   *MZ,* VII, 432; Wendehorst, *Bistum Würzburg,* II, 152; L, IV, 71–88.

7.   StAB, A 85, 6; A 160[II], 2624; *RTA, ältere Reihe,* XII, 266, note 6; Wendehorst, *Bistum Würzburg,* II, 149–51; Guttenberg, *Bistum Bamberg,* 267.

8.   StAB, A 85, 7.

9.   Julius von Minutoli, ed., *Das kaiserliche Buch des Markgrafen Albrecht Achilles, Kurfürstliche Periode 1470–1486* (Osnabrück: Zeller, 1984), 349; Heinz Quirin, "Markgraf Albrecht Achilles von Brandenburg-Ansbach als Politker," *JFFL* 31 (1971): 287–89; Wendehorst, *Bistum Würzburg,* 165–71; Schubert, *Landstände,* 85–86; Scherzer, "Das Hochstift Würzburg," 60–61.

10.   StAB, A 160, Lade 581, 2653; *RTA, ältere Reihe,* CVII, 233, note 4; Angermeier, *Königtum und Landfriede,* 415; Quirin, "Albrecht Achilles," 271–72, 290, 294; Wendehorst, *Bistum Würzburg,* 177; Scherzer, "Das Hochstift Würzburg," 64.

11.   StAB, A 160, Lade 581, 2625a; Falkenstein, I, 293, 298; Angermeier, *Königtum und Landfriede,* 418–20; Wendehorst, *Bistum Würzburg,* 177–79; Seyboth, "Johann der Alchemist," 59.

12.   Hintze, *Die Hohenzollern und ihr Werk,* 93.

13.   StAB, A 160, Lade 581, 2626a, 2327; Seyboth, *Die Markgraftümer,* 26, 110.

14.   StAB, A 160, Lade 484, 2817; C 3, 1221, prod. 3; Falkenstein, I, 324, 326, 327; L IV, 303–5; Wili Ulshamer, "Die 'Rother Richtung' 1460," in *900 Jahre Roth,* ed. Günther Rüger, 103–54 (Roth: Festaussschuss der Stadt Roth, 1960); Wendehorst, *Bistum Würzburg,* III, 5–6; Guttenberg, *Bistum Bamberg,* 263; Scherzer, "Hochstift Würzburg," 64–66; Seyboth, "Johann der Alchemist," 66–67; Seyboth, *Die Markgraftümer,* 110–11.

15.   StAB A 170, Lade 34, 1522; L IV, 307–9; Wendehorst, *Bistum Würzburg,* III, 8–10; Guttenberg, *Bistum Bamberg,* 263–64; Angermeier, *Königum und Landfriede,* 430, 442; Seyboth, *Die Markgraftümer,* 111.

16.   Stieber, *Eugenius IV,* 288–301.

17.   Scherzer, "Bistum Würzburg," 64.

18.   Angermeier, *Die Reichsreform,* 106–7, 138–40.

19.   Minutoli, *Kaiserliche Buch,* 270.

20.   StAB, C 3, 1220, fasc. 3, fol. 23; 1221, prod. 2; 1552; Minutoli, *Kaiserliche Buch,* 270–72, 360.

21.   Seyboth, *Die Markgraftümer,* 308–9.

22.   Felix Priebatsch, *Die Politische Korrespondenz des Kurfürsten Albrecht Achilles* (Osnabrück: Zeller, 1965), III, 5–7; Minutoli, *Kaiserliche Buch,* 273.

23.   StAB, C 3, 1220, prod. 8; fasc. 2, fols. 1–11; fasc. 3; Priebatsch, *Politische Korrespondenz,* III, 7–8.

24.   StAB, C 3, 1220, fasc. 3; Priebatsch, *Politische Korrespondenz,* III, 10–11.

25.   Minutoli, *Kaiserliche Buch,* 285.

26.   Priebatsch, *Politische Korrespondenz,* III, 11–14.

27.   Priebatsch, *Politische Korrespondenz,* III, 24; Minutoli, *Kaiserliche Buch,* 275, 278.

28.   StAB, C 3, 1220, prod. 14; Priebatsch, *Politische Korrespondenz,* III, 24–25.

29.   Priebatsch, *Politische Korrespondenz,* III, 16.

30.   Priebatsch, *Politische Korrespondenz,* III, 25–26.

31.   StAB, C 2, 472; Priebatsch, *Politische Korrespondenz,* III, 27–32; Minutoli, *Kaiserliche Buch,* 283–88, 368–69.

32.   StAB, A 160, 2903; Lang, *Fürstenthums Baireuth,* I, 109; Pfeiffer, "Fürst und Land," 10.

33.   August Jegel, "Geschichte der Landstände in den ehemaligen Fürstentum Ansbach-Bayreuth 1500–1533," *AO* 24 (1910): 61–63; Seyboth, *Die Markgraftümer,*

122–27; Ernest Bock, *Der Schwäbische Bund und seiner Verfassung, 1488–1534* (Aalen: Scientia, 1968), vii–xxxii, 39ff.

34.   August Jegel, "Die Landständige Verfassung in den ehemaligen Fürstentum Ansbach-Bayreuth," *AO* 25 (1912): 18–25; Pfeiffer, "Fürst und Land," 12–13; Lang, *Fürstenthums Baireuth*, I, 111–13.

35.   Lang, *Fürstenthums Baireuth*, I, 45–47, 110; Endres, "Stadt- und Landgemeinde in Franken," 104; Oestreich, 280.

36.   Lang, *Fürstenthums Baireuth*, I, 12, 109–11; Bernard Sicken, "Landesherrliche Einnahmen und Territorialstruktur: Die Fürstentümer Ansbach und Kulmbach zu Beginn der Neuzeit," *JFFL* 42 (1982): 153–248; Uwe Müller, *Die ständische Vertretung in der fränkischen Margraftümer in der erste Hälfte des 16. Jahrhunderts* (Neustadt a. d. Aisch: Degener, 1984), 12, 40–42, 238; Zmora, "Princely State-making," 42–49; Oestreich, *Geist und Gestalt*, 280–83; Eberhard, *Konfessionsbildung und Stände*, 27–28.

37.   Jegel, "Landständige Verfassung," 18–25.

38.   Seyboth, *Die Markgraftümer*, 306–13; Peter-Michael Hahn, "Kirchenschütz und Landesherrschaft in der Mark Brandenburg im späten 15. und frühen 16. Jahrhundert," *Jahrbuch für die Geschichte Mittel- und Ostdeutschlands* 28 (1979): 179–220; cf. Johanna Naendrup-Reimann, "Territorien und Kirche im 14. Jahrhundert," in Patze, *Deutsche Territorialstaat*, I, 117–74; Dieter Stievermann, *Landesherrschaft und Klosterwesen in spätmittelalterlichen Württemberg* (Sigmaringen: Jan Thorbecke, 1989); Henry J. Cohn, *The Government of the Rhine Palatinate in the Fifteenth Century* (Oxford: Clarendon, 1965), 140–51.

39.   StAB, C 7/I, 101, fols. 43–46.

40.   StAB, C 7/I, 101, fols. 47–48.

41.   Matthias Simon, *Evangelische Kirchengeschichte Bayerns* (Munich, 1943), 133–35; Heinrich Görschling, "Die Entstehung des Ansbacher Konsistoriums," *ZBKG* 4 (1929): 16; F. Lippert, "Die 400jährige Reformation im Markgrafentum Bayreuth und Georg Schmalzing," *AO* 30 (1928): 5–6; Seyboth, *Die Markgraftümer*, 344–45.

42.   StAB, C 2, 1962, prod. 1, 2, 6.

43.   StAB, A 170, Lade, 622, 602.

44.   Stievermann, *Klosterherrschaft*, 10–34; Geldner, *Langheim*, 26–28.

45.   StAB, C 3, 1415.

46.   StAB, C 3, 1384.

47.   StAB, A 180, Lade 605, 618–19.

48.   StAB, C 3, 985, 1284, 1412, 1479, 1486, 1309; Seyboth, *Die Markgraftümer*, 312.

49.   StAB, C 3, 1484, 1493; Gerhard Pfeiffer, "Die Rechtstellung des Klosters Münchsteinach," *JFFL*, 22 (1962): 239–94.

50.   Seyboth, *Die Markgraftümer*, 312–13.

51.   StAB, C 3, 1492.

52.   StAB, C 3, 1415.

53.   Seyboth, *Die Markgraftümer*, 314.

54.   Wilhelm Engel, "Dr. Theodorich Morung, General Vikar in Bamberg, Dompfarrer zu Würzburg und sein politische Prozeß (1489–1498)," *Mainfränkisches Jahrbuch für Geschichte und Kunst* 1 (1949): 2; Lorenz Kraußold, *Dr. Theodorich Morung der Vorbote der Reformation in Franken* (Erlangen: Deichert, 1877/1878).

55.   StAB, C 3, 1222, 1245, 2000; Engel, "Morung," 21–76.

56. Engel, "Morung," 4–13.

57. StAB, C 3, 1222, 1; Wilhelm Engel, "*Passio dominorum*. Ein Ausschnitt aus dem Kampf um die Landeskirchenherrschaft und Türkensteuer im spätmittelalterlichen Franken," *ZBLG* 16 (1951): 298–99.

58. StAB, C 3, 1222, 1, fol. 1.

59. StAB, C 3, 1222, 1, fols. 1–4v.

60. StAB, C 3, 1222, 1, fol. 6.

61. StAB, C 3, 1222, 1, fols. 6ff.

62. StAB, C 3, 1222, 1, fol. 4v.

63. StAB, C 3, 1222, 1, fols. 8–10v.

64. Engel, "Passio dominorum," 299–300.

65. StAB, C 3, 1222, 2, fol. 1; Engel, "Passio dominorum," 301.

66. StAB, C 3, 1222, 2, fol. 1f.

67. StAB, C 3, 1222, 2, fols. 2ff.

68. StAB, C 3, 1222, 2, fols. 4–5.

69. StAB, C 3, 1222, 2, fol. 5v.

70. StAB, C 3, 1222, 2, fols. 5v–6v.

71. Quirin, "Albrecht Achilles," 306; Hintze, *Die Hohenzollern*, 92.

72. Seyboth, *Die Markgraftümer*, 396–97.

73. Kist, *Domkapitel*, 97, 98; Wachter, 4572, 4573, 4573; Seyboth, *Die Markgraftümer*, 290–96, 396.

74. Kist, *Domkapitel*, 96; Wachter, 4570; Seyboth, *Die Markgraftümer*, 400–401; Fritz Schnelbögl, "Franken, die Heimat Albrechts," in *Albrecht von Brandenburg-Ansbach und die Kultur seiner Zeit*, ed. Walther Hubatsch, 1–5 (Düsseldorf: Rheinland-Verlag, 1968); Kurt Forstreuter, "Albrecht als Hochmeister," in Hubatsch, *Albrecht und die Kultur*, 5–10; Walther Hubatsch, *Albrecht von Brandenburg-Ansbach, Deutschordens Hochmeister und Herzog in Preußen* (Berlin: Grote, 1965).

75. Kist, *Domkapitel*, 99; Wachter, 4576; Seyboth, *Die Markgraftümer*, 395.

76. Kist, *Domkapitel*, 92–32.

77. Seyboth, *Die Markgraftümer*, 341–45; Georg Schuster and Friedrich Wagner, *Die Jugend und Erziehung der Kurfürsten von Brandenburg und Könige von Preußen* (Berlin: Hofmann, 1906), I, 178, 248–62, 366, 447–48. Joachim II was educated at Neustadt an der Aisch by some of the same tutors who had taught the sons of Friedrich the Elder.

78. Werner Meyer, "Turniergesellschaften. Bemerkungen zu sozialgeschichtlichen Bedeutung der Turnier im Spütmittelalter," in *Das ritterliche Turnier im Mittelalter*, ed. Josef Fleckenstein, 500–512 (Göttingen: Vandenhoeck and Ruprecht, 1985); Werner Rösener, "Ritterliche Wirtschaftsverhältnisse und Turnier im sozialen Wandel des Hochmittelalters," in Fleckenstein, *Das ritterliche Turnier*, 296–338; Scharrer, "Laienbruderschaften," 78–81; Guttenberg-Wendehorst, 82; Franz Machilek, "Privatfrömmigkeit und Staatsfrömmigkeit," in *Kaiser Karl IV. Staatsmann und Mäzen*, ed. Ferdinand Seibt, 99–100 (Munich: Prestel, 1978); Minutoli, *Kaiserliche Buch*, 390; Jegel, "Fürst und Adel," 226.

79. Günther Schuhmann, *Die Markgrafen von Brandenburg-Ansbach. Eine Bilddokumentation zur Geschichte der Hohenzollern in Franken* (Ansbach: Historischer Verein für Mittelfranken, 1980), 401–2; P. Cyprian Fröhlich, "Der Schwanen-Rittersorden U. L. F. mit den Sitz in Brandenburg-Ansbach: Ein Kulturbild aus der Zeit vor der Reformation," *Historisch-Politische Blätter*, 159 (1917): 1–16.

80.   Hofmann, "Adel in Franken," 107–9; Schuhmann, *Markgrafen von Branden-burg-Ansbach*, 402–5.

81.   Angermeier, *Die Reichsreform*, 110–11, 140–44.

Chapter 4

1.   Reinel, *Annotationes*, 150–60.

2.   Reinel, *Annotationes*, 429, 433.

3.   Blickle, "Communal Reformation," *passim;* cf. William Bradford Smith, "Germanic Pagan Antiquity in Lutheran Historical Thought," *Journal of the Historical Society* 4 (2004): 366–71.

4.   Seyboth, *Die Markgraftümer*, 314.

5.   Simon, *Evangelische Kirchengeschichte*, 146–47; Horst Köpstein, "Über den deutschen Hussiten Friedrich Reiser," *Zeitschrift für Geschichtswissenschaft* 7 (1959): 1068–76.

6.   A standard explanation is that records were destroyed during the Peasants' War in 1525. There are accounts of documents being destroyed, but the extent of the destruction cannot be ascertained. In a conversation about the extent and use-fulness of the parish registers (*Standbücher,* StAB Rep. A 221/XIII), Franz Machilek told the author that he did not put much stock in the destruction theory, suggesting that documents were not preserved in any systematic fashion before 1530. Changes in chancery practice explain the apparent surge of documents after the end of the Peasants' War.

7.   Simon, *Bayreuther Pfarrerbuch*, 1038, 1472, 2196; Simon, *Evangelische Kirchengeschichte*, 174; Kist, *Matrikel*, 4022, 5461; Emil Sehling, ed., *Die evangelische Kirchenordnung des XVI Jahrhunderts*, Teil Bayern-Franken (Tübingen: Mohr, 1961), 64; Bernhard Schneider, *Gutachten evangelische Theologen des Fürstentumes Brandenburg-Ansbach/Kulmbach zur Vorbereitung des Augsburger Reichstags von 1530* (Neustadt an der Aisch: Degener, 1987), 96–97; Martin Brecht, "Via antiqua, Humanismus und Reformation–der Mainzer Theologieprofesssor Adam Weiß," *ZKG* 102 (1991): 362–71; Schornbaum, *Kasimir*, 18; F. Lippert, "Die 400jährige Reformation," *AO* 30 (1928): 132–33; Claus-Jürgen Roepke, *Die Protestanten in Bayern* (Munich: Süddeutsche-Verlag, 1972), 97; Kraußold, *Geschiche der evangelische Kirche*, 20–21.

8.   Simon, *Ansbacher Pfarrerbuch*, 2501; Schornbaum, *Kasimir*, 67–68, 189–90.

9.   Schornbaum, *Kasimir*, 251–75, 278–82.

10.   Sehling, II.2, 77–78; Rudolf Endres, "Die Reformation im fränkischen Wendelstein," in *Zugänge zur bäuerlichen Reformation,* ed. Peter Blickle, 139–46 (Zürich: Chronos, 1987); Blickle, *Communal Reformation,* 15.

11.   AEB, Rep. I, 341, fol. 54.

12.   StAB, A 170, Lade 619, 366.

13.   Kist, *Matrikel*, 1918; L, IV, 909.

14.   StAB, B 49, 115, prod. 1–3, 6–9, 12–15; AEB, Rep. I, 341, fols. 12ff., 15v–55v.

15.   StAB, A 170, Lade 619, 356; C 2, 2018.

16.   Sehling, *Evangelishcen Kirchenordnungen,* II.2; Reinel, *Annotationes,* 246.

17.   Schornbaum, *Kasimir,* 30; L IV, 672; Sehling, *Evangelishcen Kirchenordnungen,* 64–65; Werner Zeissner, *Altkirchliche Kräfte in Bamberg unter Bischof Weigand von Redwitz (1522–1556)* (Bamberg: Historischer Verein, 1975), 73–74.

18.   Theodore Kolde, "Der Briefwechsel Luthers und Melanchtons mit dem Markgrafen Georg und Friedrich von Brandenburg," *ZKG* 13 (1892): 318–37.

19.   Konrad Müller, "Markgraf Georg von Brandenburg-Ansbach-Jägerndorf," in *Jahrbuch für Schlesische Kirche und Kirchengeschichte,* N.F. 34 (1955): 16.

20.   Sicken, "Landesherrliche Einnahmen," 161; Jegel, "Landstände," 61–71.

21.   StAB, Rep. A 85, Lade 356, 1551, 1560.

22.   Albert Gümbel, "Berichte Dr. Erasmus Topplers, Probsts von St. Sebald zu Nürnberg, von kaiserliche Hofe 1507–1512," *Archivalische Zeitschrift* 17 (1910): 181, 190.

23.   StAB, C 3, 247, fols. 67–68; Johann Wilhelm Holle, ed., "Videmus der Urkunde des Markgrafen Friedrich des Älteren zu Brandenburg," *AO* 3 (1845): 101–4; Seyboth, *Die Markgraftümer,* 419; Schornbaum, *Kasimir,* 7; Sicken, "Landesherrliche Einnahmen," 161–62; H. C. Erik Midelfort, *Mad Princes of Renaissance Germany* (Charlottesville: University of Virginia Press, 1994), 36–43.

24.   StAB, C 3, 247, fols. 147–153.

25.   StAB, C 3, 247, fols. 6–25; Jegel, "Landstände," 71–75; Jegel, "Landständige Verfassung," 21–22; Seyboth, *Die Markgraftümer,* 423–27; Schornbaum, *Kasimir,* 8–9; Sicken, "Landesherrliche Einnahmen," 162–63.

26.   *RTA, neuere Reihe,* IV, 149; Hartung, *Fränkische Kreis,* 159–60, 245–48; Ernst Böhme, *Das Fränkische Reichsgrafenkollegium im 16. und 17. Jahrhundert* (Stuttgart: Steiner, 1989), 89, 97; Schornbaum, *Kasimir,* 27–36; Dixon, *Reformation and Rural Society,* 16–17.

27.   The Imperial Circles (*Reichskreise*) were regional organization of states within the empire, originally established in 1500. The member states met regularly in a regional diet (*Kreistag*) to discuss policy and coordinate the execution of imperial edicts. On the origins and development of the Reichskreise, see Fritz Hartung, *Geschichte des Fränkischen Kresies (1521–1559)* (Aalen: Scientia Verlag, 1961); James Allan Vann III, *The Swabian Kreis* (Brussels: Édition de la Librairie Encyclopédique, 1975).

28.   *Ettlich artickel So der Cristlich vnd wolgeporn Fürst Casimir[us] zů brandenburg, seinen Prelatten, auch ander clöstern, vnd auch ettlich Pfarrer, vñ prediger ander, dar zů verordnet, auff ettlich überschückt artickel, den haylige[n] cristlichen glabñ betreffent, so yetz in jrru[n]g gezogen werden, zwen ratdschleg über Anttwurt seind r. c.* (Augsburg: Melchior Ramminger, 1524); Karl Schornbaum, *Zur Politik des Markgrafen Georg von Brandenburg vom Beginne seine selbständige Regierung bis zur Nürnberger Anstand 1528–1532* (Munich: Ackermann, 1906), 1; Schornbaum, *Kasimir,* 32–36; Hartung, *Fränkische Kreis,* 170–74; Kraußold, *Geschiche der evangelische Kirche,* 26–29.

29.   *Ettlich artickel,* A2v.

30.   *Ettlich artickel,* A3.

31.   *Ettlich artickel,* A3v.

32.   Roepke, *Protestanten in Bayern,* 103; Kraußold, *Geschichte der evangelische Kirche,* 34–35.

33.   Kraußold, *Geschichte der evangelische Kirche,* 40–41; Sehling, *Evangelische Kirchenordnungen,* 66; Roepke, *Protestanten in Bayern,* 103–5; Schornbaum, *Casimir,* 39–51.

34.   Kist, *Matrikel,* 5593.

35.   *Ettlich Artickel,* A3v.

36.   *Ettlich Artickel,* A3vff.; Sehling, II.3, 80. The edition in Sehling differs slightly from the 1524 printed text. See also Schornbaum, *Kasimir,* 52; Kraußold, *Geschichte der evangelische Kirche,* 43–44; Roepke, *Protestanten in Bayern,* 103–5; Dixon, *Reformation and Rural Society,* 18–19.

37.   *Ratschag: den ettliche Christenliche Pfarrherrn, Prediger, und andere Gottlicher gschrifft verstendige, Eynem fursten, wöllichen yetzugen strittigen ler halb, auf den abschyd, jüngst gehalthens Reychßtages zů Nürnberg* . . . (Augsburg: Heinrich Steiner, 1525); Smith, *Kessler,* II, 647.

38.   The use of German as a liturgical language is the only major change required. As for other ceremonies, so long as people understand "that they neither add to nor detract from our salvation" they may be performed "as in olden times." *Ratschlag,* Fol. xi, lxxiiii.

39.   *Ratschlag,* fol. 1v.

40.   *Ratschlag,* fol. 2.

41.   *Ratschlag,* fols. 7v–9. Other citations include Isaiah 28, Psalm 117, Matthew 21, Romans 9, I Corinthians 3 and 10, Ephesians 2, and I Peter 3–4.

42.   *Ratschlag,* fol. 10; cf. Luke 22:26, 31–34.

43.   *Ratschlag,* fol. 7; Galatians 2:20.

44.   *Ratschlag,* fols. 3v, 7.

45.   *Ratschlag,* fol. 4v.

46.   *Ratschlag,* fols. 4v–5.

47.   *Ratschlag,* fol. 11.

48.   Franz Bittner, "Leonhard von Egloffstein, Ein Bamberger Domherr und Humanist," *BHVB* 107 (1971): 53–159; Michael Kleiner, "Georg III. Schenk von Limpurg, Bischof von Bamberg (1505–1522) als Reichsfürst und Territorialherr," *BHVB* 127 (1991): 22–23, 40–43.

49.   Elisabeth Roth, *Hochschulgebäude Hochzeitshaus. Ein kulturhistorische Studie* (Bamberg: Fränkische Tag, 1975), 7–11.

50.   Rössler, 166–76; Roth, *Spätmittelalter,* 249, 268–75; Spitz, *Religious Renaissance,* 249.

51.   Kist, *Matrikel,* 1874, 1878; Roth, *Spätmittelalter,* 179.

52.   *Ein Missiue un Bischoff Vonn Wirtzburg Vonn herr Jakob Fuchs dem Eltern Thummherrenn außgangen. Was er helt von vereelichten geystlichen personen* (Bamberg: Georg Erlinger, 1523). The same argument appears in a contemporary pamphlet issued by the Bamberg printer Georg Erlinger. Simon Reuter von Schleiz, *Ein Christlichen frage Simonis Reuters von Schleyz, an alle Bischoffe, vnnd andere geystliche* (Bamberg: Georg Erlinger, 1523); Smith, *Kessler,* II, 503.

53.   *Eine Missiue,* A2v.

54.   *Eine Missiue,* A3v; Ephesians 5.

55.   *WA* (B), II, 538.

56.   *Furhaltung xxx artigkl, so in gegenwurtiger verwerrung auf de pan gepracht, und durch ainer neüeren beschwören den allten schlangen gerechtfertigt werden, grundtlich erclärt, durch Casparn Schatzgen barfüsser ordens* (Munich: Hans Schobser, 1525), fol. 1f; Smith, *Kessler,* II, 648.

57. *Ein Schöner Sendtbrief wolgepornen vnd Edeln herrn Johannsen, Herrn zu Schwartz-enberg, An Bischoff zu Bamberg außgangen* (Nuremberg: Jobst Gutknecht, 1524); Ozment, *When Fathers Ruled*, 3–49.

58. *Ain schöner lustiger Dialogus, von dem rechten waren Glauben, in wolchem das ewig Gottes klärich erkandt vnd gehandelt wirt on alle ergernuss, yetlichen Cristblaubigen nützlich zů leesen, Durch Vlrich Burckhart des Bischoffs zů Bamberg Capellan newlich beschriben* (Augsburg: Philipp Ulhart, 1525), A4v; Galatians 3.

59. Burchardi, *Ain schöner lustiger Dialogus*, B.

60. *Dialogus*, B2v.

61. *Dialogus*, A4, B2.

62. *Dialogus*, B3v.

63. *Dialogus*, A2.

64. *Dialogus*, A2f.

65. *Dialogus*, A3v.

66. *Dialogus*, A2.

67. *Eyn Bepstlich Breue dem radt czu Bamberg gesand widder den Luther* (Wittenberg: Johann Rhau, 1523); Smith, *Kessler*, II, 416.

68. *Der Curtisan vnd pfrundenfresser* (Bamberg: Georg Erlinger, 1522).

69. *Curtisan vnd pfrundenfresser*, A1.

70. *Curtisan vnd pfrundenfresser*, A2.

71. *Curtisan vnd pfrundenfresser*, A2v.

72. *Curtisan vnd pfrundenfresser*, A2.

73. *Curtisan vnd pfrundenfresser*, A3.

74. *Curtisan vnd pfrundenfresser*, A3v.

75. *Curtisan vnd pfrundenfresser*, A4.

76. *Curtisan vnd pfrundenfresser*, A4v.

77. StAB, B 106, 317; L, IV, 583–85, 670–71.

78. Kist, *Matrikel*, 4692; Chroust, II, 98–99; Justus Maurer, *Prediger im Bauernkrieg* (Stuttgart: Calwer, 1979), 535.

79. Kist, *Matrikel*, 99.

80. *WA* (B), II, 538; Maurer, *Prediger*, 535–36; Bensen, *Geschichte des Bauernkrieges in Ostfranken* (Erlangen, 1840), 376.

81. Kist, *Matrikel*, 5721; *WA* (B), III, 589; Maurer, *Prediger*, 531; Irmingard Geuler, "Auch Bamberg hatte seinen Reformator: Johannes Schwanhäuser, Prediger zu St. Gangolf zum Gedächtnis," address for the exhibition "Der evanglische Beitrag zum Bamberger Geistesleben," held in the chapterhouse of St. Stephan's Church, Bamberg, 23 June, 1973, TS in the Evangelische Dekanatsbibliothek, Bamberg; Horst Weigelt, "Die frühreformatorische Bewegung in Bamberg und Johann Schwannhausen," *BHVB* 134 (1998): 113–30; L IV, 569–70; Chroust, II, 98–99; cf. Reuter von Schleiz, *Christlichen Frage*, B3f.

82. *Ein Sermon geprediget durch Joānem Schwanhausen, Custor auf sant Gangolffs Stifft zů Bamberg, Anno. 1523. an dem 22. Sontag nach Trinitatis, an aller hayligen tag &c* (Bamberg: Georg Erlinger, 1523).

83. *Ein Sermon* (1523), A1–A2.

84. *Ein Sermon* (1523), A2v.

85. *Ein Sermon* (1523), B4f.

86. *Ein Sermon geprediget durch Johañem Schwanhausen custor vff sant Gangolffs styfft zu Bamberg an dem sontag, d[er] genañt wyrt, der erst in der verpottenn zeyt.* (Bamberg: Georg Erlinger, 1524).

87. *Ein Sermon* (1524), A1v.

88. *Ein Sermon* (1524), A2.

89. *Ein Sermon* (1524), A2v.

90. *Ein Sermon* (1524), A3.

91. *Ein Sermon* (1524), Bf.

92. *Ein Sermon* (1524), B2v–C.

93. *Ein Sermon* (1524), A2v, B2.

94. *Ein Sermon* (1523), A3.

95. *Ein Sermon* (1524), B2v–C.

96. (1523), B3v; (1524), A1v–A2.

97. (1523), B4v.

98. (1524), C2ff.

99. (1523), A2.

100. (1523), A1; (1524), A1v.

101. Both Justus Maurer and Bernd Moeller have concluded that Schwanhäuser's sermons represent "pure" Lutheranism. But Moeller bases his conclusions on Schwanhäuser's later writings. Maurer notes that in his works from 1525 and 1526, Schwanhäuser's teachings on authority follow Luther closely. This I would not dispute, but I would suggest that in 1523 and 1524, prior to his move to Nuremberg, Schwanhäuser's position was rather different. Maurer, *Prediger,* 139; Bernd Moeller, "Was wurde in der Frühzeit der Reformation in den deutschen Städten gepredigt?" *ARG* 75 (1984): 176–93. For a more detailed discussion of Schwanhäuser's theology, see William Bradford Smith, "Anticlericalism in Bamberg on the Eve of the Peasants' War," in *Cultures of Communication from Reformation to Enlightenment,* ed. James Van Horn Melton (Aldershot: Ashgate, 2002), 61–65.

102. Kleiner, "Georg III," 43–44.

103. Kist, *Matrikel,* 832.

104. StAB, A 231/I, 1723, fol. 62; 1726, fols. 62, 97; 1747/II, fol. 451.

105. Rudolf Endres, "Probleme des Bauernkrieges im Hochstift Bamberg," *JFFL* 31 (1971): 100–101; Endres, "Franken," in *Der deutsche Bauernkrieg,* ed. Horst Buszello, Peter Blickle, and Rudolf Endres (Munich, 1995), 139.

106. Rudolf Endres, "The Peasant War in Franconia," in *The German Peasant War: New Viewpoints,* ed. Bob Scribner and Gerhard Benecke, 65 (Boston: Allen and Unwin, 1979).

107. Blickle, *Revolution of 1525,* 166; Zeissner, *Altkirchliche Kräfte,* 80–82; Endres, "Probleme des Bauernkrieges," 105.

108. L IV, 567–68; Endres, "Probleme des Bauernkrieges," 106.

109. L IV, 454, 773–75; Schmitt, "Geistliche und weltliche Verwaltung," 78.

110. StAB, B 48, 1, prod. 1; Günther Franz, *Quellen zur Geschichte des Bauernkriegs* (Munich, 1963), 315.

111. L IV, 569; Bensen, *Geschichte des Bauernkrieges,* 377; Carl Jäger, "Markgraf Casimir und der Bauernkrieg in den südlichen Grenzämtern des Fürstentums unterhalb des Gebirgs," *Mitteilungen des Vereins für Geschichte der Stadt Nürnberg* 9 (1892): 28; Schornbaum, *Kasimir,* 68–70.

112. *CCB,* I, fols. 10–11; 19v–24.

113. Maurer, *Prediger,* 536–37.

114. Kist, *Matrikel,* 1326, 5721; Maurer, *Prediger,* 532–33; L IV, 570–71.

115. Johannes Schwanhäuser, *Ain Trostbrief an die Christlich gemayn zů Bamberg* (Nuremberg, 1525).

116. Maurer, *Prediger,* 139, 533.

117. Schwanhäuser, *Trostbrief,* fol. 7.

118. Schwanhäuser, *Trostbrief,* fols. 9–10; cf. Moeller, "Was wurde . . . gepredigt?" 185.

119. Schwanhäuser, *Trostbrief,* fols. 10–11v.

120. StAB, B 48, 1, prod. 4.

121. StAB, B 48, 1, prod. 8; Chroust, II, xxviii–xxiv, 1–8, 100–103, 161–64; Bensen, *Geschichte des Bauernkrieges,* 377–79; L IV, 574; Endres, "Franconia," 70–71; Zeissner, *Altkirchliche Kräfte,* 86–87.

122. StAB, B 48, 1, prod. 8; Chroust, II, xxix–xxxi, 8–21; L IV, 579–81; Endres, "Probleme des Baurenkrieges," 115–20; Blickle, *The Revolution of 1525,* 141.

123. StAB, B 48, 1, prod. 21, 24; Bensen, *Geschichte des Bauernkrieges,* 379.

124. StAB, B 48, prod. 15–16; Chroust, II, xxxi, 20–24; L IV, 582, 590.

125. StAB, B 48, 1, prod. 42; C 2, 160, prod. 20; Bensen, *Geschichte des Bauernkrieges,* 381.

126. StAB, B 48, 1, prod. 23, 41, 53; Chroust, II, 29–43, 116–17; L IV, 605–9, 623; Geldner, *Langheim,* 36–37; Stefan Nöth, *Ager Clavium: Das Cistercienserinnenkloster Schlüsselau, 1280–1554* (Bamberg: Historischer Verein, 1982), 64–65; Deckart, "Karmelitenkloster," 58; Endres, "Probleme des Bauernkrieges," 115–20.

127. Bachmann, "Landstände," 258–60.

128. StAB, B 48, 1, prod. 62, 67.

129. StAB, B 48, 1, prod. 62; Franz, *Quellen,* 131; Chroust, II, 50–51; L IV, 636.

130. StAB, C 2, 161; L IV, 624–28; Lang, I, 192–94; Bensen, *Geschichte des Bauernkrieges,* 403.

131. StAB, C 2, 161; L IV, 664; Kraußold, *Geschichte der evangelische Kirche,* 52.

132. StAB, C 2, 160, prod. 8; Dixon, *Reformation and Rural Society,* 21.

133. Jäger, "Casimir und Bauernkrieg," 56–68; Bensen, *Geschichte des Bauernkrieges,* 385–88.

134. Jäger, "Casimir und Bauernkrieg," 39–40; Bensen, *Geschichte des Bauernkrieges,* 395–96.

135. Franz, *Quellen,* 130, 396–410; L IV, 645, 664.

136. StAB, C 2, 160, prod. 46.

137. Bensen, *Geschichte des Bauernkrieges,* 457; Chroust, II, 59–60; L IV, 637–45.

138. Chroust, II, 59–60; Franz, *Quellen,* 130, 131; L IV, 639–41; Endres, "Probleme des Bauernkrieges," 133; Zeissner, *Altkirchliche Kräfte,* 88–89.

139. AEB, Rep. 1, 162; Zeissner, *Altkirchliche Kräfte,* 90.

140. L IV, 579, 702; Geldner, *Langheim,* 35–36.

141. Paul Wappler, *Die Täuferbewegung in Thüringen von 1526–1584* (Jena: Fischer, 1913), 2c, 240; Gottfried Seebaß, *Müntzers Erbe. Werk, Leben, und Theologie des Hans Hut* (Gütersloh: G. Mohn, 2002), 212, 220–21.

142. Karl Schornbaum, ed., *Quellen zur Geschichte der Wiedertäufer,* II (Leipzig: Heinsius, 1934), 200, 202; Gottfried Seebaß, "Bauernkrieg und Täufertum in Franken," *ZKG* 85 (1974): 285–300; Seebaß, *Müntzers Erbe,* 221; Günther Dippold, "Täufer

am Obermain," *BHVB* 119 (1983): 78–83; Günther Bauer, *Anfänge täuferische Gemeindebildungen in Franken* (Nuremberg: Verein für Bayerische Kirchengeschichte, 1966), 17–18, 25–28. Although Bauer denies a connection between the Anabaptists and the rebellion, Seebaß ("Bauernkrieg," 141–42) argues that his assertion rests not on the evidence but rather "appears [to be] more a supposition than a substantiated thesis."

143. StAB, B 86, vol. 3, fol. 406.

144. *CCB,* I, fols. 15–19v, 30–32v, 35v; L IV, 777.

145. Dippold, "Täufer," 85–90; Claus-Peter Clasen, *Anabaptism: A Social History* (Ithaca, NY: Cornell University Press, 1972), 372.

146. See James Stayer, *The German Peasants' War and Anabaptist Community of Goods* (Montreal: McGill and Queens University Press, 1991).

Chapter 5

1.   Albrecht Pius Luttenberger, *Glaubenseinheit und Reichsfriede. Konzeptionen und Wege Konfessionsneutrale Reichspolitik 1530–1552 (Kurpfalz, Jülich, Kurbrandenburg)* (Göttingen: Vandenhoek and Ruprecht, 1982), 11–26; Blickle, *Revolution of 1525,* 181–85, 189–190.

2.   Luttenberger, *Glaubenseinheit und Reichsfriede,* 46–47.

3.   *ARC,* vol. 1, 236–38; Angermeier, *Die Reichsreform,* 235–37; Heinz Durchardt, *Protestantisches Kaisertum und Altes Reich* (Wiesbaden: Steiner, 1977), 8–16; Alfred Kohler, *Antihabsburgische Politik in der Epoche Karls V.* (Göttingen: Vandenhoek and Ruprecht, 1981).

4.   Luttenberger, *Glaubenseinheit und Reichsfriede,* 62–63; Heinrich Lutz, "Kaiser, Reich, und Christenheit. Zur Weltgeschichtliche Würdigung des Augsburger Reichstages 1530," in Lutz, *Politik, Kultur und Religion,* 89–122.

5.   Felician Geß, *Akten und Briefe zur Kirchenpolitik Herzog Georg von Sachsen* (Cologne: Böhlau, 1985), II, 1139; Schornbaum, *Kasimir,* 73–87.

6.   Geß, *Akten und Briefe,* II, 1276.

7.   Schornbaum, *Kasimir,* 95ff.

8.   Sehling, *Evangelische Kirchenordnungen,* II.5, 84–86; L IV, 665–66.

9.   *Der Durchleüchtigen Hochgebornen fürsten vnd herren Herren Casimirn, vnd herren Georgen, . . . anzeygen, wie die gewesen empörung vnd auffrůrn, nit den wenigsten teyl, auß vngeschickten predigen entstanden sindt.* (Strasbourg: Matthias Schürer, 1525), fol. 3.

10. *Der Durchleüchtigen Hochgebornen fürsten,* fol. 4; cf. I Peter 3:13–17.

11. *Der Durchleüchtigen Hochgebornen fürsten,* fols. 5–6.

12. Kraußold, *Geschichte der evangelische Kirche,* 60; Schornbaum, *Kasimir,* 104–5.

13. *Abschied vñ maynung, wie sich der Durchleüchtig, Hochgeborn Fürst vnd Herr, herr Casimir, Marggraue zů Brandenburg & c., . . . zů sampt irer F. G. Landtschafft, auff nächst gehaltem Landßtag zů Onoltzbach, biß auff eyn zůkünfftig Concilium National versamlůg, oder seiner F. G. weyttern beschayd, des abschiedts halben jüngst gehaltens Reychßtag zů Speyer, in iren F. G. Land vñ Fürstenthumb zů halten vereynigt haben.* (Ansbach, 1526), A2v.

14. *Abschied vñ maynung,* A3.

15. *Abschied vñ maynung,* A3v–A4.

16. *Abschied vñ maynung,* A4v–B.

17.   *Abschied vñ maynung* A3v, B3–B4.

18.   *Abschied vñ maynung,* B4–C3.

19.   *Cristliche vnterrrichtung eins Pfarhern an seinen Herrn, ein Fursten des heligen Reychs, auff viertzig Artikel vnd puncten gestelt* (Nuremberg: Jobst Gutknecht, 1526); Bernhard Schneider, *Gutachten evangelische Theologen des Fürstentums Brandenburg-Ansbach/Kulmbach zur Vorbereitung des Augsburger Reichstages von 1530* (Neustadt a. d. Aisch: Degener, 1987), 29; Roepke, *Protestanten in Bayern,* 107.

20.   *Cristliche vnterrichtung,* C2v–C3.

21.   *Cristliche vnterrichtung,* D4v–E.

22.   *Cristliche vnterrichtung,* E2v.

23.   Simon, *Evangelische Kirchengeschichte,* 216; Schornbaum, *Kasimir,* 105.

24.   StAB, C 3, 1558, fols. 1–6.

25.   Georg the Pious was raised at the court of his uncle, King Vladislav II of Hungary, and spent most of the 1520s at the Jagellion court trying to acquire a principality in Silesia for himself and his heirs. Later Prussian claims to Silesia rested on his efforts. Ludwig Petry, "Politische Geschichte under den Habsburger," in *Geschichte Schlesiens,* 2 (Sigmaringen: Jan Thorbecke, 1988), 4–14; Seyboth, *Die Markgraftümer,* 398–99; Schuhmann, *Markgrafen von Brandenburg-Ansbach,* 77–78; Gottfried Biermann, "Jägerndorf unter der Regierung der Hohenzollern," *Zeitschrift des Vereins für Geschichte und Altertums Schleisens,* 11 (1871): 36–96.

26.   *WA* (B), IV, 1271; Kraußold, *Geschichte der evangelische Kirche,* 68; Roepke, *Protestanten in Bayern,* 111; Simon, *Ansbacher Pfarrerbuch,* 26; Kist, *Matrikel,* 2510; Simon, *Bayreuther Pfarrerbuch,* 1033; Sehling, *Evangelische Kirchenordnungen,* 113–15.

27.   Lang, II, 2–3.

28.   Falkenstein, IV.2, 434; Sehling, *Evangelische Kirchenordnungen,* 70, 102–4; Simon, *Evangelische Kirchengeschichte,* 212; Kraußold, *Geschichte der evangelische Kirche,* 67–68.

29.   StAB, C 7/I, 101, fols. 7–8.

30.   Sehling, *Evangelische Kirchenordnungen,* 108–10.

31.   StAB, C 7/I, 101, fols. 1–5; Simon, *Evangelische Kirchengeschichte,* 212.

32.   During the reign of Casimir, the state debt had risen from 170,505 gulden to 551,414 gulden, and many suspected that Georg's Silesian pretensions would only exacerbate the problem. Falkenstein, IV.2, 434; Seyboth, "Kasimir," 82; Schornbaum, *Kasimir,* 8–9; Schornbaum, *Georg,* 13; Jegel, "Landstände," 23–24.

33.   StAB, C 3, 1554.

34.   Karl Schornbaum, *Aktenstücke zur ersten Brandenburgischen Kirchenvisitation 1528* (Munich: Kaiser, 1928), 1–3.

35.   Schornbaum, *Georg,* 27–30; Schornbaum, *Aktenstücke,* 1–9.

36.   Schornbaum, *Aktenstücke,* 11–12, 42; Simon, *Evangelische Kirchengeschichte,* 217.

37.   Falkenstein, IV.2, 436.

38.   Schornbaum, *Aktenstücke,* 39; Sehling, *Evangelische Kirchenordnungen,* 115.

39.   Schornbaum, *Aktenstücke,* 10–14, 30.

40.   StAB, C 2, 2482, fols. 2f.; L IV, 1036–38.

41.   StAB, C 2, 2482, fol. 1.

42.   StAB, C 2, 2482, fol. 1v.

43.   StAB, C 2, 2482, fol. 2.

44.   StAB, C 2, 2482, fols. 2ff.

45.   StAB, C 2, 2482, fol. 3v.

46.   StAB, C 2, 2482, fol. 4.

47.   StAB, C 2, 2482, fols. 2–3; Luttenberger, *Glaubenseinheit und Reichsfriede*, 55–56.

48.   Kist, *Domkapitel*, 119–27; Zeissner, *Altkirchliche Kräfte*, 124–27, 141.

49.   Kist, *Matrikel*, 4536; L IV, 707–58; Zeissner, 141; Schmitt, "Geistliche und weltliche Verwaltung," 50–54.

50.   *CCB*, 1, fols. 10, 11–13v, 18v–21.

51.   *CCB*, 1, fols. 10v–11; 19v–20.

52.   *StAB*, B 86, vol. 3a, fol. 341, 346v; L IV, 534, 696, 758; Zeissner, *Altkirchliche Kräfte*, 96–97.

53.   AEB, Rep. I, 341.

54.   AEB, Rep. I, 341, fols. 12v–13v; Guttenberg-Wendehorst, 198–200.

55.   AEB, Rep. I, 341, fol. 54; Guttenberg-Wendehorst, 202.

56.   AEB, Rep. I, 341, fols. 54v–55v.

57.   StAB, A 232/I, 807, fol. 12; Zeissner, *Altkirchliche Kräfte*, 164–66.

58.   L IV, 816–817, 856–59; Zeissner, *Altkirchliche Kräfte*, 165, 210–12; Kist, *Matrikel*, 4764.

59.   The figures here are drawn from the *Protokollenbücher*, AEB, Rep I, 327–38, with additional information taken from Kist, *Matrikel*.

60.   AEB, Rep. I, 335, fols. 171–172; Kist, *Matrikel*, 9. Paul's son, Georg Adelhardt (Kist, *Matrikel*, 8), succeeded his father as pastor of Poppendorf, only to be imprisoned for Lutheran tendencies in 1552.

61.   AEB, Rep. I, 327, fols. 319f.; 328, fols. 14–19v; 337, fol. 278; 338, fol. 84; Kist, *Matrikel*, 4759, 3396; Wachter, 5355.

62.   AEB, Rep. I, 334, fols. 282f; Kist, *Matrikel*, 776.

63.   AEB, Rep. I, 332, fols. 360–361v; StAB, B 49, 83, fasc. 583; Kist, *Matrikel*, 621.

64.   AEB, Rep. I, 327, fols. 121–125; Kist, *Matrikel*, 875.

65.   StAB, B 49, 97; 121.

66.   AEB, Rep. I, 72, fols. 1–11; StAB, C 3, 1557; Richard Winkler, "Die Säkularisation der Kirchenkleinoden in Markgrafentum Brandenburg-Kulmbach 1529/30," *GO* 22 (1999/2000): 41–102.

67.   StAB, C 2, 1815, 1816; Winkler, 45–47.

68.   *ARC*, vol. 1, IV. 84, 88, 91, 97, 107; V. 137–38; V. 156, 394–96; Zeissner, *Altkirchliche Kräfte*, 59–61; Kohler, *Antihabsburgische Politik*, 28–29; Angermeier, *Die Reichsreform*, 263; Luttenberger, *Glaubenseinheit und Reichsfriede*, 26–27.

69.   *NBD*, I, 1, 180, 187, 190.

70.   Ernst Koch, "Die deutschen Protestanten und das Konzil von Trient," in *Die Katholische Konfessionalisierung*, ed. Wolfgang Reinhard and Heinz Schilling, 88–90 (Münster: Aschendorff, 1995); Luttenberger, *Glaubenseinheit und Reichsfriede*, 26–27, 200–205.

71.   *WA* (B) 6, 485–86.

72.   Wilhelm Gussmann, *Quellen und Forschungen zur Geschichte des Augsburgischen Glaubensbekenntnisses* (Leipzig: Teubner, 1911), I, 1.2, 95.

73.   Theobald Freudenberger, *Die Fürstbischöfe von Würzburg und das Konzil von Trient* (Münster: Aschendorff, 1989), xv–xvi.

74. StAB, C 3, 1231; *NBD,* I, 1, 144, 187.

75. *NBD,* I, 189, 190.

76. Freudenberger, 2–16.

77. *NBD,* I, 5, 204; Zeissner, *Altkirchliche Kräfte,* 202; Luttenberger, *Glaubenseinheit und Reichsfriede,* 206–12.

78. *NBD,* I, 9, 48, 147; doc. 114, 372–75; Zeissner, *Altkirchliche Kräfte,* 202–5.

79. Luttenberger, *Glaubenseinheit und Reichsfriede,* 274–81.

80. StAB, C 3, 1554, fols. 14–16; Schornbaum, *Georg,* 64–71; Wolfgang Steglich, "Die Stellung der evangelischen Reichstände und Reichstädte zu Karl V. zwischen Protestation und Konfession 1529–1530," *ARG* 62 (1971): 161–92.

81. Schornbaum, *Georg,* 102ff, 164ff.; Luttenberger, *Glaubenseinheit und Reichsfriede,* 34, 228–41; Gussmann, *Quellen,* I, 63; cf. Thomas A. Brady, Jr., "Phases and Strategies of the Schmalkaldic League: A Perspective after 450 Years," in Brady, *Communities, Politics, and Reformation in Early Modern Europe* (Leiden: Brill, 1998), 109–10.

82. Simon, *Evangelische Kirchengeschichte,* 228–30; Schornbaum, *Georg,* 83–88; Luttenberger, *Glaubenseinheit und Reichsfriede,* 54–59; Kohler, *Antihabsburgische Politik,* 128–31, 214–30.

83. StAB, C 3, 1554, fols. 39–42.

84. Sehling, *Evangelische Kirchenordnungen,* III.3, 114–15; Simon, *Evangelische Kirchengeschichte,* 219.

85. StAB, C 3, 49, fols. 13–21v.

86. StAB, C 3, 49, fols. 13f.

87. StAB, C 3, 49, fol. 14.

88. StAB, C 3, 49, fols. 15–16v.

89. StAB, C 3, 49; Sehling, *Evangelische Kirchenordnungen,* 120–22; Simon, *Evangelische Kirchengeschichte,* 233; Roepke, 122–23; Kraußold, *Geschichte der evangelische Kirche,* 95.

90. *Kirchenordnung, wie es inn des durchleuchtigen hochgeboren Fursten vnnd Herrn, Herrn Albrechts des Jungen Margrauen zu Brandenburgs . . . mit der lehr vnd Ceremonien bis auff vernere Christliche vergleichung gehalten werden sol* (Leipzig: Wolf Günther, 1552); Sehling, *Evangelische Kirchenordnungen,* III.4a; Kraußold, *Geschichte der evangelische Kirche,* 90–97; Herman Waldenmeier, *Die Entstehung der evangelischen Gottesdienstordnungen Süddeutschlands im Zeitalter der Reformation* (Leipzig: Verein für Reformationsgeschichte, 1916), 10–12.

91. StAB, C 7/I, 101, fols. 38–40.

92. StAB, C 3, 49, fols. 1–2; Sehling, *Evangelische Kirchenordnungen,* III.4c; Kraußold, *Geschichte der evangelische Kirche,* 95–96.

93. Gussmann, *Quellen,* I, 62–66.

94. Gussmann, *Quellen,* I, 67–68; Schneider, *Gutachten,* 31–33, 148–56.

95. Schneider, *Gutachten,* 82. Schnabel was the first general superintendent of the Oberland. Simon, *Bayreuther Pfarrerbuch,* 2237, 88, 407, 395; Kist, *Matrikel,* 5545, 1359, 1268.

96. Gussmann, *Quellen,* I, Beilage 1.2, 85–93.

97. Schneider, 91; Simon, *Bayreuther Pfarrerbuch,* 2595; Kist, *Matrikel,* 1571.

98. Gussmann, *Quellen,* I, Beilage 1.3, 96–99; Schneider, *Gutachten,* 101–4.

99. Schneider, *Gutachten,* 130–31; Simon, *Bayreuther Pfarrerbuch,* 830; Kist, *Matrikel,* 2243.

100. Schneider, *Gutachten,* 133–34; Simon, *Bayreuther Pfarrerbuch,* 2294; Kist, *Matrikel,* 5612.

101. StAB, C 3, 128; Otto Kneitz, *Albrecht Alcibiades, Markgraf von Kulmbach 1522–1557* (Kulmbach: Freunde der Plassenburg, 1951), 30; Volker Press, "Wilhelm von Grumbach und die deutsche Adelskrise der 1560er Jahre," *BDLG* 113 (1977): 396–431.

102. StAB, C 17/IV, 294; Kneitz, *Albrecht Alcibiades,* 31–33; Kraußold, *Geschichte der evangelische Kirche,* 105.

103. StAB, C 3, 139, 212, 213; Lang, *Fürstenthums Baireuth,* III, 2–3; Kneitz, *Albrecht Alcibiades,* 35–36; Kraußold, *Geschichte der evangelische Kirche,* 104–5; Sehling, *Evangelische Kirchenordnungen,* 291.

104. Ernst Büttner, "Der Krieg des Markgrafen Albrecht Alcibiades in Franken 1552–1555," *AO* 23 (1908): 18–21; Kneitz, *Albrecht Alcibiades,* 51–53; Luttenberger, *Glaubenseinheit und Reichsfriede,* 375, 380; Horst Rabe, *Reichsbund und Interim. Die Verfassungs- und Religionspolitik Karls V und der Reichstag von Augsburg 1547/1548* (Cologne: Böhlau, 1971), 135.

105. Luttenberger, *Glaubenseinheit und Reichsfriede,* 426–77.

106. Sehling, *Evangelische Kirchenordnungen,* IV.4; Kneitz, *Albrecht Alcibiades,* 66–67.

107. Kraußold, *Geschichte der evangelische Kirche,* 117–18; Simon, *Evangelische Kirchengeschichte,* 267; Luttenberger, *Glaubenseinheit und Reichsfriede,* 466; Rabe, *Reichsbund und Interim,* 433.

108. StAB, C 3, 1605, fol. 41.

109. StAB, C 3, 1605, fol. 1.

110. StAB, C 3, 1605, fols. 1v–2v.

111. StAB, C 3, 1605, fols. 5–7.

112. StAB, C 3, 1605, fols. 35v–36.

113. StAB, C 3, 1605, fols. 19f.

114. StAB, C 3, 1605, fols. 23v–24.

115. StAB, C 3, 1605, fols. 111–114.

116. StAB, C 3, 1605, fols. 107–110; Kraußold, *Geschichte der evangelische Kirche,* 119–21.

117. StAB, C 3, 1605, fol. 123f.

118. StAB, C 3, 1605, fol. 126.

119. StAB, C 3, 1605, fols. 126v–127.

120. StAB, C 3, 1605, fols. 127f.

121. StAB, C 3, 1605, fols. 128f.

122. StAB, C 3, 1605, fol. 129.

123. StAB, C 7/I, 101, fols. 49–53.

124. Lang, II, 211–12; Kraußold, *Geschichte der evangelische Kirche,* 122–25.

125. StAB, C 3, 1606. The estates in Württemberg and Hesse also opposed the Interim. In both cases, the patterns closely match those described here in the Oberland. William Bradford Smith, "Lutheran Resistance to the Imperial Interim in Hesse and Kulmbach," *Lutheran Quarterly* 19 (2005): 249–73; John Stalnaker, "The Emergence of the Protestant Clergy in Central Europe: The Case of Hesse" (PhD diss., University of California, Berkeley, 1970).

126. Luttenberger, *Glaubenseinheit und Reichsfriede,* 497, 578.

127. Luttenberger, *Glaubenseinheit und Reichsfriede,* 609–10, 622.

128. Chroust, II, 329–30; Lang, *Fürstenthums Baireuth*, II, 219–34; Büttner, "Krieg des Markgrafen," 20–33; Kneitz, *Albrecht Alcibiades*, 75–80; Kraußold, *Geschichte der evangelische Kirche*, 25–126; Luttenberger, *Glaubenseinheit und Reichsfriede*, 604.

129. Büttner, "Krieg des Markgrafen," 34; Luttenberger, *Glaubenseinheit und Reichsfriede*, 639–40.

130. Chroust, II, 332–33.

131. Nießen, Burgkunstadt, Maineck, Kupferberg, Leygast, Ludwigschorgast, Vilseck, Pottenstein, Veldenstein, Großweinstein, Hollfeld, Weisenstadt, Neideck, Forchheim, Neunkirchen, Hertz, Herzogenaurach, Unter- and Oberhöchstadt (Aisch), Ober Schönfeld, and Waichenrod. StAB, A 85, Lade 346, 1604, 1605; Falkenstein, IV.2, 460.

132. StAB, A 85, Lade 346, 1607, 1608; Kneitz, *Albrecht Alcibiades*, 93–96; Chroust, II, 337–38; Zeissner, *Altkirchliche Kräfte*, 216–17.

133. StAB, A 85, Lade 346, 1612; Kneitz, *Albrecht Alcibiades*, 113–17, 129–33.

Chapter 6

1.   Zeeden, *Konfessionsbildung*, 60–66; Schilling, "Konfessionalsierung im Reich"; Ziegler, "Territorium und Reformation"; Ziegler, "Typen der Konfessionalisierung in Katholischen Territorien Deutschlands," in *Die Katholische Konfessionalisierung*, ed. Wolfgang Reinhard and Heinz Schilling, 412–14 (Münster: Aschendorff, 1995).

2.   Evans, *Habsburg Monarchy*, 3–31; Forster, *Counter-Reformation*, 19–20; McHardy, *War, Religion and Court Patronage*, chapter 1.

3.   Press, "Wilhelm von Grumbach," 415; Press, "Adel im Reich um 1600," in *Spezialforschung und "Gesamtgeschichte,"* ed. Grete Klingenstein and Heinrich Lutz, 15–47 (Vienna: Verlag für Geschichte und Politik, 1981); Otto Brunner, *Adeliges Landleben und Europäischer Geist* (Salzburg: O. Müller, 1949); H. C. Erik Midelfort, "Curious Georgics: The German Nobility and Their Crisis of Legitimacy in the Late Sixteenth Century," in Fix and Karant-Nunn, *Germania Ilustrata*, 217–42.

4.   Press, "Wilhelm von Grumbach," 400–401, 430–31, Press, "Adel im Reich," 18–25, 43–45; Rudolf Endres, "Zur wirtschaftlichen und sozialen Lage in Franken vor den Dreißigjährigen Krieg," *JFFL* 28 (1968): 5–52; Ziegler, "Typen," 410–11.

5.   Nöth, *Ager Clavium*, 67–68.

6.   Zeissner, *Altkirchliche Kräfte*, 216–18.

7.   Wolfgang Ammon (Bamberg), Kist, *Matrikel*, 66; Wachter, 164; Johann Hubner (Forchheim) AEB, Rep. I, 337, fol. 314; Kist, *Matrikel*, 2919; Wachter, 4700.

8.   AEB, Rep. I, Pf.A. 189; 338, fols. 17f.

9.   Kist, *Matrikel*, 3893, 4876; Wachter, 6077, 11588.

10.   AEB, Rep. I, 332, fol. 300; Kist, *Matrikel*, 270; Wachter, 634.

11.   AEB, Rep. I, 334, fol. 332; Kist, *Matrikel*, 4759; Wachter, 7738.

12.   AEB, Rep. I, 335, fol. 171, 178v; Kist, *Matrikel*, 8; Wachter, 43.

13.   AEB, Rep. I, PfA 387; 335, fol. 57ff.; Kist, *Matrikel*, 5528; Wachter, 8984.

14.   L IV, 853–55; Zeissner, *Altkirchliche Kräfte*, 227–31.

15.   StAB, A 25, Lade 30, 53; L V, 1.

16.   *NBD*, II, 1, 346; Theobald Freudenberger, *Die Fürstbischöfe von Würzburg und das Konzil von Trient* (Münster: Aschendorff, 1989), 199; L V, 40ff.

17.   StAB, A 25, Lade 30, 54.

18.   StAB, B 84, 10; Wilhelm Hotzelt, *Veit II von Würtzburg, Fürstbischof von Bamberg 1561–1577* (Freiburg in Br.: Herder, 1918), 10–21; Freudenberger, *Konzil von Trient*, 97–98, 201.

19.   Hotzelt, *Veit II*, 47–50; L V, 53; Josef Krasenbrink, *Die Congregatio Germanica und die katholische Reform in Deutschland nach dem Tridentinum* (Münster: Aschendorff, 1972).

20.   Hotzelt, *Veit II*, 58.

21.   *Die Nuntiatur-Korrespondenz Kaspar Groppers (1573–1576),* ed. W. E. Schwarz (Paderborn: Schöningh, 1898), 49; Hotzelt, *Veit II*, 77–78; L V, 85.

22.   *Nuntiatur-Korrespondenz,* 264; Hotzelt, *Veit II*, 76; L V, 87.

23.   StAB, B 86, 12, fol. 93; *Nuntiatur-Korrespondenz,* 256, 262; Hotzelt, *Veit II*, 86–89; L V, 87–90.

24.   *Nuntiatur-Korrespondenz,* 257, 258–59, 262; L. C. Schmitt, *Geschichte des ernestinischen Klerikal-Seminars zu Bamberg* (Bamberg: Reindl, 1857); Hotzelt, *Veit II*, 77–78, 89–91; L V, 83–84.

25.   StAB, B 84, 10, fol. 188; Lothar Bauer, "Die Bamberger Weihbischöfe Johann Schöner und Friedrich Förner," *BHVB* 101 (1965): 321; Hotzelt, *Veit II*, 31, 65.

26.   *CCB,* vol. II, fols. 27–28; Hotzelt, *Veit II*, 32; L V, p. 79; cf. Reinhard Heydenreuter, *Der Landesherrliche Hofrat unter Herzog und Kurfürst Maximilian I. von Bayern (1598–1651)* (Munich: Beck, 1981), 22–23; Robert Bireley, S.J., *Maximilian von Bayern, Adam Contzen S.J. und die Gegenreformation in Deutschland, 1624–1635* (Munich, 1981), 18.

27.   Günther Dippold, *Konfessionalisierung am Obermain* (Staffelstein: Bornschlegel, 1996), 46–47.

28.   Hotzelt, *Veit II*, 75; Hotzelt, "Matricula Ordinatorum in Civitate Bamberg (1525–1598)," *BHVB* 77 (1909/1910): 33–102.

29.   *Nuntiatur-Korrespondenz,* 257; Hotzelt, *Veit II*, 89–103; L V, 91–93.

30.   Schonath, "Liturgische Drucke," 403, 409, 415.

31.   *Kurzer Auszug der christlien und Catholischen Gesäng des Ehrwürdigen Herrn Joannis Leisentritii, Thumdechants zu Budessin, Auff alle Sontag, Fest und Feyertäg, durch das gantz Jahr, in der Chatholischen Kirchen sicherlich zu singen* (Dillingen: Sebald Mayer, 1576); Hotzelt, *Veit II*, 64.

32.   StBB, Msc. Lit. 187; *CCB,* vol. V, fols. 120v–122.

33.   Wachter, 2417; Hotzelt, *Veit II*, 68–73; Bauer, "Die Bamberger Weihbischöfe," 320–23.

34.   Jakob Feucht, *Fünff Kurtze Predigen, Von Zwentzig vermeynten Ursachen: Warum etliche leut, diser zeit nit wöllen Catholisch, oder (wie sie sprechen) Bäpstisch seyn* (Cologne: Arnold Quentel, 1607), 9–10.

35.   Feucht, *Fünff Kurtze Predigen*, 3–5.

36.   Jakob Feucht, *Bescheidne und wolgegruendte Rettung des christlichen unnd kurtzen Berichts . . . Wider die vermeinte Antwort Lucae Osiandri* (Munich: Adam Berg, 1573); Jäck, *Pantheon der Literaten und Kunstler Bambergs* (Bamberg: Fränkische Merkur, 1812), 270–72, lists sixteen other works in this vein.

37.   Feucht, *Fünff Kurtze Predigen*, 7.

38.   *Fünff Kurtze Predigen*, 5–6.

39.   *Fünff Kurtze Predigen*, 158–27.

40. *Fünff Kurtze Predigen*, 78–85.

41. *Fünff Kurtze Predigen*, 89–93.

42. *Fünff Kurtze Predigen*, 245–58.

43. *Fünff Kurtze Predigen*, 35, 70.

44. *Fünff Kurtze Predigen*, 34–35, 96, 119, 227–29.

45. Rublack, *Gescheiterte Reformation*, 85; L V, 30.

46. AEB, Rep. I, 327, fols. 260–261v.

47. Weiden, Neudorf, Wunkendorf, Seubersdorf, and Görau. Weiden and Neudorf each had their own chapels. AEB, Rep. I, Pf.A. 347; Guttenberg-Wendehorst, 168–69.

48. AEB, Rep. I, Pf.A. 347.

49. StAB, B 49, 121.

50. AEB, Rep. I, Pf.A., 347; cf. L V, 29–32; Hotzelt, *Veit II*, 42.

51. StAB, B 49, 121.

52. AEB, Rep. I, Pf.A. 347.

53. Urbar A, 103–4; Urbar B, 144; Guttenberg, *Territorienbildung*, 384; Guttenberg-Wendehorst, 216.

54. Seubetenreuth, Kunsreuth, Braunersreuth, Schwand, Preineusel, Wildenstein, Schöndorf, Schlopp, Schnebes, Schlackenreuth, Trottenreuth, Kützenreuth, Enchenreuth, Ober- and Unter Brumberg, Wahl auf dem Wald, Heinersreuth, Elbersreuth. Urbar A, 103–4; Guttenberg-Wendehorst, 216.

55. AEB, Rep. I, Pf.A., 387, prod. 1.

56. AEB, Rep. I, Pf.A., 387, Prod. 2–3; Kist, *Matrikel*, 5528.

57. AEB, Rep. I, Pf.A., 387, prod. 4–6; 335, fol. 57ff.

58. AEB, Rep. I, 335, fol. 55; Wachter, 185, 5128, 4479, 10771, 1126; all but Prentel later were investigated for heresy.

59. AEB, Rep. I, 335, fols. 72v–75v.

60. Wachter, 604.

61. AEB, Rep. I, 335, fol. 54.

62. AEB, Rep. I, 335, fol. 61.

63. AEB, Rep. I, Pf.A. 387, prod. 10.

64. AEB, Rep. I, 335, fol. 63.

65. AEB, 334, fols. 13v–15v.

66. The accusations coincided with a period of particularly bad harvests, beginning in 1570 and lasting until 1575. Between 1565 and 1571, the price of a *Sümmer* of wheat rose from 23–25 d. to 60 d. The price topped out in 1574 at 90 pence. Both Georg Friedrich and Veit II issued laws prohibiting speculation and export of grain in an effort to keep supplies up and prices down. Endres, "Wirtschaftlichen und sozialen Lage," 9, 28–50.

67. StAB, B 49, 115, 8 April 1571; 26 June 1571.

68. StAB, B 49, 115, n.d. [1571]; 26 April; 12 June.

69. Cf. Joseph Patrouch, "Who Pays for Building the Rectory? Religious Conflicts in the Upper Austrian Parish of Dietach, 1540–1582," *SCJ* 26 (1995): 308–9.

70. StAB, A 95/II, Lade 297, 1334, 1335, 1338; B 49, 115, fasc. 828, 829.

71. StAB, B 68, fol. 201; C 2, 542.

72. Jürgen Petersohn, "Staatskunst und Politik des Markgrafen Georg Friedrich von Brandenburg-Ansbach," *ZBLG* 24 (1961): 229–76; Reinhard Seyboth, "Markgraf

Georg Friedrich von Brandenburg-Ansbach-Kulmbach (1556–1603) als Reichsfürst," *ZBLG* 53 (1990): 659–79.

73.   Hintze, *Die Hohenzollern,* 130; Hintze, "Calvinism and Raison d'ètat," in Felix Gilbert, ed., *The Historical Essays of Otto Hintze,* 125 (New York: Oxford University Press, 1975).

74.   StAB, C 3, 75.

75.   Jürgen Petersohn, *Markgraf Georg Friedrich von Brandenburg-Ansbach- und Bayreuth als Herzog in Preussen 1578–1603* (Bonn, 1961); Petersohn, "Georg Friedrich," 238–54; Walther Hubatsch, *Geschichte des Evangelische Kirche Ostpreussens* (Göttingen: Vandenhoek and Ruprecht, 1968), 115ff.

76.   StAB, C 2, 1821, prod. 4–6; Sehling, *Evangelische Kirchenordungen,* 295; Simon, *Evangelische Kirchengeschichte,* 306.

77.   StAB, C 3, 1608, fol. 129v; Simon, *Bayreuther Pfarrerbuch,* 186.

78.   Simon, *Bayreuther Pfarrerbuch,* 482.

79.   Simon, *Bayreuther Pfarrerbuch,* 2465; E. C. von Hagen, "Biographie des ersten General-Superintendents des Fürstentums Bayreuth, des Dr. Johannes Streitberger," *AO* 6 (1855): 69–72.

80.   Kneitz, 129–33.

81.   StAB, C 2, 1821, prod. 1, fols. 1–2.

82.   StAB, C 2, 1821, prod. 2.

83.   StAB, C 2, 1841, prod. 1–3; Sehling, *Evangelische Kirchenordnungen,* IV.8, 344–45.

84.   StAB, C 2, 1821, prod. 8, fol. 1; 1822, prod. 42; C 7/x, 1, fols. 20–25v; C 14, 29.

85.   StAB, C 7/x, 1, fols. 23–24.

86.   StAB, C 7/x, 1, fol. 25.

87.   StAB, C 2, 1821, prod. 8, fols. 22–23; prod. 10, fols. 32–33; C 2, 1835, prod. 1–3; C 3, 1223, fols. 62–66v.

88.   StAB, C 19, 1600.

89.   StAB, C 7/x, 1, fols. 5–8.

90.   StAB, C 2, 1822, prod. 41; C 7/x, 1, fols. 52ff., 261–262; Sehling, *Evangelische Kirchenordnungen,* IV.9, IV.11. Although the *Kapitelsordnung* was not published in the Oberland until 1572, it would appear that the ordinance circulated in manuscript form and had been at least partly implemented by 1566.

91.   StAB, C 7/x, 1, fol. 52–57; Sehling, *Evangelische Kirchenordnungen,* IV.9, 346–50; Simon, *Evangelische Kirchengeschichte,* 306.

92.   StAB, C 2, 1822, prod. 42; C 7/x, 1, fols. 16, 56–57.

93.   StAB, C 7/x, 1, fol. 281.

94.   StAB, C 2, 1821, prod. 3–5.

95.   StAB, C 2, 1821, prod. 8, fol. 23; C 3, 1223, fols. 62–66v; C 7/x, 1, fol. 22.

96.   StAB, C 2, 2018, prod. 1–6, 12–13.

97.   StAB, C 2, 1821, prod. 8, fol. 21; 2600, fol. 1.

98.   StAB, C 2, 2018.

99.   StAB, C 2, 2020, fols. 6–7; L IV, 906–10; Guttenberg-Wendehorst, 198–203.

100.   StAB, C 2, 2018, prod. 2–6.

101.   StAB, C 2, 2018, prod. 7–10; L IV, 906–7.

102. StAB, C 2, 2176, prod. 3, 9, 10, 12, 15, 17, 18; L IV, 955; Guttenberg-Wendehorst, 196–97.

103. StAB, C 2, 2177, 2179.

104. StAB, C 3, 2178.

105. StAB, C 2, 2180; Simon, *Bayreuther Pfarrerbuch*, 708, 730.

106. StAB, C 2, 2470; Simon, *Bayreuther Pfarrerbuch*, 86.

107. StAB, C 3, 1223, fols. 89, 115, 127–128, 132; cf. Dixon, *Reformation and Rural Society*, 92–94.

108. StAB, C 3, 1223, fols. 130–132, 151v–153v.

109. StAB, C 2, 1922; C 3, 1223, fol. 89, fol. 111–112; Simon, *Bayreuther Pfarrerbuch*, 849.

110. StAB, C 3, 1223, fol. 138.

111. StAB, C 3, 1223, fol. 138.

112. StAB, C 3, 1223, fols. 119v–120.

113. StAB, C 2, 1973.

114. StAB, B 49, 181; C 2, 2506, prod. 1–2; Reinel, *Annotationes*, 243–46, 259–60.

115. StAB, C 3, 1223, fol. 100v.

116. StAB, C 3, 1223, fol. 98v.

117. Marc R. Forster, "Clericalism and Communalism in German Catholicism," in Max Reinhart, ed., *Infinite Boundaries. Order, Disorder, and Reorder in Early Modern German Culture*, 57–58, 67–74 (Kirksville, MO: Sixteenth Century Journal Publishers, 1998); Stalnaker, "Protestant Clergy," 390–401; Patrouch, "Who Pays."

Chapter 7

1. Oestreich, *Geist und Gestalt*, 182–87, 192–97; Reinhard, "Reformation," 397–98, 403; Reinhard, "Gegenreformation oder Modernisierung?" 234–39; Schilling, "Konfessionalisierung im Reich," 3–6, 34–36; Schilling, "Konfessionalisierung von Kirche, Staat und Gesellschaft," 4–7; cf. Otto Hintze, *Staat und Verfassung*, 470–96.

2. Reinhard, "Reformation," 392–93.

3. Forster, *Counter-Reformation*, 59–60; Schorn-Schütte, "Priest, Preacher, Pastor," 15–21.

4. For a useful, if contentious, overview of the literature see Steven Ozment, *Ancestors: The Loving Family in Old Europe* (Cambridge, MA: Harvard University Press, 2001); also Joel F. Harrington, *Reordering Marriage and Society in Reformation Germany* (Cambridge: Cambridge University Press, 1995), 1–17.

5. Hamm, "Reformatio zur Reformation," 7–11; Schilling, "The Reformation and the Rise of the Territorial State," 23; Reinhard, "Reformation," 390; Schilling, "Die Konfessionalisierung im Reich," 6.

6. Susan C. Karant-Nunn, *The Reformation of Ritual: An Interpretation of Early Modern Germany* (New York: Routledge, 1997), 200.

7. Gerald Strauss, "Success and Failure in the German Reformation," *P & P* 67 (1975): 30–63. For responses to Strauss's thesis, see Steven Ozment, *When Fathers Ruled: Family Life in Reformation Europe* (Cambridge, MA: Harvard University Press,

1983); Geoffrey Parker, "Success and Failure during the First Century of the Reformation," *P&P* 136 (1992): 43–82; Hans-Christoph Rublack, "Success and Failure of the Reformation: Popular 'Apologies' from the Seventeenth and Eighteenth Centuries," in Fix and Karant-Nunn, *Germania Illustrata,* 141–65.

8. Forster, *Counter-Reformation,* 4.

9. Sabean, *Power in the Blood,* 65–68, 111–12; cf. Arnold Snyder, "Word and Power in Reformation Zurich," *ARG* 81 (1990): 263–85; Bossy, *Christianity in the West,* 100–104; Klaus Haendler, *Wort und Glaube bei Melanchthon* (Gütersloh: G. Mohn, 1968), 50–51, 97–99.

10. Hans Schieber, "Die Vorgeschichte des Bamberger Priesterseminars," in *Seminarium Ernestinum. 400 Jahre Priesterseminar Bamberg,* ed. Michael Hofmann, 18 (Bamberg: St. Otto Verlag, 1987).

11. Schieber, "Vorgeschichte," 50–51; Ernst Reiter, *Martin von Schaumberg, Fürstbischof von Eichstätt (1560–1590) und die Trienter Reform* (Münster: Aschendorff, 1965), 130–35.

12. StAB, A 25, Lade 30, 57; L V, 151–56; Weigel, *Wahlkapitulationen,* 90–91.

13. StAB, B 86, vol. 17, fol. 40f.

14. StAB, B 86, vol. 17, fol. 210; B 121, 939; *CCB,* III, fols. 104–105v; Schieber, "Vorgeschichte," 54–56; Deckert, "Karmalitenkloster," 64; L V, 174; Schmitt, *Klerikal-Seminars,* 65.

15. Deckart, "Karmelitenkloster," 65; L V, 175–76; Schmitt, *Klerikal-Seminars,* 64.

16. StAB, B 90, 940; B 121, 940; B 86, vol. 18, fols. 283–284v; Schieber, "Vorgeschichte," 59; Deckart, "Karmelitenkloster," 66–68; L V, 176–78; Schmitt, *Klerikal-Seminars,* 68–69.

17. Schmitt, *Klerikal-Seminars,* 425–30.

18. StAB, C 2, 2088, prod. 1; Jordan, *Reformation und gelehrte Bildung,* 115–213.

19. Jordan, *Reformation und gelehrte Bildung,* 80, 311–12.

20. StAB, C 2, 2088.

21. StAB, C 2, 2088; C 3, 1248; Jordan, *Reformation und gelehrte Bildung,* 326–29.

22. StAB, C 7/x, fol. 42v.

23. StAB, C 7/x, fols. 45–46v.

24. StAB, C 7/x, 1, fols. 35–42v, 47–48.

25. StAB, C 7/x, 1, fol. 233.

26. StAB, C 7/x, 1, fols. 233–234v.

27. StAB, C 2, 2088.

28. StAB, C 2, 2089, fols. 14, 24v.

29. Luise Schorn-Schütte has argued that the practice was not common, and that most pastors' wives did not spring from the parsonage. Nonetheless, in the Oberland, the practice seems quite widespread, in particular among the leading pastoral families. Schorn-Schütte, "'Gefährtin' und 'Mitregentin.' Zur Sozialgeschichte der evangelischen Pfarrfrau in der Frühen Neuzeit," in *Wandel der Geschlechterbeziehungen zu Beginn der Neuzeit,* ed. Heide Wunder and Christina Vanja, 123–31 (Frankfurt: Suhrkamp, 1991); cf. Po-Chia Hsia, *Social Discipline,* 14–15; Martin Brecht, "Herkunft und Ausbildung der protestantischen Geistlichen der Herzogtum Württemberg im 16. Jahrhundert," *ZKG* 80 (1969): 163–75.

30. Simon, *Pfarrerbuch,* 1146.

31. StAB, C 3, 1248, fols. 32–63.

32. StAB, C 3, 1248, fols. 21–26; C 2, 2089, fol. 1, Simon, *Bayreuther Pfarrerbuch,* 482, 483.

33. Simon, *Bayreuther Pfarrerbuch,* 301, 304, 306.

34. StAB, C 2, 2088; Roth, *Oberfranken in der Neuzeit,* 288, 576–78, 617.

35. StAB, C 2, 2154, fols. 37–38, 43, 58–60v; Pietsch, *Gelehrte Bildung,* 109–10, 123.

36. Pietsch, *Gelehrte Bildung,* 123.

37. StAB, C 2, 2154, fols. 15–16, 21.

38. StAB, C 2, 2154, fols. 127–129; Simon, *Bayreuther Pfarrerbuch,* 2545.

39. StAB, C 2, 2154, fol. 137; Simon, *Bayreuther Pfarrerbuch,* 2543.

40. StAB, C 2, 2089, fol. 2v.

41. StAB, C 2, 2358. Breutla subsequently hanged himself in despair over his pastoral duties.

42. StAB, C 2, 2088.

43. Schorn-Schütte, "Priest, Preacher, Pastor," 20–21.

44. StAB, C2, 2125, fols. 4–24v; Simon, *Bayreuther Pfarrerbuch,* 1146.

45. Although the evidence is very slight, data from Kist, *Matrikel,* as well as from the *Protokollenbücher* indicate that after 1560, it became increasingly rare for the sons of priests to enter the priesthood. After 1583, it was essentially impossible, as legitimate birth became an absolute prerequisite for admission to the Ernestinum. Schmitt, *Klerikal-Seminars,* 397; cf. Schorn-Schütte, "Priest, Preacher, Pastor," 16–19.

46. Bauer, "Die Bamberger Weihbischöfe," 317–18, 325–26.

47. Schorn-Schütte, "Lutherische Konfessionalisierung?" 184–89; John Stroup, *The Struggle for Identity in the Clerical Estate* (Leiden: Brill, 1984), 24–28; Schilling, "Konfessionalisierung im Reich," 38–39.

48. Mark. R. Forster, "Clericalism and Communalism in German Catholicism," 57–58, 67–74.

49. Pörtner, *Counter-Reformation,* 188–93.

50. James A. Brundage, *Law, Sex, and Christian Society in Medieval Europe* (Chicago: University of Chicago Press, 1987); R. H. Helmholz, *Marriage Litigation in Medieval England* (Cambridge: Cambridge University Press, 1974).

51. Hans-Günter Gruber, *Christliches Eheverständnis im 15. Jahrhundert. Eine moralgeschichtliche Untersuchung zur Ehelehre Dionysius des Kartäusers* (Regensburg: F. Pustet, 1989).

52. StBB, Theol. Msc. 38, fols. 295–289.

53. Kramer, *Ansbach,* 217–18.

54. *CCB,* vol. II, fols. 7v–8.

55. StAB, B 26^c, 126^ii, Oct. 14, 1566.

56. *CCB,* vol. II, fols. 255v–258v; StAB, B 26^c, 107, Feb. 17, 1574.

57. StAB, B 26^c, 107; Karant-Nunn, *Reformation of Ritual,* 37–38.

58. StAB, B 26^c, 3^i, prod. 1. Jan. 29, 1587; Brundage, 565.

59. StAB, B 26^c, 131, May 16, 1562; Jan. 7, 1580.

60. L V, 203–7.

61. StAB, C 2, 1822, prod. 38, fol. 63v.

62. StAB, C 2, 1821, prod. 8, fol. 21v.

63.   StAB, C 2, 11; 1832; C 7/I, 102; Petersohn, "Georg Friedrich," 243–44.

64.   StAB, C 2, 1832; Kraußold, *Geschichte der evangelische Kirche,* 235–36.

65.   Sehling, *Evangelische Kirchenordnungen,* IV.17, 379–96.

66.   StAB, C 2, 11; C 7^i, 102, Oct. 18, 1567.

67.   Josef Kohler and Willy Scheel, eds., *Die Bamberger Halsgerichtsordung* (Aalen: Scientia, 1968); cf. Thomas Max Safley, *Let No Man Put Asunder: The Control of Marriage in the German Southwest: A Comparative Study 1550–1600* (Kirksville, MO: Sixteenth Century Journal Publishers, 1984), 38.

68.   Cf. Brundage, *Law, Sex, and Christian Society,* 493, 517–20.

69.   StAB, B 68, 890.

70.   StAB, B 68, 877, fols. 208f.

71.   StAB, B 68, 877, fol. 226.

72.   StAB, C 3, 18, Lit. H, fols. 48–50.

73.   Kramer, *Volksleben Im Fürstentum Ansbach,* 221–23; Kramer, *Bamberg,* 143–44; Dixon, *Reformation and Rural Society,* 123–24; Thomas Robisheaux, *Rural Society and the Search for Order in Early Modern Germany* (Cambridge: Cambridge University Press, 1989), 114–15. *Fenster* was a practice in which girls left their windows open at night and allowed young gallants to lie with them. The practice involved female choice, and did not always end in sexual relations, though this was a common result. *Fenster* appears to have constituted a part of spousal arrangements in some communities and frequently occurred the evening before the wedding. C. L. Powell, *English Domestic Relations 1487–1653* (New York: Columbia University Press, 1917), 3–4; Ozment, *When Fathers Ruled,* 34–36.

74.   StAB, B 68, 876, fols. 1005–1006, 1036.

75.   Kramer, *Ansbach,* 216–17; Brundage, *Law, Sex, and Christian Society,* 497–98; Helmholz, *Marriage Litigation,* 12–15; Safley, *Control of Marriage,* 15–31; Ozment, *When Fathers Ruled,* 38–39.

76.   StAB, C 2, 1814, Lit. A.

77.   StAB, C 2, 1814, fasc. 3, 1577.

78.   StAB, B 68, 877, fol. 204.

79.   StAB, C 7^i, 102, Jun. 10, 1573.

80.   *CCB,* vol. III, fol. 247.

81.   StAB, C 2, 14, prod. 4.

82.   StAB, C 2, 1842.

83.   StAB, C 2, 18, prod. 1.

84.   StAB, C 2, 1814, Lit. A.

85.   StAB, B 68, 876, fol. 1018; cf. Ozment, *Ancestors,* 61–65; Wunder, *He Is the Sun,* 120–26.

86.   Kramer, *Ansbach,* 202–3.

87.   Gruber, *Christliche Eheverständnis,* 78–81; Robisheaux, *Rural Society,* 106–9.

88.   Ozment, *When Fathers Ruled,* 43.

89.   StAB, C 2, 22; Kramer, *Ansbach,* 218–19; Dixon, *Reformation and Rural Society,* 108.

90.   Kramer, *Ansbach,* 141–42, 205–10; Ingrid Ahrendt-Schulte, "Schadenzauber und Konflikte. Sozialgeschichte von Frauen im Spiegel der Hexenprozesse des 16. Jahrhundert in der Grafschaft Lippe," in Wunder and Vanja, *Wandel der Geschlechterbeziehungen,* 213–28.

91. AEB, Rep. I, 327, fol. 181 (1594); Robisheaux, *Rural Society*, 116–19.

92. Harline, 242; Ozment, *When Fathers Ruled*, 30–32; Wunder, *He Is the Sun*, 53–54; Harrington, *Reordering Marriage*, 14–16, 277.

93. Harrington, *Reordering Marriage*, 6, 276.

94. Karant-Nunn, *The Reformation of Ritual*, 39–40, here summarizing Mary Douglas, *Natural Symbols: Explorations in Cosmology* (London: Barrie and Jenkins, 1973), 93–112, and Ray Porter, "History of the Body," in *New Perspectives on Historical Writing*, ed. Peter Burke, 206–32 (University Park: Pennsylvania State University Press, 1992). Giles Constable makes a convincing argument that it was in the twelfth and thirteenth centuries that the monastic ideal permeated secular society. Between 1100 and 1160, he writes, the reform movements "can be seen as an effort to monasticize first the clergy, by imposing on them a standard of life previously reserved for monks, and then the entire world. The influence of monasticism permeated society." Constable, *The Reformation of the Twelfth Century*, 6; Constable, *Three Studies in Medieval Religious and Social Thought* (Cambridge: Cambridge University Press, 1995), 324–41; see also Hans Baron, *In Search of Florentine Civic Humanism* (Princeton, NJ: Princeton University Press, 1988), chapters 7–8. In any event, the spread of confraternal piety during the fourteenth and fifteenth centuries, noted in chapter 1, testifies to the popular acceptance of quasi-monastic discipline as well as more "urban" forms of religious devotion in the countryside a good century prior to the beginnings of confessionalization.

95. Forster, *Counter-Reformation in the Villages*, 19–20; Dixon, 77–78; Ozment, *Ancestors*, 41–42.

96. Blickle, *Revolution of 1525*, 190.

97. StAB, C 2, 1922; Simon, *Bayreuther Pfarrerbuch*, 2058.

98. StAB, C 3, 758.

99. StAB, C 2, 2125; C 3, 19, fols. 179v–181v; Simon, *Bayreuther Pfarrerbuch*, 313, 334.

100. StAB, C 2, 14, prod. 4.

101. StAB, C 2, 14, prod. 5; C 3, 1842.

102. Martin Honecker, "Sozialethik des Luthertums," in Hans-Christoph Rublack, ed., *Die lutherische Konfessionalisierung in Deutschland*, 316–40 (Gütersloh: Mohn, 1992); Schorn-Schütte, "'Gefährtin' und 'Mitregentin,'" 109–18, 148–52; Wunder, *He Is the Sun*, 48–49.

103. Dixon, *Reformation and Rural Society*, 122; Harrington, *Reordering Marriage*, 276–78; Oestreich, *Geist und Gestalt*, 185.

104. Rebel, *Peasant Classes*, 245–47.

105. Rebel, *Peasant Classes*, 269.

106. Heide Wunder, "Hexenprozesse und Gemeinde," in *Hexenverfolgung und Regionalgeschichte. Die Grafschaft Lippe im Vergleich*, ed. Gisela Wilbertz, Gerd Schwerhoff, and Jürgen Scheffler, 61–70 (Bielefeld: Verlag für Regionalgeschichte, 1994); Walter Rummel, *Bauern, Herren, und Hexen. Studie zur Sozialgeschichte sponheimische und kurtrierische Hexenprozesse 1574–1664* (Göttingen: Vandenhoeck and Ruprecht, 1991), 26–41.

107. Evans, *Habsburg Monarchy*, 113; Oestreich, *Geist und Gestalt*, 35–79.

108. Frances Yates noted the extent to which, in the early years of the seventeenth century, mathematics had been tainted on account of its association with cabalistic

studies and the occult. Yates, *The Rosicrucian Enlightment* (London: Routledge, 1972), 42–56, 157–64.

109. Evans, *Habsburg Monarchy,* 427–33.

110. Evans, *Habsburg Monarchy,* 80–116.

111. Günther Dippold, *Konfessionalisierung am Obermain* (Staffelstein: Bornschlegel, 1996), 351–52, cf. 245–54; Rebel, *Peasant Classes,* 259–65.

112. Evans, *Habsburg Monarchy,* 400–401; Forster, *Counter-Reformation,* 246–47.

Chapter 8

1. Schilling, "The Reformation and the Rise of the Early Modern State," 27–28.

2. Reinhard, "Katholische Konfessionalisierung," 450–51.

3. Forster, *Counter-Reformation;* Forster, *Catholic Renewal;* MacHardy, *War, Religion, and Court Patronage;* Pörtner, *Counter-Reformation in Central Europe;* Patrouch, *Negotiated Settlement.* Significant earlier studies of the Habsburg Counter-Reformation include Rebel, *Peasant Classes;* Bireley, *Religion and Politics,* and Evans, *The Making of the Habsburg Monarchy.*

4. Erwin Riedenauer, "Reichsritterschaft und Konfession. Ein Diskussionsbeitrag zum Thema 'Adel und Konfession,'" in *Deutscher Adel, 1555–1740,* ed. Hellmuth Rössler, 1–63 (Darmstadt: Wissenschaftliche Buchgesellschaft, 1695); Press, "Adel im Reich," 28–30; Christ, "Selbstverständnis," *passim.* We await the publication of Richard Ninness's study of the Bamberg cathedral chapter in the seventeenth century.

5. Schubert, "Gegenreformation," 276–78; Ziegler, "Territorium und Reformation," 62–67.

6. *CCB,* II, fols. 43–43v (1564); fols. 63–63v (1566); fol. 91v (1566); fols. 101v–103v (1566); fols. 117–119v, 124v–125 (1566); fols. 192v–193 (1569); fols. 198v–199 (1570); fols. 202–202v (1571); fols. 217–219 (1571); fols. 233–233v (1572); fols. 241v–242 (1573); fols. 252–254v (1574); fols. 270v–271 (1575); fols. 234–235 (1576); vol. III, fols. 58–59v (1584); fols. 70–71v (1585); fols. 93–96v (1586); fols. 139–140 (1587); fols. 148–153 (1588); fols. 153v–155 (1589); fols. 173–175 (1589); fols. 195v–196 (1589); fols. 197–199 (1590); fols. 217v–218v (1590); fols. 224–224v (1591); StAB, B 26^c, 106 (1566); 126^{ii} (1566); 129 (1584).

7. *CCB,* II, fol. 103.

8. *CCB,* III, fols. 58–59v; fols. 70–71v.

9. *CCB,* II, fols. 117–119v.

10. *CCB,* II, fols. 217–219, 233f., 270v–271.

11. *CCB,* III, fols. 139–140, 217v–218v.

12. *CCB,* II, fols. 58–59v.

13. *CCB,* II, fols. 151f., 220v–222, 226–228, 246–248, 264v–266.

14. StAB, B 26^c, 140^i.

15. *CCB,* III, fols. 111–114v.

16. Schubert, "Gegenreformation," 277.

17. Schubert, "Gegenreformation," 278–84; Ziegler, "Territorium und Reformation," 67–74; Pörtner, *Counter-Reformation,* 170ff.; cf. Ziegler, "Typen der Konfessionalisierung," *passim.*

18.   *CCB,* IV, fols. 6–7v; Zagel, *Neithard von Thüngen,* 34.

19.   *CCB,* IV, fols. 20f.

20.   Schubert, "Gegenreformation," 298.

21.   L V, 225–38.

22.   *CCB,* IV, fols. 3, 14v–15v, 17–18, 20, 30–31, 32–34, 41–50v, 58–61v, 77–79v, 89–91.

23.   StAB, B 26ᶜ, 3ⁱ, prod. 2; Zagel, *Neithard von Thüngen,* 44–45.

24.   *CCB,* IV, fols. 95v–98; Zagel, *Neithard von Thüngen,* 6–48; Schubert, "Gegen-reformation," 298–99.

25.   L V, 242–43.

26.   *CCB,* IV, fols. 109v–111v; StAB, B 26ᶜ, 135ⁱ, May 17, 1595; L V, 248–250; Zagel, *Neithard von Thüngen,* 48–49.

27.   *CCB,* IV, fols. 235v–256, 268v–269v.

28.   *CCB,* IV, fols. 182ff.

29.   *CCB,* IV, fols. 117v–122.

30.   StAB, B 26ᶜ, 140ⁱ, Aug. 5, 1595.

31.   *CCB,* IV, fols. 162–164v, 207–215.

32.   *CCB,* IV, fols. 285v–286v.

33.   L V, 264.

34.   AEB, Rep. I, 337, fol. 6v.

35.   AEB, Rep. I, 336, fol. 261v.

36.   AEB, Rep. I, 333, fol. 504.

37.   L V, 263–64; Zagel, *Neithard von Thüngen,* 69–70.

38.   AEB, Rep. I, 334, fols. 294f.

39.   AEB, Rep. I, 335, fols. 53–57; PfA. 387.

40.   AEB, Rep. I, 335, fols. 56v–57, 71.

41.   AEB, Rep. I, 335, fols. 68–69v.

42.   Wachter, 11374.

43.   AEB, Pf.A. 387, prod. 8; Wachter, 4587.

44.   StAB, B 49, 149.

45.   AEB, Rep. I, 327, fols. 191–203v; 335, fols. 178–183; Guttenberg-Wende-horst, 140–43; Wachter, 1633; Kist, *Matrikel,* 1070.

46.   AEB, Rep. I, 335, fol. 178.

47.   AEB, Rep. I, 331, fols. 152v–153.

48.   AEB, Rep. I, 325, fol. 49; 331, fol. 160v.

49.   AEB, Rep. I, 331, fols. 154f.

50.   Wachter, 708.

51.   AEB, Rep. I, 331, fols. 153–154, 155–156.

52.   AEB, Rep. I, 327, fols. 319v, 327; 331, fols. 156v–159.

53.   AEB, Rep. I, 327, fols. 356–357v.

54.   Zeumer, 163, §26.

55.   Riedenauer, "Reichsritterschaft," 18–19; Press, "Adel im Reich," 27–30; MacHardy, "Einfluss von Status," 56; MacHardy, *War, Religion and Court Patronage,* 51–52, 58–59.

56.   Zagel, *Neithard von Thüngen,* 70–71.

57.   Zagel, *Neithard von Thüngen,* 71, 83–84.

58.   Merz, "Landstadt," 76–77.

59. Rublack, *Gescheiterte Reformation,* 87–90, 255–58.

60. L V, 262; Zagel, *Neithard von Thüngen,* 111–13.

61. StAB, B 86, vol. 21, fols. 408v–409; B 86, 296k; Zagel, *Neithard von Thüngen,* 95–97; 112–13; Rublack, *Gescheiterte Reformation,* 87.

62. StAB, A 45, 67; Zagel, *Neithard von Thüngen,* 116–19; L V, 260.

63. StAB, C 2, 214; C 3, 1231.

64. StAB, B 41^i, vol. 42, fols. 249–256.

65. *B. u. A.* IV, 390–91; V, 309; L V, 263; Rublack, *Gescheiterte Reformation,* 89.

66. StAB, B 86, vol. 22, fols. 234, 263, 267, 286, 309, 321, 352, 366, 375; vol. 23, fols. 16, 19, 38, 41, 46.

67. Josef Heller, "Jakob Ayrer's bamberger Reim-Chronik, vom Jahre 900–1599," *BHVB* 3 (1838): 101.

68. Lother Bauer, "Fürstbischof Johann Philipp von Gebsattel (1599–1609) im Urteil der Nachwelt," *BHVB* 100 (1964): 407–13.

69. AEB Rep. I, A 3, prod. 1, fols. 26v–29v.

70. *B. u. A.,* IV, 381.

71. *B. u. A.,* IV, 394; L V, 290–91; Bauer, "Die Weihbischöfe," 344.

72. Lothar Bauer, "Der Informativprozeß für den Bamberger Fürstbischof Johann Philipp von Gebsattel (1599–1609)," *JFFL* 21 (1961): 1–3.

73. *B. u. A,* IV, 394–99; L V, 239, 279–86; Bauer, "Informativprozeß," 4–7, Beilage I; Bauer, "Die Bamberger Weihbischöfe," 345; Wachter, 1470.

74. L V, 343; Bauer, "Informativprozeß," 12–14; Bauer, "Die Bamberger Weihbischöfe," 346–49.

75. *CCB,* V, fols. 6v–7v, 15–16v, 20–21, 27–28, 53–55, 88–90, 107–108v, 125–127, 142–144, 150v–152, 228f.; StAB, B 26^c, 134, July 22, 1606, May 28, 1608; 135^i, 1599, 1600, 1602, 1605, 1609.

76. AEB, Rep. I, 333, fols. 148–149.

77. AEB, Rep. I, 333, fols. 149–152.

78. AEB, Rep. I, 333, fols. 152–153.

79. AEB, Rep. I, 333, fols. 178f.; Guttenberg-Wendehorst, 114–15.

80. AEB, Rep. I, 327, fol. 320.

81. AEB, Rep. I, 327, fols. 320, 323f., 325ff., 327v; Guttenberg-Wendehorst, 86.

82. AEB, Rep. I, 327, fols. 320v–321.

83. Nöth, *Ager Clavium,* 67–68, 101–14.

84. AEB, Rep. I, 328, fols. 49–59; see Patrouch, "Who Pays," 300–301; Pörtner, *Counter-Reformation,* 172–78, 187–88.

85. Georgium Frenhofer, *Ain kurzen Psalter auß allen Psalmen Davids, nach ordnung und zal der hundert und fünfftzig Psalmen* (1574).

86. L V, 312–15; Bauer, "Die Bamberger Weihbischöfe," 349–50.

87. StAB, B 73, fols. 113f.

88. StAB, B 73, fols. 2v–3, 27–35.

89. StAB, B 73, fols. 44–50v.

90. StAB, B 73, fols. 55f.

91. StAB, B 73, fols. 2–3v, 68–69v; *B. u. A.,* IV, 518–23.

92. StAB, B 73, fols. 70–74v, 84–85v, 111–112; Bauer, "Die Bamberger Weihbischöfe," 356.

93. StAB, B 73, fol. 68; L V, 318; Bauer, "Die Bamberger Weihbischöfe," 357–58.

94. Friedrich Förner, *Vom Ablaß und Jubeljar, Orthodoxisches vnd Summarischer Bericht* (Ingolstadt: Andrea Angermeyr, 1600), A2v.

95. *B. u. A.,* IV, 400.

96. AEB, Rep. I, A 27; StAB, B 73, fols. 124f., 139f.; L V, 343–44; Bauer, "Die Bamberger Weihbischöfe," 375–77.

97. Bauer, "Die Bamberger Weihbischöfe," 384–85.

98. StAB, A 46, 25–28; L V, 347–48; Bauer, "Die Bamberger Weihbischöfe," 389–91.

99. AEB, Rep. I, A 27; *B. u. A.,* V, 928–29; Bauer, "Die Bamberger Weihbischöfe," 394–97.

100. AEB, Rep. I, A 3, prod. 2; StAB, H 2, 352, Aug. 17/27, 1607; *B. u. A.,* IV, 401–3; Lothar Bauer, "Die Rolle Herzog Maximilians von Bayern bei der Wahl des Bamberger Fürstbischofs Johann Gottfried von Aschhausen, 1609," *ZBLG* 25 (1961): 558–71; Bauer, "Die Kurie und Johann Philipp von Gebsattel, 1608/1609," *Quellen und Forschungen aus Italienischen Archive und Bibliotheken,* 40 (1960): 89–115.

101. StAB, B 73, 2, fols. 173f.

102. Anton Ruland, ed., "Die Briefe des Bamberger Dompredigers und späteren Weihbischofs Friedrich Förner," *BHVB* 34 (1871): V, 179–81; Bauer, "Die Bamberger Weihbischöfe," 405–6.

103. Ruland, "Briefe," VI, 183–84, 24 Jun. 1609.

104. Bauer, "Die Rolle Maxilimian I," 563–65, Beilage II–III, 569–70; Ruland, "Briefe," VII, 185.

105. StAB, A 25, Lade 30, 62, 62a; AEB, Rep. I, A 4; Bauer, "Die Rolle Maximilian I," 565–67, Beilage IV; Ruland, "Briefe," VII, 185.

106. L V, 317; Bauer, "Die Bamberger Weihbischöfe," 409.

107. Ruland, "Briefe," VIII, 185–86; Bauer, "Die Bamberger Weihbischöfe," 410–15.

108. AEB, Rep. I, A 4, *Heroicus applausus Rom. Et Ill. Principias Dño, Dño Johannis Godefrido ab Aschausen,* fols. 6v, 33v–34.

109. Bauer, "Johann Philipp im Urteil der Nachwelt," 409–10.

110. L V, 384, 386–87.

111. Dippold, *Konfessionalisierung am Obermain,* 457.

112. *CCB,* VI, fols. 1–11.

113. *CCB,* VI, fol. 12v–13v; L V, 373; Kanzler, "Landkapitel," II, 36.

114. *CCB,* VI, fols. 30v–31; StAB, B 26/c, 135/I, prod. 16, 17; L V, 375.

115. L V, 376; Dippold, *Konfessionalisierung am Obermain,* 460–61.

116. Dippold, *Konfessionalisierung am Obermain,* 462–63.

117. AEB, Rep. I, 327, fols. 265f.

118. AEB, Rep. I, 331, fols. 164f; cf. Pörtner, *Counter-Reformation,* 178.

119. AEB, Rep. I, Pf.A., 569, prod. 1–4.

120. StAB, B 49, 285; L V, 408; Georg Denzler, "Die Religiöse Entwicklung Deutschlands im Dreissigjährigen Krieg verdeutlicht am Beispiel des Bistums Bamberg," *BHVB* 104 (1968): 383–405.

121. AEB, Rep. I, PfA. 569, prod. 4.

122. AEB, Rep. I, Pf.A., 569, prod. 4

123. AEB Rep. I, 337, fols. 379v–380; 338, fols. 657v–660v.

124. Friedrich Förner, *Notwehr vnd Ehrnrettung, Der Catholischen Religions, vnd etlich ihrer fürnembsten Glaubens Articuln, als vom Ablaß und Iubilaeo* (Ingolstadt: Andrea Angermeyr, 1600), 5–6, 15.

125. Förner, *Vom Ablaß und Jubeljar,* 6–8; Förner, *Notwehr vnd Ehrnrettung,* 6.

126. Förner, *Notwehr vnd Ehrnrettung,* 13–14, 36; cf. Evans, *Habsburg Monarchy,* 109–12.

127. Förner, *Notwehr vnd Ehrnrettung,* 15, 31–33, 36; Förner, *Vom Ablaß und Jubeljar,* 1, 6–7.

128. Förner, *Vom Ablaß und Jubeljar,* A2v, B2.

129. Friedrich Förner, *Relatio Historico-Paranetica de Sacrosanctis, Sacri Romani Imperii, Reliquiis, Et Ornamentis* (1629), 71–76; on the interpretation of Catholic rhetoric generally, see Evans, *Habsburg Monarchy,* 68–72; MacHardy, *War, Religion and Court Patronage,* 108–16.

130. Evans, *Habsburg Monarchy,* 419.

131. Friedrich Förner, *Beneficia Miraculosa tam vetera quam Recentia Virginis Deiparæ Weyerensis* (Cologne: Johann Kinch, 1620), **2v.

132. Förner, *Relatio Historico-Paranetica,* 71–72.

Chapter 9

1. StAB, A 245/I 40/I, *Annotationes Domini M. Pauli Reinelii Diaconis Selbensis Anno 1612;* StAB, C 2, 2089, fols. 64–65; Simon, *Bayreuther Pfarrerbuch,* 1937.

2. Reinel, *Annotationes,* 147–50.

3. Reinel, *Annotationes,* 157.

4. Reinel, *Annotationes,* 58, 160–61.

5. *Außschreiben, Wie vnd aus was Vrsachen, Inn des Durchleuchtigen Hochgebornen Fürsten vnd Herrn Herr Christiani, Marggraffen zu Brandenburg . . . Landen vnd Fürstenthum, ein Christliches Evangelische Jubelfest zu feiern sey.* (1617).

6. *Außschreiben,* A2–[A3v].

7. *Außschreiben,* [A2v].

8. Reinel, *Annotationes,* 5.

9. Although Reinel identifies David Chytraeus as a source, his chronology derives primarily from his reckoning of local history. Cf. Robin Barnes, *Prophecy and Gnosis: Apocolypticism in the Wake of the Lutheran Reformation* (Stanford: Stanford University Press, 1988), 100ff.

10. *Außschreiben,* A4v.

11. *Außschreiben,* A3f.

12. Reinel, *Annotationes,* 156–57, 246–47, 429–30.

13. Psalm 94:20.

14. StAB, H 2, 351, fols. 31–36, 79–82.

15. StAB, B 41^{i}, vol. 12, fols. 152–157; vol. 13, fol. 15; H 2, 351, fols. 127ff.

16. StAB, B 41^{i}, vol. 22, fol. 195; vol. 30, fols. 17–28; H 2, 351, fol. 253.

17. Karl Schornbaum, "Die Bündnisbestrebungen der deutschen evangelischen Fürsten und Markgraf Georg Friedrich von Brandenburg-Ansbach, 1566–1570," *ZKG* 38 (1920): 262–82; Schornbaum, "Markgraf Georg Friedrich von Brandenburg als Vermittler zwischen den evangelischen Fürsten, 1567–1570," *ARG* 26 (1929): 208–11.

18. StAB, C 2, 1833, prod. 2, 4, 5, 7; StBB, Msc. Theol. 206; Schornbaum, "Bündnisbestrebungen," 263ff.

19. StAB, C 2, 1833, prod. 1, 7; Sehling, *Evangelische Kirchenordnungen,* 298–301, IV.16, 377–78; Simon, *Evangelische Kirchengeschichte,* 307; Karl Schornbaum, "Markgraf Georg Friedrich von Brandenburg und die evangelische Stände Deutschlands 1570–1575," *ARG* 22 (1925): 268–70; Schornbaum, "Markgraf Georg Friedrich von Brandenburg als Vermittler," 209, 219–24; Evans, *Making of the Habsburg Monarchy,* 53–57.

20. *B. u. A.,* I, 181, 271–72; 241, 317–19; 301, 380–83; Hans-Jörg Herold, *Markgraf Joachim Ernst von Brandenburg-Ansbach als Reichsfürst* (Göttingen: Vandenhoek and Ruprecht, 1973), 49–50.

21. *B. u. A.,* I, 284, 355; 292, 361–62; Herold, *Joachim Ernst,* 50–52.

22. *B. u. A.,* I, 295, 374–75.

23. *B. u. A.,* I, 183, 272; Falkenstein, IV.2, 492; Otto Veh, "Der Bayreuther Landstände unter dem Markgrafen Christian 1605–1655," Teil 1, *AO* 33 (1938): 10; Herold, *Joachim Ernst,* 30–36.

24. Falkenstein, IV.2, 494; Lang, III, 380–83; Veh, 11; Herold, *Joachim Ernst,* 31–32; Ernst Sticht, *Markgraf Christian von Brandenburg Kulmbach und der 30jährige Krieg in Ostfranken 1618–1635* (Kulmbach: Freunde der Plassenburg, 1965), 4.

25. Jegel, "Landständische Verfassung," 30; Veh, "Bayreuther Landstände," 9–12; Herold, *Joachim Ernst,* 36.

26. *B. u. A.,* I, 322, 416–17; Herold, *Joachim Ernst,* 53–55.

27. StAB, H 2, 352, May 7/April 27, 1605; Herold, *Joachim Ernst,* 63–64; Evans, 9–10, 51–53.

28. *B. u. A.,* I, 442, 539–40; 459, 556–57; Herold, *Joachim Ernst,* 65–76.

29. *B. u. A.,* I, 529; Herold, *Joachim Ernst,* 86–93.

30. *B. u. A.,* I, 529, 658–59.

31. Herold, *Joachim Ernst,* 94–95.

32. StAB, C 47, 4–5, 9; *B. u. A.,* I, 571, 704–8; Herold, *Joachim Ernst,* 101–3.

33. StAB, C 47, 6–7; *B. u. A.,* II, 41, 96–99; 74, 156–58; 87, 174–75; 132, 270; 3, 20, 102–4; Veh, "Bayreuther Landstände," 14–16; Evans, 52–59.

34. *B. u. A.,* I, 529, 659; 2, 132, 266; 3, 19, 38–41; 20, 93.

35. Dippold, *Konfessionalisirung am Obermain,* 329–33.

36. StAB, C 7^X, 1, fols. 213–215; Veh, "Bayreuther Landstände," 16–17; Herold, *Joachim Ernst,* 107–13; Jegel, "Landständische Verfassung," 31; Wolf and Tausenpfund, "Obrigkeit und jüdische Untertanen," 92–93; Roland-Götz Foerster, *Herrschaftsverständnis und Regierungsstruktur in Brandenburg-Ansbach 1648–1701* (Ansbach: Historischer Verein für Mittelfranken, 1975), 259–60.

37. Veh, "Bayreuther Landstände," 17–23; Jegel, "Landständische Verfassung," 31–32.

38. Kraußold, *Geschichte der evangelische Kirche,* 186–88; Simon, *Bayreuther Pfarrerbuch,* 17; cf. Bodo Nischan, "The Exorcism Controversy and Baptism in the Lutheran Reformation," *SCJ* 18 (1987): 31–50.

39. Veh, "Bayreuther Landstände," 23–26.

40. Veh, "Bayreuther Landstände," 27–33.

41. Veh, "Bayreuther Landstände," 36–42; Pfeiffer, "Fürst und Land," 16–17; Jegel, "Landständische Verfassung," 32–33; Sticht, *Markgraf Christian,* 17–18.

42. StAB, A 160^{II}, 1252.

43. StAB, A 160^{II}, 1263, fols. 18v–20v; 1234, 28–29; Jegel, "Fürst und Adel," 244–46; Pfeiffer, "Fürst und Land," 11–12.

44.   StAB, A 160^{II}, 1263, fols. 19v–24v; 1234, fols. 29–30.

45.   Pfeiffer, "Fürst und Land," 12; Jegel, "Fürst und Adel," 272–73; Sticht, *Markgraf Christian,* 17.

46.   Press, "Adel im Reich," 26–29; 34; MacHardy, "Einfluss von Status," 67–79.

47.   StAB, A 160^{II}, 1254, fols. 29–30; Jegel, "Fürst und Land," 272–73.

48.   StAB, A 160^{II}, 1263, fol. 22; 1234, 31v.

49.   StAB, C 14, 90.

50.   Pfeiffer, "Fürst und Land," 12–13; Press, "Adel im Reich," 6.

51.   Veh, "Bayreuther Landstände," 59–64; Sticht, *Markgraf Christian,* 94–109.

52.   Cf. Press, "Adel im Reich," 40–41; Schorn-Schütte, "Lutherische Konfessionalisierung?" 191–92.

53.   StAB, B 26^{a}, 3^{I}; Bachmann, "Landstände," 148–50, Beilage 38, 276. Ernst ordered the expulsion of the Jews in March 1585, but many still lived on noble estates near Aisch and Höchstadt. AEB, Rep. I, 327, fols. 356–357v; Eckstein, *Geschichte der Juden,* 16, 265–66.

54.   StAB, A 85, Lade 341, 193, 194; Bachmann, "Landstände," 150, Beilage 39–40, 277–80.

55.   Bachmann, "Landstände," 151–53, Beilage 41, 281–83; Press, "Adel im Reich," 40–41.

56.   AEB, Rep. I, A 8, prod. 3–10. Johann Schöner died in penury in 1646. L V, 412–32; Bauer, "Die bamberger Weihbischöfe," 422–42.

57.   *CCB,* IV, fols. 18v–19v; L V, 380–81.

58.   L V, 406–8.

59.   StAB, B 49, 96/I; Kanzler, "Die Landkapitel," II, 34–35; Ruland, "Briefe," IX, 190–92; Schmitt, *Die Synoden,* 35; Bauer, "Die Bamberger Weihbischöfe," 448.

60.   Schmitt, *Die Synoden,* 40–42; Kanzler, "Die Landkapitel," II, 49.

61.   Reinhard Weber, *Würzburg und Bamberg im Dreißigjährigen Krieg* (Würzburg: Echter Verlag, 1979), 456–57.

62.   StAB, B 26^{a}, 135^{I}.

63.   AEB, Rep. I, Pf.A. 569, prod. 7, fols. 11–15; cf. Bauer, "Die Bamberger Weihbischöfe," 447–48; L V, 409.

64.   AEB, Rep. I, Pf.A. 556; Kanzler, "Die Landkapitel," II, 46–48.

65.   StAB, B 26/c, 135/I, 1613 Feb. 15, 1615, Mar. 6.

66.   L V, 433–37; Bauer, "Die Bamberger Weihbischöfe," 448–49; F. J. Riedler, "Das Dominkanerinnenkloster zum Heiligen Grab und Bischof Johann Gottfried von Aschhausen," *BHVB* 60 (1899): 3–107.

67.   L V, 438–45, 470. The deficit had risen to 1.2 million gulden by 1623, largely on account of the cost of quartering troops. Bachmann, "Landstände," 159.

68.   StAB, B 86, 287c; L V, 454; Weigel, *Wahlkapitulationen,* 97–99.

69.   Evans, 53, 62–63.

70.   Friedrich Förner, *Duo Specula Principis Ecclesiastici e Duorum Laudatissimorum Præsulu ac Principum* (Ingolstadt, 1623), 2.

71.   Förner, *Duo Specula,* 7–8. The argument closely follows that found in a letter written by Aschhausen to Maximilian of Bavaria in July 1618; cf. *B. u. A,* N.F. 1.1, 41.

72.   Förner, *Duo Specula,* 9–10.

73.   Förner, *Duo Specula,* 34–36, 41–42; cf. 27–24.

74.   Friedrich Förner, *Palma Triumphalis Miraculorum Ecclesiae Catolicae* (Ingolstadt: Wilhelm Eder, 1620), §2-§§§§7, 447–58; Yates, 137.

75.   Lupold of Bebenburg, *De Zelo Catholicae Religionis,*)(2v-)(3.

76.   Förner, *Duo Specula,* 42; cf. *De Zelo Catholicae Religionis,* 51ff.

77.   StAB, A 25, Lade 30, 64–65; AEB, Rep. I, A 5; L VI, 7–9; Michael Deinlein, "Fürstbischof Johann Georg II Fuchs von Dornheim 1623–1633," *BHVB* 40 (1878): 1–41; Bauer, "Die Bamberger Weihbischöfe," 451.

78.   L VI, 82; Bauer, "Die Bamberger Weihbischöfe," 451–54; Weber, *Würzburg und Bamberg,* 6.

79.   Denzler, "Religiöse Entwicklung," 396–404.

80.   StAB, B 49, 4^I; B 49, 95^I, fasc. 1; AEB, Rep. I, 327, fols. 265f., 328, fols. 133–134; L VI, 80–81.

81.   AEB, Rep. I, Pf. A, 569, prod. 9.

82.   AEB, Rep. I, 569, prod. 9.

83.   StAB, B 49, 95^I, fasc. 1.

84.   Schmitt, "Die Synode," 191; Kanzler, "Die Landkapitel," II, 50; L VI, 86.

85.   StAB, B 26^a, 135^I.

86.   StAB, B 26^c, 104; 136; 137.

87.   StAB, B 26^c, 137.

88.   StAB, B 49, 95^I, fasc. 1; cf. Weber, *Würzburg und Bamberg,* 457–58; Riedenauer, "Adel und Konfession," 20.

89.   StAB, B 49, 81^I; L VI, 88.

90.   L VI, 87–88.

91.   AEB, Rep. I, 335, fols. 75–94; Pf.A., 387; StAB, B 49, 58, 149, 298, 299; C 7/x, 4; L VI, 92–93, 126–27.

92.   StAB, B 41, vol. 98, fols. 14–18.

93.   Valentin Loch, "Fürstbischof Johann Georg II als Präsident der kaiserliche Commission für der fränkischen Kreis zur Durchführung der Restitutionsedicts im Jahr 1629," *BHVB* 39 (1877): 33–108; L VI, 136–38; Bauer, "Die Bamberger Weihbischöfe," 460; Sticht, *Markgraf Christian,* 64–65; Bireley, *Religion and Politics,* 74.

94.   Bauer, "Die Bamberger Weihbischöfe," 465–66; Riedenauer, "Adel und Konfession," 49; Gerhard Pfeiffer, "Studien zur Geschichte der fränkischen Reichsritterschaft," *JFFL* 22 (1962): 77–215; Bachmann, "Landstände," 104–5.

95.   StAB, A 85, 320; Bauer, "Die Bamberger Weihbischöfe," 462–63.

96.   Förner, *Relatio,* 1–14; *Norimbergae in Flora,* 18–28.

97.   Förner, *Relatio,* 44–49; *Norimbergae in Flora,* A2, 37–40, 45–92; Kist, *Matrikel,* 1733.

98.   Förner, *Relatio,* 71–76.

99.   StAB, C 2, 1835; L VI, 139–40.

100.   Kraußold, *Geschichte der evangelische Kirche,* 198–202.

101.   Sticht, *Markgraf Christian,* 65–66; Robert Bireley, *Maximilian von Bayern, Adam Contzen, S.J. und die Gegenreformation in Deutschland 1624–1635* (Göttingen: Vandenhoek and Ruprecht, 1975), 75–89, 95–98; Bireley, *Religion and Politics,* 74–78.

102.   StAB, C 48, 153; Kraußold, *Geschichte der evangelische Kirche,* 203–4; Sticht, *Markgraf Christian,* 66.

103.   StAB, C 48, 153; Sticht, *Markgraf Christian,* 67; Weber, *Würzburg und Bamberg,* 4–5.

104. StAB, B 34, 8, prod. 17; *B. u. A.,* NF, 2.5, 170, 680–85. The discussion of Protestant grievances coincided with requests by the emperor for aid against the Swedes. StAB, B 41, vol. 99, fols. 78–79, 90–92, 128–130.

105. *B. u. A.,* NF, 2.5, 170, 685–90; cf. 177, 757–60.

106. Bireley, *Religion and Politics,* 131; cf. Bireley, *Maximilian von Bayern,* 133–38.

107. Förner, *Relatio,* 76.

108. StAB, A 85, 320; Bireley, *Religion and Politics,* 113–32, 151–52; Bauer, "Die Bamberger Weihbischöfe," 464–68.

109. L VI, 159–61; Bireley, *Religion and Politics,* 167–68; Bireley, *Maximilian von Bayern,* 161–65. Förner died two weeks after his return from Regensburg. Bauer, "Die Weihbischöfe," 468.

110. *B. u. A.,* NF, 2.5, 177, 757–60.

111. StAB, A 45, II, 69.

112. StAB, B 34, 8, prod. 53; Ludewig, 102–27; Michel Hofmann, "Cuius regio?" 345–55.

113. Hofmann, "Cuius regio?" 350–53; MacHardy, *War, Religion and Court Patronage,* 36–46.

114. Hofmann, "Cuius regio?" 350–53.

115. Hofmann, "Cuius regio?" 353–55.

116. A similar argument is made in another document, dated August 30 and addressed to the duke of Württemberg. The author–possibly Winter–claims that the duke is "no territorial prince" but merely a nobleman with a slightly more elevated title. StAB B 41, vol. 101, fols. 256ff.

117. Weber, *Würzburg und Bamberg,* 439–40.

118. StAB, C 48, 174, 182.

119. L VI, 164–65; Weber, *Würzburg und Bamberg,* 464–66.

120. StAB, C 48, 170, 174; L VI, 166–213; Weber, *Würzburg und Bamberg,* 130–32.

Chapter 10

1. The author is currently working on a comprehensive study of the Bamberg witch-hunts. The most recent work on the subject is Britta Gehm, *Die Hexenverfolgung im* Hochstift *Bamberg und das Eingreifen des Reichshofrates zu ihrer Beendung* (Hildesheim: Olms, 2000). This book largely supercedes the older treatments of the witch-hunts in Bamberg. Other recent studies are Andrea Renczes, *Wie löscht man eine Familie aus? Eine Analyse Bamberger Hezenprozesse* (Pfaffenweiler: Centaurus, 1990); Andrea Stickler, *Eine Stadt im Hexenfieber. Aus dem Tagebuch des Zeiler Bürgermeisters Johann Langhans (1611–1628)* (Pfaffenweiler: Centaurus, 1994). Older works frequently cited include Pius Wittmann, "Die Bamberger Hexen-Justiz (1595–1631)," *Archiv für das katholische Kirchenrecht* 50 (1883): 177–223; Georg von Lamberg, *Criminal-Verfahren vorzüglich bey Hexenprozessen im ehemaligen Bißthum Bamberg während der Jahren 1624 bis 1630* (Nuremberg: Kiegel and Wiessner, 1835); cf. Friedrich Merzbacher, *Die Hexenprozesse in Franken* (Munich: Beck, 1970); L VI, 33–71.

2. Cf. Robin Briggs, "'Many Reasons Why': Witchcraft and the Problem of Multiple Explanation," in *Witchcraft in Early Modern Europe,* ed. Jonathan Barry, Marianne Hester, and Gareth Roberts, 62–63 (Cambridge: Cambridge University Press, 1996).

3. Wolfgang Behringer, *Hexenverfolgung in Bayern* (Munich: Oldenbourg, 1997), 400–430.

4. Behringer, *Hexenverfolgung,* 52–55, 96–121; Schremmer, *Wirtschaft Bayerns,* 184–206.

5. Behringer, *Hexenverfolgung,* 401.

6. Behringer, *Hexenverfolgung,* 413.

7. Behringer, *Hexenverfolgung,* 423–26.

8. Behringer, *Hexenverfolgung,* 419; cf. Larner, *Witchcraft and Religion: The Politics of Popular Belief* (Oxford: Blackwell, 1984).

9. Behringer, *Hexenverfolgung,* 429.

10. Larner, *Witchcraft and Religion,* 139; Brian P. Levack, "State-building and Witch-hunting in Early Modern Europe," in Barry, *Witchcraft,* 96–115.

11. Lyndal Roper, *Witch-Craze: Terror and Fantasy in Baroque Germany* (New Haven, CT: Yale University Press, 2004). The argument is in many ways an elaboration of the suggestion first put forward by Eric Midelfort that the persecution of witches was connected to changes in the structures of family and marriage. For Roper, the issue is not marriage so much as fertility. Midelfort, *Witch-hunting in Southwestern Germany 1562–1684* (Stanford: Stanford University Press, 1972); cf. Roper, *Witch-Craze,* 303, note 5.

12. Roper, *Witch-Craze,* 158–59.

13. Roper, *Witch-Craze,* 128–31, 247–56.

14. See above, chapter 7.

15. Roper (*Witch-Craze,* 131) notes that questions concerning the accused's reproductive history were standard in Würzburg, but this was not the case in Bamberg.

16. William Bradford Smith, "Food and Deception in the Discourse on Heresy and Witchcraft in Bamberg," in *At the Table: Metaphorical and Material Cultures of Food in Medieval and Early Modern Europe,* ed. Juliann Vitullo and Timothy J. Tomasik, 107–22 (Brugge: Brepols, 2007).

17. Evans, *Habsburg Empire,* 394–99; Rebel, *Peasant Classes,* 271–75; Smith, "Friedrich Förner," 124–25.

18. Behringer, *Hexenverfolgung,* 162, note 154.

19. StAB, C 2, 3235; Lang, III, 338; Behringer, *Hexenverfolgung,* 162; the episode is described in great detail by Dixon, *Reformation and Rural Society,* 193–202.

20. StAB, C 2, 3235, fols. 5–7, 46.

21. StAB, C 2, 3235, fols. 54–55.

22. StAB, C 2, 3235, 9 June, 1569.

23. StAB, C 2, 3236; Dixon, *Reformation and Rural Society,* 183–85.

24. StAB, C 2, 3238.

25. StAB, C 2, 3240; Dixon, *Reformation and Rural Society,* 182–83.

26. Lang, *Fürstentum Baireuth,* III, 338–39.

27. The visitation of 1611 noted the presence of "*incantationitrices*" in Kupferberg, but none were identified by name. AEB, Rep. I, Pf.A. 569, prod. 1, fol. 65v; StAB, B 49, 99.

28.	See above, 110–12.

29.	Labouvie, *Zauberei und Hexenwerk,* 27–31; Herbert Pohl, *Hexenglaube und Hexenverfolgung im Kurfürstentum Mainz* (Stuttgart: Steiner, 1988), 301; Franz Irsigler, "Zauberei und Hexenprozeße im Köln," in *Hexenglaube und Hexenprozeße im Raum Rhein-Mosel-Saar,* ed. Gunther Franz and Franz Irsigler, 173 (Trier, 1995).

30.	StAB, B 26ᶜ, 44, fasc. 1; Behringer, *Hexenverfolgung,* 163–64, 196; Merzbacher, *Hexenprozesse,* 57–58.

31.	Lang, *Fürstentum Baireuth,* III, 340–41; Behringer, *Hexenverfolgung,* 215.

32.	Behringer, *Hexenverfolgung,* 163–66, 226–28; cf. Rummel, *Bauern, Herren, und Hexen,* 157–82; Gerd Schwerhoff, "Hexerei, Geschlecht und Regionalgeschichte. Überlegungen zur Erklärung des scheinbar Selbstverständlichen," in Wilbertz, *Hexenverfolgung und Regionalgeschichte,* 351.

33.	Behringer, *Hexenverfolgung,* 162–63. Dixon (*Religion and Rural Society,* 193) states that in 1591, "twenty-two witches were executed in Bayreuth," but this is a misreading of an admittedly confusing remark by Merzbacher. Merzbacher writes "im gleichen Jahr 1591 sind in Bayreuth*ischen* zwei und zwanzig Hexen verbrannt" (*Hexenprozesse,* 59; emphasis added). The trials that Merzbacher is referring to did not occur in the city of Bayreuth, but rather in the county of Oettingen-Wallerstein, a Catholic enclave in the southernmost part of the Niederland. The number of victims ultimately derives from Lang (*Fürstentum Baireuth,* III, 341). There was a series of trials in Wallerstein between 1587 and 1594. The actual number of victims is uncertain; Behringer gives a tentative figure of thirty-eight. Behringer, *Hexenverfolgung,* 140, 436, 439–40.

34.	StBB, RB. Msc. 148, 2.

35.	StBB, RB. Msc. 148, 1–5; L VI, 29; Gehm, *Hexenverfolgung,* 42; Wittmann, "Bamberger Hexen-Justiz," 178–79; Smith, "Food and Deception."

36.	StAB, B 68, 876, fols. 1019–1020, 1032.

37.	StBB, RB. Msc. 148, 7–11; Gehm, *Hexenverfolgung,* 46; Wittmann, "Bamberger Hexen-Justiz," 178.

38.	*CCB,* V, fols. 186–191v; StAB, B 26ᶜ, 129.

39.	*CCB,* VI, fols. 33v–34v; StAB, B 26ᶜ, 44, fasc. 2; L VI, 29–30; Wittmann, "Bamberger Hexen-Justiz," 180.

40.	StAB, B 49, 285, fols. 3f.

41.	AEB, Rep. I/III, Pf.A., 569, prod. 4.

42.	AEB, Rep. I/III, Pf.A., 569, prod. 4., fols. 36v–37.

43.	AEB, Rep. I/III, Pf.A., 569, prod. 8, fol. 20; Kramer, *Bamberg,* 174, 187.

44.	AEB, Rep. I/III, Pf.A., 569, prod. 4, fols. 18v, 36v.

45.	AEB, Rep. I/III, Pf.A., 569, prod. 4, fols. 31f.

46.	AEB, Rep. I/III, Pf.A., 569, prod. 4, fol. 46v.

47.	StBB, RB. Msc. 148, 12–13; L VI, 33; Gehm, *Hexenverfolgung,* 57–58; Wittmann, "Bamberger Hexen-Justiz," 180.

48.	StBB, RB. Msc. 13–14; Gehm, *Hexenverfolgung,* 59.

49.	StBB, RB. Msc.16, 880, 88; Gehm, *Hexenverfolgung,* 59–61.

50.	StBB, RB. Msc. 148, 20–21, 854, 883; Gehm, *Hexenverfolgung,* 61–62.

51.	StBB, RB. Msc. 148, 21, 23–24; L VI, 33–34; Wittmann, "Bamberger Hexen-Justiz," 180.

52.	StBB, RB. Msc. 148, 27, 31.

53.	StBB, RB. Msc. 148, 856, 857; Gehm, *Hexenverfolgung,* 63.

54. StBB, RB. Msc. 148, 49–53, 56; 855, 864; Gehm, *Hexenverfolgung*, 62–64.

55. StBB, RB. Msc. 148, 37–39.

56. StBB, RB. Msc. 148, 40, 41, 859, 860.

57. StBB, RB. Msc. 148, 47, 859, 861.

58. StBB, RB. Msc. 148, 34, 34a, 35, 862; Gehm, *Hexenverfolgung*, 64.

59. AEB, Rep. I, Pf.A. 569, prod. 4, fols. 50–54.

60. StBB, RB. Msc. 148, 39.

61. Given that Schnabrich was also the name of the most notorious of the Pressecker preachers, one cannot help but wonder whether there was any connection between the two. The sources are silent on this point.

62. Wittmann, "Bamberger Hexen-Justiz," (54) and Looshorn (VI, 34) give one trial for the year 1614. The trial in question actually took place in 1674. StBB, RB. Msc. 148, 724–26; Gehm, *Hexenverfolgung*, 69.

63. Behringer, *Hexenverfolgung*, 236–37.

64. Gehm, *Hexenverfolgung*, 72, 89; Stickler, *Stadt im Hexenfieber*, 48.

65. StBB, RB. Msc. 148, 61. Dorothea's fate is unknown, although Gehm, *Hexenverfolgung*, 73, suggests that she either died in prison or was eventually executed.

66. StBB, RB. Msc. 148, 60.

67. StBB, RB. Msc. 148, 865; L VI, 35–36; Gehm, *Hexenverfolgung*, 74; Wittmann, "Bamberger Hexen-Justiz," 181–83.

68. StBB, RB. Msc. 148, 866.

69. StBB, RB. Msc. 148, 868, 870–72.

70. StBB, RB. Msc. 148, 873.

71. StBB, RB. Msc. 148, 865, 866.

72. Gehm, *Hexenverfolgung*, 69–71.

73. Gehm, *Hexenverfolgung*, 70, Wittmann, "Bamberger Hexen-Justiz," 182.

74. *New, Vnerhörte, erschröcklische, warhafftige Wundergeschicht* (Ingolstadt, 1602), 10–17; Bauer, "Die bamberger Weihbischöfe," 455–56.

75. Friedrich Förner, *Panoplia Armaturae Dei, Adversus Omnem Superstitionum, Divinitionum, Excantationum, Daemonolatriam, et Universas Magorum, Veneficorum, & Sagarum, & ipsiusmet Sathanae insidias praestigias & inventiones* (Ingolstadt, 1626); Bauer, "Die bamberger Weihbischöfe," 509–10; Gehm, *Hexenverfolgung*, 115–18.

76. Förner, *Panoplia,*)(2v,)(4v, 45–47, 128–29; AEB, Rep. I, A2, prod. 2; A 3, prod. 1, fol. 4, 9, 17f., 19, 23v; Smith, "Friedrich Förner," 117–19.

77. Förner, *Panoplia,*)(2-)()(,

78. Förner, *Panoplia,*)(3r; *Duo Specula*, 10, 34.

79. StBB, RB. Msc. 148, 886.

80. Gehm, *Hexenverfolgung*, 95–97.

81. StBB, RB. Msc. 148, 1119; Gehm, *Hexenverfolgung*, 97.

82. Neustetter-Stürmer's opposition may have derived from the fact that his mother, Magdelena von Rechenberg, had been accused of witchcraft. Förner, *Vom Ablaß und Jubeljar*, B2.

83. L V, 438–39, 459–61; Gehm, *Hexenverfolgung*, 100–103.

84. StBB, RB. Msc. 148, 673–75; CUL, 4620, Box 5, fol. 1; Gehm, *Hexenverfolgung*, 119.

85. Gehm, *Hexenverfolgung*, 107–14.

86. Gehm, *Hexenverfolgung*, 69–72, 109–12.

87.   Stickler, *Stadt im Hexenfieber,* 61.

88.   L VI, 50–56; the case is described in detail by Renczes, *Wie löscht man eine Familie aus?* See note 1 above.

89.   CUL, 4621++ Bd. Mss. 32, 12.

90.   StBB, RB. Msc. 148, 800, 801, 804–7, 811–12; Stickler, *Stadt im Hexenfieber,* 62–63. It is not entirely clear how all of the accused were related.

91.   Gehm, *Hexenverfolgung,* 190–92.

92.   Günther Dippold, "Aspekte der Hexen-Verfolgung im Hochstifts Bamberg," *BHVB* 135 (1999): 291–305; Renczes, *Wie löscht man eine Familie aus?* 107–12. The most famous of these "good people" was Mayor Junius, whose letter to his daughter has been widely reprinted. Original letter = StBB, RB. Msc. 148, 300.

93.   Stickler, *Stadt im Hexenfieber,* 48–58, 62–65; cf. Midelfort, *Witch-Hunting,* 187–88.

94.   Förner, *Panpolia,* 14, 102–3,)(3f.; Stuart Clark, *Thinking with Demons. The Idea of Witchcraft in Early Modern Europe* (Oxford, 1997), 572–81.

95.   StBB, RB. Msc. 148, 672, 905; cf. Evans, *Habsburg Monarchy,* 42.

96.   CUL, 4621++ Bd. Mss. 32, 7.

97.   Förner, *Panoplia,* 4.

98.   Förner, *Panoplia,* 5–6, 97–99, 109–11; *Notwehr und Ehrenrettung,* 15, 31–32; *Vom Ablaß und Jubeljar,* 8–9, 160–70; cf. Clark, *Thinking with Demons,* 360–61.

99.   Förner, *Duo Specula,* 7–10, 34–36.

100.   Förner, *Panoplia,* 108–9; Smith, "Friedrich Förner," 126–28.

101.   StAB, B 26c, 44; L VI, 40, 44; Wittmann, "Bamberger Hexen-Justiz," 190–91.

102.   StAB, B 68, 889, fols. 253, 262, 295–296v; 895, fols. 73v, 79, 87v, 101, 349.

103.   CUL, 4621, ++ Bd. Mss. 32, 4; StAB, B 73, 3, prod. 6; Wittmann, "Bamberger Hexen-Justiz," 191.

104.   StAB, B 73, 3, prod. 7–8.

105.   L VI, 73.

106.   StBB, RB. Msc. 148, 489; L VI, 68–69.

107.   StBB, RB. Msc. 148, 443; CUL, 4621, ++ Bd. Mss. 32, 2.

108.   StBB, RB. Msc. 148, 580; Gehm, *Hexenverfolgung,* 214–28.

109.   CUL, 4621, ++ Bd. Mss. 32, 9; L VI, 73; Wittmann, "Bamberger Hexen-Justiz," 194.

110.   Wittmann, "Bamberger Hexen-Justiz," 194–95.

111.   StBB, RB. Msc. 148, 588; CUL, 4621, ++ Bd. Mss. 32, 25, fol. 1; 30; Wittmann, "Bamberger Hexen-Justiz," 196–97.

112.   StBB, RB. Msc. 148, 583; CUL, 4621, ++ Bd. Mss. 32, 29; L VI, 73–74; Wittmann, "Bamberger Hexen-Justiz," 198–200.

113.   StBB, RB. Msc. 148, 599, 600; CUL, 4621, ++ Bd. Mss. 32, 28; Wittmann, "Bamberger Hexen-Justiz," 199–203; Behringer, *Hexenverfolgung,* 316–17.

114.   Wittmann, "Bamberger Hexen-Justiz," 203–5; Behringer, *Hexenverfolgung,* 317.

115.   StBB, RB. Msc. 148, 601; CUL, 4621, ++ Bd. Mss. 32, 26; Wittmann, "Bamberger Hexen-Justiz," 205–6.

116.   CUL, 4621, ++ Bd. Mss. 32, 25, fols. 1–2v; L VI, 74–75; Wittmann, "Bamberger Hexen-Justiz," 206–8; Lamberg, *Criminal-Verfahren,* 20.

117.   CUL, 4621, ++ Bd. Mss. 32, 25, fols. 1v–3; cf. *CCC,* § 66; Merzbacher, *Hexenprozesse,* 127–28.

118.   CUL, 4621, ++ Bd. Mss. 32, 25, fols. 3f.

119. CUL, 4621, ++ Bd. Mss. 32, 24; Wittmann, "Bamberger Hexen-Justiz," 209–10, Behringer, *Hexenverfolgung,* 317–18.

120. CUL, 4621, ++ Bd. Mss. 32, 21; Wittmann, "Bamberger Hexen-Justiz," 210.

121. Behringer, *Hexenverfolgung,* 318.

122. Gehm, *Hexenverfolgung,* 228–37.

123. CUL, 4621, ++ Bd. Mss. 32, 22; Wittmann, "Bamberger Hexen-Justiz," 210; Behringer, *Hexenverfolgung,* 319. Franz von Hatzfeld was no supporter of witch-hunts. He was appointed bishop of Bamberg after Johann Georg's death in 1633 and did not resume the trials. Weber, *Würzburg und Bamberg,* 481–83.

124. StBB, RB. Msc. 148, 148–74; CUL, 4621, ++ Bd. Mss. 32, 23.

125. StBB, RB. Msc. 148, 625; Wittmann, "Bamberger Hexen-Justiz," 211–12; Lamberg, *Criminal-Verfahren,* 18; Behringer, *Hexenverfolgung,* 319; Merzbacher, *Hexenprozesse,* 132–33.

126. StBB, RB. Msc. 148, 630.

127. StBB, RB. Msc. 148, 908; Wittmann, "Bamberger Hexen-Justiz," 214.

128. Wittmann, "Bamberger Hexen-Justiz," 214–16.

129. CUL, 4621, ++ Bd. Mss. 32, 20.

130. On the forms of torture, see Gehm, *Hexenverfolgung,* 254–57.

131. CUL, 4621, ++ Bd. Mss. 32, 41, fols. 1–2v; Wittmann, "Bamberger Hexen-Justiz," 218.

132. CUL, 4621, ++ Bd. Mss. 32, 30; 41, fols. 3–4.

133. CUL, 4621, ++ Bd. Mss. 32, 41, fol. 1v; cf. Clark, *Thinking with Demons,* 183; Evans, *Habsburg Monarchy,* 384.

134. StBB, RB. Msc. 148, 695, 699; CUL, 4621, ++ Bd. Mss. 32, 41, fols. 4–5; Wittmann, "Bamberger Hexen-Justiz," 215–16.

135. CUL, 4621, ++ Bd. Mss. 32, 40; Wittmann, "Bamberger Hexen-Justiz," 218–19.

136. CUL, 4621, ++ Bd. Mss. 32, 30; Wittmann, "Bamberger Hexen-Justiz," 220.

137. Gehm, *Hexenverfolgung,* 260–67.

138. Behringer, *Hexenverfolgung,* 234.

139. The sociologist Hans Sebald has drawn an interesting parallel between the witch trials of the sixteenth and seventeenth centuries and the spate of bizarre accusations of child abuse that surfaced in the United States in the mid-1980s. In both cases, a set of professional "advocates"—in the modern sense, child welfare advocates and social service professionals—were able to conduct inquisitions, sometimes in direct violation of the rule of law. Despite the dubious methods used to secure testimony and the frankly absurd character of some of the accusations, convictions were returned by judges unwilling, for one reason or another, to question the admissibility of the evidence brought forward by the professionals. Moreover, in both the witch trials and the child-abuse cases Sebald mentions, the accusation itself was often taken as proof of guilt. The media circus that surrounded the child abuse trials, most of which involved lurid tales of devil worship, spurred copycat cases in other places, including Germany. In all of these aspects, Sebald sees clear structural parallels between the character of the witch-hunts and the child-abuse cases. Although his examination of the trials (in particular his treatment of religion) has serious problems, the basic argument is compelling and worthy of serious consideration. Sebald, *Witch Children: From Salem Witch-Hunts to Modern Courtrooms* (Amherst, MA: Prometheus Books, 1995).

140. Cf. Rebel, *Peasant Classes,* 280.

141. AEB, Rep. I, 329, fols. 66–69, 105v–135v; Förner, *New, Vnerhörte, erschröck-lische, warhafftige Wundergeschicht.*

142. Bireley, *Religion* and *Politics,* 74, 152–53.

143. See above, note 6.

144. The *Centbücher* for the years 1616–29 (StAB, B 68, 889–96) show about five to six cases a year, most of which appear to have ended in acquittals. These cases have not, to my knowledge, been dealt with in any systematic fashion.

145. On the notion of options, see Evans, *Habsburg Monarchy,* 410–18.

146. Smith, "Friedrich Förner," 127–28.

Conclusion

1. Eberhard, *Konfessionsbildung und Stände,* 30–36.

2. Trexler, "Florentine Religious Experience," 10.

3. Reinhard, "Katholische Konfessionalisierung."

4. Marc Raeff, *The Well-Ordered Police State. Social and Institutional Change through Law in the Germanies and Russia, 1600–1800* (New Haven,CT: Yale University Press, 1983), 167–69.

5. Vann, *The Making of a State,* 19.

6. Evans, *Habsburg Monarchy,* 447.

7. Gershom Scholem, "Toward an Understanding of the Messianic Idea in Judaism," in Scholem, *The Messianic Idea in Judaism and other Essays on Jewish Spirituality* (New York: Schocken, 1971), 10.

8. This point was central to Troeltsch's criticism of the social and political character of Lutheranism. In his critique of the "passivity of Lutheranism," Troeltsch described the Lutheran "habit of falling back upon whatever power happen[ed] to be dominant at that time . . . The yielding spirit of its wholly interior spirituality adapted itself to the dominant authority of the day." Ernst Troeltsch, *The Social Teachings of the Christian Churches,* trans. Olive Wyon (Chicago: University of Chicago Press, 1981), II, 574. In the *Oberland,* Lutheranism did adapt, but to the power of the estates, not the prince. As shown in the visitation of 1528, the debates over the Augsburg Confession, and the diets of 1548 and 1608, the central position of the Lutheran clergy was marked by a resistance to princely authority in spiritual matters and the desire to place distinct limits on the power of the prince. Their resistance, moreover, did not involve a return to a "medieval" conception of society, as Troeltsch would have it, but rather, as Karl Holl pointed out in his response to Troeltsch, rested on the confessional state as "something superior to the individual will, an institution which served to direct all the efforts of the people" while setting "a rigid limit to the absolute power of the state." Holl, *The Cultural Significance of the Reformation,* trans. Karl and Barbara Hertz and John H. Lichtblau (New York: Meridian, 1959), 53; Schorn-Schütte, "Ernst Troeltschs 'Soziallehren,'" 139–51.

9. H. C. Erik Midelfort, "Witchcraft and Religion in Sixteenth Century Germany: The Formation and Consequences of an Orthodoxy," *ARG* 62 (1971): 266–78.

BIBLIOGRAPHY

Manuscript Collections

Archiv des Erzbistums Bamberg
    Repertorium I
        Urkunden
        Pfarreiakten
        Bischofsakten
        Weihbischofsakten
Cornell University Library, Division of Rare Books and Manuscripts
    Witchcraft Collection
Staatsarchiv Bamberg
    A: Urkunden

25	Bischofswahlen
45	Theologica bzw. ecclesiastica
46	Weihbischofsurkunden
50	Testamenta
85	Einungen, Kreisrezesse, Landtagsabschiede, Bündnisse und Staatsverträge
90	Urkunden über Orten der Hochstifts Bamberg
95	Urkunden über Bamberg Pfarreien und Benefizien
105	Bauernkrieg
149	Unterrichts und Wohltätigkeitsanstalten
153	Spitäler
160	Brandenburger Urkunden
165	Urkunden über Orten der Markgrafschaft Bayreuth
170	Bayreuther Pfarrei Urkunden
221/XIII	Spitäler, Gotteshäuser
245	Handschriften Sammlung

    B: Bamberger Akten

23	Bamberger Korrespondenz
26c	Verordnungen
34	Bamberger Reichskorrespondenz
41	Ältere Kreisakten
46a	Differenzen mit Brandenburg, Oberpfalz und Sachsen
49	Pfarreiakten
67/XII	Hochstift Bamberg Regierungsakten betr. Kloster Langheim
68	Malefizamt
73	Weihbischofsakten
84	Wahl- und Sterbeakten

85	Rezeßbücher, Literalien und Akten des Domkapitels
106	Kloster Langheim
113	Kloster Neunkirchen am Brand

C: Brandenburger Akten

2	Hauptmann und Räthe a. d. Gebirg
3	Hofrat, Ansbach-Bayreuth (vor 1603)
7/I	Verordnungen und Gemeinbücher
7/V	Krieg- und Domänenkammer Bayreuth, Regierung, Nachbarliche Verhältnisse und Differenzen
7/X	Kirchen- und Schulakten
14	Bayreuther Konsistorium
40	Kreistagakten
47	Unionsakten
48	Bayreuther 30jährige Kriegsakten
49	Bayreuther Pfarreiakten und Literalien

H: Fränkischen Kriesakten

| 2 | Akten der fränkischen Kreises (1508–1808) |

Staatsbibliothek Bamberg

Bibl. Msc.	Biblische Handschriften
Theol. Msc.	Theologische Handschriften
Lit. Msc.	Liturgische Handschriften
RB. Msc.	Bamberger Sammlung

Printed Sources

Abschied vñ maynung, wie sich der Durchleüchtig, Hochgeborn Fürst vnd Herr, herr Casimir, Marggraue zů Brandenburg & c., . . . zů sampt irer F. G. Landtschafft, auff nächst gehaltem Landßtag zů Onoltzbach, biß auff eyn zůkünfftig Concilium National versamlüg, oder seiner F. G. weyttern beschayd, des abschiedts halben jüngst gehaltens Reychßtag zů Speyer, in iren F. G. Land vñ Fürstenthumb zůhalten vereynigt haben. Ansbach, 1526.*

Acta Reformationis Catholicae Ecclesiam Germaniae Concernentia Saeculi XVI. Edited by Georg Pfeilschifter. Vol. I. Regensburg: F. Pustet, 1959.

Arnold, Klaus. "Johannes Trithemius und Bamberg. '*Oratio ad clerum Bambergensem*'" *BHVB* 107 (1971): 161–89.

Außschreiben, Wie vnd aus was Vrsachen, Inn des Durchleuchtigen Hochgebornen Fürsten vnd Herrn Herr Christiani, Marggraffen zu Brandenburg . . . Landen vnd Fürstenthum, ein Christliches Evangelische Jubelfest zu feiern sey. 1617.

Die Bamberger Halsgerichtsordung. Edited by Josef Kohler and Willy Scheel. Aalen: Scientia Verlag, 1968.

Blebelius, Thomas. *Oratio continens praecipua capita laudationis VRBIS CURIANAE Variscorum.* Leipzig, 1599. Reprinted in *Chronik der Stadt Hof,* vol. VI, 16–66. Hof: Selbstverlag der Stadt Hof, 1966.

Briefe und Akten zur Geschichte des Dreißigjährigen Krieges in den Zeiten des vorwaltenden Einflusses der Wittelsbacher. Munich: Oldenbourg, 1870–1978.

1: Die Gründung der Union 1598–1608, ed. M. Ritter (1870)

2: Die Union und Heinrich IV. 1607–1609, ed. M. Ritter (1874)

3: Der Jülicher Erbfolgkrieg, ed. M. Ritter (1877)

4–5: Die Politik Bayerns 1591–1607, ed. F. Stieve (1878)

6: Vom Reichstag 1608 biz zum Gründung der Liga, ed. F. Stieve (1895)

12: Die Reichspolitik Maximilian von Bayern 1613–1618 ed. Hugo Alterman (1978)

Neue Folge: Die Politik Maximilian von Bayern und seiner Verbündeten 1618–1651

1.1: Januar 1618–Dezember 1620, ed. Karl Mayr-Deisinger und Georg Franz (1966)

1.2: Januar 1621–Dezember 1622, ed. Arno Duch (1978)

2.4: 1628–Juni 1629, ed. Walter Goetz (1948)

2.5: Juli 1629–Dezember 1630, ed. Dieter Albrecht (1964)

Bundschuh, Johann Caspar. *Geographisches Statistisch-topographisches Lexicon von Franken*. 6 vols. Ulm: Bundschuh, 1799–1804.

Burchardi, Ulrich. *Ain schöner lustiger Dialogus, von dem rechten waren Glauben, in wolchem das ewig Gottes klärlich erkandt vnd gehandelt wirt on alle ergernuss, yetlichen Cristglaubigen nützlich zů leesen.* Augsburg: Philipp Ulhart, 1525.

Chroust, Anton, ed. *Chroniken der Stadt Bamberg*. Vols. I–II. Leipzig: Quelle and Meyer, 1907, 1910.

Der Curtisan vnd pfrundenfresser. Bamberg: Georg Erlinger, 1522.

Del Rio, Martin. *Investigations into Magic.* Translated by P. G. Maxwell-Stuart. Manchester: University of Manchester Press, 2000.

Der Durchleüchtigen Hochgebornen fürsten vnd herren Herren Casimirn, vnd herren Georgen, . . . anzeygen, wie die gewesen empörung vnd auffrůrn, nit den wenigsten teyl, auß vngeschickten predigen entstanden sindt. Vnnd das herwiderumb durch frum, gelert, geschickt, Christlich Prediger, vil auffrůr fürkummen weren mög. Strassburg: Matthias Schürer, 1525.

Ettlich artickel So der Cristlich vnd wolgeporn Fürst Casimir[us, zů brandenburg, seinen Prelatten, auch ander clöstern, vnd auch ettlich Pfarrer, vñ prediger ander, dar zů verordnet, auff ettlich überschückt artickel, den haylige[n] cristlichen glabñ betreffent, so yetz in jrru[n]g gezogen werden, zwen ratdschleg über Anttwurt seind r. c. Augsburg: Melchior Ramminger, 1524.

Eyn Bepstlich Breue dem radt czu Bamberg gesand widder den Luther. Wittenberg: Johann Rhau, 1523.

Falkenstein, Johann Heinrich von, ed. *Antiquitatem Nordgaviensium. Tom. IV, Codex Dipolomaticus od. Probationun.* Leipzig: Enderes, 1788.

Feucht, Jacob. *Bescheidne und wolgegruendte Rettung des christlichen unnd kurtzen Berichts . . . Wider die vermeinte Antwort Lucae Osiandri.* Munich: Adam Berg, 1573.

——. *Fünf Kurze Predigen, Von Zwentzig vermeynten Ursachen: Warumb etliche leut, dieser zeit nit wöllen Catholisch, oder (wie sie sprechen) Bäpstische seyn.* Cologne: Quentel, 1607.

Förner, Friedrich. *Beneficia Miraculosa tam vetera quam Recentia Virginis Deiparæ Weyerensis.* Cologne: Johann Kinch, 1620.

——. *Duo Specula Principis Ecclesiastici e Duorum Laudatissimorum Præsul ac Principum.* Ingolstadt, 1623.

——. *Norimberga in Flore Avitae Romano-Catholicae Religionis.* 1629.

——. *Notwehr vnd Ehrnrettung, Der Catholischen Religions, vnd etlich ihrer fürnembsten Glaubens Articuln, als vom Ablaß und Iubilaeo.* Ingolstadt: Andrea Angermeyr, 1600.

——. *Palma Triumphalis Miraculorum Ecclesiae Catolicae.* Ingolstadt: Wilhelm Eder, 1620.

——. *Panoplia Armaturae Dei, Adversus Omnem Superisitionum, Divinationum, Excantationum, Dæmonolatriam, et Universas Magorum Veneficorum, & Sagarum.* Ingolstadt: Gregory Haenlein, 1626.

——. *Relatio Historico-Paranetica de Sacrosanctis, Sacri Romani Imperii, Reliquiis, Et Ornamentis.* 1629.

——. *Vom Ablaß und Jubeljar, Orthodoxisches vnd Summarischer Bericht.* Ingoldstadt: Andrea Angermeyr, 1600.

Förner, Friedrich, et. al. *New, Vnerhörte, erschröcklische, warhafftige Wundergeschicht . . .* Ingolstadt, 1602.

Franz, Günther. *Quellen zur Geschichte des Bauernkriegs.* Munich: Oldenbourg, 1963.

Fronhofer, Georg. *Ain kurzer Psalter auß allen Psalmen Dauids, nach ordnung und zal den hundert und fünfftzig Psalmen, durch der H. Augustinum sinen mů ter Monica zů samen gezogen et. c.* 1574.

Fuchs von Wallburg, Jakob. *Ein Missiue an Bischoff Vonn Wirtzburg Vonn herr Jakob Fuchs dem Eltern Thumherrenn außgangen. Was er helt von vereelichten geystlichen personen.* Bamberg: Georg Erlinger, 1523.

Geldner, Ferdinand, ed. *Das älteste Urbar des Cistercienserklosters Langheim (um 1390).* Würzburg: Schöningh, 1952.

Gess, Felician. *Akten und Briefe zur Kirchenpolitik Herzog Georgs von Sachen.* 2 vols. Cologne: Böhlau, 1985.

Gümbel, Albert. "Berichte Dr. Erasmus Topplers, Probsts von St. Sebald zu Nürnberg, von kaiserliche Hofe 1507–1512." *AZ* 16 (1909): 257–95; 17 (1910): 125–229.

Guttenberg, Erich Freiherr von, and Alfred Wendhorst. *Das Bistum Bamberg,* zweiter Teil. *Germania Sacra,* zweiter Abteilung: Die Bistümer der Kirchenprivinz Mainz, vol. 1. Berlin: De Gruyter, 1966.

Guttenberg, Erich Freiherr von. *Urbare und Wirtschaftsordnungen des Domstifts zu Bamberg.* I Teil. Würzburg: Schöningh, 1969.

Gussmann, Wilhelm. *Quellen und Forschungen zur Geschichte des Augsburgischen Glaubensbekenntnisses.* Leipzig: B. G. Teubner, 1911.

Höfler, Constantin, ed. *Friedrich von Hohenlohe, Rechtsbuch (1348).* Bamberg: Buchner, 1852.

Holle, Johann Wilhelm, ed. "Videmus der Urkunde des Markgrafen Friedrich des Älteren zu Brandenburg." *AO* 3 (1845): 101–4.

Jäck, Joachim. *Bambergische Jahrbücher vom Jahre 741 bis 1829.* Bamberg: Selbstverlag des Autors, 1829.

——. *Pantheon der Literaten und Kunstler Bambergs.* Bamberg/Erlangen: Fränkische Merkur, 1812.

Kirchenordnung, wie es inn des durchleuchtigen hochgeboren Fursten vnnd Herrn, Herrn Albrechts des Jungen Margrauen zu Brandenburgs . . . mit der lehr vnd Ceremonien bis auff vernere Christliche vergleichung gehalten werden sol. Leipzig: Wolf Günther, 1552.

Kolde, Theodore. "Der Briefwechsel Luthers und Melanchtons mit dem Markgrafen Georg und Friedrich von Brandenburg." *ZRG* 13 (1892): 318–37.

Lang, Karl Heinrich. *Neuere Geschichte des Fürstenthums Baireuth.* 3 vols. Göttingen: J. C. D. Schneider, 1798–1811.

Looshorn, Johannes. *Geschichte des Bistums Bamberg.* 6 vols. Munich and Bamberg: Verlag der Handelsdrückerei, 1889–1906.

Ludewig, Johann Peter. *Scriptores rerum Episcopatus Bambergensis.* Frankfurt/Leipzig, 1718.

Lupold of Bebenburg. *De Zelo Catholicae Religionis, Veterum Germaniae Principum Romanorum Regum, Imperatorum.* Edited by Friedrich Förner. Ingolstadt: Gregory Heinlin, 1624.

——. *Tractatus de iuribus regni et imperii Romani.* In Matthias Flacius Illyricus, *De translatione Imperii Romani ad Germanos,* vol. II. Basel: Petrum Pernam, 1566.

Minutoli, Julius von, ed. *Das kaiserliche Buch des Markgraften Albrecht Achilles. Kurfürstliche Periode 1470–1486.* Osnabrück: Zeller, 1984.

Nöth, Stefan. "'Item darnach sol man fragen . . . ' Weistümer in Urbaren der Bamberger Domprobstei aus dem 15. Jahrhundert." *JFFL* 44 (1984): 49–64.

Nuntiaturberichte aus Deutschland

I: Abteilung (1533–1559)

Vol. 1: Nunitaturen des Vergerio 1533–1536. Edited by Walter Friedensburg. Frankfurt: Minerva, 1968.

Vol. 5: Nutiaturen Morones und Poggios, Legation Farneses und Cervinus 1539–1540. Edited by Ludwig Cardauns. Frankfurt: Minerva, 1968.

Vol. 9: Nuntiatur des Verallo 1546–1547. Edited by Walter Friedensburg. Gotha: Minerva, 1968.

II: Abteilung (1560–1572)

Vol. 1: Die Nuntien Hosius und Delphino 1560–1561. Edited by S. Steinherz. Vienna, 1897.

Parigger, Harald, ed. *Das Bamberger Stadtrecht.* Würzburg: Schöningh, 1983.

Pfeiffer, Gerhard, ed. *Quellen zur Geschichte der fränkisch-bayerischen Landfriedensorganisation im Spätmittelalter.* Munich: Beck, 1975.

Priebatsch, Felix, ed. *Die Politische Korrespondenz des Kurfürsten Albrecht Achilles.* Osnabrück: Zeller, 1965.

Ratschag: den ettliche Christenliche Pfarrherrn, Prediger, und andere Gottlicher gschrifft verstendige, Eynem fursten, wöllichen yetzugen strittigen ler halb, auf den abschyd, jüngst gehalthens Reychßtages zů Nürnberg. Augsburg: Heinrich Steiner, 1525.

Reuter von Schleiz, Simon. *Ein Christlichen frage Simonis Reuters von Schleyz, an alle Bischoffe, vnnd andere geystliche.* Bamberg: Erlinger, 1523.

Roppelt, Johann Babtist. *Historisch-topographischen Beschreibung des Kaiserlichen Hochstifts und Fürstenthums Bamberg.* Nuremberg: Schneider and Weigel, 1801.

Ruland, Anton. "Briefe des Bamberger Dompredigers und späteren Weibischof Friedrich Förner." *BHVB* 34 (1871): 147–201.

Rürer, Johann. *Cristliche vnterrrichtung eins pfarhern an seinen herr, einz fursten des heligen Reychs, auff viertzig Artikel vnd puncten gestellt.* Nuremberg: Jobst Gutknecht, 1526.

Schatzgeyer, Kaspar. *Furhaltung xxx artigkl, so in gegenwurtiger verwerrung auf de pan gepracht, und durch ainer neüeren beschwören den allten schlangen gerechtfertigt werden.* Munich: Hans Schobser, 1525.

Scherzer, Walter. "Das älteste Bamberger Bischofsurbar 1323/28 (Urbar A)." *BHVB* 108 (1972).

Schmitt, Lothar Clemens. *Die Bamberger Synoden.* Bamberg: Reindl, 1851.

Schornbaum, Karl. *Aktenstücke zu ersten Brandenburgischen Kirchenvisitations 1528.* Munich: Kaiser, 1928.

——. *Quellen zur Geschichte der Wiedertäufer.* Leipzig: Heinsius, 1934.

Schwanhäuser, Johann. *Ein Sermon geprediget durch Joãnem Schwanhausen, Custor auf sant Gangolffs Stifft zů Bamberg, Anno. 1523. an dem 22. Sontag nach Trinitatis, an aller hayligen tag &c.* Bamberg: Georg Erlinger, 1523.

——. *Ein Sermon geprediget durch Johañem Schwanhausen custor vff sant Gangolffs styfft zu Bamberg an dem sontag, d[er] genañt wyrt, der erst in der verpottenn zeyt.* Bamberg: Georg Erlinger, 1524.

——. *Ain Trostbrief an die Christlich gemayn zů Bamberg. Johannes Schwannhauser.* Nuremberg, 1525.

Schwarzenberg, Johann von. *Ein Schöner Sendtbrief wolgepornen vnd Edeln herren, Johannsen, Herrn zu Schwartzenberg, An Bischoff zu Bamberg außgegangen, Dariñ der treffenliche vñ Christenliche vusachñ, wie vñ warůmb er sein Tochter auß dem Closter daselbst (zum Heyligen Grab genant) hinweg gefůrt.* Nuremberg: Jobst Gutknecht, 1524.

Schwartz, W. E., ed. *Die Nuntiatur-Korrespondenz Kaspar Groppers nebst verwandten Aktenstücken (1573–1576).* Paderborn: Schöningh, 1898.

Sehling, Emil, Ed. *Die Evangelishcen Kirchenordnungen des XVI. Jahrhunderts.* Vol. 11, *Teil Bayern, Franken.* Tübingen: Mohr, 1961.

Simon, Matthias. *Ansbacher Pfarrerbuch. Die Evangelische-Lutherische Geistlichkeit der Fürstentums Brandenburg-Ansbach 1528–1806.* Nuremberg: Verein für Bayerische Kirchengeschichte, 1955–57.

——. *Bayreuther Pfarrerbuch. Die Evangelisch-Lutherische Geistlichkeit des Fürstenbums Kulmbach-Bayreuth (1528/29–1810).* Munich: Kaiser, 1930.

Smith, William Bradford, ed. *The Richard C. Kessler Reformation Collection: An Annotated Bibliography.* 4 vols. Atlanta: Scholars Press, 1999.

Stillfried, Rudolf Graf, and Traugott Maerker, eds. *Monumenta Zollerana, Urkundenbuch zur geschichte des Hauses Hohenzollern.* 8 vols. Berlin: Ernst and Korn, 1852–66.

Wachter, Friedrich. *General-Personal-Schematismus der Erzdiözese Bamberg, 1007–1907.* Bamberg: Nagengast, 1908.

Wappler, Paul. *Die Täuferbewegung in Thüringen von 1526–1584.* Jena: Fischer, 1913.

Zeumer, Karl. *Quellensammlung zur Geschichte der Deutschen Reichsverfassung in Mittelalter und Neuzeit.* Leipzig: C. L. Hirschfeld, 1904.

Literature

Angermeier, Heinz. *Königtum und Landfriede in Deutschen Spätmittelalter.* Munich: Beck, 1966.

——. *Die Reichsreform 1410–1555.* Munich: Beck, 1984.

Arnold, Benjamin. *Count and Bishop in Medieval Germany.* Philadelphia: University of Pennsylvania Press, 1991.

Arnold, Klaus. "Dorfweistümern in Franken." *ZBLG* 38 (1975): 819–76.

——. *Johannes Trithemius.* Würzburg: Schöningh, 1971.

Bachmann, Siegfried. "Die Landstände des Hochstifts Bamberg." *BHVB* 98 (1962): 1–337.

Bader, Karl Siegfried. *Der deutsche Südwesten in seiner territorialstaatlichen Entwicklung.* Sigmaringen: Jan Thorbecke, 1978.

——. *Dorfgenossenschaft und Dorfgemeinde.* Weimar: Böhlau, 1968.

——. *Das mittelalterliche Dorf als Friedens- und Rechtsbereich.* Weimar: Böhlau, 1957.

Barnes, Robin Bruce. *Prophecy and Gnosis: Apocolypticism in the Wake of the Lutheran Reformation.* Stanford: Stanford University Press, 1988.

Barry, Jonathan, et. al., eds. *Witchcraft in Early Modern Europe: Studies in Culture and Belief.* Cambridge: Cambridge University Press, 1996.

Bauer, Günther. *Anfänge täuferische Gemeindebildungen in Franken.* Nuremberg: Verein für Bayerische Kirchengeschichte, 1966.

Bauer, Lothar. "Die Bamberger Weihbischöfe Johann Schöner und Friedrich Förner." *BHVB* 101 (1965): 306–528.

——. "Fürstbischof Johann Philipp von Gebsattel (1599–1609) im Urteil der Nachwelt." *BHVB* 100 (1964): 407–13.

——. "Die Informativprozeß Johann Philipp von Gebsattel." *JFFL* 21 (1961): 1–27.

——. "Die Kurie und Johann Philipp von Gebsattel." *Quellen und Forschungen aus italienischen Archiven und Bibliotheken* 40 (1960): 89–118.

——. "Die Rolle Herzog Maximilians von Bayern bei der Wahl des Bamberger Fürstbischofs Johann Gottfried von Aschhausen 1609." *ZBLG* 25 (1962): 558–71.

——. "Vatikanische Quellen zur neueren Bamberger Bistumsgeschichte." *BHVB* 99 (1963): 171–316.

Bäumer, Remigius, ed. *Concilium Tridentinum.* Darmstadt: Wissenschaftliche Buchgesellschaft, 1979.

Behringer, Wolfgang. *Die Hexenverfolgung in Bayern.* Munich: Oldenbourg, 1997.

Beisbart, Helmut. "Marktschorgast–Ein Stadt kämpft um ihre Rechte. Ein Beitrag zu oberfränkische Stadtgeschichte." *GO* 21 (1997/98): 27–40.

Bensen, Heinrich Wilhelm. *Geschichte des Bauernkriegs in Ostfranken.* Erlangen, 1840.

Berg, Gustav. "Beiträge zur Geschichte des Markgrafen Johann von Cüstrin." *Schriften des Vereins für Geschichte der Neumark,* 14 (1903): 1–142.

Bireley, Robert, S.J. *Maximilian von Bayern, Adam Contzen S.J. und die Gegenreformation in Deutschland, 1624–1635.* Göttingen: Vandenhoeck and Ruprecht, 1975.

——. *Religion and Politics in the Age of the Counterreformation. Emperor Ferdinand II, William Lamormaini, S.J. and the Formation of Imperial Policy.* Chapel Hill: University of North Carolina Press, 1981.

Bittner, Franz. "Leonhard von Egloffstein, Ein Bamberger Domherr und Humanist." *BHVB* 107 (1971): 53–159.

Blänkner, Reinhard. "'Absolutismus' und 'frühmoderner Staat.' Probleme und Perspektiven der Forschung." In *Frühe Neuzeit–Frühe Moderne? Forschungen zur Vielgeschichtigkeit von Übergangsprozessen,* edited by Rudolf Vierhaus, 45–74. Göttingen: Vandenhoeck and Ruprecht, 1992.

Blaschke, Karlheinz. "Dorfgemeinde und Stadtgemeinde in Sachsen zwischen 1300 und 1800." In *Landgemeinde und Stadtgemeinde in Mitteleuropa,* edited by Peter Blickle, 119–43. Munich, Oldenbourg, 1991.

——. "Fiskus, Kirche und Staat in Sachsen vor und während der Reformation." *ARG* 80 (1989): 194–212.

——. "The Reformation and the Rise of the Territorial State." In *Luther and the Modern State in Germany,* edited by James D. Tracy, 61–75. Kirksville, MO: Sixteenth Century Journal Publishers, 1986.

Blickle, Peter. *Communal Reformation. The Quest for Salvation in Sixteenth Century Germany.* Translated by Thomas Dunlap. New Brunswick, NJ: Humanities Press, 1992.

——. "Communal Reformation and Peasant Piety: The Peasant Reformation in its Late Medieval Origins." *CEH* 20 (1987): 216–28.

——. *From the Communal Reformation to the Revolution of the Common Man.* Translated by Beat Kümin. Leiden: Brill, 1998.

——. ed. *Landgemeinde und Stadtgemeinde in Mitteleuropa. Ein struktureller Vergleich.* Munich: Oldenbourg, 1991.

——. *The Revolution of 1525.* Translated by Thomas Brady and Erik Midelfort. Baltimore: Johns Hopkins University Press, 1985.

Bog, Ingomar. *Die bäuerliche Wirtschaft im Zeitalter des Dreißigjährigen Krieges.* Erlangen: Veste Verlag, 1952.

——. *Dorfgemeinde, Freiheit und Unfreiheit in Franken.* Stuttgart: Fischer, 1956.

——. "Geistliche Herrschaft und Bauer in Bayern und die spätmittelalterliche Agrarkrise." *VSJWG* 45 (1958): 62–75.

Böhme, Ernst. *Das Fränkische Reichsgrafenkollegium im 16. und 17. Jahrhundert.* Stuttgart: Steiner, 1989.

Brady, Thomas A., Jr. *Communities, Politics, and the Reformation in Early Modern Europe.* Leiden: Brill, 1998.

——. "From the Sacral Community to the Common Man: Reflections on German Reformation Studies." *CEH* 20 (1987): 230–45.

——. *The Politics of the Reformation in Germany. Jacob Sturm (1489–1553) of Strasbourg.* Atlantic Highlands, NJ: Humanities Press, 1997.

——. "Some Peculiarities of German Histories in the Early Modern Era." In *Germania Ilustrata,* edited by Andrew C. Fix and Susan C. Karant-Nunn, 197–216. Kirksville, MO: Sixteenth Century Journal Publishers, 1992.

——. *Turning Swiss: Cities and Empire 1450–1550.* Cambridge: Cambridge University Press, 1985.

Braun, Karl. *Nürnberg und die Versuch zur Wiederherstellung der alten Kirche im Zeitalter der Gegenreformation (1555–1648).* Nuremberg: Verein für bayerische Kirchengeschichte, 1925.

Brecht, Martin. "Via antiqua, Humanismus und Reformation–der mainzer Theologieprofessor Adam Weiß." *ZRG* 102 (1991): 362–71.

Brodek, Theodore. "Lay Community and Church Institutions of the Lahngau in the Late Middle Ages." *CEH* 2 (1969): 22–47.

——. "Society and Politics of Late Medieval Ulm." PhD diss., Columbia University, 1970.

Brundage, James A. *Law, Sex, and Christian Society in Medieval Europe.* Chicago: University of Chicago Press, 1987.

Brunner, Otto. *Adeliges Landleben und Europäischer Geist.* Salzburg: O. Müller, 1949.

——. *Land and Lordship. Structures of Governance in Medieval Austria.* Translated by Howard Kaminsky and James Van Horn Melton. Philadelphia: University of Pennsylvania Press, 1992.

Büttner, Ernst. "Der Krieg des Markgrafen Albrecht Alcibiades in Franken 1552–1555." *AO* 23 (1908): 1–164.

Christ, Günther. "Selbsverständnis und Rolle der Domkapitel in der Geistlichen Territorien des alten Deutschen Reiches in der Frühneuzeit." *ZHF* 16 (1989): 257–328.

Christian, William A., Jr. *Local Religion in Sixteenth-Century Spain.* Princeton, NJ: Princeton University Press, 1981.

Clark, Stuart. *Thinking with Demons: The Idea of Witchcraft in Early Modern Europe.* Oxford: Clarendon, 1997.

Clasen, Claus-Peter. *Anabaptism: A Social History.* Ithaca, NY: Cornell University Press, 1972.

Constable, Giles. *The Reformation of the Twelfth Century.* Cambridge: Cambridge University Press, 1996.

——. *Three Studies in Medieval Religious and Social Thought.* Cambridge: Cambridge University Press, 1995.

Deckart, Adalbert, O. Cist. "Das ehemalige Karmelitenkloster zu Bamberg in der Au." *BHVB* 91 (1952): 1–372.

Deinlein, Michael von. "Johann Gottfried von Aschausen." *BHVB* 39 (1877): 1–31.

Demandt, Dieter, and Hans-Christoph Rublack. *Stadt und Kirche in Kitzingen. Darstellungen und Quellen zu Spätmittelalter und Reformation.* Stuttgart, 1978.

Dietrich, Klaus Peter. *Territorial Entwicklung, Verfassung und Gerichtswesen im Gebiet um Bayreuth bis 1603.* Kallmünz: Lassleben, 1958.

Dipple, Geoffrey. *Antifraternalism and Anticlericalism in the German Reformation.* Alsdershot: Ashgate, 1996.

Dippold, Günther. "Aspekte der Hexen-Verfolgung im Hochstifts Bamberg." *BHVB* 135 (1999): 291–305.

——. *Konfessionalisierung am Obermain.* Staffelstein: Bornschlegel, 1996.

——. "Die Städtegründung der Andechs-Meranier in Franken." In *Die Andechs-Meranier in Franken. Europäische Fürstentum in Hochmittelalter,* edited by Lothar Hennig, Ursula Vorwerk, and Wolfram Unger, 183–96. Heidelberg: Vernissage-Verlag, 1998.

——. "Täufer am Obermain." *BHVB* 119 (1983): 78–83.

Dixon, C. Scott. *The Reformation and Rural Society: The Parishes of Brandenburg-Ansbach-Kulmbach, 1528–1603.* Cambridge: Cambridge University Press, 1996.

Dollinger, Philippe. *Der bayerische Bauernstand vom 9. bis zum 13. Jahrhundert.* Translated by Ursula Irsigler. Munich: Beck, 1982.

Dotterweich, Ranier. "Die Rolle Bischofs Lambert von Brunn in der Reichspolitik unter Kaiser Karl IV. und König Wenzel." *BHVH* 118 (1982/83): 31–82.

Durchhardt, Heinz. *Protestantisches Kaisertum und Altes Reich.* Wiesbaden: Steiner, 1977.

Eberhard, Winfried. *Konfessionsbildung und Stände in Böhmen, 1478–1530.* Munich: Oldenbourg, 1981.

Eckstein, A. *Geschichte der Juden im ehemaligen Fürstbistum Bamberg.* Bamberg: Handesdruckerei, 1886.

Endres, Rudolf. "The Peasant War in Franconia." In *The German Peasant War: New Viewpoints,* edited by Robert Scribner and Gerhard Benecke, 63–83. Boston: Allen and Unwin, 1979.

——. "Probleme des Bauernkrieges im Hochstift Bamberg." *JFFL* 31 (1971): 91–138.

——. "Die Reformation in fränkischen Wendelstein." In *Zugänge zur bäuerlichen Reformation,* edited by Peter Blickle, 127–46. Zürich: Chronos, 1987.

——. "Stadt- und Landgemeinde in Franken." In *Landgemeinde und Stadtgemeinde in Mitteleuropa. Ein struktureller Vergleich,* edited by Peter Blickle, 101–17. Munich, Oldenbourg, 1991.

——. "Zur wirtschaftlichen und sozialen Lage in Franken vor den Dreißigjährigen Krieg," *JFFL* 28 (1968): 5–52.

Engel, Wilhelm. "Dr. Theodorich Morung, General Vikar in Bamberg, Dompfarrer zu Würzburg und sein politische Prozeß." *MJGK* 1 (1949): 1–76.

——. "*Passio dominorum.* Ein Ausschnitt aus dem Kampf um die Landeskirchenherrschaft und Türkensteuer im spätmittelalterlichen Franken." *ZBLG* 16 (1951): 265–316.

Evans, R. J. W. *The Making of the Habsburg Monarchy.* Oxford: Clarendon, 1979.

Fix, Andrew C., and Susan C. Karant-Nunn, eds. *Germania Ilustrata.* Kirksville, MO: Sixteenth Century Journal Publishers, 1992.

Fleckenstein, Josef, ed. *Herrschaft und Stand. Untersuchungen zur Sozialgeschichte im 13. Bis zum 14. Jahrhundert.* Göttingen: Vandenhoeck and Ruprecht, 1979.

——, ed. *Das ritterliche Turnier im Mittelalter.* Göttingen: Vandenhoeck and Ruprecht, 1985.

Foerster, Roland-Götz. *Herrschaftsverständnis und Regierungsstruktur in Brandenburg-Ansbach 1648–1701.* Ansbach: Historischer Verein für Mittelfranken, 1975.

Forster, Marc. *Catholic Revival in the Age of the Baroque: Religious Identity in Southwest Germany, 1550–1750.* Cambridge: Cambridge University Press, 2001.

——. "Clericalism and Communalism in German Catholicism." In *Infinite Boundaries: Order, Disorder, and Reorder in Early Modern German Culture,* edited by Max Reinhart, 55–76. Kirksville, MO: Sixteenth Century Journal Publishers, 1998.

——. *The Counter-Reformation in the Villages: Religion and Reform in the Bishopric of Speyer, 1560–1720.* Ithaca, NY: Cornell University Press, 1992.

Forstreuter, Kurt. "Albrecht als Hochmeister." In *Albrecht von Brandenburg-Ansbach und die Kultur senier Zeit,* edited by Walther Hubatsch, 5–10. Düsseldorf: Rheinland-Verlag, 1968.

Franz, Günther. *Der Deutsche Bauernkrieg.* Darmstadt: Wissenschaftliche Buchgesellschaft, 1975.

Freudenberger, Theobald. *Die Fürstbischöfe von Würzburg und das Konzil von Trient.* Münster: Aschendorff, 1989.

Fröhlich, P. Cyprian. "Der Schwanen-Rittersorden U. L. F. mit den Sitz in Brandenburg-Ansbach: Ein Kulturbild aus der Zeit vor der Reformation." *Historisch-Politische Blätter* 159 (1917): 1–16.

Fuchs, Heinrich. *Marktschorgast. Pfarrei, Amt und Markt.* Bamberg, 1959.

Gehm, Britta. *Die Hexenverfolgung im Hochstift Bamberg und das Eingreigen des Reichshofrates zu ihrere Beendigung.* Hildesheim: Georg Olms, 2000.

Geldner, Ferdinand. *Langheim: Wirken und Schicksal eines fränkischen Zisterzienser Klosters.* Kulmbach: Freunde der Plassenburg, 1966.

Goez, Werner. "Karl IV. und das politische System seiner Zeit." *JFFL* 39 (1979): 41–61.

——. *Translatio Imperii. Ein Beitrag zur Geschichte des Geschichtsdenkens und der politischen Theorien im Mittelalter und in der frühen Neuzeit.* Tübingen: Mohr, 1958.

Göldel, Caroline. "Zur Entwicklung der Bamberger Stadtvefassung im 15. Jahrhundert im Spannungsfeld Rat-Gemeinde-Klerus." *BHVB* 135 (1999): 7–44.

Görschling, Heinrich. "Die Entstehung des Ansbacher Konsistoriums." *ZBKG* 4 (1929): 13–48.

Gruber, Hans-Günter. *Christliches Eheverständnis im 15. Jahrhundert. Eine moralgeschichtliche Untersuchung zur Ehelehre Dionysius des Kartäusers.* Regensburg: Friedrich Pustet, 1989.

Guth, Klaus. "Das Entstehen Fränkischen Wallfahrten." *MJGK* 29 (1977): 39–53.

——. "Kirche und Religion." *Oberfranken im Spätmittelalter und zu Beginn der Neuzeit,* edited by Elisabeth Roth, 149–278. Bayreuth: Oberfrankenstiftung, 1975.

Guttenberg, Erich Freiherr von. *Das Bistum Bamberg.* Berlin: De Gruyter, 1937.

——. *Die Territorienbildung am Obermain.* Bamberg: Historischer Verein, 1966.

Hahn, Peter-Michael. "Kirchenschütz und Landesherrschaft in der Mark Brandenburg im späten 15. und frühen 16. Jahrhundert." *Jahrbuch für die Geschichte Mittel- und Ostdeutschlands* 28 (1979): 179–220.

Haimerl, Franz Xaver. *Das Prozessionswesen des Bistum Bamberg im Mittelalter.* Munich: Kösel-Pustet, 1937.

Hamm, Bernd. "Von der spätmittelalterlichen reformatio zur Reformation: der Prozeß normativer Zentrierung von Religion und Gesellschaft in Deutschland." *ARG* 84 (1993): 7–81.

Harrington, Joel F. *Reordering Marriage and Society in Reformation Germany.* Cambridge: Cambridge University Press, 1995.

Harrington, Joel F., and Helmut Walser Smith. "Confessionalization, Community, and State Building in Germany, 1555–1870." *JMH* 69 (1997): 77–101.

Hartung, Fritz. *Geschichte des Fränkischen Kreises (1521–1559).* Aalen: Scientia Verlag, 1961.

Haussherr, Rainer, ed. *Zeit der Staufer. Geschichte–Kunst–Kultur.* 5 vols. Stuttgart: Württembergisches Landesmuseum, 1977.

Helmholz, R. H. *Marriage Litigation in Medieval England.* Cambridge: Cambridge University Press, 1974.

Hennig, Lothar, Ursula Vorwerk, and Wolfram Unger, eds. *Die Andechs-Meranier in Franken. Europäische Fürstentum im Hochmittelalter.* Heidelberg: Vernissage-Verlag, 1998.

Herold, Hans-Jörg. *Markgraf Joachim Ernst von Brandenburg-Ansbach als Reichsfürst.* Göttingen: Vandenhoeck and Ruprecht, 1973.

Hesslinger, Helmo. *Die Anfänge des Schwäbischen Bundes. Ein Beitrag zur Geschichte der Einungswesen unter der Kreichsreform unter Kaiser Friedrich III.* Ulm and Stuttgart: W. Kohlhammer, 1970.

Heydenreuter, Reinhard. *Der Landesherrliche Hofrat unter Herzog und Kurfürst Maximilian I. von Bayern (1598–1651).* Munich: Beck, 1981.

Hintze, Otto. *Die Hohenzollern und ihr Werk.* Berlin: P. Parey, 1915.

——. *Staat und Verfassung. Gesammelte Abhandlungen zur Allgemeinen Verfassungsgeschichte* Edited by Gerhard Oestreich. Göttingen: Vandenhoek and Ruprecht, 1962.

Hlaváček, Ivan. *Das Urkunden- und Kanzleiwesen des böhmischen und römischen Königs Wenzel (IV.) 1376–1419.* Stuttgart: Hiersemann, 1970.

Hofmann, Hanns Hubert. "Adel in Franken." In *Deutscher Adel 1430–1555,* edited by Hellmuth Rössler, 95–126. Darmstadt: Wissenschaftliches Buchverlag, 1965.

——. "Freibauern, Freidörfer, Schutz und Schirm im Fürstentum Ansbach." *ZBLG* 23 (1960): 195–327.

——. "Territorienbildung in Franken im 14. Jahrhundert." In *Der deutsche Territorialstaat im 14. Jahrhundert,* edited by Hans Patze, vol. II, 255–300. Sigmaringen: Jan Thorbecke, 1970–71.

Hofmann, Michel. "Die Außenbehörden des Hochstifts Bamberg und des Markgrafschafts Bayreuth." *JFFL* 3 (1937): 58–95.

——. "Cuius regio? Ein Beitrag zum historischen Staatsrecht Frankens." *JFFL* 11/12 (1953): 345–55.

——. "Die Dorfverfassung im Obermaingebiet." *JFFL* 6/7 (1941): 140–96.

——. "Studien über fränkische Bauern-Weistümern I. Beiträge zur Rechtsgeschichte Frankens." *MJGK* 13 (1964): 101–20.

Hotzelt, Wilhelm. *Veit II von Würtzburg, Fürstbischof von Bamberg 1561–1577.* Freiburg in Br.: Herder, 1918.

Hsia, R. Po-Chia. "The Myth of the Commune: Recent Historiography on City and Reformation in Germany." *CEH* 20 (1987): 203–15.

——. *Social Discipline in the Reformation: Central Europe 1550–1750.* New York: Routledge, 1989.

Hubatsch, Walther, ed. *Albrecht von Brandenburg-Ansbach und die Kultur seiner Zeit.* Düsseldorf: Rheinland-Verlag, 1968.

——. *Albrecht von Brandenburg-Ansbach, Deutschordens Hochmeister und Herzog in Preußen.* Berlin: Grote, 1965.

——. *Geschichte der Evangelischen Kirche Ostpreußens.* Göttingen: Vandenhoeck and Ruprecht, 1968.

Irsigler, Franz. "Zauberei und Hexenprozeße im Köln." In *Hexenglaube und Hexenprozeße im Raum Rhein-Mosel-Saar,* edited by Gunther Franz and Franz Irsigler, 169–79. Trier: Spee, 1995.

Jäger, Carl. "Markgraf Casimir und der Bauernkrieg in den südlichen Grenzämtern des Fürstentums unterhalb des Gebirgs." *Mitteliungen des Vereins für Geschichte der Stadt Nürnberg* 9 (1892): 18–90.

Jegel, August. "Fürst und Adel in der ehemaligen Fürstentümern Ansbach-Bayreuth." *AZ* 3 (1915): 211–75.

——. "Geschichte der Landstände in den ehemaligen Fürstentümern Ansbach-Bayreuth, 1500–1533." *AO* 24 (1910): 60–85.

——. "Die landständige Verfassung in den ehemaligen Fürstentümern Ansbach-Bayreuth." *AO* 25 (1912): 1–52.

Johanek, Peter. "Zur kirchlichen Reformtätigkeit Bischof Lamprechts von Brunn." *BHVB* 102 (1966): 235–54.

Johnson, Trevor. "'Everyone Should Be Like the People': Elite and Popular Religion and the Counter Reformation." In *Elite and Popular Religion,* edited by Kate Cooper and Jeremy Gregory, 206–24. Woodbridge, UK: Boydell, 2006.

Jordan, Hermann. *Reformation und gelehrte Bildung in der markgrafschaft Ansbach-Bayreuth.* Leipzig: Deichert, 1917.

Kaminsky, Howard. "Estates, Nobility, and the Explanation of Estate in the Late Middle Ages." *Speculum* 68 (1993): 684–709.

Kanzler, Georg. "Die Landkapitel im Bistum Bamberg." *BHVB* 83 (1931): 1–71, 84 (1934): 1–119.

Karant-Nunn, Susan C. *The Reformation of Ritual: An Interpretation of Early Modern Germany.* London: Routledge, 1997.

Kaufmann, Thomas. *Universität und lutherische Konfessionalisierung.* Gütersloh: G. Mohn, 1997.

Kist, Johannes. *Das Bamberger Domkapitel von 1399–1556.* Weimar: Böhlau, 1943.

——. "Hieronymus von Reitzenstein, O. Cist., Weihbischof von Bamberg (1474–1503)." *BHVB* 90 (1950): 322–27.

——. *Klerus und Wissenschaft im spätmittelalterlichen Bistum Bamberg.* Bamberg: Philosophische-Theologische Hochschule, 1964.

——. *Das Matrikel der Geistlichkeit des Bistums Bamberg.* Würzburg: Schöningh, 1955.

Klassen, Johannes M. "Ownership of Church Patronage and the Czech Nobility's Support for Hussitism." *ARG* 66 (1975): 36–49.

Kleiner, Michael. "Georg III. Schenk von Limpurg. Bischof von Bamberg (1505–1522) als Reichsfürst und Territorialherr." *BHVB* 127 (1991): 13–117.

Klingenstein, Grete, and Heinrich Lutz, eds. *Spezialforschung und "Gesamtgeschichte."* Vienna: Verlag für Geschichte und Politik, 1981.

Kneitz, Otto. *Albrecht Alcibiades, Markgraf von Kulmbach 1522–1557.* Kulmbach: Freunde der Plassenburg, 1951.

Kohler, Alfred. *Antihabsburgische Politik in der Epoche Karls V.* Göttingen: Vandenhoeck and Ruprecht, 1982.

Kolb, Peter, and Ernst-Günter Krenig, eds. *Unterfränkische Geschichte.* II. Würzburg: Echter, 1992.

Kraemer, Horst. *Der deutsche Kleinstaat des 17. Jahrhunderts im Spiegel von Seckendorffs "Teutschem Fürstenstaat."* Darmstadt: Wissenschaftliche Buchgesellschaft, 1974.

Kramer, Karl-Siegmund. *Volksleben im Fürstentum Ansbach und seinen Nachbargebieten (1500–1800).* Würzburg: Schöningh, 1961.

——. *Volksleben im Hochstift Bamberg und im Fürstentum Coburg (1500–1800).* Würzburg: Schöningh, 1967.

Kraußold, Lorenz. *Geschichte der evangelischen Kirche im ehemaligen Furstenthum Bayreuth.* Erlangen: Deichert, 1860.

——. *Dr. Theodorich Morung der Vorbote der Reformation in Franken.* Erlangen: Deichert, 1877/78.

Labouvie, Eva. *Zauberei und Hexenwerk. Ländliche Hexenglaube in der frühen Neuzeit.* Frankfurt: Fischer, 1991.

Lahner, Andreas. "Die ehemalige Benediktiner-Abtei Michelsberg zu Bamberg," *BHVB* 51 (1889): 139–74.

Lamberg, Georg von. *Criminal-Verfahren vorzüglich bey Hexenprozessen im ehemaligen Bißthum Bamberg während der Jahren 1624 bis 1630.* Nuremberg: Kiegel and Wiessner, 1835.

Lambert, Malcolm. *Medieval Heresy.* Oxford: Basil Blackwell, 1992.

Landwehr, Götz. "Mobilisierung und Konsolidierung der Herrschafts ordnung im 14. Jahrhundert." In In *Der deutsche Territorialstaat im 14. Jahrhundert,* edited by Hans Patze, vol. II, 484–505. Sigmaringen: Jan Thorbecke, 1970–71.

——. *Die Verpfändung der Deutschen Reichsstädte im Mittelalter.* Cologne: Böhlau, 1967.

Larner, Christina. *Witchcraft and Religion: The Politics of Popular Belief.* Oxford: Basil Blackwell, 1984.

LeBras, Gabriel. "Les confréres chrétiennes." *Études de sociologie religieuse* 2 (1965): 423–62.

Leff, Gordon. *Heresy in the Later Middle Ages.* Manchester: Manchester University Press, 1967.

Lippert, F. "Die 400jährige Reformation in Markgrafentum Bayreuth und Georg Schmalzing." *AO* 30 (1928): 1–146.

Losher, Gerhard. *Königtum und Kirche zur Zeit Karls IV.* Munich: Oldenbourg, 1985.

Luttenberger, Albrecht Pius. *Glaubenseinheit und Reichsfriede. Konzeptionen und Wege Konfessionsneutrale Reichspolitik 1530–1552.* Göttingen: Vandenhoeck and Ruprecht, 1982.

Lutz, Heinrich. *Politik, Kultur und Religion im Werdeprozeß der frühen Neuzeit.* Klagfurt: Universitäts-Verlag Carinthia, 1982.

MacHardy, Karin J. "Der Einfluss von Status, Konfession und Besitz auf das Politische Verhalten des Niederösterreichischen Ritterstandes 1580–1620." In *Spezialforschung und 'Gesamtgeschichte,'* edited by Grete Klingentsein and Henrich Lutz, 56–83. Vienna: Verlag für Geschichte und Politik, 1981.

——. *War, Religion and Court Patronage in Habsburg Austria.* New York: Palgrave, 2003.

Machilek, Franz. "Hus und die Hussiten in Franken." *JFFL* 51 (1991): 15–37.

——. "Privatfrömmigkeit und Staatsfrömmigkeit." In *Kaiser Karl IV. Staatsmann und Mäzen,* edited by Ferdinand Seibt, 98–103. Munich: Prestel, 1978.

Maierhöfer, Isolde. "Bambergs Verfassungstopographische Entwicklung vom 15. bis zum 18. Jahrhundert." In *Bischofs- und Kathedralstädte des Mittelalters und der frühen Neuzeit,* edited by Franz Petri, 146–62. Cologne: Böhlau, 1976.

Maurer, Helmut. *Der Herzog von Schwaben.* Sigsmaringen: Jan Thorbecke, 1978.

——. "Das Herzogtum Schwaben in staufischer Zeit." In Haussherr, *Zeit der Staufer. Geschichte–Kunst–Kultur,* edited by Rainer Haussherr, vol. V, 91–106. Stuttgart: Württembergisches Landesmuseum, 1977.

Maurer, Justus. *Prediger im Bauernkrieg.* Stuttgart: Calwer, 1979.

Meyer, Christian. *Geschichte der Burggrafschaft Nürnberg und der späteren Markgrafschaften Ansbach und Bayreuth.* Tübingen: Laupp, 1908.

Meyer, Werner. "Turniergesellschaftern. Bemerkungen zur socialgeschichtlichen Bedeutung der Turniere im Spätmittelalter." In *Das ritterliche Turnier in Mittelalter,* edited by Josef Fleckenstein, 500–512. Göttingen: Vandenhoeck and Reprecht, 1985.

Merz, Johannes. "Die Landstadt im Geistlichen Territorium." *Archiv für Mittelrheinischen Kirchengeschichte* 46 (1994): 55–82.

Merzbacher, Friedrich. *Die Hexenprozesse in Franken.* Munich: Beck, 1970.

——. *Iudicium provinciale ducatus Franconiae. Das Kaiserliche Landgericht des Herzogtum Franken-Würzburg im Spätmittelalter.* Munich: Beck, 1965.

Midelfort, H. C. Erik. "Curious Georgics: The German Nobility and Their Crisis of Legitimacy in the Late Sixteenth Century." In *Germania Ilustrata,* edited by Andrew C. Fix and Susan C. Karant-Nunn, 217–42. Kirksville, MO: Sixteenth Century Journal Publishers, 1992.

——. *Mad Princes of Renaissance Germany.* Charlottesville: University of Virginia Press, 1994.

——. "Witchcraft and Religion in Sixteenth Century Germany: The Formation and Consequences of an Orthodoxy," *ARG* 62 (1971): 266–78.

——. *Witch-Hunting in Southwestern Germany, 1562–1684.* Stanford: Stanford University Press, 1972.

Miethke, Jürgen. "Karrierechancen eines Theologiestudiums im späteren Mittelalter." In *Gelehrten im Reich. Zur Sozial- und Wirkungsgeschichte akademische Eliten des 14. bis 16 Jahrhunderts,* edited by Rainer C. Schwinges, 181–209. Berlin: Duncker and Humblot, 1996.

Mitteis, Heinrich. *Lehnsrecht und Staatsgewalt.* Weimar: Böhlau, 1958.

Moeller, Bernd. *Reichstadt und Reformation.* Gütersloh: G. Mohn, 1962.

——. "Was wurde in der Frühzeit der Reformation in den deutschen Städte gepredigt?" *ARG* 75 (1984): 176–93.

Mötsch, Johannes. "Das Ende der Andeschs-Meranier–Streit ums Erbe." In *Die Andechs-Meranier in Franken. Europäische Fürstentum im Hochmittlealter,* edited by Lothar Hennig, Ursula Vorwerk, and Wolfram Unger, 129–41. Heidelberg: Vernissage-Verlag, 1998.

Müller, Konrad. "Markgraf Georg von Brandenburg-Ansbach-Jägerndorf." *Jahrbuch für Schlesische Kirche und Kirchengeschichte,* N.F. 34 (1955): 1–29.

Müller, Uwe. *Die ständische Vertretung in der fränkischen Margraftümer in der erste Hälfte des 16. Jahrhunderts.* Neustadt a. d. Aisch: Degener, 1984.

——. "Markgraf Georg der Fromme. Ein protestantische Landesherr im 16. Jahrhundert." *JFFL* 45 (1985): 107–23.

Myers, W. David. *Poor, Sinning Folk: Confession and Conscience in Counter-Reformation Germany.* Ithaca, NY: Cornell University Press, 1996.

Neukam, Wilhelm. "Immunitäten und Civitas in Bamberg von der Gründung bis zum Ausgang des Immunitätenstreit 1440." *BHVB* 78 (1922/23/24): 189–367.

——. "Territorium und Staat der Bischöfe von Bamberg und seine Außenbehörden." *BHVB* 89 (1948/49): 1–35.

Neuer-Landfried, Franziscka. *Die katholische Liga–Gründung, Neuordnung und Organisation eines Sonderbundes 1608–1620.* Kallmünz: Lassleben, 1968.

Nischan, Bodo. "The Exorcism Controversy and Baptism in the Lutheran Reformation." *SCJ* 18 (1987): 31–50.

Nöth, Stefan. *Ager Clavium: Das Cistercienserinnenkloster Schlüsselau, 1280–1554.* Bamberg: Historischer Verein, 1982.

——. *Urbare und Wirschaftsordnungen des Domstifts zu Bamberg.* II Teil. Neustadt a. d. Aisch: Degener, 1986.

Oberman, Heiko. "*Gelehrten die Verkehrten:* Popular Response to Learned Culture in the Renaissance and the Reformation." In *Religion and Culture in the Renaissance and Reformation,* edited by Steven Ozment, 43–62. Kirksville, MO: Sixteenth Century Journal Publishers, 1989.

——. "The Present Profile and Future Face of Reformation History: A Review Article." *SCJ* 28 (1997): 170–71.

Oestreich, Gerhard. *Geist und Gestalt des frühmodernen Staates. Ausgewählte Aufsätze.* Berlin: Duncker and Humblot, 1969.

O'Malley, John, S.J. *Trent and All That: Renaming Catholicism in the Early Modern Era.* Cambridge, MA: Harvard University Press, 2000.

Ozment, Steven. *Ancestors: The Loving Family in Old Europe.* Cambridge, MA: Harvard University Press, 2001.

——. *When Fathers Ruled: Family Life in Reformation Europe.* Cambridge, MA: Harvard University Press, 1983.

——. *The Reformation in the Cities.* New Haven, CT: Yale University Press, 1975.

Palacký, František. *Dějiny Národu Čeckého.* Prague: Mazač, 1937.

Paschke, Hans. "Das Franziskanerkloster an der Schranne zu Bamberg." *BHVB* 110 (1974): 167–318.

Patrouch, Joseph F. *A Negotiated Settlement: The Counter-Reformation in Upper Austria under the Habsburgs.* Leiden: Brill, 2000.

——. "Who Pays for Building the Rectory? Religious Conflicts in the Upper Austrian Parish of Dietach, 1540–1582." *SCJ* 26 (1995): 297–310.

Patze, Hans, ed. *Der deutsche Territorialstaat im 14. Jahrhundert.* 2 vols. Sigmaringen: Jan Thorbecke, 1970–71.

——. "Herrschaft und Territorium." In *Zeit der Staufer. Geschichte–Kunst–Kultur,* edited by Rainer Haussherr, vol. III, 37–38. Stuttgart: Württembergisches Landesmuseum, 1977.

——. "Neue Typen des Geschäftsschriftgutes im 14. Jahrhundert." In *Der Deutsche Territorialstaat im 14. Jahrhundert,* edited by Hans Patze, vol. I, 9–64. Sigmaringen: Jan Thorbecke, 1970–71.

Petersohn, Jürgen. *Herzogsmacht und Ständetum in Preußen während der Regierung Herzog Georg Friedrichs 1578–1603.* Würzburg: Holzner-Verlag, 1963.

——. "Staatskunst und Politik des Markgrafen Georg Friedrich von Brandenburg-Ansbach and Bayreuth 1539–1603." *ZBLG* 24 (1961): 229–76.

Petry, Ludwig. "Politische Geschichte unter den Habsburger." In *Geschichte Schlesiens,* edited by Ludwig Petry et al., vol. 2, 4–14. Sigmaringen: Jan Thorbecke, 1988.

Pfändter, Bernhard. "Die Belagerung Bamberg im Jahre 1435. Ein Zeitgenössische Gedicht, Eingeleitet und Kommentiert." *BHVB* 118 (1982): 83–95.

Pfeiffer, Gerhard. "Fürst und Land: Betrachtungen zur Bayreuther Geschichte." *AO* 57/58 (1978): 7–20.

——. "Die königliche Landfriedenseinungen in Franken." In *Der Deutsche Territorialstaat im 14. Jahrhundert,* edited by Hans Patze, vol. II, 229–53. Sigmaringen: Jan Thorbecke, 1988.

——. "Studien zur Geschichte der fränkischen Reichsritterschaft." *JFFL* 22 (1962): 173–280.

——. "Die Rechtstellung des Klosters Münchsteinach." *JFFL* 22 (1962): 239–94.

Pietsch, Franz. *Geschichte der gelehrten Bildung in Kulmbach.* Kulmbach: Freunde der Plassenburg, 1974.

Pohl, Herbert. *Hexenglaube und Hexenverfolgung im Kurfürstentum Mainz.* Stuttgart: Steiner, 1988.

Pörtner, Regina. *The Counter-Reformation in Central Europe: Styria 1580–1630.* Oxford: Clarendon, 2001.

Powell, Chilton Latham. *English Domestic Relations 1487–1653.* New York: Columbia University Press, 1917.

Prechtl, Alexander. "Bayreuths religiose Bruderschaften des ausgehenden Mittelalters." *AO* 79 (1999): 91–145.

Press, Volker. "Adel im Reich um 1600." in Klingenstein and Lutz, *Spezialforschung und Gesamtgeschichte,* 15–47.

——. "Das Römisch-Deutsche Reich–Ein politische System in verfassungs- und sozialgeschichtlicher Fragestellung." In *Spezialforschung und Gesamtgeschichte,* edited by Grete Klingenstein and Heinrich Lutz, 221–42. Vienna: Verlag für Geschichte und Politik, 1981.

——. "Wilhelm von Grumbach und die deutsche Adelskrise der 1560er Jahre." *BDLG* 113 (1977): 396–431.

Quirin, Heinz. "Markgraf Albrecht Achilles von Brandenburg-Ansbach als Politiker." *JFFL* 31 (1971): 261–308.

Rabe, Horst. *Reichsbund und Interim. Die Verfassungs- und Religionspolitik Karls V und der Reichstag von Augsburg 1547/1548.* Cologne: Böhlau, 1971.

Rebel, Herman. *Peasant Classes: The Bureaucratization of Property and Family Relations under Early Habsburg Absolutism, 1511–1636.* Princeton, NJ: Princeton University Press, 1983.

Reindl, Alwin. "Die Vier Immunitäten des Domkapitels zu Bamberg." *BHVB* 105 (1969): 213–509.

Reinhard, Wolfgang. "Gegenreformation als Modernisierung? Prologomena zu einer Theorie des konfessionellen Zeitalters," *ARG* 68 (1977): 226–51.

——. "Reformation, Counter-Reformation, and the Early Modern State: A Reassessment," *Catholic Historical Review* 75 (1989): 383–404.

——. "Was ist Katholische Konfessionalisierung?" In *Die Katholische Konfessionalisierung,* edited by Wolfgang Reinhard and Heinz Schilling, 419–52. Münster: Aschendorff, 1995.

——. "Zwang zur Konfessionalisierung? Prologomena zu einer Theorie des konfessionellen Zeitalters," *ZHF* 10 (1983): 257–98.

Reinhard, Wolfgang, and Heinz Schilling, eds. *Die Katholische Konfessionalisierung.* Münster: Aschendorff, 1995.

Reiter, Ernst. *Martin von Schaumberg, Fürstbischof von Eichstätt (1560–1590) und die Trienter Reform.* Münster: Aschendorff, 1965.

Remling, Ludwig. *Bruderschaften in Franken. Kirchen und Sozialgeschichtlich Untersuchungen zur spätmittelalterlsichen und frühneuzeitlichen Bruderschaftswesen.* Würzburg: Schöningh, 1986.

Renczes, Andrea. *Wie löscht man eine Famile aus? Eine Analyse Bamberger Hexenprozesse.* Pfaffenweiler: Centaurus Verlag, 1990.

Riedenauer, Erwin. "Reichsritterschaft und Konfession." In *Deutscher Adel, 1555–1740,* edited by Hellmuth Rössler, 1–63. Darmstadt: Wissenschaftliche Buchgesellschaft, 1965.

Robisheaux, Thomas. *Rural Society and the Search for Order in Early Modern Germany.* Cambridge: Cambridge University Press, 1989.

Rödel, Dieter. "Grundherrschaft un Landesausbau im Hochmittelalter am Beispiel Mainfrankens." In *Grundherrschaft und bäuerliche Gesellschaft im Hochmittelalte,* edited by Werner Rösener, 294–319. Göttingen: Vandenhoeck and Ruprecht, 1995.

Roepke, Claus-Jürgen. *Die Protestanten in Bayern.* Munich: Süddeutsche-Verlag, 1972.

Roper, Lyndal. *Witch Craze: Terror and Fantasy in Baroque Germany.* New Haven, CT: Yale University Press, 2004.

Rösener, Werner. "Ministerialität, Vasallität und niederadelige Ritterschaft im Herrschaftsbereich der Markgraften von Baden vom 11. Bis zum 14. Jahrhundert." In *Herrschaft und Stand. Untersuchungen zur Sozialgeschichte im 13. Bis zum 14. Jahrhundert,* edited by Josef Fleckenstein, 40–91. Göttingen: Vandenhoeck and Ruprecht, 1979.

——. *Peasants in the Middle Ages.* Translated by Alexander Stützer. Urbana: University of Illinois Press, 1992.

——. "Ritterliche Wirtschaftsverhältnisse und Turnier im sozialen Wandel des Hochmittelalters." In *Das ritterliche Turnier im Mittelalter,* edited by Josef Fleckenstein, 296–338. Göttingen: Vandenhoeck and Ruprecht, 1985.

Rössler, Hellmuth. *Fränkischer Geist: Deutsches Schicksal–Ideen–Kräfte–Gestalten im Franken, 1500–1800.* Kulmbach: Freunde der Plassenburg, 1953.

Roth, Elisabeth. *Hochschulgebäude Hochzeitshaus. Ein kulturhistorische Studie.* Bamberg: Fränkische Tag, 1975.

——, ed. *Oberfranken in der Neuzeit bis zum Ende des Alten Reiches.* Bayreuth: Oberfrankenstiftung, 1984.

——, ed. *Oberfranken im Spätmittelalter und zu Beginn der Neuzeit.* Bayreuth: Oberfrankenstiftung, 1975.

Rothkrug, Lionel. *Religious Practices and Collective Perceptions: Hidden Homologies in the Renaissance and Reformation.* Waterloo, ON: Department of History, University of Waterloo, 1980.

Rublack, Hans-Christoph. *Gescheiterte Reformation: früreformatorische und protestantische Bewegungen in süd- und westdeutsche geistliche Residenzen.* Stuttgart: Klett-Cotta, 1978.

——, ed. *Die lutherische Konfessionalisierung in Deutschland.* Gütersloh: G. Mohn, 1992.

——. "Lutherische Predigt und sozial Wirklichkeiten," in *Die lutherische Konfessionalisierung,* 344–95.

——. "Zur Sozialstruktur der protestantischen Minderheit in der geistlichen Residenz Bamberg am Ende des 16. Jahrhunderts." In *The Urban Classes, the Nobility, and the Reformation,* edited by Wolfgang Momsen, Peter Alter, and Robert W. Scribner, 130–48. Stuttgart: Klett-Cotta, 1979.

Rummel, Walter. *Bauern, Herren, und Hexen. Studie zur Sozialgeschichte sponheimische und kurtrierische Hexenprozesse 1574–1664.* Göttingen: Vandenhoeck and Ruprecht, 1991.

Ruß, Herbert. "Das Baunacher Stadtrecht von 1328 und 1341." *Frankenland* 41 (1989): 93–98.

Sabean, David. *Power in the Blood.* Cambridge: Cambridge University Press, 1984.

Safley, Thomas Max. *Let No Man Put Asunder: The Control of Marriage in the German Southwest; A Comparative Study 1550–1600.* Kirksville, MO: Sixteenth Century Journal Publishers, 1984.

Scharrer, Werner. "Laienbruderschaften in der Stadt Bamberg vom Mittelalter bis zum Ende des Alten Reiches." *BHVB* 126 (1990): 21–392.

Scherzer, Walter. "Das Hochstift Würzburg." In *Unterfränkische Geschichte,* edited by Peter Kolb and Ernst-Günter Krenig, II, 17–84. Würzburg: Echter, 1992.

Schieber, Hans. "Die Vorgeschichte des Bamberger Priesterseminars." In *Seminarium Ernestinum. 400 Jahre Priesterseminar Bamberg,* edited by Michael Hofmann, 17–86. Bamberg: St. Otto-Verlag, 1986.

Schilling, Heinz. "Die Konfessionalisierung im Reich. Religiöser und gesellschaftlicher Wandel in Deutschland zwischen 1555 und 1620." *HZ* 246 (1988): 1–45.

——. "Die Konfessionalisierung von Kirche, Staat und Gesellschaft–Profil, Leistung, Defizite und Perspektiven eines geschichtwissenschaftlichen Paradigmas." In *Die Katholische Konfessionalisierung,* edited by Wolfgang Reinhard and Heinz Schilling, 1–49. Münster: Aschendorff, 1995.

——. "The Reformation and The Rise of the Early Modern State." In *Luther and the Modern State in Germany,* edited by James D. Tracy, 21–30. Kirksville, MO: Sixteenth Century Journal Publishers, 1986.

——, ed. *Die reformierte Konfessionalisierung in Deutschland–Das Problem der "Zweiten Reformation."* Gütersloh: G. Mohn, 1986.

Schimmelpfennig, Bernhard. *Bamberg im Mittelalter. Siedelgebiete und Bevölkerung bis 1370.* Lübeck/Hamburg: Mathiesen, 1964.

Schlesinger, Gerhard. *Die Hussiten in Franken.* Kulmbach: Stadtarchiv, 1974.

Schlesinger, Walter. "Zur Geschichte der Landesherrschaft in der Marken Brandenburg und Meissen während des 14. Jahrhunderts." In *Der deutsche Territorialstaat im 14. Jahrhundert,* edited by Hans Patze, vol. II, 101–26. Sigmaringen: Jan Thorbecke, 1970–71.

Schmitt, Hans-Jürgen. "Die Geistliche und Weltliche Verwaltung der Diözese und des Hochstifts Bamberg zur Zeit des Bischofs Weigand von Redwitz (1522–1556)." *BHVB* 106 (1970): 33–184.

Schmitt, Lothar Clemens. *Geschichte des Ernestinischen Klerikal-Seminars zu Bamberg.* Bamberg, 1857.

Schneider, Bernhard. *Gutachten evangelische Theologen des Fürstentums Brandenburg-Ansbach/Kulmbach zur Vorbereitung des Augsburger Reichstages von 1530.* Neustadt a. d. Aisch: Degener, 1987.

Schnelbögl, Fritz. "Franken, die Heimat Albrechts." in Hubatsch, *Albrecht von Brandenburg-Ansbach und die Kultur seiner Zeit,* edited by Walther Hubatsch, 1–5. Düsseldorf: Rheinland-Verlag, 1968.

——. "Siedlungsbewegungen im Veldener Forst." *JFFL* 11/12 (1953): 221–35.

——. "Zur Siedlungsgeschichte des Raumes Erlangen-Forchheim-Gräfenberg." *JFFL* 14 (1954): 141–51.

Schonath, Wilhelm. "Die Liturgische Drucke des Bistums und späteren Erzbistums Bamberg." *BHVB* 103 (1967): 307–419.

Schornbaum, Karl. "Die Bündnisbestrebung der deutschen evangelischen Fürsten und Markgraf Georg Friedrich von Brandenburg-Ansbach 1566–1570." *Zeitschrift für Kirchengeschichte* 38 (1920): 262–82.

——. "Markgraf Georg Friedrich von Brandenburg als Vermittler zwischen den evangelischen Fürsten 1667 bis 1570." *ARG* 26 (1929): 204–49.

——. "Markgraf Georg Friedrich von Brandenburg und die evangelische Stände Deutschlands 1570–1575." *ARG* 22 (1925): 268–300.

——. *Die Stellung des Markgrafen Kasimir von Brandenburg zur reformatorischen Bewegung in den Jahren 1524–1527.* Nuremberg: Knoll, 1900.

——. *Zur Politik des Markgrafen Georg von Brandenburg von Beginne seine selbständige Regierung bis zur Nürnberger Anstand 1528–1532.* Munich: Ackermann, 1906.

Schorn-Schütte, Luise. "Ernst Troeltschs 'soziallehren' und die gegenwärtige Frühneuzeitforschung. Zur Disckussion um die Bedeutung von Luthertum und Calvinismus für die Entstehung der modernen Welt." In *Ernst Troeltschs Soziallehren. Studien zu ihrer Interpretation,* edited by Friedrich Wilhelm Graf and Trutz Rendtorff, 133–52. Gütersloh: G. Mohn, 1993.

——. "'Gefährtin' und 'Mitregintin.' Zur Sozialgeschichte der evangelischen Pfarrfrau in der Frühen Neuzeit." In *Wandel der Geschlechterbeziehungen zu Beginn der Neuzeit,* edited by Heide Wunder and Christina Vanja, 123–31. Frankfurt: Suhrkamp, 1991.

——. "Lutherische Konfessionalisierung? Das Beispiel Braunschweig-Wolfenbüttel (1589–1613)." In *Die lutherische Konfessionalisierung in Deutschland,* edited by Hans-Christoph Rublack, 163–94. Gütersloh: G. Mohn, 1992.

——. "Priest, Preacher, Pastor: Research on Clerical Office in Early Modern Europe." *CEH* 33 (2000): 1–40.

Schreiner, Klaus. "Die Staufer als Herzöge von Schwaben." In *Zeit der Staufer. Geschichte–Kunst–Kultur,* edited by Rainer Haussherr, vol. III, 8. Stuttgart: Württembergisches Landesmuseum, 1977.

Schremmer, Eckart. *Die Wirtschaft Bayerns*. Munich: Beck, 1970.

Schubert, Ernst. "Franken als Königsnahe Landschaft unter Karl IV." *BDLG* 114 (1978): 865–90.

——. "Gegenreformation in Franken." *JFFL* 28 (1968): 275–307.

——. *Landständische Verfassung des Hochstifts Würzburg*. Würzburg: Schöningh, 1967.

Schuhmann, Günther. *Die Markgrafen von Brandenburg-Ansbach. Eine Bilddokumentation zur Geschichte der Hohenzollern in Franken*. Ansbach: Historischer Verein für Mittelfranken, 1980.

Schuster, Georg, and Wagner, Friedrich. *Die Jugend und Erziehung der Kurfürsten von Brandenburg und die Könige von Preußen*. Berlin: Hofmann, 1906.

Schwerhoff, Gerd. "Hexerei, Geschlecht und Regionalgeschichte. Überlegungen zur Erklärung des scheinbar Selbstverständlichen." In *Hexenverfolgung und Regionalgeschichte*, edited by Giesla Wilbertz, Gerd Schwerhoff, and Jürgen Scheffler, 325–53. Bielefeld: Verlag für Regionalgeschichte, 1994.

Schwinges, Rainer C., ed. *Gelehrte im Reich. Zur Sozial- und Wirkungsgeschichte akademische Eliten des 14. bis 16. Jahrhunderts*. Berlin: Duncker and Humblot, 1996.

——. "Karriermuster. Zur sozialen Rolle der Gelehrten im Reich des 14. bis 16. Jahrhunderts. Eine Einführung." In *Gelehrte im Reich. Zur Sozial- und Wirkungsgeschichte akademische Eliten des 14. bis 16. Jahrhunderts*, edited by Rainer C. Schwinges, 11–22. Berlin: Duncker and Humblot, 1996.

Scribner, Robert. "Communalism: Universal Category or Ideological Construct? A Debate in the Historiography of Early Modern Germany and Switzerland." *Historical Journal* 37 (1994): 199–207.

Seebaß, Gottfried. "Bauernkrieg und Täufertum in Franken." *ZKG* 85 (1974): 285–300.

——. *Müntzers Erbe. Werk, Leben, und Theologie des Hans Hut*. Gütersloh: G. Mohn, 2002.

Seibt, Ferdinand. *Karl IV. Ein Kaiser in Europa 1326 bis 1378*. Munich: Süddeutsche Verlag, 1994.

Seyboth, Reinhard. *Die Markgraftümer Ansbach und Kulmbach unter der Regierung Markgraf Friedrich des Ältern (1485–1515)*. Göttingen: Vandenhoeck and Ruprecht, 1985.

——. "Markgraf Georg Friedrich von Brandenburg-Ansbach-Kulmbach (1556–1603) als Reichsfürst." *ZBLG* 53 (1990): 659–79.

——. "Markgraf Johann der Alchemist von Brandenburg (1406–1464)." *JFFL* 51 (1991): 39–65.

Shank, Michael H. *"Unless You Believe, You Shall Not Understand": Logic, University and Society in Late Medieval Vienna*. Princeton, NJ: Princeton University Press, 1988.

Sicken, Bernhard. "Landesherrliche Einnahmen und Territorialstruktur. Die Fürstentümer Ansbach und Kulmbach zu Beginn der Neuzeit." *JFFL* 42 (1982): 153–248.

Sieben, Hermann Josef. *Die Partikularsynode. Studien zur Geschichte der Konzilsidee*. Frankfurt: Josef Knecht, 1990.

Simon, Matthias. *Evangelische Kirchengeschichte Bayerns*. Munich: Paul Müller, 1942.

Smith, William Bradford. "Anticlericalism in Bamberg on the Eve of the Peasants' War." In *Cultures of Communication from Reformation to Enlightenment*, edited by James Van Horn Melton, 48–65. Aldershot: Ashgate, 2002.

——. "Food and Deception in the Discourse on Heresy and Witchcraft in Bamberg." In *At the Table: Metaphorical and Material Cultures of Food in Medieval and Early Modern Europe,* edited by Juliann Vitullo and Timothy J. Tomasik, 107–22. Brugge: Brepols, 2007.

——. "Friedrich Förner, the Catholic Reformation, and Witch Hunting in Bamberg." *SCJ* 36 (2005): 115–28.

——. "Germanic Pagan Antiquity in Lutheran Historical Thought." *Journal of the Historical Society* 4 (2004): 351–74.

——. "Lutheran Resistance to the Imperial Interim in Hesse and Kulmbach." *Lutheran Quarterly* 19 (2005): 249–73.

——. "Some Territorial Implications of Rural Confraternities in Upper Franconia." *Confraternitas* 6 (1995): 13–18.

Spitz, Lewis. *The Religious Renaissance of German Humanism.* Cambridge, MA: Harvard University Press, 1963.

Stayer, James. *The German Peasants' War and Anabaptist Community of Goods.* Montreal: McGill and Queens University Press, 1991.

Sticht, Ernst Ludwig. *Markgraf Christian von Brandenburg Kulmbach und der 30jährige Krieg in Ostfranken 1618–1635.* Kulmbach: Freunde der Plassenburg, 1965.

Stickler, Andrea. *Eine Stadt im Hexenfieber. Aus dem Tagebuch des Zeiler Bürgermeisters Johann Langhans (1611–1628).* Pfaffenweiler: Centaurus-Verlag, 1994.

Stieber, Joachim W. *Pope Eugenius IV, the Council of Basel, and the Secular and Ecclesiastical Authorities of the Empire.* Leiden: Brill, 1978.

Stievermann, Dieter. *Landesherrschaft und Klosterwesen in spätmittelalterlichen Württemberg.* Sigmaringen: Jan Thorbecke, 1989.

Störmer, Wilhelm. "Die Gesellschaft. Lebensformen und Lebensbedingungen." In *Unterfränkische Geschichte,* edited by Peter Kolb and Ernst-Günter Krenig, 495–521. Würzburg: Echter, 1992.

——. "Die Gründung von Kleinstädten als Mittle herrschaftlichen Territorienaufbaus, gezeigt auf fränkischen Beispielen." *ZBLG* 36 (1973): 563–85.

Stroup, John. *The Struggle for Identity in the Clerical Estate.* Leiden: Brill, 1984.

Thumser, Matthias. *Das Konflikt um die Wahlkapitulation zwischen dem Bamberger Domkapitel und Bischof Philipp von Henneberg.* Bamberg: Historischer Verein, 1990.

Tracy, James D., ed. *Luther and the Modern State in Germany.* Kirksville, MO: Sixteenth Century Journal Publishers, 1986.

Trexler, Richard C. "Florentine Religious Experience: The Sacred Image." *Studies in the Renaissance* 19 (1972): 7–41.

Trinkaus, Charles. "Humanism, Religion, Society: Concepts and Motivations of Some Recent Studies." *Renaissance Quarterly* 29 (1976): 676–91.

Ulshamer, Wili. "Die 'Rother Richtung' 1460." In *900 Jahre Roth,* edited by Günther Rüger, 103–54. Roth: Festausschuss der Stadt Roth, 1960.

Unger, Ludwig. *Die Reform des Benediktiner Klosters St. Michael bei Bamberg in der 2. Hälfte des 15. Jahrhunderts.* Bamberg: Historischer Verein, 1987.

van Eickels, Klaus. "Die Andechs-Meranier und das Bistum Bamberg." In *Die Andechs-Meranier in Franken. Europäische Fürstentum im Hochmittelalter,* edited by Lothar Hennig, Ursula Vorwerk, and Wolfram Unger, 145–56. Heidelberg: Vernissage-Verlag, 1998.

Vann, James Allen, III. *The Making of a State: Württemberg 1590–1790.* Ithaca, NY: Cornell University Press, 1984.

——. "New Directions for Study of the Old *Reich*." *JMH* 58, supplement (1986): S3–S22.

Veh, Otto. "Der Bayreuther Landstände unter dem Markgrafen Christian 1605–1655," Teil 1. *AO* 33 (1938): 1–64.

Waldenmeier, Hermann. *Die Entstehung der evangelischen Gottesdienstordnungen Süddeutschlands im Zeitalter der Reformation.* Leipzig: Verein für Reformationsgeschichte, 1916.

Walker, Mack. *German Home Towns: Community, State, and General Estate 1648–1871.* Ithaca, NY: Cornell University Press, 1971.

Weber, Reinhard. *Würzburg und Bamberg im Dreißigjährigen Krieg.* Würzburg: Echter Verlag, 1979.

Wefers, Sabine. *Das politische System Kaiser Sigismunds.* Stuttgart: Steiner, 1989.

Weigel, Georg. *Die Wahlkapitulationen der Bamberger Bischöfe 1328–1693.* Bamberg: Schmidt, 1909.

Weigelt, Horst. "Die frühreformatorische Bewegung in Bamberg und Johann Schwannhausen." *BHVB* 134 (1998): 113–30.

Wendehorst, Alfred. *Das Bistum Würzburg,* Teil 2: *Die Bischofsreihe von 1224 bis 1455.* Berlin: De Gruyter, 1968.

——. *Das Bistum Würzburg,* Teil 3. *Die Bischofsreihe von 1455 bis 1617.* Berlin: De Gruyter, 1978.

Wilbertz, Gisela, Gerd Schwerhoff, and Jürgen Scheffler, eds. *Hexenverfolgung und Regionalgeschichte.* Bielefeld: Verlag für Regionalgeschichte, 1994.

Winkler, Richard. "Die Säkularisation der Kirchenkleinoden in Markgrafentum Brandenburg-Kulmbach 1529/30." *GO* 22 (1999/2000): 41–102.

——. "Weismain und die Andechs-Meranier." *BHVB* 136 (2000): 33–45.

Wittmann, Pius. "Die Bamberger Hexen-Justiz (1595–1631)." *Archiv für das katholische Kirchenrecht* 50 (1883), 177–223.

Wolf, Gerhard Philipp, and Walter Tausenpfund. "Obrigkeit und jüdische Untertan in der Fränkischen Schweiz." In *Jüdische Leben in der Fränkischen Schweiz,* 79–174. Erlangen: Palm and Enke, 1997.

Wunder, Heide. "Die ländliche Gemeinde als Strukturprinzip der spätmittelalterlich-frühneuzeitlichen Geschichte Mitteleuropas." In *Landgemeinde und Stadtgemeinde in Mitteleuropa. Ein struktureller Vergleich,* edited by Peter Blickle, 385–402. Munich: Oldenbourg, 1991.

——. *He is the Sun, She is the Moon: Women in Early Modern Germany.* Translated by Thomas Dunlap. Cambridge, MA: Harvard University Press, 1998.

——. "Hexenprozesse und Gemeinde." In *Hexenverfolgung und Regionalgeschichte,* edited by Gisela Wilbertz, Gerd Schwerhoff, and Jürgen Scheffler, 61–70. Bielefeld: Verlag für Regionalgeschichte, 1994.

Wunder, Heide, and Christina Vanja, eds. *Wandel der Geschlechterbeziehungen zu Beginn der Neuzeit.* Frankfurt: Suhrkamp, 1991.

Würdinger, Joseph. *Kriegsgeschichte von Bayern, Franken, Pfalz, und Schwaben 1347–1506.* Munich: Literarisch- Artistische Anstalt, 1868.

Yates, Frances. *The Rosicrucian Enlightenment.* London: Routledge, 1972.

Zagel, Georg. *Die Gegenreformation im Bistum Bamberg unter Fürstbischof Neithard von Thüngen 1581–1598*. Kulmbach, 1899.

Zeeden, Ernst Walter. *Die Entstehung der Konfessionen. Grundlagen und Formen der Konfessionsbildung*. Munich: Oldenbourg, 1965.

——. *Konfessionsbildung. Studien zur Reformation, Gegenreformation, und katholischen Reform*. Stuttgart: Klett-Cotta, 1985.

Zeeden, Ernst Walter, and Hansgeorg Moliter, eds. *Die Visitation im Dienst der kirchlichen Reform*. Münster: Aschendorff, 1977.

Zeißner, Werner. *Altkirchliche Kräfte in Bamberg unter Bischof Weigand von Redwitz (1522–1556)*. Bamberg: Historischer Verein, 1975.

Ziegler, Walter. "Territorium und Reformation." *Historisches Jahrbuch* 110 (1990): 52–75.

——. "Typen der Konfessionalisierung in katholischen Territorien Deutschlands." In *Katholische Konfessionalisierung*, edited by Wolfgang Reinhard and Heinz Schilling, 405–18. Münster: Aschendorff, 1995.

Zmora, Hillay. "Princely State-Making and the 'Crisis of the Aristocracy' in Late Medieval Germany." *P & P* 153 (1996): 37–63.

——. *State and Nobility in Early Modern Germany*. Cambridge: Cambridge University Press, 1997.

Index